90 mi

ART AS PLUNDER

This book examines the ancient origins of debate about art as cultural property. What happens to art in time of war? Who should own art, and what is its appropriate context? Should the victorious ever allow the defeated to keep their art? These questions were posed by Cicero during his prosecution of a Roman governor of Sicily, Gaius Verres, for extortion. Cicero's published speeches had a very long afterlife, affecting debates about collecting art in the eighteenth century and reactions to the looting of art by Napoleon. The focus of the book's analysis is theft of art in Greek Sicily, Verres' trial, Roman collectors of art, and the later impact of Cicero's arguments. The book concludes with the British decision after Waterloo to repatriate Napoleon's stolen art to Italy and an epilogue on the current threats to art looted from archaeological contexts.

Margaret M. Miles, an archaeologist and art historian, is Professor of Art History and Classics at the University of California, Irvine. She has held fellowships at the American School of Classical Studies in Athens, the Institute for Advanced Study in Princeton, and the American Academy in Rome. She has excavated at Corinth and Athens and did architectural fieldwork at Rhamnous in Greece and at Selinunte and Agrigento in Sicily. Her earlier publications include a study of the Temple of Nemesis at Rhamnous (*Hesperia*, 1989) and a volume in the Agora excavation series on the City Eleusinion, the downtown Athenian branch of the Eleusinian Mysteries (*The Athenian Agora*, Vol. 31: *The City Eleusinion*, 1998).

ART AS PLUNDER

THE ANCIENT ORIGINS OF DEBATE ABOUT CULTURAL PROPERTY

MARGARET M. MILES

University of California, Irvine

CAMBRIDGE
UNIVERSITY PRESS

CAMBRIDGE UNIVERSITY PRESS
Cambridge, New York, Melbourne, Madrid, Cape Town, Singapore, São Paulo, Delhi

Cambridge University Press
32 Avenue of the Americas, New York, NY 10013-2473, USA

www.cambridge.org
Information on this title: www.cambridge.org/9780521872805

First published 2008

Printed in the United States of America

A catalog record for this publication is available from the British Library.

Library of Congress Cataloging in Publication Data

Miles, Margaret Melanie.
Art as plunder : the ancient origins of debate about cultural property / Margaret M. Miles.
  p.   cm.
Includes bibliographical references and index.
ISBN 978-0-521-87280-5 (hardback)
1. Art thefts – Rome.   2. Art treasures in war – Greece.   3. Cicero, Marcus Tullius –
Political and social views.   4. Cultural property – Protection – Europe – History.
I. Title.
N9114.M55   2008
709 – dc22   2007024636

ISBN   978-0-521-87280-5 hardback

For the people of Sicily, past and present

CONTENTS

ILLUSTRATIONS

PLANS

MAPS

PREFACE AND ACKNOWLEDGMENTS

ON A BRIGHT SPRING MORNING IN SICILY IN 2000, I WAS STANDING by the side of the Temple of Athena at Syracuse with a group of Fellows from the American Academy in Rome and telling them about the history of the temple. Here they could see and enter a standing classical Doric temple, preserved so well because it was converted into a Christian church in the seventh century. It now serves as the Duomo of Syracuse, with an elegant façade added in the early eighteenth century. We had gone inside and looked at its furnishings and the chapel dedicated to St. Lucy, patron of Syracuse, whose left arm only is there because the rest of her body was taken off to Venice. When it was first built, the temple had beautiful gold and ivory doors with carved panels and gold bosses. They were stripped off by the Roman governor of Sicily, Gaius Verres, in 73 BCE. He also took from the temple a series of historical paintings of famous Greek rulers of Syracuse and stole many statues from other temples in Sicily. After I pointed out the architectural features to the group, I read aloud some passages from Cicero's *Verrines* that describe the Roman governor's theft of art from Syracuse. Cicero's vivid descriptions bring to life what the Sicilian Greeks suffered under Verres. As an archaeologist, it seemed to me then that not enough had changed, that ancient sanctuaries and archaeological sites had been vulnerable for two thousand years and were still being looted, despite all current international law. I had been studying the architecture of Sicilian temples for some time but resolved that morning to make a detour and investigate further Cicero's account. This book is the result.

Like many other places in the Mediterranean, Sicily is still vulnerable to *clandestini*, people who rob archaeological sites in order to sell their finds on the art market. When *clandestini* rob a site, we lose history because an object loses its historical value if we have no archaeological context. For example, a statue of Aphrodite, such as the one acquired some years ago by the Getty Museum in Malibu, California (which is to be returned to Italy), although perhaps "beautiful" as an art object, would be far more significant and interesting if we knew for certain where it came from, how it was used, and its contextual date. In my view, modern customers of the *clandestini* are little different from Verres because they are encouraging the destruction of the historical record by the removal of art from its context. Although this book is about events far in the past, I hope to show that those events have contemporary resonance and, indeed, that our modern views about the ownership of art have been shaped by previous experiences going all the way back to Cicero's life-time.

It is a pleasure to acknowledge the various institutions that have generously allowed me to make use of their resources for my research. I am grateful to the American Academy in Rome, not only for the use of its Library and Rare Book Room but also for hosting me as a Resident in the winter of 2000. I also thank the Blegen Library of the American School of Classical Studies in Athens, the British Library, the Prints and Drawings department of the British Museum, the Library and Archives of the Royal Institute of British Architects, and the Vatican Library. I owe a special debt to the Wellington Archives at the University of Southampton and its head, C. M. Woolgar, for their generous assistance. My work could not have been accomplished without the dedicated help of the Interlibrary Loan Department of the Langson Library at the University of California, Irvine.

Interested and responsive audiences offered helpful suggestions after lectures I gave on Cicero's *Verrines* at the annual meeting of the Archaeological Institute of America held in Dallas, Texas, in December 1999 (abstract in *AJA* 104[2000]: 322) and at the American Academy in Rome in March 2000. Many friends and colleagues have generously shared their interest in the topics of this book and helped me in various ways, and I thank them warmly. At the Academy in Rome, Lester Little (its then Director), Christopher Johns, Sandra Phillips, and Jerrold Seigel encouraged me to pursue the whole range of art plunder. In Irvine, Linda and George Bauer, Anna Gonosová, and Maria Pantelia offered helpful advice on my manuscript, and Richard Frank, James Herbert, Richard Kroll, Patrick Sinclair, and Margaret Smith suggested useful bibliography. Kim Hartswick and Patricia Rosenmeyer also took the time to read my manuscript carefully and offer many useful suggestions. Claire Lyons, a passionate advocate for the protection of antiquities, urged me to publish a short version of my findings in the *International Journal of Cultural Property* (2002), and I also had the benefit of Patty Gerstenblith's suggestions, the journal's then editor. On a trip through Sicily with Connie and Ronald Stroud and the Mungerites, Verres and Cicero became a frequent topic of fruitful conversation. Others who have worked on related matters were very generous, and I thank especially Beryl Barr-Sharrar, Malcolm Bell, John Camp, Stephen Dyson, Helena Fracchia, Christopher Frei, Crawford H. Greenewalt, Jr., Otto and Grete Heinz, Nicholas Horsfall, Michael Ierardi, Dale Kinney, Kenneth Lapatin, Clemente Marconi, Miranda Marvin, Olga Palagia, Ingrid D. Rowland, Michele Salzman, Adele Scafuro, H. Alan Shapiro, Elizabeth Simpson, Gretchen Umholtz, and Ann Vasaly. While writing, I was always encouraged by Theodore H. Chenoweth, Linda Miles Coppens, and Karen and Thomas Voigts, and I was glad for constant support from Rocco Leonardis. I owe especially warm thanks to Beatrice Rehl, my editor, for her patience and ongoing interest in this project. My appreciation of Sicily and its people (past and present) is reflected in the dedication of this book to them.

INTRODUCTION

◉▣◉

The charge against Gaius Verres is that during a period of three years he has laid waste the province of Sicily: that he has plundered Sicilian communities, stripped bare Sicilian homes, and pillaged Sicilian temples. Here before you, here with their tale of wrong, stand the whole Sicilian people.

(In Caecilium div. *3.11*)

THIS BOOK IS ABOUT THE ORIGINS OF ART AS CULTURAL PROPERTY AND the competing claims that arise when it is seized, appropriated, and collected by a stronger authority. In the long experience of frequent, almost constant warfare in the ancient Mediterranean, we can trace evolving attitudes and expectations about what should happen to this category of an enemy's property during and after battle. Greek and Roman authors comment on art captured in war because art was of central importance to both cultures, and its fate reflected the effects of war on people. Art was also vulnerable to seizure by other agencies with the power to do so: magistrates, governors, and emperors sometimes took coveted items for their own use, and such confiscations were remembered and deplored.

The seizure of statues, paintings, and other art in peacetime, not by an enemy but by the Roman magistrate who had been chosen to govern prosperous Sicily under Roman law, is a central theme in a set of speeches written to prosecute that governor by Marcus Tullius Cicero. This famous Roman legal case of the first century BCE provides

1

vivid evidence illustrating how issues of ownership of art were then regarded. Because of the continuing prestige of its author, the legal case became an ancient but compelling precedent used in debates during the eighteenth century on the same topics of ownership of art, its fate in wartime, and the ethics of collecting art.

Cicero used the topic of stolen and confiscated art, taken by the very magistrate who was supposed to guarantee stability and security on the island, as a way of making his case urgent to a Roman audience that might otherwise be inclined toward indifference to details of maladministration in a foreign province. Cicero's speeches prosecuting the governor Gaius Verres were never lost and have had a wide audience over many centuries.

Here I address the questions posed by Cicero's use of art in his prosecution of Verres and the impact of his discussion on modern views about the ethics of ownership of art: Why do we [Romans] value art? Who should "own" art? Does art have a fixed location where it belongs? What should happen to it in time of war? When should the victors in war allow the defeated to retain their art, and why should they? Cicero is the first author to discuss these critical questions. Roman experience helped shape the reasoning that provided the historical genesis and foundation for our current laws on the ownership of art.

Greek art in quantity first arrived in Rome as plunder, a result of Rome's expansion into southern Italy and Sicily and then mainland Greece. Roman victories over Greeks resulted in huge amounts of captured booty, including bullion, human captives, moveable goods, and works of art of all sorts. As their military power expanded across the Mediterranean in the first three centuries BCE, the Romans developed a fairly systematic way of dealing with such a vast amount of plunder: a portion was usually dedicated to the gods, including significant captured statues of gods; the sale of captives provided slaves that became ubiquitous in society; money helped fund the army and state treasury;

and other Greek statues, paintings, furniture, tapestries, dishes, clothing, and jewelry were eagerly sought by the wealthy, whose appetite for them did not escape criticism.

The blend of Greco-Roman styles into a notably "Roman" art that would characterize the first and second centuries CE had not yet been realized, and ancient authors depict this as a time when tension was still felt around the opposition between Greek and Roman cultural norms. In part, this was due to the means of acquisition: much of Greek art (often representations of gods) had been taken from Greeks in war as booty, from religious contexts in sanctuaries. Also at work for ancient authors such as Polybius, Cato, Livy, Sallust, and Seneca was nostalgia for the allegedly simpler observances of the Roman past that did not depend on elegant statuary and for the more rustic, plain houses of past heroic Romans, whose austerities were thought to have contributed to their sterling characters. Less than two decades after Cicero's death, any actual cultural tensions began to dissolve into a new and creative cultural synthesis under the emperor Augustus.

Rome faced problems administrating her vast territorial holdings by the first century BCE. The political and legal superstructure that had served Republican Rome so well while she was expanding her control over all of Italy and much of Europe was being undermined by the very people who were entrusted with government. Gaius Verres, a member of the Senate, was brought to trial at the request of the Sicilians because his actions as governor of Sicily had been particularly egregious. When Cicero agreed to prosecute Verres on behalf of the Sicilians, he was then a young lawyer still building his reputation and eager to participate in a prominent case. The prosecution of Verres opened on August 5, 70 BCE, and Cicero's first short speech and the documentary evidence he presented were so damning that Verres immediately went into exile.

Soon after the trial, Cicero published the speech he gave together with five further speeches, written as though they had been actually delivered in the Forum. Cicero draws a vivid portrait of Verres as an administrator who acted with extreme avarice and duplicity in all aspects of his office and who, in addition, was a peculiarly unscrupulous collector of art. The theme of Verres' improper acquisition of art is the main topic of one of the speeches, and many references to his theft of art occur throughout the others, including the one Cicero had delivered in the Forum. After Cicero published them, the speeches were circulated widely and soon became a model for students of rhetoric, then an essential tool for any participant in public life. Among the earliest literary papyri in Latin found in Egypt is a section of the *Verrines*, perhaps dating to about 20 BCE, just fifty years after the trial.

Cicero was following literary precedents by taking such an interest in art, especially statues. Ancient literary interest in statues – their theft, ownership, and restitution – reflected a deep, pervasive, cultural respect for statuary. This respect included recognition of a spectrum of potency for images of gods and significant humans, from the merely decorative to the potentially numinous, a vehicle for divine manifestation and communication of divine will. Statues were a striking and memorable part of the visual environment in public spaces and temples, and they symbolized power, authority, and celebrity. They were so numerous that they comprised a kind of "second population" in ancient cities and, like living citizens, they belonged in a particular place. The interest in statuary is a part of the ancient authors' larger, primary topic of what happens in war and its aftermath, to those who win and those who lose, including the bronze and marble population: the fate of captured statuary is a symbolic parallel for human fate.

I begin with an overview of the major episodes of plundering in the ancient Near East and in classical Greece that are documented by inscriptions, ancient authors, and the archaeological record. There is a clear record of unease felt over artistic plunder taken from temples and sanctuaries, where most of the captured art had been dedicated, because its seizure was a serious religious violation and could have retributory consequences. Military episodes of plunder in Greece served as "case law" for Cicero in his prosecution of Verres and offered a body of well-known precedents that he could use to persuade the jurors. Cicero's case was so effective and widely disseminated that we can see its impact in the attitudes expressed by later Roman authors. The ambivalence felt by some Romans about taking art as plunder, as detailed by Cicero in the *Verrines*, becomes an underlying theme in subsequent historical accounts of earlier events projected into the more distant Roman past, such as those described by Livy. Cicero's idealized portraits of compassionate generals who return art to the defeated (drawn as a contrast to Verres) are implicit in later texts and inscriptions referring to the protection of art by Julius Caesar, Augustus, and Claudius.

In the second chapter, I provide an account of Greek Sicily in the time of Cicero, the setting for Verres' depredations, his trial in Rome, and the aftermath, including Cicero's publication of the speeches. The Greeks in Sicily and southern Italy had always been Rome's neighbors, but now Rome ruled them and, although close geographically, they were still viewed ambivalently as foreigners, weak militarily but part of an older, more sophisticated culture. I describe the particulars of the trial and details about the publication of the speeches because the historical context and its explicit cultural tensions are crucial for understanding why Cicero discusses art as he does and why the speeches from this legal case had such an impact.

Next, I discuss views about the social place of art presented by Cicero: at the time of the trial, the appetite of the elite for owning Greek art was increasing, with growing private wealth making acquisition and collection possible. For the modern student of ancient art history, the extensive text of the *Verrines* yields considerable insight into the expectations and assumptions of one particular class of Romans – Cicero, his associates, and readers in the earlier part of the first century BCE – about

Greek statuary, painting, and other portable art. Cicero is the first author to make careful distinctions between public and private uses of art, and he conveys a sense of what is appropriate for each sphere of expression.

Pervasive in his speeches is his view that the primary purpose of art is usually religious expression, that content, context, and veneration elevate art from the merely decorative and utilitarian. Through vivid anecdotes in the *Verrines*, Cicero presents indirectly the first extended commentary from antiquity on the social uses and purposes of art, through the filter of his rhetorical denunciation of one exceptionally avaricious individual, the defendant Verres. His ideas about the social place and ownership of art may seem familiar, since they became embedded in subsequent discussions in antiquity, most notably that of Pliny the Elder. But Cicero's views were not unique. He organized his material according to appropriate rhetorical categories that he expected would persuade his readers, and he must have used preexisting ideas about art and its purposes that they would have understood and appreciated. These widely held views, articulated with skill and elegance by Cicero, were then taken up and repeated in new contexts by subsequent Latin authors, who together convey a distinctively "Roman" set of attitudes about art and its ownership.

Crucial to the success of Cicero's rhetorical strategy is his assumption that art does have a larger significance than just a simple possession, an assumption we still hold. For affluent Romans of Cicero's time, collecting and owning Greek art had become possible only recently, and it soon became indispensable to a suitably furnished life. Gaius Verres was exceptional for his criminal excess and greed, not for his taste. Yet appetite for Greek art, for both private and public uses, continued unabated, and in Chapter 4, I discuss how notable Romans resolved the issues raised by Verres' negative example, including his late-first-century antithesis Novius Vindex. When Constantine moved the capital of the empire to Constantinople, once again Greek sanctuaries were plundered for the sake of decorating the new capital with furnishings considered necessary for a "new Rome."

In the last chapter, I follow the path of reception of Cicero's ideas about art and their impact in the early modern period. When Cicero's *Verrines* were brought into wider circulation in the Renaissance, they were read avidly and helped to form the general opinion then held that Cicero was the greatest stylist ever. Sicily and Sicilian Greeks are the constant foil for Verres, and when scholarly attention now shifted to Sicilian history, the *Verrines* provided important historical background because Cicero had to educate his immediate listeners about Sicily and its history. In the sixteenth century, Sicily was beginning to be viewed as a part of Italy once again: the Dominican monk Leandro Alberti, for example, had hoped to write a history of Sicily as a continuation of his larger projects on Italy. That was accomplished by another Dominican monk, Tomaso Fazello, author of the first topographical account of Sicily (published in 1558), who used Cicero's speeches as an authority for factual detail. His book in turn influenced the learned treatise of P. Cluverius (1619) and many subsequent descriptions and travel accounts of Sicily written during the following two centuries. This kept alive awareness of the events of Verres' governorship and his nefarious acquisition of art among an audience eager to participate (even if only by reading) in this part of the "Grand Tour."

Because of Cicero's skillful rhetoric and superb prose, the speeches continued to influence later generations of readers, and his views about the appropriate use of art had a decided impact. In eighteenth-century England and France, the speeches were read appreciatively as models of colorful rhetoric – once again important for public careers – and as a component of standard education in Latin. Cicero's strategy includes depicting ideal behavior for administrators and the military as a contrast to Verres' venality and ruthlessness. For readers in the eighteenth century, this idealism set the tone in public debates on topics ranging from the responsibilities of imperial administration abroad to the ethics of collecting art from Greece and Italy and the fate of art in wartime.

The actual charges brought against Verres were for extortion as governor, and that part of Cicero's text served as a model for Edmund Burke in his lengthy prosecution of Warren Hastings (1788–1793), the first governor of India. For seven years, readers of London newspapers received heavy doses of Ciceronian arguments used by Burke, and some editors provided exegesis and discussion of the original case against Verres. This kept in the public eye tales of art theft in the Roman period, as well as peculation and excessive taxation, as a comparison with contemporary events.

Napoleon and Lord Elgin were excoriated in print for behaving like Verres, and when the opportunity came after Waterloo in the autumn of 1815, the Duke of Wellington arranged for art plundered by Napoleon's army to be returned to Italy, where it belonged, he believed, rather than in Windsor Castle. Although the *Verrines* are just a small portion of Cicero's preserved writings, Cicero's authority in eighteenth- and early-nineteenth-century England and France was so great that even his idealism on these issues was taken up as a model and contributed to the concept of "cultural property." Our basic assumptions about art and its ownership have evolved since then but still owe much to Roman antecedents.

In our own time, looted, stolen, and confiscated art – whether taken in peace or war – has again provoked ongoing debate and litigation, discussed briefly in the Epilogue. Art is highly valued, just as it was in Cicero's time, and so too is there debate about issues of mode of acquisition and ownership. Cicero's comments on art and how later readers used them are worth investigating because they provided the historical genesis for our concepts of "cultural property" and "cultural heritage." Questions about proper ownership of art considered cultural property have become perennial human concerns; an examination of Cicero's views and their subsequent impact will clarify the fundamental basis for current law and even our own attitudes. I hope to demonstrate in this book the continuing relevance of Cicero's ethical commentary on the acquisition of art.

It is surprising that no modern, full commentary on the *Verrines* exists, even though they have been admired since antiquity and are rich with historical detail: we truly need such a commentary. A thorough, very useful commentary on one of the speeches has been published by Gianluigi Baldo (*In C. Verrem actionis secundae, Liber Quartus* [*De Signis*], 2004). Yet the speeches have not been neglected by classicists: numerous articles and chapters in recent books deal with particular aspects and how they illuminate Roman history and culture in the first century BCE. Certain individual selections of the speeches have been published with commentaries as textbooks for students of Latin, some of them excellent. Students of archaeology and art history will be familiar with the *Verrines* from the excerpts given in sourcebooks on Greek and Roman art used to illustrate Roman appetite for Greek art. Scholars have analyzed rhetorical characteristics of the speeches, most notably Ann Vasaly in *Representations: Images of the World in Ciceronian Oratory* (1993). Shane Butler investigated Cicero's use of written evidence in the case and draws attention to the very significant implications of this legal case for our understanding of literacy and the use of documents in the Roman world (*The Hand of Cicero*, 2002). Frank Cowles's historical study of Gaius Verres, a short monograph published in 1917, and his effort to discern the man behind Cicero's rhetorical presentation remains the fullest modern treatment of the speeches as a whole. The modern scholarly bibliography on Cicero and his other writings is already enormous and rapidly growing (we are in the midst of a Ciceronian revival), but the *Verrines* still need further study. My focus on Cicero's comments on the social place of art and on the impact of his speeches in later generations is just one of many possible topics one could take up from the *Verrines*.

So vivid is Cicero's text that it becomes cinematic, as we follow Verres' early career as a magistrate, manipulating inheritances and cheating on construction of the Temple of Castor and Pollux in the Forum of Rome; taking gold from the Parthenon, statues from Delos, and images from the Temple of Hera on Samos on his trip overseas as quaestor; forcing himself on young women in Asia Minor; and thus setting up a "pattern of behavior" that he will repeat in full as propraetor in Sicily. Verres' cupidity evidently had many targets but also a special goal: the collection of Greek art.

As I use the term here, *art* includes a range of traditional artifacts that have more than just the intrinsic value of their material: antique statues are the foremost category desired by Verres, but he also wanted paintings, tapestries, and special garments; vessels of every sort, made of gold, silver, or bronze; and lots of ornate and luxurious furniture. It is precisely in this period in Roman history, the first half of the first century BCE, that art begins to emerge as a category of objects considered valuable for its aesthetic qualities; however, throughout antiquity, any aesthetic evaluation tends to be subordinate to other religious, social, or political values. The nineteenth-century concept of "art for art's sake" lay far in the future. Nonetheless, it is here, in the activities of Verres, that we can see the first well-documented attempt of a private individual (not a pharaoh, king, or prince) to build a private "collection" of art, extracted from its religious and public settings and gathered with a connoisseur's attitude.

Cicero's rhetorical portrait of Verres is intended to prosecute and succeeds in overwhelming condemnation, even though the legal charge is extortion, not theft of art. Stolen art, however, is the topic of enduring interest over two millennia. My account of the development of ideas about the fate of art in war, and art as plunder more generally, is intentionally focused on events in ancient Greece and Rome and early modern western Europe. A more global account would consider the many notable and well-documented episodes of plundering in the New World, Africa, and Asia. Here, I have restricted my discussion to follow the path of the genesis and impact of Cicero's speeches because they contributed to the development of international law on cultural property during the Enlightenment in Europe and, thus, indirectly to current law. Verres' lurid behavior, however, and even the contrasting ideals expressed by Cicero, could also be illustrated globally, since plundering art seems to be a persistent human characteristic as is deliberate forbearance from plundering (although that is much less common).

In a further restriction of my topic, I pass over a great many instances of art plundered simply for its potential value as bullion or other raw material, such as the shiploads of bronze statuary taken in the sack of Rome in 410 CE, destined to be melted down, or art destroyed for ideological or religious motives. My interest here is in plundered art that was still valued as art by the plunderers. I do not attempt to discuss plundered art over two millennia (sadly, that would require several volumes) but rather in Roman antiquity for the most part, and in the late eighteenth and early nineteenth centuries in Europe and England, when new views on the ethics of acquisition of art were being formulated under the duress of the Napoleonic wars.

I conclude with the events in Paris in the aftermath of Waterloo: the repatriation of art plundered by Napoleon was the first-ever wartime repatriation of art on a large scale, an event that had no equal anywhere on the globe. It was accomplished under the aegis of the Duke of Wellington and set a new precedent. But with the end of eighteenth-century attitudes and ideals came also the waning of Cicero's direct influence in public discourse. The experience of classical antiquity was no longer taken as an important model for the present. If we contemplate the depredations of art in the twentieth and twenty-first centuries, both in wartime and peacetime, they seem to have little in common with any Ciceronian thread. Nevertheless, the outraged reaction we feel to more recent events shares much with Cicero's indignation at Verres. The plundering of art in World War II has received extensive and excellent treatment elsewhere and lies outside the scope of this book.

In the last three decades, the looting of antiquities by illegal diggers for sale to private collectors and museums has escalated greatly, especially in Italy, Greece, Mali, Nigeria, Peru, and Cambodia. The brute force of illegal commerce (rather than traditional warfare) is now plundering art, with grievous loss of historical context. The legal solutions that have already emerged and are still evolving were modeled on international agreements made concerning plunder in wartime and are discussed briefly in the Epilogue. Especially important passages on the subject of art as plunder are given in the Appendix. There and throughout the text, I quote ancient authors in English, either using my own translations or standard translations.

Readers have come to Cicero's *Verrines* motivated by various expectations, but what has been recalled and reused above all are the stories about Verres' excessive passion for acquiring art. Cicero's piercing commentary and eloquent denunciations of Verres' conduct seem fresh and much needed once again, when the aftermath of seizures of art by the Nazis is still unfolding, paintings are sold at hugely exorbitant prices, the ownership of art designated as "cultural heritage" is bitterly disputed, and at any moment, vulnerable archaeological sites all over the world are being robbed and their contents and sold to private collectors. The permanent destruction of the historical context of art is ongoing. Fecklessness in warfare permitted art to become plunder once again in April 2003, with looting and damage in the Baghdad Museum. Just as Verres' robberies diminished not only Sicilians but also all Greeks and Romans, the current acts of looting diminish all of us.

1 ART AS ROMAN PLUNDER

◎▣◎

For the law among all people is eternal,
that when a city is captured by enemies,
both the bodies of those in the city and
their goods belong to those who capture
it. Therefore it is not by injustice that
you will acquire whatever you may
get, but it will be out of humanity that
you do not take something away, if you
allow them to keep anything.
(Xenophon, Cyr. *7.5.73)*

ROMAN TRADITION DEPICTS ROMULUS, THE FOUNDER OF ROME, AS
the first victor to dedicate in the Temple of Jupiter Feretrius spoils taken
by him from an enemy chieftain killed in single combat: the famous
spolia opima. Only two other Roman generals would match Romulus'
personal feat, but during the many wars after Romulus, such blood-
stained arms and armor were proudly accumulated in Rome's other
temples as trophies of Roman valor, taken in battles against enemies
in Italy. Occasionally, images of gods worshipped by defeated enemies
were also captured, dedicated, and cared for in Roman temples, a physical expression of respect for the enemies' gods and a way of getting them
to change sides. As Roman power expanded through Italy to the south,
where Greek cities had flourished for centuries, plunder from those
captured cities flowed into Rome. But new types of booty, including
statues, paintings, luxurious furniture, and furnishings, now distracted
Romans from their main business of supporting Rome – or so some
ancient authors tell the story: Romans were proud and valorous, content

13

with simple furnishings until they met the corrupting influence of the more sophisticated Greeks, whose art and luxury would make the Romans soft, distracted, and unfit for war.

This moralizing discourse on Rome's response to captured art is phrased as a warning to future builders of empire by the Greek historian Polybius. He was himself a Roman hostage, deported to Rome from Greece in the aftermath of the Roman victory at Pydna in 167 BCE. One of the central issues of his time was the intersection of Greek and Roman culture. Because Rome had become dominant in the Mediterranean in Polybius' own life-time, talking about Greek art and Romans taking it as plunder was a way of coming to grips with some of the larger cultural perplexities – in particular, the Greek inability to cooperate with each other that left an opening, even an invitation, to Roman military power.[1] In the following century, Cicero continued the ongoing discussion of art and its acquisition in his prosecution of Verres, but he took up the topic as a way of illustrating Verres' criminal activities as a Roman governor over a Greek province.

The sacking and burning, raping and killing, pillage and destruction of cities is a running theme in both Greek and Roman history and literature, beginning with Homeric epic. Warfare was an ongoing event and its aftermath familiar to everyone. But it was carried out within a set of conventions and expectations that changed over time. When Cicero accused Verres of stealing art from temples, agoras, and shrines, his listeners were well aware of the long history of such actions in a military context. Cicero uses the military history of conquest and plunder strategically, careful not to condemn Rome's own historical and ongoing practices but rather to fashion parallels and contrasts

---

[1] As E. Gruen has fully demonstrated, the interaction between Greek culture and Roman culture was in fact longstanding and positive for Romans: to them, "the attraction of Hellas lay deep and started early." For full discussion, E. S. Gruen, *Culture and National Identity in Republican Rome* (Ithaca, 1992), especially 223–271; quotation on p. 269.

with those legitimate actions on behalf of the Republic and Verres' illegitimate, private thefts.[2]

Because this is a crucial part of Cicero's rhetorical strategy and a theme of his speeches that would have a profound effect on much later readers, the traditions and attitudes surrounding the acquisition of art by war in antiquity deserve closer scrutiny. Furthermore, an ancient consensus held that Romans first developed a taste for Greek art through warfare (although this consensus may be questioned). I begin here with a brief account of Near Eastern and Greek antecedents, since they too formed part of the background for perceptions of Roman customs. Within these variegated antecedents, two themes emerge that we can follow through several centuries: first, plundering was legitimate only in formal, declared wars (otherwise, it was considered piracy, looting, or theft); and second, plundering of sacred property, even in a legitimate, declared war, had consequences of many kinds. In effect, the past episodes of Greek and Roman plundering – well known to educated contemporaries of Cicero from the histories of Herodotus, Thucydides, and Polybius – form case law for Cicero: not legal precedents in the strict sense but rather a body of cultural experience and historical memories that he could draw on for support of his own points. This case law, a wellspring of experience, furnished many of his rhetorical *exempla*. Even the ideal of the humane conqueror who returns revered items to

---

[2] The extensive Greek and Latin vocabulary for plundering, looting, stealing, pillaging, and piracy is not always used by ancient authors precisely or consistently, and, just as in English, the words can take on different tones depending on context. Here I use the verb "plunder" to refer to removing an enemy's property in wartime; "looting" as a more predatory form of plundering, used more derogatorily about a less legitimate situation; "pillaging" suggests destructive but less thorough plundering. *Spolia* in Latin originally meant arms and armor captured from the enemy but came to mean booty more generally. In the later Roman periods, artistic *spolia* came to refer to art removed from one context and put into another. *Spoliatio* is used by Cicero (in the *Verrines*) specifically for removing art or architectural decoration out of its proper context. On *spolia* and *spoliatio* see further D. Kinney, "Rape or Restitution of the Past? Interpreting *Spolia*," in S. C. Scott, ed., *The Art of Interpreting. Papers in Art History from The Pennsylvania State University*, 9 (1995): 52–67.

the defeated, used so effectively by Cicero, appears as a theme earlier in Hebrew and Greek histories. Conscientious restitution of revered items is still at the heart of current discussions about cultural property.

NEAR EASTERN ANTECEDENTS

One of the oldest works of art known to have been plundered in antiquity is the famous victory stele of the Akkadian ruler Naram-Sin, now in the Louvre Museum in Paris (Fig. 1). The stele is an upright slab of sandstone, more than 6 feet tall. On its front is a carved relief showing Naram-Sin ascending a mountain, followed by his soldiers, who slash down enemy soldiers as they go up. A sun and stars above show the favor of the gods in the battle. This stele commemorates Naram-Sin's victory over the Lullubi, a people who lived in the Zagros Mountains between modern Iraq and Iran, in a battle fought around 2250 BCE. About a thousand years later, the victory stele was still in the city of Sippar (on the Euphrates River southwest of modern Baghdad) when the area was conquered by Elamites, who lived across the Zagros Mountains in southwestern Iran. The Elamites took Naram-Sin's stele – by then an antique – as booty off to their capital city Susa in Iran, where it was found by French excavators in 1898. An inscription in Elamite carved across the mountaintop opposite Naram-Sin records the successful raid of King Shutruk-Nahhunte I in 1158 BCE and celebrates the Elamite triumph over Naram-Sin's much later descendants.[3]

Shortly after the death of Naram-Sin, the Akkadian empire had collapsed. A Sumerian poem entitled *The Curse of Akkad* charges Naram-Sin with the responsibility for it: he had looted and destroyed the Temple of Enlil, god of winds and storms, in Nippur (southeast of Babylon) and brought down the wrath of the gods. There was no rain, a famine

[3] The cache of booty found by the excavators of Susa also included the famous stele of Hammurabi and the obelisk of Manishtushu: discussed recently, e.g., by M. Van De Mieroop, *King Hammurabi of Babylon. A Biography* (Oxford, 2005): 129–130.

FIGURE 1. Stele of Naram-Sin, ca. 2230 BCE. Originally from Mesopotamia, found in Susa, Iran. Louvre Museum, Paris, France. Photo credit: Erich Lessing / Art Resources, NY.

ensued after a severe and prolonged drought, and thus ended a golden age that had begun under his grandfather, Sargon. *The Curse of Akkad* (in wide circulation by ca. 2150) emphasizes and laments the terrible punishment on the community because of the looting and destruction of the temple, described in great detail in fifty lines of text. Unsurprisingly, plundering other people's monuments, sacking temples of their treasures, and anxiety about the repercussions of sacrilege have a long history.[4]

According to biblical accounts, in the following millennium the Temple of Solomon in Jerusalem was plundered and destroyed by King Nebuchadnezzar II of Babylon in 586 BCE. His soldiers removed elaborately worked bronze pillars, stands and temple furnishings, incense burners and ritual vessels, and then burned down the four-hundred-year-old Temple. The greater part of the population was forcibly deported to Babylon (2 Kings 25:13). After living in Babylon for a whole generation, the captured Jewish people were released, thanks to a new, more compassionate ruler. The Persian king, Cyrus the Great, conqueror and founder of the Persian Empire in the mid-sixth century, is said to have allowed the return of the deported Jewish people, giving them permission to rebuild the Temple. Biblical authors depict Cyrus as sending back with them 5,400 gold and silver vessels from the original Temple that Nebuchadnezzar had taken and dedicated in Babylon (Ezra 1:9, 5:14). After considerable delay, the Temple was rebuilt by 516 BCE,

---

[4] Although the plundering of the temple may have been a poetic invention, such plundering is boasted in many other accounts of this era. The devastating drought ca. 2200 is proving to be historical: summary of evidence (from the Aegean to the Indus) in H. Weiss, "Late Third Millennium Abrupt Climate Change and Social Collapse in West Asia and Egypt," in H. N. Dalfes et al., *Third Millennium BC Climate Change and Old World Collapse* (Berlin, 1997): 711–723. For an edition and translation of the poem, J. S. Cooper, *The Curse of Agade* (Baltimore and London, 1983): destruction of temples, lines 98–148. A general account of Weiss's findings by E. Kolbert appeared in *The New Yorker*, May 2, 2005: 64–73, and forms chapter 5 of her *Field Notes from a Catastrophe: Man, Nature and Climate Change* (New York, 2006).

and life could continue with the Temple in Jerusalem as the focal point. During the course of its biblical history from Solomon onward, however, the Jewish Temple was sacked and the contents plundered at least seventeen times before it was finally destroyed by the Romans under Titus in 70 CE.[5]

King Cyrus' humane treatment of the Jewish captives and his "compassionate return" of sacred items to Jerusalem (as depicted in the Hebrew Bible) also illustrate a corollary, what Xenophon calls *philanthropeia*. Writing in the 360s BCE, Xenophon in the epigraph at the beginning of this chapter has his hero, the great Cyrus, exhort his troops and reassure them of the right of the victors to booty in the course of a confrontation with Assyrians. In this, the Persian king is no different from his Assyrian antagonist, who in the same essay also exhorts his men from his chariot on the battlefield by reminding them that they will lose land, houses, family, and all property if they lose but keep all those things and win everything from the enemy if they prevail in battle: "For who does not know that victors save their own possessions and take in addition what belongs to the defeated?" says the Assyrian king (*Cyr.* 3.3.44). With these sentiments, the Greek historian Xenophon sums up a long tradition in the ancient Near East: the winner takes all – unless, out of humanity (*philanthropeia*), the conquerors are generous. Xenophon himself fought for Cyrus' namesake in Mesopotamia and knew the tradition well. He understood the ambivalence about destruction a soldier might feel that would require such reassurance of the sort he has his fictional Cyrus give. These two linked models of behavior in war, that the winner takes all and that some winners might show humane qualities in the aftermath of victory, are thus firmly rooted in historical memory.

---

[5] Excellent discussion in E. Cline, *Jerusalem Besieged* (Ann Arbor, 2004): tally on p. 129 and footnote 97. For a study of Jewish cultural survival, despite constant plunder, between 586 BCE and 70 CE, see S. Weitzman, *Surviving Sacrilege. Cultural Persistence in Jewish Antiquity* (Cambridge, MA, 2005).

GREEK ANTECEDENTS

The oldest and perhaps most significant stolen statue in western literature is the Palladion, a small, wooden, armed statue of Athena that protected Troy as the city's talisman. The conquest of Troy (see Map 1) was made possible (so it was widely believed in antiquity) because a pair of Greeks had managed to sneak into the city and steal the Palladion from the Temple of Athena. Without the protection of the Palladion, the Trojans were susceptible to stratagems like the gift of the Wooden Horse. Yet the Trojans were not the only ones who faced calamity after the loss of the Palladion, in part because stealing the statue was a sacrilegious act. According to a long literary tradition, many of the victorious Greeks themselves suffered afterward, including Odysseus, who masterminded the theft.

Possession of statues and stories of their theft in time of war help explain the fate of cities and of heroes from the beginning of western literary tradition. Even before Virgil's great epic, in earlier Greek accounts Aeneas survives the sack of Troy largely because he carries with him not only his aged father but also his *penates*, small statues of his household gods. Roman authors naturally found various plot-devices to move the sacred Palladion itself to Rome as its final destination: in one version, Diomedes alone had stolen it and then gave it to Aeneas in Lavinium, and so Rome, founded by descendants of the Trojan Aeneas and protected by the recovered Palladion, would be invincible forever. In these literary accounts, we see both the potency of a talismanic statue and the repercussions of its theft.[6]

---

[6] For the Palladion as a talisman, C. A. Faraone, *Talismans & Trojan Horses* (Oxford 1992): 6–7, 136–169; for the literary versions of the story and visual representations of the Palladion, J. Boardman and C. E. Vafopoulou-Richardson, "Diomedes I," in *LIMC* 3 (1986): 396–409, and Roscher III.1 (1897–1909): 1301–1309, s.v. "Palladion" (E. Wörner); for the Palladion as a complement to the Wooden Horse: M. J. Anderson, *The Fall of Troy in Early Greek Poetry and Art* (Oxford, 1997): 17–20.

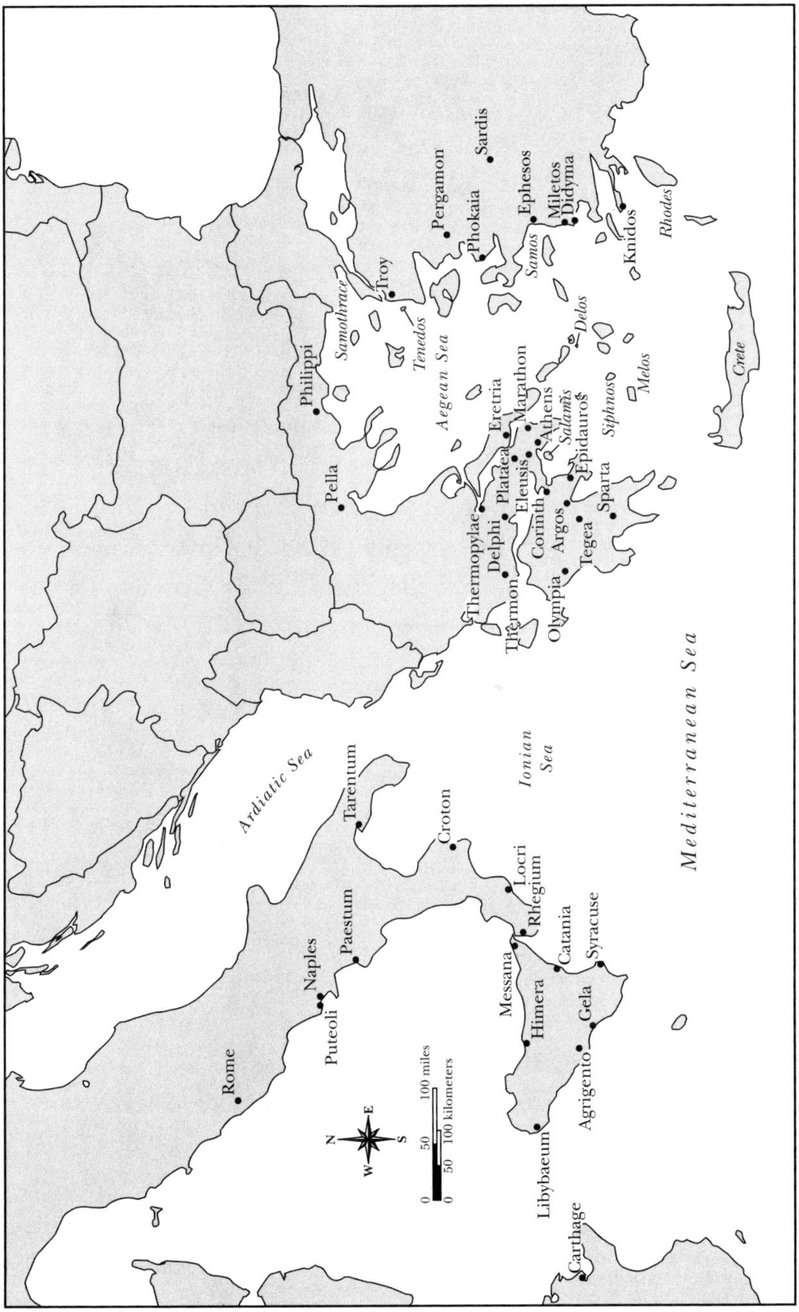

Sardis

Pergamon

Phokaia Ephesos

Troy Samos Miletos
Didyma

Knidos

Rhodes

Samothrace

Tenedos

Philippi

Aegean Sea

Delos

Melos

Crete

Pella

Eretria
Marathon
Delphi Plataea Athens
Thermopylae Eleusis Salamis Siphnos
Thermon Corinth Epidauros
Olympia Argos Sparta
Tegea

Adriatic Sea

Tarentum

Croton

Ionian
Sea

Locri
Rhegium

Naples

Paestum Messana Catania
Himera Syracuse

Rome

Puteoli Gela

Agrigento

Mediterranean Sea

N
W E
S

0   50   100 miles
0   50   100 kilometers

Libybaeum

Carthage

MAP 1. Southern Italy and Greece

21

Homeric epic also features piracy as an accepted way of life. Telema-chos, son of Odysseus, is asked, "Are you a pirate?" when he arrives at the court of Nestor (*Od.* 3.80–83), a question that Thucydides asserts was a common greeting in that earlier age to those who arrive by sea (1.5). There seems to have been little distinction in practice between piracy and warfare in this period (assuming that such details in Homer's epics reflect his own era, ca. 700 BCE), but piracy was looked upon with some disdain, even though heroes could acquire status through booty won even by piracy.[7] The acquisition and possession of booty, in the form of material goods even more so than captives, was a clear marker of heroic status. When Odysseus finally nears home in Ithaca after twenty years away, he was not supposed to arrive empty-handed: Zeus sends Hermes to the Phaeacians to let them know they should send Odysseus off with bronze, gold, and robes, more than he could have won at Troy (*Od.* 5.41–44).

Disapproval of piracy accelerates with the rise of organized maritime trade by cities, and the distinction between piracy and warfare also is made clear in historical accounts. Thucydides credits Corinth and her rising wealth as the force that initially cleared the seas of pirates (1.13). Piracy persisted throughout antiquity, rising in chaotic times and ebbing when there was organized opposition from regular naval fleets and adequate protection of harbors. As P. de Souza has shown, the character of piracy and the way it was viewed changes considerably through antiquity.[8]

Pirates became especially notorious not for targeting temples or sanc-tuaries, however, but rather for their common practice of kidnapping

---

[7] On the complexities of interpretation of piracy in Homer and Thucydides' account of the era, see P. de Souza, *Piracy in the Greco-Roman World* (Cambridge, 1999): 15–26; also on raids and piracy in the Classical and Hellenistic periods, W. K. Pritchett, *The Greek State at War* 5 (Berkeley and Oxford, 1991): 312–363.

[8] de Souza (1999).

travelers and other vulnerable people and ransoming or selling them into slavery. (The capture by pirates of a hero or heroine becomes a stock plot device in later Greek novels.) Pirates demonstrate their spiritual myopia in just such an episode recounted in Homeric Hymn 7: they capture the god Dionysos, thinking he is a young prince they can ransom. Soon the ship fills with wine, and grapevines and ivy grow from the mast. Still they fail to recognize his divinity, even when warned by the helmsman, who recognizes the signs. Eventually, the pirates jump overboard and are changed into dolphins, a metamorphosis depicted in Greek and Roman art.[9] Literary myth made the pirates' transgression even more direct than seizing statues.

Another mythical robbing of a temple was Herakles' effort to carry off Apollo's tripod from his oracle at Delphi, perhaps because the Pythia refused to answer him. The incident is represented as early as the mid-sixth century BCE in a sculptured metope from the Heraion at Foce del Sele (near Paestum), but the story is narrated only in much later literary accounts. They attribute various motives to Herakles, generally depicted as a freebooting adventurer who also performs difficult tasks and rids the world of nuisance creatures.[10] Elaborately worked tripods that support cauldron-like bowls were a favored form of dedication in sanctuaries, but at Delphi, the tripod is also associated with the oracle itself, as a seat for the Pythia where she could become inspired by the god. In some versions of the story, Herakles is not simply pillaging but also wishes to set up his own oracle. In the small pediment of the Siphnian treasury at Delphi (ca. 525 BCE), we see Herakles and Apollo each pulling on a leg of the tripod, with a tall Zeus standing behind in the process of adjudicating between them (Fig. 2). In this didactic

[9] C. Gasparri and A. Veneri, *LIMC* 3: 414–420, 423, 489, 496–514, and 541–558 (Dionysos/Bacchus).

[10] For sources, T. Gantz, *Early Greek Myths. A Guide to Literary and Artistic Sources* (Baltimore and London, 1993): 437–438; visual representations, S. Woodford, *LIMC* 5 (19): 133ff.

and possibly metaphorical sculpture, Zeus enforces Apollo's rightful possession of the tripod and the oracle, and the robbing of the temple is forestalled.

ATHENS PLUNDERED

As an archaeologist, I have seen firsthand how the destructive results of warfare in ancient cities could leave a clear trace evident even two thousand years later. While excavating in the Agora of Athens some years ago, diggers encountered a layer of ash filled with architectural fragments, which proved to be "Sullan destruction debris," a result of the Roman general Sulla's sack of Athens in 86 BCE, vengeance on the Athenians for siding with Mithradates of Pontus against Rome. Sullan destruction debris has been found in several areas of the Agora, the Kerameikos, and elsewhere around the city, and it confirms historical accounts of the siege. Especially notable among the plunder Sulla is said to have taken from Athens were some antique inscribed shields from the Stoa of Zeus in the Agora, a famous painting by Zeuxis, some columns from the Temple of Zeus Olympios (perhaps destined for the Temple of Jupiter on the Capitoline in Rome), and Aristotle's library.[11]

As we dug down farther, pits of destruction debris provided vivid support for Herodotus' description of the Persian sack of Athens in 479 BCE (8.52–53). King Xerxes had come in person, with a fleet and a huge army, determined to avenge Greek actions in Asia Minor and to make Greece a part of the Persian Empire. The Persians plundered and burned the temples on the Akropolis, smashed its statuary and other

---

[11] Sullan plunder: shields, Pausanias 10.21.6; painting, Lucian, *Zeuxis or Antiochos* 3; columns: Pliny, *HN* 36.45; library, Plut. *Sulla*, 26. For the extent of damage in Athens caused by Sulla, M. Hoff, "*Laceratae Athenae*: Sulla's Siege of Athens in 87/6 B.C. and its Aftermath," in M. C. Hoff and S. I. Rotroff, eds., *The Romanization of Athens* (Oxford, 1997): 33–51. For the library, J. Barnes, "Roman Aristotle," in J. Barnes and M. Griffin, eds., *Philosophia Togata II. Plato and Aristotle at Rome* (Oxford, 1997): 1–21.

FIGURE 2. Pediment of Siphnian Treasury, ca. 525 BCE. Delphi Museum, Greece. The photograph has been cropped. Photo credit: Alison Frantz Collection, The American School of Classical Studies, Athens.

votive offerings, and devastated the whole city below it. Even more dramatic than our pits of debris were the seventeen wells excavated in the Agora during the 1960s and 1970s. After the Persian sack, the wells had been abandoned as a water supply – probably they were believed to be poisoned – and were found by excavators packed with mud-brick, pieces of wood, and broken crockery, cleaned up from the destroyed households that had used the wells before the Persians invaded.[12]

During that invasion, Xerxes is believed to have taken at least four statues from Athens back to his capital at Susa, among them the

[12] T. L. Shear, Jr., "The Persian Destruction of Athens: Evidence from Agora Deposits," *Hesperia* 62 (1993): 383–482.

pair known as the "Tyrannicides," statues of Harmodios and Aristo-geiton (Fig. 3). The Tyrannicides had killed a member of the autocratic Peisistratid family, which had dominated Athens in the sixth century BCE, in an uprising that led to the foundation of the first democratic constitution in Athens. So important to the Athenians had been these statues that after Xerxes was driven out of Greece, they immediately commissioned a new pair for the Agora. More than 150 years later, Alexander the Great, in a gesture of respect for Athens (over which he had won complete control a short time earlier), is said to have sent back the original statues from the Persian palace, and there they stood as a constant reminder of democratic spirit, along with the replacements, in the heart of the Agora for at least five hundred years.[13]

The Athenians had in their collective memory invasions of the city by Thracians and Amazons, and remembered being in thrall to King Minos of Crete, but those events were safely far back in the distant, mythic past. Now they were stunned by the Persian devastation of Athens and especially by the damage to the Akropolis, sacred to Athena. In the fourth century BCE, Athenian orators, looking back on the Persian Wars, assert that all the victorious Greeks (or just the Athenians and Ionians) swore an oath not to rebuild the destroyed temples, but to leave them in ruins as a memorial to the impiety of the barbarians. Although the oath is now generally regarded as a fiction of the fourth century, it is an archaeological fact that in Athens the temples were not rebuilt until the 460s. As part of the cleaning up of the Akropolis after the Persian sack, the Athenians took apart the scorched and cracked blocks of the Older Parthenon and the Old Temple of Athena and built many

---

[13] Alexander is given the credit for this "compassionate" return by Pliny (*HN* 34.70) and Arrian (3.16.7, 7.19.2), generally accepted; Seleucus is named by Valerius Maximus (2.10, ext. 1, with the additional comment that on the way back, the statues were given a public banquet in the city of Rhodes); Antiochos is the donor in Pausanias (1.8.5). Pausanias saw the two pairs together in the Agora about 160 CE. For discussion of scholarly speculations about the various attributions, see J.-L. Ferrary, *Philhellénisme et Impérialisme* (Rome, 1988): 582–587.

FIGURE 3. The Tyrannicides Harmodios and Aristogeiton, Roman version of Greek original. National Archaeological Museum, Naples. Photo credit: Alinari / Art Resource, NY.

of them facing outward into the north wall of the Akropolis, where they may be seen today (Fig. 4).

Besides Athenian temples, the Persians burned temples on the islands of Chios, Lesbos, Tenedos, and Euboea but, seeking to account for this sacrilege, Herodotus comments twice that the Persians burned Greek temples in reprisal for the burning of the Temple of Cybele at Sardis by Greeks earlier in the 490s (5.102, 6.101). Herodotus also illustrates Persian respect for Greek sanctuaries. The day after the temples on the Akropolis in Athens were burned down, Xerxes felt uneasy and ordered Athenian survivors to go up to the Akropolis and make sacrifices there according to their usual custom. Herodotus speculates that he might have been urged to do so in a dream or because of a troubled conscience (*enthumion*, 8.54–55). Despite Xerxes' attempted expiation, Herodotus has the Greek judgment of Xerxes' actions summed up by Themistocles in the course of his (possibly duplicitous) advice to the Athenians not to pursue the Persian fleet, on the grounds of potential divine retribution: they should let the fleet go, because the gods and heroes "were jealous that one man should be king of both Asia and of Europe, who was wicked and presumptuous, who considered sacred property and private property the same, who burnt and overthrew the statues of the gods, and lashed the sea with whips and bound it with fetters" (8.109).[14]

In the course of the earlier Persian invasion by Xerxes' father Darius, the Persian admiral Datis offered a huge quantity of frankincense on the altar of Apollo in the sanctuary on Delos and even chastised the Delians for running away (6.97–98). While returning to Asia Minor after defeat at the battle of Marathon, Datis was prompted by a dream to inspect the cargo holds of the fleet under his command and discovered a gold-covered statue of Apollo in a Phoenician ship. He took it on his own ship and sailed back to Delos, where he left it for safekeeping, until it was

[14] For discussion of retribution as a theme in Greek historical accounts, see G. W. Trompf, *Early Christian Historiography. Narratives of Retributive Justice* (London and New York, 2000): 10–33.

FIGURE 4. North wall of Akropolis, Athens. Photo credit: Author.

claimed later by its owners at Delion, a coastal town in Boeotia opposite Euboea (6.118). Sacred plunder was believed to have the potential
to bring unwanted consequences. Herodotus, writing in the 440s BCE
about events early in the century, presents the Persian Wars as a conflict
with suffering, destruction, and reprisals directed at humans on both
sides, but with Persian antagonists still (intermittently) observant of
the sanctity of Greek sanctuaries.

The battles at Marathon and Plataia yielded quantities of Persian
booty that amazed the victorious Greeks, and the memory of it lasted for
centuries. Even as late as the second century CE, Pausanias, who traveled
throughout mainland Greece and wrote an account of the temples and
monuments, was shown items said to have been taken from Persians
in the famous battles. Especially interesting are the "Persian" relics he
saw in the Erechtheion (Temple of Athena Polias) on the Akropolis

of Athens, presumably dedicated after the collective Greek victory at Plataia (1.27.1). Pausanias mentions the cuirass of Masistios, a Persian cavalry commander second in Persian esteem only to Mardonios, whose gold-plated iron cuirass, death, and the ensuing struggle for his body are described in detail by Herodotus (9.22). Pausanias also was shown the golden Persian dagger of Mardonios himself but was rightly skeptical about its authenticity because, as he says, the Spartans would have kept this trophy for themselves.[15] (If they were authentic, they would have been about 650 years old when he saw them.) Clearly, some "booty" might have been forged over the years in response to famous historical descriptions of battles, such as Herodotus' account of the events at Plataia.

GREEK BOOTY

W. K. Pritchett has given us a masterly, thorough account of the many aspects of Greek booty, and I give here only a summary of some principal points as a background for Roman practices.[16] We shall see that among Greeks art was created as a result of victory, often from booty, more frequently than it was specifically targeted for plunder. Evidence for Greek attitudes toward booty and its acquisition is abundant in ancient historians' accounts because war is their main subject. This is supplemented by inscriptions, especially from sanctuaries

---

[15] Furthermore, the dagger (even if inauthentic) was possibly subject to a famous theft in the fourth century BCE; on booty from defeated Persians on the Akropolis, see D. Harris, *The Treasures of the Parthenon and Erechtheion* (Oxford, 1995): 204–205. On the cultural impact on Athenians of the Persian spoils from Marathon and Plataia and spoils as a form of cultural exchange, see M. C. Miller, *Athens and Persia in the Fifth Century BC. A Study in Cultural Receptivity* (Cambridge, 1997): 29–62.

[16] Pritchett, *Greek State at War* 1 (1971), 3 (1979), and 5 (1991). Among earlier discussions, Ducrey on the treatment, sale, and profit from human captives is thorough: P. Ducrey, *Le traitement des prisonniers de guerre dans la Grèce antique* (Paris, 1968). For a more general, interpretive essay on symbolic uses of booty in representations of power among both Greeks and Romans, see T. Hölscher, "The Transformation of Victory into Power: From Event to Structure," in S. Dillon and K. Welch, eds., *Representations of War in Ancient Rome* (Cambridge, 2006): 27–48.

where dedications were made after victories. Finds include inscribed dedications, often with the victory advertised, and magistrates' inventories of the treasuries in temples. Actual victory dedications (sculpture, arms and armor, and buildings) have been preserved or found in excavations.

According to ancient Greek custom, the deity of a sanctuary owned all its votives, statues, and other dedications and any sacred grove, orchard, or other land associated with the sanctuary (the god could even make loans and charge interest, with the temple as the bank). Because this was the god's property, the sacred space, temples and other buildings, and all contents were considered inviolable – immune from war. Sacred land was marked out with boundary stones or sometimes surrounded by walls or, in the case of the small island Delos, the water's edge marked the boundary. Respectful behavior was required within sacred property: bodily functions, giving birth, dying, and dogs were typically prohibited. This expectation is attested by numerous warning inscriptions from various sanctuaries and references in ancient authors to polluting behavior and its punishment.[17]

The temples had practical protection from common thieves. Security measures have left traces in the archaeological record, such as cuttings for placing grills between columns, locked stone chests, and walls around some sanctuaries. In Athens, annual inventories were made of the temple treasures on the Akropolis, for which magistrates were directly responsible, in an effort to prevent embezzlement. Even raw materials purchased for statues were under protection: we hear of (false, politically motivated) accusations against Pheidias, that he peculated gold or ivory intended for the image of Athena Parthenos. It was considered fair and reasonable to use some of the god's treasure in very dire circumstances, as long as it was paid back; hence, the gold drapery on

---

[17] R. Parker, *Miasma. Pollution and Purification in Early Greek Religion* (Oxford, 1983): 160–163, 235–256; on inviolability, K. J. Rigsby, *Asylia. Territorial Inviolability in the Hellenistic World* (Berkeley and London, 1996): 1–19, 25–26.

Pheidias' Athena Parthenos was made so that it could be removed and weighed.[18] Related to the inviolability of a sanctuary was the custom that suppliants fleeing from civic or even familial authority could claim protection in sanctuaries. This was not always respected and we hear of violations of asylum of prominent individuals, but it remained for many centuries an ideal, from a sense of natural reciprocity with the gods.[19]

Usually sanctuaries and their precious contents were respected by Greek adversaries in the Archaic and Classical periods. Historical accounts that include violations begin with Herodotus' history of the Persian Wars and the preceding era. While we hear of earlier disputes over control of sacred land, presumably the normative ethics of respecting the contents within sanctuaries prevailed in the earlier era, although mythical antecedents such as the struggle over the Delphic tripod hint at potential violations. Accounts of the sack of Greek sanctuaries from the late fifth century BCE onward, however, include staggering figures of accumulated wealth; even allowing for some exaggeration, it is obvious that such wealth could accumulate over time because the inviolability of the sanctuary had been respected previously. In his account of the siege and sack of wealthy Akragas (modern Agrigento) in Sicily by Carthaginians in 406, Diodorus says specifically that the city and temples had never been plundered since its founding in 581 (Diod., 13.90.3). Among the items taken was the bronze Bull of Phalaris, an antique revered by Akragentines as commemorative of their earlier

---

[18] Thucydides has Pericles list among the resources of the Athenians as they faced the Spartans 40 talents of gold on the statue (2.13.5); for Pheidias, Plutarch (*Per.* 31.2); for inventories, Harris (1995); for references to temple robbery (*hierosylia*), considered an exceptionally heinous crime, and its punishment, Pritchett, *Greek State at War* 5: 161 and n. 211.

[19] Ducrey (1968): 289–311; U. Sinn, "Greek Sanctuaries as Places of Refuge," in N. Marinatos and R. Hägg, eds., *Greek Sanctuaries. New Approaches* (London and New York, 1993): 88–109. Violations of this aspect of "sanctuary" date back to Homeric poetry: Ajax seizes and rapes Cassandra, who is shown in Greek sculpture and in Greek and Roman paintings as clinging to an image of Athena within her temple; eventually he is punished.

tyrant, an important symbol of political reversal like the Tyrannicides in Athens.

It was customary to offer to major deities a portion ("best parts" or "top parts") of whatever booty was gained in war. Typically, money from the ransom or sale of captives into slavery or from items taken in war would be used to commission a new monument or statue – or even a temple, treasury, or stoa – for the sanctuary, which was usually inscribed with a record of the event. Arms and armor were very common dedications and many have been excavated at Olympia, where the soil conserves bronze well. Dedications were set up in the victors' own home sanctuaries, but major victories were also publicized in the Panhellenic sanctuaries: Delphi and Olympia are still filled with the foundations and inscribed bases for such offerings. Because of this, the Panhellenic sanctuaries became artistic centers, where innovative displays and techniques influenced subsequent creations. Such public offerings were carefully positioned for maximum impact: at Delphi, Spartan and Athenian statue-groups of heroes and generals could posture to each other just yards apart across the Sacred Way. Another large portion of the booty typically would be deposited into the city's central treasury for further wars or improvements to the city.[20]

Whereas sanctuaries were the primary places for the display of art, the public spaces of the agoras in Greek cities were also furnished with statuary and other sculptural decoration. The agora of Athens contained shops, law courts, meeting places, offices of magistrates, archives, and other public buildings, but it also had the character of a sanctuary with boundary markers, and there were numerous smaller shrines within it. The statues of the Tyrannicides were set up near the Altar of the Twelve Gods – considered the center marker of the city and itself decorated

---

[20] On division of spoils, Pritchett, *Greek State at War* 5: 363–437; fate of captives, 5: 203–312; armor, 3: 240–295; dedications generally, 1: 93–100 and 3: 240–242; legal ownership of booty, 1: 85–104.

with sculptured reliefs – and many other statues and statue-groups are documented by inscriptions or ancient authors who mention them.[21]

As for private ownership of art, expensive artistic objects were not commonly made for general private use in the fifth century BCE, and only gradually in the fourth century was there a rising standard of private consumption. This was a consequence of viewing the public, religious sphere as the appropriate place for display of public and private surplus wealth: in the Greek world, stone temples are the most characteristic form of architecture, not impressive private houses or palaces. The case of the Athenian Alcibiades, a rich aristocrat, general, political leader, and athlete, serves as an example: his household property was confiscated as a result of a conviction for impiety in 415 BCE. Preserved inscriptions (although incomplete) list the contents, and they are not impressive furnishings.[22] Elsewhere in the Greek world, wealthy Akragas was unusual in providing the Carthaginian plunderers with precious and artistic items that had been in private possession. In his account of the Carthaginian sack of 406, Diodorus describes at length the extraordinary private wealth of the citizens of Akragas, who had a thriving trade in olive oil with the Carthaginians themselves. These merchants had built large houses and had amassed extensive collections of paintings and statues. The temples and agora of Akragas were also full of rich dedications. Here was the realized potential for both private and public luxury, as early as the late fifth century BCE.[23] In contrast,

[21] Shrines and statues in the agora, *Agora* 3: 48–125.
[22] *IG* I³ 421–432; *Agora* 31: 65–66, 203–205. Plutarch, commenting on Alcibiades' faults, says he once kept the painter Agatharcus imprisoned in his house until he painted the whole of it but then paid him (*Alc.* 16.4). Illustrated wall-painting in private houses such as that at Pompeii, however, is a much later phenomenon. Plutarch also comments on an expensive chariot Alcibiades bought and horses and other equipment people gave him. See further Pritchett, *Greek State at War* 5: 193, n. 276.
[23] It is possible that Diodorus is retrojecting into his account some of the Roman *luxuria* of his own time into the past but the wealth of Akragas is attested by other authors, and the number, quality, and size of Doric temples in the city shows that they had unusual public

Sparta had strong taboos and legislation against luxury and ostentation and served as an exemplar over several centuries for austere living and (consequent) military might.[24]

The excavations of the city Olynthus in northern Greece provide further insight into private ownership and the increasing standard of living. The city was destroyed and thoroughly looted by Philip II in 348 BCE and was not rebuilt. Ordinary household objects, not valuable or too difficult to move, were found in quantity by the excavators on the floors of the houses, some of them fallen from upper stories. In a meticulous study of the find-spots of the artifacts, N. Cahill has shown that some expected equipment, such as sympotic vessels (drinking equipment) for the androns (rooms used for men's dinner parties), was absent. This suggests that they commonly used metal rather than ceramic vessels, which were either taken by fleeing survivors or pillaged carefully by Philip's troops.[25] By the mid-fourth century, then, ordinary people in a small town in northern Greece evidently could afford metal vessels for entertainment. Other fine crafts, such as carpets and tapestries, probably existed in many households but have left only reflections in patterns on other more durable media. Fine jewelry has been found in graves of all periods. Objects of potentially artistic value, as well as intrinsic value, were now not just the exclusive property of the wealthy, heroes, and gods. Even so, the best items were dedicated to the gods.

---

wealth, rivaled only by Selinous. Diodorus was from Agyrium in Sicily and probably lived in Rome; he was a younger contemporary of Cicero, writing ca. 60–30 BCE. For historiographical issues concerning his use of sources, see K. Sacks, *Diodorus Siculus and the First Century* (Princeton, 1990) and P. Green's introductory essay in *Diodorus Siculus, Books 11–12.37.1. Greek History, 480–431 BC. The Alternative Version* (Austin, 2006).

[24] Nonetheless, Spartan households did possess valuables: detailed discussion in S. Hodkinson, *Property and Wealth in Classical Sparta* (London, 2000): on booty, 153–154, 358–359; on restrictions of private wealth, 209–235.

[25] N. Cahill, *Household and City Organization at Olynthus* (New Haven and London, 2002): 45–49, 187–190.

During the Peloponnesian War in the later fifth century BCE, belligerents occasionally violated the custom of respecting sanctuaries, not through pillage but through profane use, which could still cause shock and protest.[26] What we see in the course of the fourth and third centuries is a loosening of these standards of behavior because of kaleidoscopic changes in the economics of warfare and its social support, the institutional strengths of the polis, and wider interactions among people around the Mediterranean. The need to pay mercenaries (rather than relying on civic defense or civic conscription as in preceding generations) seems to drive the initial violations noted by ancient authors.

When the inviolability began to be broken, what may have started out as a "loan" from a sanctuary in a time of emergency became, in the eyes of the perpetrators, a necessity for survival. Many anecdotes concerning this type of violation were circulated in antiquity about Dionysios I of Syracuse (ca. 430–367 BCE), who emerged in the western Mediterranean after the Carthaginian sack of Akragas as an extremely effective military leader and became a king (*basileus*), archon, tyrant, or warlord (depending on who is describing him).[27] Eventually, he dominated most of Sicily and parts of southern Italy, after first driving out the Carthaginians. He needed to pay mercenaries in order to accomplish all of this, and so we hear of many depredations in sanctuaries, where he could find concentrated wealth. Here are just a few of his plunderings mentioned by ancient authors: in Syracuse itself, he is

[26] E.g., the episode of Athenian encampment at Boeotian Delion in 424, and the claims and counterclaims about violation of the sanctuary (but not theft) and the sacred spring (Thuc. 4.97–98). Pritchett, *Greek State at War* 5: 160–168, collects and discusses this and several other episodes of violating sanctuaries; he also tabulates all instances of mention of booty in Herodotus, Thucydides, Xenophon's *Hellenica* and *Anabasis*, Polybius, Diodorus (after 480), and Polyainos, pp. 505–541. For Spartan scrupulousness, M. D. Goodman and A. J. Holladay, "Religious Scruples in Ancient Warfare," *CQ* 36 (1986): 151–171.

[27] For the difficulties of discerning a true portrait of Dionysios, see B. Caven, *Dionysius I. War-Lord of Sicily* (New Haven and London, 1990): 1–6, 222–253; also L. J. Sanders, *Dionysios I of Syracuse and Greek Tyranny* (London, New York, and Sydney, 1987).

said to have taken a gold mantle from the sanctuary of Zeus Olympios (Aelian, *VH* 1.20), and he customarily took statuettes of Victory, gold cups, and crowns from the hands of statues of gods, saying that he was availing himself of these offerings (Cicero, *Nat. D.* 3.84). From the sanctuary of Hera at Croton, preeminent among Greek sanctuaries in Italy, he took an especially magnificent cloak that had been dedicated by a wealthy Sybarite more than a hundred years earlier; he then sold it to the Carthaginians, who appreciated fine textiles, for the very large sum of 120 talents (Athenaeus, 12.541A). He attacked the Etruscan port Pyrgi and robbed its Temple of Leukothea in a campaign that yielded a total of 1,500 talents (Polyainos, 5.2.21).[28] In his speeches on Verres, Cicero invokes Dionysios I's activities as parallel for Verres' rapaciousness.

In old Greece, Xenophon reports embezzlement from the sanctuary of Zeus at Olympia in 364 BCE by a small group of magistrates of the Arcadian Confederacy in order to pay mercenaries. This so disturbed the Mantineans that they voluntarily sent their share of the pay so as not to be responsible for sacrilege.[29] Just a few years later, starting in 356, the Phocians incurred enormous opprobrium by plundering the sanctuary of Apollo at Delphi in order to pay mercenaries and thus precipitated a Sacred War.[30] As some years went by, the money was all spent, and they had already melted and coined the accumulated dedications. They then

---

[28] Other references in Pritchett, *Greek State at War* 5: 163–165. In an incident illustrating respect for the gods, Dionysios is said to have tried to dedicate statues worked in gold and ivory at Delphi and Olympia that were seized as plunder and sold by Iphicrates, the Athenian general, with Athenian assent (Diod., 16.57.2–3). Diodorus cites this incident as an example of Athenian arrogance, hypocrisy, and impiety and quotes a letter of protest from Dionysios written to the Athenians.

[29] Xen. *Hell.* 7.4.33–34, discussed by J. A. O. Larsen, *Greek Federal States. Their Institutions and History* (Oxford, 1968): 188–193. The magistrates were also accused of enriching themselves from the sanctuary.

[30] The origins and politics are discussed by J. Buckler, *Philip II and the Sacred War*, Mnemosyne, Supp. 109 (Leiden, 1989): 9–29, 37–57. A fragmentary inscription records items they took, discussed by C. Habicht, "Pausanias and the Evidence of Inscriptions," *ClAnt* 3 (1984): 47 (the inscribed list includes a huge silver bowl dedicated by King Alyattes of Lydia, father of Croesus, a gift also mentioned by Herodotus [1.25]).

desperately dug up the floor of the temple, still under reconstruction after the earthquake of 373, in the belief that they would find more gold and silver. Their depredations could not be considered "loans" because what they took had been dedicated by other cities, now doubly affronted by the sacrilegious behavior.

Their brief ascendancy was eventually blocked by Philip II of Macedon, and their generals came to fatefully bad ends that were viewed by ancient authors as just recompense. They were also supposed to pay back an indemnity of 60 talents a year. In ancient accounts, not only the mercenaries and leaders suffer in the end but also their wives, who wore gold jewelry stolen from the sanctuary, such as necklaces that were said to have belonged to Helen and Eriphyle. They were eventually forced into prostitution, punished, or killed in fates that mirrored the destinies of the original owners of the jewelry. Especially interesting in the stories of the offenders' deaths is that the end comes with some indirection: being forced to jump off a cliff, drowned at sea, or burned alive in one's house in a fire set by a maddened son – so that the recompense seems to come from the offended god, not from direct bloodshed by a human hand.[31]

The plundering of Delphi brought into circulation a huge quantity of precious metals, more than 10,000 talents, and bronze and iron was melted down for new weaponry. Some of the items melted and coined had been dedicated some two hundred years earlier by King Croesus of Lydia. The sacrilege of using Delphic treasure was considered so serious that at least one city is said to have rounded up all coined silver known to have come from Delphi, melted it down, made a new dedication out of it, and sent it back. What was especially egregious about this violation was that it was perpetrated not by barbarian invaders but by the Phocians,

---

[31] For the sacrilege, Diod. 16.14.3, 23–39, 56–64; full citations of ancient references and further discussion in H. W. Parke and D. E. W. Wormell, *The Delphic Oracle* (Oxford, 1956): 221–232, with n. 31 on p. 232; see also Parker, *Miasma*: 172–175, on recompense for sacrilege.

Greeks themselves in whose territory the traditionally independent oracle at Delphi was the most resplendent sanctuary of Greece.

One famous object the Phocians melted down was a large gold tripod that had been collectively dedicated to Apollo by the Greeks who defeated the Persians at Plataia. It was made and dedicated as a tithe from Persian booty left on the battlefield. The gold tripod was supported by a bronze column representing three intertwined snakes, with the names of the Greek communities that had participated inscribed on individual coils of the snakes' bodies. The bronze Serpent Column was spared and today stands in the Hippodrome in Istanbul, having been taken from Delphi by Constantine I in the fourth century CE to decorate his new city[32] (Fig. 5). Fragments of the circular base that supported the snakes and tripod still exist at Delphi.

By the Hellenistic period, conquering generals took on the ancient Near Eastern view and seized whatever they wanted when they sacked a city or sanctuary. Often a primary motive in war, or even for war, was the booty: it was needed to pay mercenaries, the fundamental necessity to maintain the claim to monarchical power that was now widespread, and to sustain a suitably luxurious way of life that included lavish display and gifts to others.[33] Alexander operated on that basis throughout his eastern campaigns and victories. Like the French legionnaires under Napoleon, the troops were expected to live off the land through

[32] One of the three snake's heads is also preserved in the Istanbul Archaeological Museum. For the inscription on the snake coils, *ML* 27; Herod. 9.81; Thuc. 1.132.2–3; Diod. Sic. 11.33.2; Paus. 10.13.3; for the Phocian theft, Paus. 10.13.9; for the monument as a dedication, W. Gauer, *Weihgeschenke aus den Perserkriegen, AM Beiheft* 2 (1968): 75–96; D. Laroche, "Nouvelles observations sur l'offrande de Platées," *BCH* 113 (1989): 183–198, and M. Steinhart, "Bemerkungen zu Rekonstruktion, Ikonographie und Inschrift des platäischen Weihgeschenkes," *BCH* 121 (1997): 33–69. For the removal of the Serpent Column to Istanbul, see S. Bassett, *The Urban Image of Late Antique Constantinople* (Cambridge, 2004): 224–227, and Chapter 4 in this book.

[33] Booty as the motive in and for war discussed by M. M. Austin, "Hellenistic Kings, War, and the Economy," *CQ* 36 (1986): 465; avowals of booty as a purpose of war even earlier, Pritchett, *Greek State at War* 5: 439–445.

which they were passing. When he captured the Persian capital Susa, an enormous sum of bullion (at least 40,000 talents of gold and silver) and 9,000 talents of minted gold was found there that was subsequently distributed or spent (Diod. 19.46); at Persepolis, 120,000 talents of silver were taken. Pack animals and three thousand camels had to be rounded up to carry it westward. Here, the Macedonians also found Athens' statues of the Tyrannicides and many other statues, luxurious furniture, vessels, tapestries, vessels of Nile and Danube water, and the bejeweled Golden Vine in the Persian king's bedroom. This storied wealth had been accumulating since the days of King Cyrus more than two centuries earlier.[34] No subsequent conquest could compete with this one for the sheer quantity of bullion and artistic objects.

In the century following Alexander's death, Delphi was threatened once again, this time by groups of Gauls who had been migrating eastward for some decades from the area of modern France and entered into central Greece in 279 BCE. They came close to sacking Delphi, but the sanctuary was staunchly defended under the leadership of the Aetolians, whose homeland lay to the west of Phocis and whose territory had already been invaded by rogue bands of Gauls. The Aetolians had an unsavory reputation in antiquity, largely because they had retained even into this period the freebooting brigandage and piratical customs that had seemed somewhat acceptable back in the Homeric era but now were considered uncivilized.[35] At Delphi, however, they had taken a

---

[34] Booty at Susa: Diodorus, 17.65.5–66.1–2; Arrian, 3.16.6–7 (Harmodius and Aristogeiton); Curt. 5.2.8–12; and Plutarch, *Alex.* 36 (ancient fabric, Nile and Danube water); booty at Persepolis: Diodorus, 17.70–71.2 (mules, camels); Curt. 5.6.2–9 (art and statues hacked into pieces); Plutarch, *Alex.* 37 (mules, camels, colossal statue of Xerxes); and Athen. 12.514e–f (golden vine with clusters of jewels).

[35] On the Aetolians, Polybios says in a summary statement: "The Aetolians had for long been dissatisfied with peace and with an outlay limited to their own resources, as they had been accustomed to live on their neighbors, and required abundance of funds, owing to that natural covetousness, enslaved by which they always lead a life of greed and aggression, like beasts of prey, with no ties of friendship but regarding everyone as an enemy" (4.3.1, trans. Paton [Loeb]).

FIGURE 5. Serpent Column, Hippodrome, Istanbul. Photo credit: Carolyn L. Connor.

heroic stand against barbarian invaders and saved Greece's most important oracle. Afterward, they even set up dedications of Gallic armor there
in ways that recalled Athenian dedications from the Persian Wars.[36] The
victory strengthened the Aetolian Confederacy, which in the next several decades expanded its territory and political influence. This aura
of legitimacy was squandered when they raided four temples in the
Peloponnesos.[37] In 218, they were emboldened to venture into Thessaly
and sack the city and sanctuary of Dion, and soon after they sacked the
famous and venerable oracle at Dodona in Epirus (Polyb., 4.62, 67).

The Aetolians' own primary sanctuary and meeting place was that
of Apollo at Thermon, whose main temple dates back to the seventh
century BCE.[38] This temple and sanctuary were sacked and plundered
in reprisal by Philip V of Macedon shortly after the Aetolians had
plundered Dion and Dodona, an episode that eventually culminated
in the first serious Roman intervention in mainland Greece. In this
first sack of Thermon, Philip V, although angered by the sack of Dion
and Dodona, showed some restraint and toppled 2,000 statues but left
alone statues of gods and those inscribed as dedications to gods in the
sanctuary. His troops did take for their own use or burn some 15,000
items of arms and armor from the stoas in the sanctuary, and they
left taunting graffiti on the walls. They also pillaged the houses and
local stores of goods owned by the Aetolian elite, who had left their
possessions there thinking they were safe (Polyb., 5.8, 9).

Philip V returned to Thermon in 207, however, and this time savagely
destroyed everything. Deliberate destruction in sanctuaries became

---

[36] For the Aetolians and the role in repelling the Gauls, J. B. Scholten, *The Politics of Plunder.
Aitolians and Their Koinon in the Early Hellenistic Era, 279–217 B.C.* (Berkeley and London,
2000): 31–37; on dedications that reflected Athenian monuments, 39–42. The Phocians also
fought very hard against the Gauls because they wanted to rectify their earlier sacrilege
(Pausanias, 10.3.4).

[37] *Ibid.*, 117, with ancient sources.

[38] For the sanctuary at Thermon and its history, C. Antonetti, *Les Étoliens. Image et religion* (Paris, 1990): 151–208. Archaeological evidence confirms Polybius' description of the
magnificence of the sanctuary and its devastation.

his standard operating policy: Athens and Attica, and a sanctuary at Pergamon were subject to this as well.[39] This deliberate pulling down of temples – he was not content just to take statues, offerings, and other wealth – was a new form of sacrilege among Greeks (three centuries earlier the Persian invaders had burned temples). These episodes of despoliation were followed by Greek appeals to the Roman Senate for assistance and intervention.

The range of actions over several centuries taken by Greeks and Macedonians to acquire booty by and from their neighbors is thus well documented, as is the nature of that booty. In addition to the Persian treasures, human captives sold into slavery proved the most reliable and enduring source of income, but military equipment, livestock, food supplies, and ships could also be sold. What the evidence demonstrates is that "art" was not a common target of acquisition in war in the Archaic and Classical periods but rather more often a product of victory in war. Most of what we might now consider art was dedicated in sanctuaries, often as a result of war and created as a victory dedication. This included small buildings, statues, paintings, elaborate vessels in precious metals, fine textiles, and furniture made of exotic woods or ivory, such as the Chest of Cypselus: all items attested by ancient authors. To be sure, dedications were made in sanctuaries for a wide variety of purposes: they could commemorate sudden bursts of prosperity (a large catch of tuna fish off Corfu, a lucky strike in a gold mine on Siphnos) and equestrian or athletic triumphs by individuals in festival games. Military victories were the richest and most elaborate, however, because they were usually communal and had yielded the greatest wealth from

[39] Philip V's incursions in Athens and Attica are attested by Polybius (16.27), Diodorus (28.7), and Livy (31.24.8–18, 31.30); see further F. W. Walbank, *Philip V of Macedon* (Cambridge, 1940): 129–131, 139–141. Archaeological evidence for deliberate destruction of temples in Attica supports their accounts: M. M. Miles, "A Reconstruction of the Temple of Nemesis at Rhamnous," *Hesperia* 58 (1989): 235–236. His ferocious destruction of statues, altars, and temples in the sanctuary of Athena Nikephoros at Pergamon (outside the citadel) is described in detail by Polybius, 16.1 (Walbank, *Commentary* II: 500–503).

which the tithe was taken. In the Hellenistic period, newly created artistic displays to honor military victories became ever more elaborate, such as the Altar of Zeus and Athena at Pergamon, and the Attalid dedications after their victories over the Gauls. When Romans did begin to assert military control over Greece and Asia Minor, they reaped a rich harvest of artistic booty.

SACKING THE CITY, DIVIDING THE BOOTY

Romans also had a collective memory of foreign invasion of their city, not in the distant, mythic past but in the historic record, and after the traumatic sack they made revolutionary changes in their methods of waging war. Rome was plundered for the first time about 386 BCE by the Senones, a Gallic tribe that migrated across the Alps into northern Italy and gathered in the area around modern Bologna and Ravenna. The evidence for the sack in Rome depends completely on historical accounts: although layers of ash and burning have been excavated in the Forum and in the sanctuary near Sant' Omobono in the Forum Boarium, they date to the sixth century BCE and are associated with turmoil around the end of the monarchy.[40] Unlike the Persian sack of Athens, the Gallic sack of Rome left no physical traces so far discovered.

In a reconstruction of events pieced together by T. J. Cornell from ancient historians' accounts, the impetus for the Gauls' presence as far south as Rome was not that they had been called in to avenge an adulterous affair in the Etruscan city Clusium or that they were looking for good vineyards (the traditional reasons). More likely, they expected to be hired by Dionysios I of Syracuse, who was seeking mercenaries to support his ambitions against the Greek communities in southern Italy.

---

[40] F. Coarelli, *Il foro romano, I: Periodo arcaico* (Rome, 1983): 137–138, and *idem, Il foro Boario* (Rome, 1988): 205–244.

The Gauls found in Rome, still enjoying the wealth of Etruscan Veii taken just a decade earlier, a ripe target. After the city was sacked and pillaged, eventually the Romans probably paid ransom to the Gauls or simply lost their gold to them entirely. The gold is said to have been retrieved later, most likely at Caere by the Etruscans, who defeated the Gauls on their way back from the south. This was just about the time when Dionysios I attacked Pyrgi, the vulnerable harbor town of Etruscan Caere (where he sacked the Temple of Leukothea). The confrontation with the Gauls may have been a coordinated land assault.[41]

Many attractive legends adhere to this bare-bones reconstruction, some of them possibly historical.[42] The best are told by the Roman historian Livy (59 BCE–CE 17), who started writing his history of Rome early in the reign of Augustus in the generation after Cicero. I focus on his version of two events that occurred some four hundred years before he was writing because they illustrate legal issues surrounding plunder in war that he presents as controversial and unresolved in the fourth century BCE. In the fifth book of his history, Livy links together the two pivotal events: the Roman capture of the neighboring Etruscan city Veii (396 BCE) and, about ten years later, the Gallic sack of Rome.[43] The first episode punctuates Rome's already growing hegemony within Italy, whereas the second is Rome's first military confrontation with unfamiliar foreigners and a staggering setback that had to be overcome.

[41] Comments about the sack of Rome date back to Greek authors in the fourth century BCE. For sources, discussion, and the reconstruction given here, see T. J. Cornell, *CAH* 7^2.2: 302–398 and *The Beginnings of Rome. Italy and Rome from the Bronze Age to the Punic Wars (c. 1000–264 BC)* (London and New York, 1995): 313–322.

[42] For an overview of the complexities in finding "facts" in the sources, T. J. Cornell, "The Value of the Literary Tradition Concerning Archaic Rome," in K. A. Raaflaub, ed., *Social Struggles in Archaic Rome. New Perspectives on the Conflict of the Orders* (Berkeley and London, 1986): 52–76; on legend in the sack of Rome, N. Horsfall, in J. N. Bremmer and N. M. Horsfall, *Roman Myth and Mythography*, BICS Supp. 52 (London, 1987): 63–75.

[43] The date of the sack as given by Livy's contemporary, Varro, is 390 BCE, apparently four years off from the chronology of several Greek sources. See *CAH* 7^2.2: 347–350.

Livy includes booty and its acquisition as a motivating theme in his retrospective account of both events.

The two sacks, of Veii by Romans and Rome by Gauls, are also linked and framed with references to religious events and personnel: portents and prodigies appeared (common throughout Livy's history), a *lectisternium* (a ceremonial banquet for statues of the gods) was held, it was felt necessary to consult the Delphic oracle, information was gleaned from a captured Etruscan haruspex, priestesses had to take refuge, and a divine warning voice was heard on the Nova Via in Rome. Both sacks represent Rome's progress toward her glorious destiny, Livy's main subject, fulfilled by right action and Roman *virtus* (valor or manly courage). In his treatment of these stories, ambivalence over the subject of booty and the transfer of an enemy's cult image is resolved by careful, pious action and a reverent attitude toward the gods: it becomes one of Livy's *exempla*, a didactic illustration of right behavior.

The sacks of Veii and Rome are historical events, and some incidental details are factual, but the whole is presented by Livy with literary flourishes (and some anachronisms) that support his primary goal of "celebrating the history of the greatest nation on earth" while providing a model for right action. Livy was overwhelmingly successful: so popular in his life-time were his books that one appreciative reader traveled all the way from Gades (Cadiz in Spain) just to see him and then went home.[44] His history is still wonderful to read. In current scholarship on Livy, emphasis has shifted from dissecting his text as a factual "source" to renewed appreciation of his literary and rhetorical skills and a better understanding of how religion and religious rituals figure in his presentation of history.[45]

[44] Pliny, *Ep.* 2.3.8.

[45] T. J. Luce, *Livy. The Composition of His History* (Princeton, 1977): xv–xxvii; useful recent analyses of Livy's literary sophistication in G. B. Miles, *Livy. Reconstructing Early Rome*

In Livy's account of the Roman siege of Etruscan Veii and its capture, the expectation, acquisition, and disposition of booty is a running theme that serves an instrumental role to move the plot along and as a basis for political commentary. Livy uses dissent and confusion over the division of the booty to illustrate deficiency of proper pious attitude and discord among different sectors of the population (the "Conflict of the Orders" between patricians and plebeians). People upset over the booty are especially angered because they are expected to give back a tenth of it in fulfillment of a vow to Apollo made before the battle by the commanding general, Marcus Furius Camillus. The preoccupation and resentment over booty even led to his exile and, as a result, Camillus, then Rome's most effective general, is absent during the sack of Rome by the Gauls some years later. As has been pointed out in recent studies, *avaritia* (greedy acquisitiveness) and its results are recurring motifs in Livy's history.[46] In book 5, however, the quarrels over booty are quite specific and an intrinsic part of the story, told with considerable elaboration.

According to Livy, Rome had besieged Veii, only some 16 miles to the north, for ten years (in a literary parallel with the siege of Troy), when an unusual portent caused the Senate to send envoys to consult the oracle at Delphi for an explanation.[47] Meanwhile, they force an elderly Etruscan

---

(Ithaca and London, 1995); M. Jaeger, *Livy's Written Rome* (Ann Arbor, 1997); C. S. Kraus, in C. S. Kraus and A. J. Woodman, *Latin Historians* (Oxford, 1997): 51–81; A. Feldherr, *Spectacle and Society in Livy's History* (Berkeley and London, 1998); J. D. Chaplin, *Livy's Exemplary History* (Oxford, 2000); on Livy's use of religion, D. S. Levene, *Religion in Livy* (Leiden, 1993): 175–203; J. P. Davies, *Rome's Religious History: Livy, Tacitus and Ammianus on their Gods* (Cambridge, 2004): 21–142.

[46] Emphasized by G. Miles (1995): 76–88, and Feldherr (1998): 37–50.

[47] The portent (an unusual rise in the water level of the Alban Lake) is one of many warning prodigies listed by Livy that he uses to frame unusual events, including incidents of sacrilege. See *RoR*: 37–39 and references in n. 111 on 37; S. W. Rasmussen, *Public Portents in Republican Rome* (Rome, 2003), with a useful chart, 53–116; excellent analysis in Davies (2004): 27–78.

haruspex (a specialized priest with technical competence in signs and portents) to explain its significance. Soon, remedies were put into place and when the city was about to be stormed, Camillus, the general in charge, seeks advice from the Senate about the proper disposition of the booty anticipated from the city: "When the dictator saw that victory was now in his grasp, that a very wealthy city was on the point of capture and that the plunder would be greater than in all of Rome's previous wars put together, he was afraid that in distributing the booty tight-fistedness would make the soldiers angry or prodigality create resentment among the senators" (5.20, trans. Luce). Livy recounts the resulting senatorial debate at length; the conclusion was that anyone who wanted booty ought to go to the Roman camp at Veii and participate, and a huge mob sets out. Meanwhile, Camillus vows to Pythian Apollo (of Delphi) a tenth of the booty and to Juno, the protecting deity of Veii, a new temple in Rome.

After the city is sacked and plundered, they next turn to the Veientine temples. There they are far more careful, "acting more like worshippers than despoilers" (5.22). Selected young men chosen from the army bathe and dress in white garments and then hesitantly enter the temple of Juno. One of them asks the goddess whether she wants to go to Rome, and the others see her nod yes and hear her say she is willing. They pick up the statue, which seems light and easy to move (thus showing the goddess's agreement), and take it to the Aventine Hill in Rome, where Camillus eventually builds a temple to the goddess in fulfillment of his vow. This was the first Roman occasion of *evocatio*, a ceremony transferring an enemy's god to Rome – in this instance, along with the actual image of the goddess.[48]

---

[48] Discussion in R. M. Ogilvie, *A Commentary on Livy, Books 1–5* (Oxford, 1965): 673–675. Most of the known instances of *evocatio* are of Etruscan gods; the major exception is Carthage (in 146 BCE), apparently a deliberate revival of an archaic custom. See also *RoR*: 62, 82–83, 132–133.

As the narrative continues, division and disposition of the booty becomes problematic. Some are displeased that the proceeds from the sale of captives as slaves were put into the state treasury by Camillus. Although it was up to the commander to decide this (Livy says), he had deferred the matter to the Senate, which allowed the people to have booty, and so any credit (so the critics thought) should go to the senators. Nonetheless people rejoice at the victory and its rewards, but then in his Triumph they feel resentment to see Camillus in a chariot pulled by four white horses because such conveyance should be reserved for the gods.[49] Soon the debate begins over the proper gift for Apollo at Delphi: to what should "tenth" refer? Because everyone had gone home with what was taken individually, how could it be retrieved from the populace? Eventually it was decided that the amount given back would be up to each individual's conscience. Livy remarks that this increased the animosity against Camillus. (In fact, the vow of a specific tenth to Apollo, common among Greeks, was quite unusual here and is clearly tied to the emergency consultation of the oracle.) Camillus himself declares that the captured city and its territory were also part of the vow, and a tithe should be made from that as well. Gold is taken from the state treasury to cover this, but there was still a shortfall. Then the married women get together and decide to offer up all their personal jewelry, for which they are rewarded (by the men) with new social privileges.

Finally, a huge gold bowl is made and sent off to Delphi under escort of a single warship. Before reaching the straits of Messina near Sicily, the ship is boarded by pirates from the Lipari Islands. Their chief magistrate, Timasitheus, however, is impressed by the pious nature of the mission, gives the envoys warm hospitality, and sends them off to

[49] White horses were said to have been used by Romulus for a Triumph, thus linking Camillus to Romulus as a "second founder"; Julius Caesar also used white horses in his Triumph of 46 BCE, which leant color to Livy's detail about Camillus (noted by Ogilvie, 678–680, interpreted differently by S. Weinstock, *Divus Julius* [Oxford, 1971]: 71–75).

Delphi with an escort.[50] There they place the golden bowl in the treasury of the Massaliotes (modern Marseilles, then a Greek city friendly to Rome), where its bronze pedestal stood for centuries: although the bowl itself was melted down by the Phocians forty years later, the support for it could still be seen. The aftermath of a battle is what counts most, and throughout Livy's history, the disposition of booty captured in war is necessarily intertwined with religious concerns that must be resolved before risk is truly over: booty extends the risks of war into an uncertain realm in which the gods must be satisfied or at least not offended. The successful dedication of the golden bowl at Delphi in fulfillment of the vowed tithe closes the episode.

I have recounted Livy's story of the sack of Veii and its aftermath because it contains many paradigmatic elements that are featured in numerous accounts of Romans sacking cities in the following centuries. The tedium of long sieges, decisions about conscription and pay of soldiers, discipline during the actual sack, authority over booty and its distribution (including portions for the state treasury and for the gods), and appropriate arrangements for the general's triumphal procession are all presented by the historian as problematic and a cause of dissension, implicitly because in this still-formative stage of the city, the later solutions to them had not yet been achieved. Veii's image of Juno was treated respectfully and the vows fulfilled, but all else is depicted as a chaotic scene that plainly contributes to the vulnerability of Rome itself, which is then sacked. The bickering over booty and Camillus' consequent exile had weakened Rome.

According to Livy, just before the Gallic sack of Rome, the Vestal Virgins pack up the sacred objects (and the Palladion) and are escorted by a plebeian from Rome to Etruscan Caere, where they are given

---

[50] The Romans give Timasitheus honorary guest-citizenship and, in 242 BCE, they award special privileges to the descendants of Timasitheus on Lipara in acknowledgment of their ancestor's generous actions.

shelter. During the sack, elderly senators sacrifice themselves for the benefit of the younger Roman families in refuge on the Capitoline Hill. They put on their regalia and sit in curule seats in their houses like statues, awaiting slaughter. During the siege, a young man fearlessly walks through the enemy line to perform a sacrifice on the Quirinal Hill, a traditional obligation of his family. On the Capitoline Hill, the defenders are alerted and saved by the honking and wing-flapping of the sacred geese when the invaders try to sneak up at night. In Livy's account, the Roman general Camillus arrives just as the gold is being weighed out for the ransom and prevents it. Thus, Livy has all elements of the population contribute to the preservation of the sanctity of the Capitoline and the most sacred objects, even though the lower city was sacked, and the city escaped the humiliation of paying a gold ransom to the Gauls. He concludes the book with a moving speech by Camillus, extolling Roman gods and their veneration, and the significance of Rome as a locality, sacred because of her history. During the time of greatest peril, when they finally realize how desperate was the situation, the otherwise quarrelling Romans behave properly and together preserve the sanctity of the city.

In Livy's history, this ability to overcome a crisis with unity and the collective political instinct lead the city to future greatness. As D. Potter has pointed out in an essay on the development of the Roman army, within a generation after the sack of Rome and under its impetus as a psychological shock, the army was completely reorganized and became far more effective. The restructuring and reorganizing and a shift to the sword as the primary weapon (rather than the hoplite's spear) over time were truly revolutionary and created efficient, disciplined legionaries who could undertake extensive conquest.[51] As represented

---

[51] D. Potter, "The Roman Army and Navy," in H. Flower, ed., *The Cambridge Companion to the Roman Republic* (Cambridge, 2004): 66–88. On the deep cultural significance of Roman

in Livy's narrative, the formative experiences of Veii and Gauls in Rome neatly predict future success because the problems were faced with determination and *virtus*.

Livy's account of the sack of Veii also stands as an antithesis to Polybius' frequently cited description of the highly systematic, organized, and very disciplined Roman method of sacking and pillaging. The Greek historian Polybius (c. 200–c. 118 BCE) wrote in the century previous to Livy for a Greek audience about the sudden and swift rise of Rome as the dominant power in the Mediterranean.[52] Because military maneuvers figure so prominently, he includes a full description of the Roman army, its equipment and camps (in book 6). His detailed description of the Roman way of destroying a city is set in the context of the Roman sack in 209 of Carthago Nova in Spain (New Carthage, modern Cartagena), a wealthy Carthaginian colony that had been refounded by Hasdrubal in 228.

When P. Cornelius Scipio (the future Africanus) as commanding general decides the city is sufficiently subdued, he sends in troops to kill indiscriminately until the signal for plundering is given. Before the signal is eventually given, the troops are organized into various duties, with only a part designated to collect booty. They have all sworn an oath to divide the booty equally, even with the sick or those out on reconnaissance or other duties (Polyb., 10.15.4–16). In a thorough analysis of this passage and others describing Roman sacks, A. Ziolkowski has shown that despite Polybius' implication that this orderly procedure was standard practice, the Polybian model for sacking is, in

---

warfare that accelerates in this period, see K. Welch's introduction and the essays in Dillon and Welch (2006).

[52] As mentioned previously, he himself was among a thousand prominent Achaeans who were deported to Rome and detained there after the Roman victory at Pydna (in 168). He became acquainted with the young Scipio Aemilianus when they exchanged books and discussed them; Polybius then became his friend and mentor. Subsequently, he traveled widely with Romans and was present at the sack of Carthage in 146.

fact, exceptional. Although commanders did maintain control initially, during the phase of pillage that included extensive rape and slaughter (*direptio*), control could not be maintained and some private acquisition of booty was the norm.[53] Ziolkowski's discussion is primarily concerned with sacking, however. A set of customs and expectations surrounding the division of booty was developed over time, and Polybius' account, perhaps reflecting an ideal procedure, nonetheless is surely correct in its emphasis on booty and concern about its appropriate disposition.

What happened next, and who got what, is a matter of continuing scholarly controversy.[54] This seems to be one of those cultural topics of such familiarity that they are taken for granted by ancient authors as understood – hence, a relative dearth of any direct discussion, even though the actual words for *booty* appear frequently. *Praeda* is the most common, and *manubiae* appears to refer to a subset of *praeda*, reserved for the general in command; yet, even that distinction is not always maintained. (*Spolia* is a more general term, originally used for arms and armor captured from the enemy.) The central issues are those raised at Veii: Who owns the booty? Who decides what to do with it? What about a share for the gods? According to Livy, possibly depicting the issues anachronistically, it was up to the commander to decide what to do with it, although to be sure, individual soldiers would have taken what they could during the actual sack. Exactly how ownership and

[53] A. Ziolkowski, "*Urbs direpta*, or How the Romans Sacked Cities," in J. Rich and G. Shipley, eds., *War and Society in the Roman World* (London and New York, 1993): 69–91. A. K. Goldsworthy emphasizes the difficulty of discipline during a sack because of the emotional state of the besiegers (*The Roman Army at War, 100 BC–AD 200* [Oxford, 1996]: 259–261).

[54] The most persuasive resolution: J. B. Churchill, "*Ex qua quod vellent facerent*: Roman Magistrates' Authority over *Praeda* and *Manubiae*," *TAPA* 129 (1999): 85–116, with full citations of previous discussions. Churchill challenges the view that a general was free to use his portion however he wished with no restrictions, argued by I. Shatzman, "The Roman General's Authority over Booty," *Historia* 21 (1972): 177–205, and followed in part by E. Orlin, *Temples, Religion and Politics in the Roman Republic* (Leiden, 1997): 117–161.

claims to the booty were perceived and acted upon changed over the centuries.[55]

More significant amounts of plunder would be divided and dispersed as the general decided. A portion set aside for him, the *manubiae* (from which derives the term *manubial*, referring to a general's spoils), was his to use on behalf of public interest – it should not go directly into his private treasury – but it could be kept in his custody (even in his house) with the understanding that it was intended for public benefit. By the time of Cicero's prosecution of Verres, it was customary for a general to give a full accounting of each item: in his narrative of the trial, such a list is read aloud at the trial from an account submitted to the Aerarium[56] by Publius Servilius (then sitting as a juror in the trial), who seven years earlier had sacked Olympus, a pirates' city on the coast of Lycia. Not only are the numbers of statues taken listed, but also their size, shape, and pose are described (*Verr.*, 2.1.57). This catalogue of statues as *manubiae* provides a contrast with the illicit acquisition and sloppy bookkeeping of Verres.

The *manubiae* could be distributed to soldiers and colleagues as largesse from the general: such gifts and the broad discretion afforded the general obviously had considerable potential political benefit. It was also at times simply deposited in the state treasury. Typically, a general used a portion of the *manubiae* as a dedication to gods in temples, the Forum, porticoes, or other public spaces: the dedication itself is usually an item taken from the enemy, such as statues or paintings or, in some cases, a whole new temple.[57] (These temples and dedications are often

---

[55] A development traced by legal historians: see discussion in A. Watson, *The Law of Property in the Later Roman Republic* (Oxford, 1968): 63–74.

[56] The Aerarium contained the state treasury and also held state archival records in the substructure of the Temple of Saturn in the Forum.

[57] Orlin (1997) discusses the documented cases of manubial temples and concludes that fewer new temples were constructed than generally assumed (127–139). Not all preserved temples are firmly correlated with literary or epigraphical evidence, however, so that the number may be higher than he allows. See also A. Ziolkowski, *The Temples of Mid-Republican Rome*

referred to in modern discussions as "manubial temples," or "manubial dedications" – i.e., offerings from the *manubiae*, the general's portion of the spoils.) The infrastructure of Rome was improved with other public works from manubial funds, such as new aqueducts and roads. Even in the imperial period, when booty belonged to the emperor, the Republican overtones of triumph could be invoked in projects such as the Colosseum, built *ex manubiis* (by Vespasian and Titus out of booty from Judea) as proclaimed in very large, prominent inscriptions placed in the interior, of which one is preserved.[58]

TRIUMPHAL PROCESSIONS

The Senate had a continuing interest in the disposition of booty and had ultimate authority in a related matter, the awarding of the Triumph, by far the most significant public procession held in Rome and the highest peak of glory for which a Roman man could hope. Initially, a victory celebration with purificatory overtones, the Triumph became increasingly elaborate through time. Those celebrated in the second century BCE after victories over Greeks initially astonished and always impressed the populace with displays of Greek art.[59] The elaboration of the Triumph also owed inspiration to magnificent processions staged

---

and *Their Historical and Topographical Context* (Rome, 1992); M. Aberson, *Temples votifs et butin de guerre dans la Rome républicaine* (Rome, 1994); L. Pietilä-Castrén, Magnificentia publica: *The Victory Monuments of the Roman Generals in the Era of the Punic Wars* (Helsinki, 1987); R. D. Weigel, "Roman Generals and the Vowing of Temples, 500–100 B.C.," *C&M* 49 (1998): 119–142.

[58] G. Alföldi, "Eine Bauinschrift aus dem Colosseum," *ZPE* 109 (1995): 195–226.

[59] The bibliography on the Triumph is extensive. See W. Ehlers, s.v. "Triumphus" *RE* VIIA: 493–511; H. S. Versnel, *Triumphus* (Leiden, 1970); M. Lemosse, "Les éléments techniques de l'ancien triomphe romain et le problème de son origine," *ANRW* 1.2 (Berlin and New York, 1972); E. Künzl, *Der römische Triumph* (Munich, 1988); T. C. Brennan, "Triumphus in Monte Albano," in R. W. Wallace and E. M. Harris, eds., *Transitions to Empire* (Norman and London, 1996): 315–337; on literary descriptions, M. Beard, "The Triumph of the Absurd: Roman Street Theatre," in C. Edwards and G. Woolf, eds., *Rome the Cosmopolis* (Cambridge, 2003b): 21–43, and "Writing Ritual: The Triumph of Ovid," in A. Barchiesi, J. Rüpke, and S. Stephens, eds., *Rituals in Ink* (Stuttgart, 2004): 115–126. The best overview is in P. J. Holliday, *The Origins of Roman Historical Commemoration in the Visual Arts* (Cambridge, 2002): 22–62.

in the Hellenistic east, such as those of Ptolemy II in Egypt (ca. 276 BCE) and Antiochus IV in Daphne (166 BCE).

The main features are as follows: the procession entered through a ceremonial gate in the Campus Martius of Rome, outside the pomerium (the religious boundary of the city), then wound through the cheering, applauding populace on a fixed, traditional path for maximum visibility (see Plan 1). It went around the western side of the Capitoline, through the Forum Boarium and the Circus Maximus, where many thousands could be seated while watching, around the eastern base of the Palatine, turned left to go through the Forum and up to the top of the Capitoline, where it ended at the Temple of Jupiter Optimus Maximus, for sacrifices and offerings. Today the arches of Constantine and Titus mark parts of the route, as did other arches no longer preserved.

Magistrates and the senate with accompanying musicians were followed by the *triumphator* in a four-horse chariot with any older sons and officers on horseback as escorts (and possibly riding in the chariot was a slave who held a gold oakleaf wreath over the general's head and murmured constantly in his ear, "Remember you are mortal"). Then came the troops, who on that day were allowed to sing and chant obscenities, with particular reference to their general. Many cartloads of spoils and booty and manacled prisoners were processed as a visible justification for the war. There were large didactic paintings of battles and placards to explain the origins of especially notable booty. If possible, the defeated chieftain, king, or queen was made to process with the prisoners and then executed.[60] In earlier days, the *triumphator* wore red paint on his face and red clothes, believed to be in imitation

---

[60] Because Cleopatra had committed suicide, Octavian had to substitute an effigy (probably in wax), representing her dead in a tableau on a float in his Triumph for victory over Egypt (Cassius Dio, 51.21). About three hundred years later, Queen Zenobia of Palmyra was required to process in Aurelian's Triumph. Rather than executing her afterward, they gave her a villa outside Rome and she retired there.

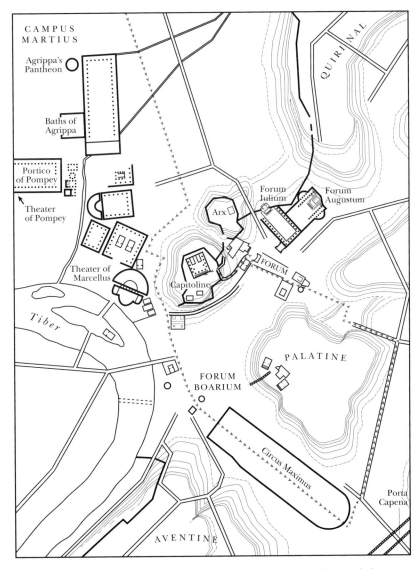

PLAN I. Plan of central Rome, Augustan period, with route of the Triumphal procession.

of the image of Jupiter, but later he wore very elaborate embroidered regalia.

Whether a Triumph would be granted was subject to a popular vote, but first the Senate had to agree that a Triumph could be held, which meant that political intrigue was a factor. (It became such a focal point of contention that in the imperial period Triumphs were soon reserved for the imperial family; this also neatly vitiated effective senatorial input.) The Senate was to determine whether strict conditions were met: in theory, the victor had to have killed at least 5,000 men in a declared war against a foreign enemy (slave wars, native rebellions, and civil wars did not count); the army had to return with the victor to Rome, showing that the enemy was completely pacified; the victor had to have held official *imperium*, which included appointment as highest magistrate of a province and the right to take military auspices. When these conditions (or the Senators) could not be satisfied, the alternative was to receive an *ovatio*, a lesser celebration.[61] In practice, the senate could be more flexible in its determination if it so wished.

The names of the *triumphatores* were carved onto *fasti triumphales*, marble inscriptions that provided a permanent calendric record and were displayed on an arch in the Forum and elsewhere as a public monument. Romulus was regarded as the first *triumphator*; if so, the ritual was staged for more than 1,000 years. This quintessentially Roman event brought together religious ritual, the rewards of military glory and personal initiative, the material benefits of war, and broad participation for the people of Rome in the whole endeavor of warfare.

In antiquity, the potential for metaphorical use of the Triumph, and even its parody, was exploited in representations (and even stagings, in Alexandria) of the Triumph of Dionysos, returning from India or

---

[61] For a brief period, a third alternative was a triumph staged on the Alban Mount, about 17 miles southeast of Rome. After his victory over Syracuse, M. Claudius Marcellus staged both an Alban Triumph and an *ovatio*. For political maneuvering in awarding triumphs, see Brennan (1996).

ascending to Mt. Olympos, or Triumphs of marine deities or satyrs. While Suetonius' account of the cruel emperor Caligula is far from humorous, one exception is the description of Caligula's (deranged?) attack on the English Channel and the requirement of his soldiers to gather great volumes of seashells as the *spolia* for a Triumph over Oceanus (*Calig.* 46). Because numerous actual military Triumphs are mentioned and described by Livy and other authors, this central cultural feature of the Roman Republic was also represented and imitated in subsequent contexts as a way of evoking Roman Republican values and eliciting comparison with Roman military glory. Napoleon staged a triumphal procession of sculpture and paintings he had taken from Italian churches and private collections in a showy entrance to Paris, complete with placards proclaiming the names of various captured Italian cities.

As a result of Rome's success at war, during the 310 years between the sack of Veii and Sulla's sack of Athens, there was a massive transfer to Rome of precious metals from cities in southern Italy and Sicily, Spain and north Africa, Gaul, mainland Greece, and Asia Minor. In the earlier periods, because there was no Roman coinage, divisions of booty would have been resolved by weight. The early Roman unit of monetary exchange was a copper *aes*, about 11.5 oz. While silver coinage was a widespread feature of the Greek economy since the archaic period, and bronze coinage was first introduced in southern Italy in the fifth century BCE, Romans did not mint coins themselves until some sporadic issues in the later fourth century BCE and not regularly until the wars with Pyrrhus in the 270s BCE.[62] Beginning with the indemnity paid by Carthage after the First Punic War, silver and some gold flowed into Rome. Livy states that at the end of the Second Punic War, Carthage was to pay 10,000 talents of silver over fifty years (30.37.5), and in Scipio's

---

[62] M. H. Crawford, *Coinage and Money under the Roman Republic* (Berkeley, 1985): 1–51. For a superb discussion of the impact of "monetization," D. M. Schaps, *The Invention of Coinage and the Monetization of Ancient Greece* (Ann Arbor, 2004).

Triumph, he brought (into the Aerarium) 123,000 pounds of silver, of which each soldier received 400 asses (30.45.3).[63]

This raises the inevitable question of whether economic gain was a motive for war, a question that lurks even in Livy's account of the sack of Veii: a short, if equivocal, answer is that is was surely sometimes a factor, especially for individuals, but not a primary motive for the state.[64] Of narrower interest but more germane here is whether acquiring art (with aesthetic, totemic, religious, or prestigious value) was ever a factor in initiating Roman warfare: it was not. Hence, Cicero used warfare and its attendant customs as a pointed contrast with Verres' extraordinarily aggressive behavior in Sicily, a protectorate of Rome, in peacetime. Roman practitioners of war usually followed rules, but Verres did not.

GREEK ART ON DISPLAY

Ancient comments on Greek art in Roman possession occur often in the context of military narratives and descriptions of what was paraded in Triumphs. Because the triumphal processions were so highly sought by the elite, they were politically charged and often controversial: Livy adopts the realistic atmosphere of dissent in his retrospective account of the sack of Veii, in which Camillus is criticized for his four white horses in the Triumphal procession afterward. The spoils also excited

---

[63] The sums and evidence are conveniently collected in T. Frank, ed., *Economic Survey of Ancient Rome* I (Baltimore, 1933): 67–68, 74–75, 127–138, 230–231, 324–326. For the effects on the supply of money, C. Howgego, "The Supply and Use of Money in the Roman World," *JRS* 82 (1992): 1–31.

[64] Discussion of the nature and motives of Roman territorial expansion began in antiquity with Polybius and has continued ever since; it was invigorated more recently by W. H. Harris, *War and Imperialism in Republican Rome* (Oxford, 1979), which elicited many responses. For subsequent, moderate assessments, see, e.g., essays in *CAH* 7².2 (1989), *CAH* 8² (1989); J. Rich, "Fear, Greed and Glory: The Causes of Roman War-Making in the Middle Republic," in J. Rich and G. Shipley, eds., *War and Society in the Roman World* (London and New York, 1993): 38–68, and K. A. Raaflaub, "Born to Be Wolves? Origins of Roman Imperialism," in Wallace and Harris (1996): 273–314. The definitive account of Roman expansion into the eastern Mediterranean, different in character from earlier expansion within and near Italy, is Gruen, *HWCR*; on the economic benefits of war (welcome but not a motive for war), see esp. pp. 288–315.

criticism as well as admiration. They were overt displays of the material "benefits" of successful war, but whether they actually benefited Rome was a question raised early on by Polybius. Well before Verres' trial for extortion, art as triumphal plunder was one focal point for framing Rome's relationship to Greeks. Captured art brought into the city served as a convenient symbol for foreign territories brought under Roman governance and took on fresh nuance when that art actually had an impact on Romans in its new home. There were many victories to celebrate: the first Greek cities conquered were in the west, in Sicily and southern Italy. Then in the second century BCE, successive Triumphs celebrated victories over Greeks and their neighbors farther east: Macedonians, Aetolians, Ambracians, Greeks in Asia Minor, and, finally, Corinth, sacked in 146 BCE, the same year as the sack of Carthage. They have been described and analyzed often.[65] I comment on just a few of them here to illustrate the issues that were raised in the course of acquiring art by warfare.

Ancient authors agree that the first major display of Greek art in Rome was during a triumphal procession of M. Claudius Marcellus, after the fall of Syracuse in 211. Embroiled in the struggle between Rome and Carthage, the political leaders who had taken power in Syracuse had made the calculated but poor decision to side with Carthage. Syracuse fell after a siege that lasted three years, in large part because of the clever mechanisms of Archimedes that allowed the city to defend herself for so long. This was the first capture and sack of a major Greek city by Romans.[66] Despite the great significance of the victory, Marcellus

---

[65] For discussion of the cultural ideology of the triumphs over Greeks, Gruen (1992): 84–130; for a detailed account of the plunder in the various triumphs, see M. Pape, *Griechische Kunstwerke aus Kriegsbeute und ihre öffentliche Aufstellung in Rom* (Hamburg, 1975); L. Pietilä-Castrén, *Magnificentia publica: The Victory Monuments of the Roman Generals in the Era of the Punic Wars* (Helsinki, 1987).

[66] Although Tarentum (Greek Taras, on the inner side of the heel of the Italian peninsula) had been defeated by Rome earlier in 272, the aftermath had been relatively benign. Florus (second century CE), the author of an *Epitome* of Roman history, states that statues were

was not awarded a proper Triumph, with the stated reason that his army was not present; however, political opposition was likely behind this senatorial decision. Instead, he was given an *ovatio*, but he staged a Triumph on the Alban Mount outside of Rome the day before entering the city for the *ovatio*.[67] He brought into Rome the *spolia* from Syracuse, and later some of it was displayed in the Temple of Honos and Virtus (Honor and Valor) that he had vowed years earlier at Clastidium. The temple was not completed until after his death, by his son. This simple outline of events seems clear in the sources, but the details of the various accounts differ considerably and are colored by moralizing comments about the effects of the plunder on Romans and about Marcellus' character. The sack of Syracuse was widely viewed as a turning point in Roman appreciation of Greek art, for better or worse. Here, I examine the literary evidence for Marcellus' actions and the booty from Syracuse (a focal point also for ancient criticism of looting, discussed further on p. 83)

Marcellus had such outstanding talents that during his life he had to endure constant opposition and efforts to limit his achievements from competitors and rivals. The rivalries in Rome seem always to have been intense but were then especially acute because of tensions over the ongoing war against Hannibal and the Carthaginians. He had been only the third (and last) Roman after Romulus to win the *spolia opima* by killing a Gallic chieftain in single combat in 222, the year of his first consulship.[68] Ancient historians represent Marcellus and his sack of Syracuse in both positive and critical ways, depending on how his

taken from Tarentum then (1.13.27), but this is probably a confusion with the more famous sack in 209; see C. Brauer, Jr., *Taras. Its History and Coinage* (New York, 1986): 170. Brauer's point is persuasive in view of the extensive comments on the two later sacks of Tarentum and Syracuse, and the comparisons made between them (*pace* Gruen, *HWCR*: 252, and Gruen [1992]: 89). Romans had also taken over Cumae, Neapolis (modern Naples), and Poseidonia (Paestum) earlier, but those cities had already lost their independence.

[67] Brennan (1996) sees this as a protest by Marcellus (pp. 323–324).

[68] On his dedication of the *spolia opima*, H. Flower, "The Tradition of the Spolia Opima: M. Claudius Marcellus and Augustus," *ClAnt* 19 (2000): 34–64.

story was being used and their own affiliations.[69] Polybius' account, the closest in date to the actual event, is only preserved in fragments. Livy is presumed to have followed Polybius in historical detail, but he offers his own judgments and conclusions. Since Marcellus' descendants included one of the jurors in Verres' trial, Cicero had all the more reason to praise the successful general and emphasize his humane qualities, in contrast to Verres. Another even later descendant was Marcellus, nephew of Augustus (and his potential heir until his early death). Virgil found it only apt to include the deceased young man walking alongside his famous ancestor, the general Marcellus, in the great parade of heroes in the underworld whom Anchises points out to Aeneas as predictive of Rome's greatness.[70]

Plutarch writes of Marcellus from the distance of three hundred years as an exemplar of a Roman who understood and appreciated Greek culture and was himself properly imbued with appreciation of Greek culture. Plutarch was impressed that Marcellus gave his son proper *paideia* (Greek cultural education), and yet he tells the story of the siege of Syracuse as though from a Roman rather than Syracusan (Greek) viewpoint.[71] Since the time Polybius wrote his account (soon after the actual event), the "Fall of Syracuse" became a *topos*, a story

---

[69] Ferrary (1988): 573–578; H. Flower, "'Memories' of Marcellus. History and Memory in Roman Republican Culture," in U. Eigler et al., eds., *Formen römische Geschichtsschreibung von den anfängen bis Livius* (Darmstadt, 2003): 39–52; for Livy's use of Syracuse as a parallel to Rome, M. Jaeger, "Livy and the Fall of Syracuse," in *ibid.*: 213–234; on reactions to spolia in Rome, Jaeger (1997): 124–131; for a reassessment of the impact of the looted art, M. McDonnell, "Roman Aesthetics and the Spoils of Syracuse," in Dillon and Welch (2006): 68–90.

[70] *Aeneid*, 6.855–859. These and the following lines about the recently deceased Marcellus are said to have caused Octavia, his mother and sister of Augustus, to faint when she heard them recited.

[71] C. Pelling, "Plutarch: Roman Heroes and Greek Culture," in M. Griffin and J. Barnes, eds., *Philosophia Togata. Essays on Philosophy and Roman Society* (Oxford, 1989): 199–208. S. C. R. Swain discusses Plutarch's representation of Marcellus' character and the use of Greek material culture as part of its definition: "Hellenic Culture and the Roman Heroes of Plutarch," in B. Scardigli, ed., *Essays on Plutarch's Lives* (Oxford, 1995): 229–264.

repeated often with some variation of emphasis, because it offered useful illustration of the complex issues of Roman military dominance over Greece, intertwined with Roman appreciation of Greek cultural accomplishments.

Even though the Syracusan booty was much talked about in antiquity, in fact, remarkably little is said about exactly what was taken. No one seemed to remember. Polybius, perhaps showing his hostility to Marcellus (or because his text is incompletely preserved), simply says in the extant passage that he took "everything" (9.10). Livy criticizes him for taking so much art because it stimulated an appetite for art that led eventually to spoliation of sacred and profane buildings up to the present (25.40). He also comments that the booty was almost as great as if it had been Carthage that was taken (25.31.11), but he gives no precise tallies as he does in his other descriptions of booty, including that from Carthage. He does say somewhat more specifically that the procession into the city for the *ovatio* included catapults, artillery, and other engines of war (presumably the ones designed by Archimedes); the "adornments of a long peace and royal wealth" (a reference to King Hiero II and his long rule); silver and bronze vessels; textiles and precious furnishings; many noble statues; and eight elephants (taken from the Carthaginians who had ensconced themselves at Agrigento). Aside from the elephants, the list seems formulaic.[72] Livy remarks that in his life-time, hardly any of the items dedicated by Marcellus in the Temple of Honos and Virtus could be seen (25.40) : apparently, they were taken off during subsequent disturbances in the city or lost in fires; hence, the vagueness of his description.[73]

---

[72] 26.21.6–10. The royal treasure is mentioned in the course of the description of the capture of the city, but no figures are given. T. Frank (1933) provides estimates, p. 81. Because this was an *ovatio* rather than a full Triumph, perhaps there was no proper record of the booty, hence the formulaic description. Artillery was often paraded in a Triumph.

[73] The temples were located just outside the Porta Capena, on the Via Appia (just southeast of the curved end of the Circus Maximus). Pliny states that they were restored by Vespasian

Pliny the Elder is no help either: he does not mention any specific statues taken by Marcellus. Plutarch, following the earlier authors, comments that most of the statues and offerings in Syracuse were taken but whereas Rome previously was filled with crude blood-stained booty, now the city had Hellenic grace and truth to nature (*Marc.* 21). No one could say just what was taken, but what was remembered was the high quality of the art and the social reaction to it, looked upon with disapproval by critics because of the inevitable loss of the sense of sanctity surrounding art and because the Greek style of art was seemingly preferred to what was familiar. The critics were writing long after the fact, and they found the introduction of Marcellus' Syracusan booty to be a convenient historical "peg" to mark a change in attitudes toward art, even if they could not say just what the art was.

In the *Verrines*, where the purpose is legal prosecution, not narrative history, Cicero gives a favorable picture of Marcellus and his activities in Sicily to contrast with the depredations of Verres, and he does provide more detail. His fullest description of Marcellus' booty, however, occurs in a dialogue written much later in his life. He describes in detail two globes that had belonged to Archimedes and were taken to Rome. At least one of the globes was set in an intricate orrery that displayed the movements of the sun, moon, and planets in relationship to the earth. Marcellus had kept the simpler one, the only item he kept from all the booty, and dedicated the more complex one in the Temple of Honos and Virtus.[74] In addition to the globes, in the *Verrines* we are told about many other specific items Marcellus did *not* take but were taken later by Verres. Cicero here speaks not only as the prosecutor but also as

---

(*HN* 35.120) and painted by Cornelius Pinus and Attius Priscus, who were highly esteemed painters of the day. For the temples and their location, A. Ziolkowski, *The Temples of Mid-Republican Rome and Their Historical and Topographical Context* (Rome, 1992): 58–60; Haselberger, *MAR*: 138–139.

[74] *Rep.* 1.22, written in 54 BCE. For later references to the same orrery, K. Büchner, *De re publica, Kommentar* (Heidelberg, 1984a): 102–105.

an eyewitness: he had been to Syracuse in the course of his duties as quaestor (assistant governor) in Sicily in 75 BCE.

He says that Marcellus left the city richly adorned and unharmed, with its treasures unplundered (*Verr.* 2.2.4), that Marcellus was a conqueror and a humane man who knew that it would not be a credit to Rome if he destroyed the city's beauty, who did not strip the city bare but had preserved it from destruction (*Verr.* 2.4.120). What booty he did take was all put in the Temple of Honos and Virtus (not in his house, garden, or villa), and he did not touch or profane the gods (*Verr.* 2.4.121). But Verres, in contrast, took a set of historical paintings and twenty-seven other portraits of Syracusan rulers from the walls of the Temple of Athena (immured into the present day Duomo); he wrenched off ivory carvings from the temple's doors and its gold bosses; he took from it even curiosities such as giant bamboo stalks. There follows a long recitation of statuary from public places such as the prytanion (a statue of Sappho, whose empty base inscribed in beautiful Greek Verres left behind because he couldn't read it, Cicero adds sarcastically), and statues from other temples: one of Apollo, from the temple of Asklepios; one of Aristaeus, from the temple of Dionysus; one of Zeus, from the temple of Zeus. Cicero states that all this had been left by Marcellus, although the possibility remains that something might have been dedicated in the intervening 140 years.

The events before and after the sack are also recounted in detail by Livy, with an emphasis on Marcellus' emotions just before the final charge:

> When Marcellus stood on the heights of Epipolae and looked down at the city below him – in those days the most beautiful, perhaps, in all the world – he is said to have wept, partly for joy in the accomplishment of so great an enterprise, partly in grief for the city's ancient glory. He remembered the sinking, long ago, of the Athenian fleets, the two great armies wiped out with their two famous commanders, and the perils she

had passed through in all her wars with Carthage. He saw again in
fancy her rich tyrants and kings, Hieron above all, still vivid in men's
thoughts, and glorious for his generosity to the people of Rome....

(25.24, trans. de Sélincourt)

And so moved, he tried once again for a peace parley, to no avail, and then renewed the final attack.[75] Back in Rome, after the sack and the Alban triumph, Marcellus' political enemies find some Syracusans willing to go to Rome to complain about Marcellus' behavior and despoliation of Syracuse. The Senate hears them, debates, and exonerates Marcellus. The Syracusans then fall at Marcellus' feet and beg him to become a patron of their city, to which he agrees. As others have pointed out, the speed with which Marcellus became a patron of the city and the fact that a festival was enacted in Syracuse in his honor soon afterward – continued until Verres tried to substitute one in his own honor – suggest a more positive reception than the (ancient) critics allow.[76]

Marcellus set a pattern of post-victory gifts to Greek cities and Greek sanctuaries that would be followed by other generals. After his single combat with Viridomarus, the Gallic chieftain, the Romans collectively sent another gold bowl to Delphi and gifts to their allies, including Hieron of Syracuse (Plut., *Marc.* 8.6). Of the dedications Marcellus made personally in Rome, two inscribed bases are preserved, one found on the Esquiline and the other near the Porta Capena, in the vicinity of the Temple of Honos and Virtus.[77] Marcellus is said by Plutarch to

---

[75] On Marcellus' weeping, A. Rossi, "The Tears of Marcellus. History of a Literary Motif in Livy," *G&R* 47 (2000): 56–66. She suggests that Livy was paying indirect homage to Polybius, who saw Scipio Aemilianus weep before Carthage, and the Greek tradition going back to Achilles receiving Priam.

[76] Flower (2003), Jaeger (2003); P. Gros thinks that Plutarch's more favorable portrait shows that he used an independent Greek source for his life of Marcellus, perhaps by Poseidonius ("Les Statues de Syracuse et les 'dieux' de Tarente," *REL* 57 [1979]: 85–114); J. Rives suggests that the festival was established for Marcellus but honored his great-great-grandson (a juror in the trial) as well ("Marcellus and the Syracusans," *CPh* 88: 32–35).

[77] *ILS* 12, 13. No. 12 supported a statue taken from the Sicilian city of Henna.

have donated a gymnasium at Catania in Sicily, set up statues and other offerings to the Cabiri in Samothrace, and offerings to Athena at Lindos, where there was a statue of him whose base was inscribed with an epigram recorded by Poseidonius, quoted in Plutarch's text (*Marc.* 30.6–8).[78]

Marcellus' actions at Syracuse are frequently compared by ancient authors to those of Q. Fabius Maximus (nicknamed "Cunctator:" the Delayer, for his policy of attrition against Hannibal). Fabius Maximus capped his distinguished and long career by the recapture of Tarentum in 209, just two years after the fall of Syracuse. Years earlier, in 233, Fabius had celebrated a Triumph for his victory over the Ligurians, and he had vowed the original Temple to Honos (later modified and doubled to include Virtus by Marcellus). The events at Tarentum were another bitter and prolonged episode of betrayal and intrigue during the war against Carthage. Tarentum had been under Roman aegis since 272 but in 212 had fallen to Hannibal.

After a siege, the city was betrayed by Bruttians, and Fabius Maximus sacked the city in the usual way (with indiscriminate slaughter) but is credited with showing restraint in gathering up statues.[79] A secretary asked him what to do about the largest images of the gods, and he famously replied, "Let us leave these angry gods to the Tarentines." He took 30,000 people as slaves (it is not clear whether they were citizens or already slaves), 3,080 pounds of gold bullion, and "an enormous amount" of coins. Livy says he took almost as many statues and paintings as had Marcellus but, when it came to statues of the gods, he showed more restraint than Marcellus (27.16). The overall impression a reader

---

[78] Like other Roman dedications, Marcellus' dedication(s) at Lindos is not mentioned in the Lindian chronicle, but whether this was deliberate is uncertain because of lacunae in the text: C. Higbie, *The Lindian Chronicle and the Greek Creation of Their Past* (Oxford, 2003): 166–167.

[79] Livy, 27.16; Plutarch, *Fab.* 22.5–6, *Marc.* 21.1–5; complete ancient sources listed in Broughton, *MRR*, 285. Augustine, *Civ. dei*, 1.6, cites Livy on Fabius Maximus' moderation and Marcellus' weeping at the destruction of Syracuse as a comparison to the sack of Rome in 410 CE. On rivalry between Marcellus and Fabius, see McDonnell (2006): 77–82.

might take from Livy's comparison of the two generals is that Marcellus was the more clement to the defeated people while removing images of gods, but Fabius was the more brutal to the enemy yet left images of gods behind.

Left behind in Tarentum was a colossal Zeus, about 60 feet high, by Lysippos, apparently because it was too difficult to move despite being perfectly balanced (so says Pliny, *HN* 34.40). One colossal image Fabius Maximus did scruple to take was a bronze seated statue of the weary Herakles, also by the celebrated sculptor Lysippos. He dedicated it on the Capitoline, along with an equestrian statue of himself, and it may be that he had more interest in this statue than the others because of legendary connections between his family and Herakles. The base for it is still preserved in the Capitoline Museums, but the statue itself was taken off about 325 CE by Constantine I to Constantinople to decorate his Basilica and was later moved to the Hippodrome there. It was melted down in the crusader sack of 1204.[80]

Some two decades later, after the final Roman victory over the Aetolians in 187, M. Fulvius Nobilior took plundered art from Ambracia, fairly rich in possessions because Pyrrhus had lived there a hundred years earlier and had booty from elsewhere, perhaps even from Athens.[81] He did not sack the city fully and was given a gold crown by the defeated following the peace negotiations. After debate in the Senate over whether he should be allowed a Triumph, Fulvius Nobilior was granted one and processed with 785 bronze statues, 230 marble statues, gold crowns totaling 112 pounds, 83,000 pounds of silver, 243 pounds of gold, large quantities of coined money, arms and armor, and artillery. With the encouragement of Fulvius' political enemies in Rome, complaints

---

[80] Plut. *Fab.* 22; Pliny, *HN* 34.39–41. For the weary Herakles, see discussion and sources in Bassett (2004): 152–154; associations of Fabius' family, Gruen (1992): 102, n. 87.
[81] Pyrrhus: Livy, 38.9.13, Polybius 21.30.9; booty perhaps from Athens, Pape (1975): 12, other booty of Fulvius, 12–14. On Fulvius' use of the booty in Rome for the Temple of Hercules of the Muses, Pietilä-Castrén (1987): 95–103.

were lodged against Fulvius by the Ambracians, who accused him of despoiling their temples and taking cult images: they claimed they had to offer prayers to bare walls and doorposts (Livy, 38.43.5).

In his own defense, Fulvius invoked the siege of Syracuse and its booty as a parallel (39.4). In this case, the Senate decided that the college of pontiffs should examine the booty and determine whether it was sacred or profane, as they had done earlier in 210 BCE after the capture of Capua, when a similar investigation was made (38.44, 26.34.12). Besides the clear political maneuvering, this episode illustrates the continuing respect of the Senate for the religious aspect of the booty. As E. Gruen points out, Fulvius himself was not an indiscriminate looter; he was a cultured author of a treatise on religion and a patron of Greek artists, several of whom even attended his triumphal games out of respect for him.[82] Following the Marcellan pattern, he also built and furnished the Temple of Hercules of the Muses in Rome, where he dedicated the spoils to the Muses. This was the first capture and (partial) sack of a Greek city in mainland Greece.

As the next century wore on, triumph after triumph brought still more art, and bullion, and *spolia* to Rome. What is noticeable in the descriptions is the growing choosiness about what was taken and what was kept personally by the commanding general. The thematic selection of certain kinds of images from the enemy that represented particular gods (Herakles, Zeus, Apollo, Venus, Athena) or Alexander the Great is emphasized by M. Pape and B. Ridgway. This is discernable over time in literary references to booty, up to the Augustan period. Thus the meaning or content of images eventually seems to have become more important in selecting art for booty than whether it was made by a noted artist.[83]

---

[82] On Fulvius' interests, Gruen (1992): 107–110; artists' respect for Fulvius: Livy, 39.22.1–2.

[83] Pape (1975): 61–68; B. Ridgway, *Roman Copies of Greek Sculpture: The Problems of the Originals* (Ann Arbor, 1984): 17–19.

Plutarch has Marcellus asserting proudly in his own defense that his captured art had instructed Romans to admire and appreciate Greek art (*Marc.* 21), but he himself, as we have seen, kept only Archimedes' second-best globe. Fulvius is said to have left behind terra-cotta statues, even those by Zeuxis, preferring the finer material of bronze and marble (Pliny, *HN* 35.66). L. Aemilius Paullus is said to have kept only Perseus' library, allowing his sons to take what books they liked from it, of all the plunder from the Macedonian king (Plut., *Aem.* 28.11). L. Mummius, destroyer of Corinth in 146 BCE, is said to have kept nothing for his own house (Cic., *Off.* 2.76) and not to have left enough for a dowry for his daughter after he died (Pliny, *HN* 34.36). Scipio Aemilianus, after the final destruction of Carthage (also in 146), not only abstained from taking or purchasing any of the booty but also forbade his slaves and freedmen to participate in the pillaging or to buy any of the booty for themselves.[84]

The human cost in Greece of L. Aemilius Paullus' victory at Pydna in 168 BCE was enormous. Because his troops had been allowed to pillage only four towns in the area of Macedon and Thessaly, the Roman Senate granted permission to the army to plunder the towns of Epirus that had gone over to Perseus (the king of Macedon) four years earlier. Through guile and treachery, leading citizens were encouraged to bring out all gold and silver into the various agoras; meanwhile, the troops were sent out at staggered intervals according to the distance of the towns so that the various cohorts could be turned loose all at once on all the towns. Seventy towns were sacked, their walls demolished, and 150,000 people were sold as slaves (Livy, 45.34). All proceeds went to the troops. Even so, the soldiers begrudged Aemilius Paullus (and the Aerarium) the Macedonian king's treasure.

---

[84] Polyb. 18.35.9; complete references (numerous) in A. E. Astin, *Scipio Aemilianus* (Oxford, 1967): 76, footnote 2, 78.

After his defeat of Perseus, Aemilius Paullus first staged a victory celebration in Amphipolis, to which he invited rulers and dignitaries from all over Greece and Asia Minor. This spectacle was organized specifically for an eastern Mediterranean audience and combined traditional Greek features with Roman display – he had the booty spread out for all the guests to examine.[85] Later, Aemilius Paullus sailed up the Tiber to Rome in a huge ship formerly owned by Perseus, laden with gold, silver, arms and armor, and textiles from the Macedonian palace, all on display to the throngs that filled both banks of the river. Despite initial opposition to a Triumph (led by soldiers disappointed that they had not received enough themselves), when it was held, three days were needed for the triumphal procession (Livy, 45.32–35). The first day was entirely devoted to the display of the captured statues, paintings, and colossal statues: this required 250 wagons, says Plutarch (*Aem.* 32). Of them all, only one statue was remembered as a "masterpiece" by a named artist: an Athena by Pheidias (Pliny, *HN* 34.54), which Aemilius Paullus dedicated in the Temple of Fortuna Huiusce Diei (Today's Fortune, now identified as Temple B on the Largo Argentina). Aemilius Paullus also sent to Athens to request a painter for the paintings to be made for his Triumph and a philosopher to tutor his children. The Athenians sent Metrodorus, who, they said, would be the best for both jobs (Pliny, *HN* 35.135). In addition, there was so much money put into the Aerarium by Aemilius Paullus that various taxes on citizens could be ended.

Most interesting for the developing relationship between Greek and Roman culture, however, is Aemilius Paullus' tour and pilgrimage to the famous sanctuaries of old Greece: he made sacrifices at most of them, including an especially large one at Olympia, because he had

---

[85] On the politics of the celebration, Ferrary (1988): 547–572; for analysis of Aemilius' celebration as a Hellenistic spectacle, see J. C. Edmonson, "The Cultural Politics of Public Spectacle in Rome and the Greek East, 167–166 BCE," in B. Bergmann and C. Kondoleon, eds., *The Art of Ancient Spectacle* (*Studies in the History of Art,* 56) (New Haven and London, 1999): 77–95.

felt so moved by Pheidias' chryselephantine cult image of Zeus, which, he declared, captured Homer's Zeus perfectly. He provided the more sumptuous sacrifice there as though it were meant for Jupiter on the Capitoline, Livy remarks (45.28). His tour included Delphi, where he had an equestrian statue of himself set on a pillar carved with an extant relief showing the battle of Pydna that had been destined for a statue of Perseus, and made a sacrifice there (Fig. 6). He went to the Asklepieion at Epidauros; Corinth, Sicyon, and Argos; the oracles of Trophonios at Lebadia and Amphiaraos at Oropos; and spots famous in literature, such as the Temple of Artemis and harbor at Aulis, used by Agamemnon, then on to Athens, where he sacrificed on the Akropolis. As he returned to Demetrias in Thessaly, the tour was cut short because of administrative problems, but Livy's description (followed by Plutarch) contributes to the image of Aemilius Paullus as a Roman respectful of Greek sanctuaries and Greek ritual – but viewing all of it from a Roman perspective, with Rome as the proper center of the world.[86] There is no way to gauge the motives for his sacrifices, but that he made them certainly shows a wish to present a respectful image.

GRABBING THE INCENSE

For the Greeks, the greatest shock came at the Roman destruction of Corinth in 146 BCE. After consecrating the city to the gods of the underworld in a ritual *devotio*, L. Mummius took everything and then destroyed the city, at least enough so that it remained fairly deserted until it was refounded by Julius Caesar 102 years later.[87] Mummius'

---

[86] Livy, 45–27–28, based on Polybius 30.10.3–6 (fragmentary, see Walbank, *Commentary* III: 431–433); for the Romanocentric imagery in Livy's version, see U. Eigler, "Aemilius Paullus: ein Feldherr auf Bildungsreise?" in Eigler (2003):250–267. W. Reiter sees specifically political, controlling motives in the tour and, in general, views Aemilius' positive reputation with considerable skepticism (*Aemilius Paullus. Conqueror of Greece* [London, New York, and Sydney, 1988]: on the tour, 136–137).

[87] For details of the historical background, R. Morstein Kallet-Marx, *Hegemony to Empire. The Development of the Roman Imperium in the East from 148 to 62 B.C.* (Berkeley and London, 1995): 84–96.

FIGURE 6. Battle of Pydna, Monument of Aemilius Paullus, 168 BCE, Delphi Museum, Greece. Photo credit: Foto Marburg / Art Resource, NY.

supposed avarice and ignorance about the art among the booty became a stock part of the story, told and retold: the soldiers played dice on a painting; Mummius only withdrew a painting for sale when a Pergamene bid a high price; Mummius thought one painting could be substituted for another, if damaged; he confused Zeus with Philip and called statues of youths Nestor and Priam, and so forth: a mocking tradition that perhaps sought to minimize what must have been a truly staggering, unprecedented haul of Greek art.[88]

Yet Mummius also followed the Marcellan tradition of using the art booty from Corinth as dedications elsewhere. He is said to have decorated all of Italy with the art from Corinth. In fact, more inscriptions are preserved documenting his gifts in more places in Italy, Rome, and sanctuaries in mainland Greece than from any other Roman general of the Republic, and the list keeps growing as more are found.[89]

In his description of the sack of Corinth, Pausanias (who visited Corinth around 160 CE), although normally reticent on such things, emphasizes the killing and slavery after the sack of Corinth, the human

---

[88] For analysis of the ancient comments, see Gruen (1992): 123–129, where Mummius' intelligence and integrity are defended and restored.

[89] Most recent list of ancient evidence, including Greek and Latin inscriptions, with discussion in L. Graverini, "L. Mummio Acaico," *Maecenas* I (2001): 105–148; see also H. Philipp and W. Koenigs, "Zu den basen des L. Mummius in Olympia," *AM* 94 (1979): 193–216; G. Waurick, "Kunstraub der Römer: Untersuchungen zu seinen anfängen anhand der Inschriften," *JRGZ* 22 (1975): 1–46.

cost of the destruction, and the loss of autonomy in Greece, but he also disapproves of the loss of sanctity in removing votive offerings (7.16.7–10).[90] At Olympia, Pausanias notes that Mummius dedicated twenty-one gilded shields that were hung onto the exterior metopes of the Temple of Zeus (the dowel holes and circular weathering can still be seen on the blocks). He offered them after he had captured Corinth and after he had "driven out the Dorian Corinthians" (5.10.4). Pausanias also comments (incorrectly) that Mummius was the first Roman, private person or senator, who dedicated an offering (*anathema*) in a Greek sanctuary, with reference to a bronze image of Zeus, then standing next to the first column on the right of the front façade of the same temple (5.24.4).

Presumably, Mummius had the shields and the Zeus made specifically for Olympia out of the proceeds from the sack and recycled actual Corinthian statues elsewhere. Some sixty years later, Sulla, after pillaging many places in Greece, was not so discreet. In the case of a noteworthy statue of Dionysus by Myron that Sulla dedicated at Helikon, Pausanias comments with some asperity that "he dedicated it not from his own means, but after he took it from the Minyan Orchomenians: this is called among the Greeks 'worshipping the gods with other people's incense'" (9.30.1). Evidently such behavior had become proverbial.

Within the military context of a declared war against a foreign enemy, we see that Roman conquerors developed a set of customs surrounding the booty that grew ever more publicly ostentatious. Some generals tried to compensate in part with personal austerity (that too would vanish in the next century). By their personal abstemiousness, they also hoped to avoid the ever-growing controversy over booty and

[90] K. Arafat makes the point about humanitarian concern and religious scruple, in K. W. Arafat, *Pausanias' Greece. Ancient Artists and Roman Rulers* (Cambridge, 1996): 93, with further useful analysis, 92–97. On the historical and literary context of Pausanias' views on Greek freedom and on the gods, see S. Swain, *Hellenism and Empire. Language, Classicism, and Power in the Greek World AD 50–250* (Oxford, 1996): 333–347.

perhaps dampen the sense of entitlement in the army. At the same time, analogous with the principle behind *evocatio*, they decorated new and old temples in Rome with the finest of the spoils and the best of the art.

Other instances of "plundering" of sanctuaries should be labeled "looting" or even just "theft" because although they were carried out with indirect military authority by representatives of Rome, they did not occur during direct warfare. One episode was the looting of the goddess Persephone's sacred treasure in Locri, on the southern coast of the toe of Italy, in 204 BCE (it had accumulated for more than 450 years and had been left sacrosanct by Hannibal).[91] A senatorial commission investigated and made full restitution of the looted treasure, making up from the Aerarium what could not be retrieved from the perpetrators, who were led by Q. Pleminius. The commission also performed expiatory rites to the Goddess.[92] A similar incident occurred in 106 BCE, when the consul Q. Servilius Caepio took the sacred gold of the Tectosages near Tolosa (modern Toulouse) in Gaul. He was eventually tried, found guilty, and went into exile.[93] To the credit of the Roman Senate, these incidents were severely punished, largely because it was felt that the religious violation would fall on the people of Rome as a whole

[91] The Locri Tablets record a staggering sum that was given to Pyrrhus in the 270s: 11,240 silver talents were paid to him over six years: 295 metric tons of silver. The Tablets are an archive of bronze inscriptions found packed in a stone cylinder that had been set underground and capped by a stone lid that has a large bronze ring; in 1959, the ring was caught by the plow of a farmer and the repository was discovered. The "king" could be Agathocles rather than Pyrrhus; the amazing wealth they record shows why the sanctuary was an attractive target. For a summary discussion with further bibliography, see P. Franke, *CAH²* 7.2: 471–472.

[92] Both Livy and Diodorus give an account of this episode, with some variation in degrees of culpability: Livy, 29.8–9; Diod. 27.4; other sources in Broughton, *MMR*: 304. For modern discussions, A. J. Toynbee, *Hannibal's Legacy. The Hannibalic War's Effects on Roman Life* (Oxford, 1965) II: 613–621 (where the suggestion that Scipio was knowingly responsible for the looting is not credible); on the perpetrator Q. Pleminius' rank and the legal implications, Brennan, *Praetors*: 141–142. Much to the Senate's annoyance, the looting was repeated by unnamed Romans in 200 BCE and again was restored and the same expiatory rites performed (Livy, 31.12–13).

[93] Cic. *Nat. D.* 3.74; other sources in Alexander, *Trials*, no. 65. The incident was especially worrisome because some of the gold was believed to been taken from Delphi.

because the perpetrators represented them. This parallels exactly the situation that Cicero seeks to establish with his lengthy discussion of Verres' looting of art from Sicily.

An especially egregious incident of looting and wanton destruction was directed against another venerable Italiote Greek sanctuary: the Temple of Hera Lacinia at Croton was stripped of at least half of its white marble roof by Q. Fulvius Flaccus. This ancient sanctuary lay on the promontory outside the city that had been the adopted home of Pythagoras. The temple had been left inviolate by Hannibal. Livy refers to theft of the roof tiles as a *sacrilegium* (42.3.3). With this action, looting was ratcheted up to include an actual temple, not simply an individual piece of art ripped out of context, or bullion, or treasure but part of the context itself.

At the time of this theft in 173 BCE, Fulvius Flaccus had been elected censor, a senior magisterial office whose wide range of duties included not only the maintenance of the roll of Roman citizens and letting public contracts but also scrutiny of reprehensible moral conduct. It was under the protection of this office that he was able to despoil the temple because the people of Croton were afraid to resist or even to object to it. Seven years earlier, this man had vowed a temple to Fortuna Equestris during a battle with the Celtiberians in Spain; he won the battle and a subsequent one against the Ligurians in southern France in 174 and was awarded Triumphs for both.[94] Livy comments that no money and only enemy weapons were displayed in the second Triumph, and that it was generally thought that he was awarded it only because of his influence (his family was distinguished) and not because he had made a significant achievement (40.59). Fulvius Flaccus wanted to make his new temple in Rome distinctive but lacked any distinctive plunder to dedicate in it (as Marcellus was able to do with Syracusan

[94] The temple in Rome is discussed in Pietilä-Castrén (1987): 11–116; *LTUR* s.v. Fortuna Equestris (F. Coarelli). For Fulvius Flaccus, Broughton, *MRR*: 404; whole incident summarized by Valerius Maximus, 1.1.20.

plunder), so he went to Croton to steal the white marble roof from its famous temple.

Fulvius Flaccus tried to keep silent the origin of the marble roof tiles, but word got out. He was summoned before the Senate in the Curia, where they individually and as a body upbraided him furiously. Livy vividly depicts the deep anger of the Senate. Here is an excerpt from his account:

> *This, the most venerable temple in the region, which neither Pyrrhus nor Hannibal had violated, he was not content with violating but had shamefully robbed its covering and nearly destroyed it. The top of the temple had been ripped off, and the framing left bare to be rotted by rain. Was it for this that a censor is chosen to control behavior? That the very magistrate who was entrusted, by ancestral custom, with the duty of repairing public temples and contracting their maintenance was now roving through the cities of allies, plundering their temples and stripping the roofs from sacred buildings! And, if he were to do so to private buildings this would seem shameful enough, now he does it to the temples of the immortals gods, so as to bind the Roman people with impiety, building temples with the ruins of temples, as though the immortal gods were not the same everywhere, but that some should be adorned and decorated with the* spolia *from others!*
>
> (*Livy, 42.3*)

The Senators voted to let a contract for the return of the tiles and to have sacrifices of atonement (*piacularia*) made to the goddess. But all the contractor did was dump the tiles near the temple, supposedly because no craftsman could figure out how to put them back.[95] Fulvius

---

[95] Livy, 42.3.11: *tegulas relictas in area templi, quia reponendarum nemo artifex inire rationem potuerit, redemptores nuntiarunt.* The excuse for the incomplete restitution is patently absurd and should be read with a disgusted, sarcastic inflection. Although to be sure the masons and workmen of Croton were likely killed off or sold into slavery by either Romans or Carthaginians, they could have looked elsewhere or found the men Fulvius Flaccus

Flaccus was not punished by the Senate: he was not dismissed from the pontifical college, nor prohibited from dedicating the new temple or celebrating games. Evidently, in their eyes, he was not held personally responsible; rather, all Romans were.[96]

Nonetheless, in the next year, Fulvius Flaccus, having heard of the death of one son in battle in Illyricum and the grave illness of another, became overwhelmed with grief and fear and hung himself in his bedroom. Livy comments that it had been noticed after his time as censor he was not behaving normally, and it was thought that because of the wrath of Juno (Hera) Lacinia, he had become mentally unbalanced (Livy, 42.28). Thus, Livy implies, looting a temple for its parts, even to build another one, does have consequences. Today one column of this temple, built in the early fifth century BCE, still stands on the remains of the foundations and some of the stylobate (Fig. 7). Some pieces of the white island marble roof tiles have been found.[97]

Not long after Fulvius Flaccus dismembered the Temple of Juno Lacinia, Polybius visited the sanctuary and saw there a bilingual inscription on a bronze stele that Hannibal had set up as a record of his military accomplishments. There was also an altar dedicated by

intended to use in Rome for his temple. Moreover, while requiring some skill, fitting marble roof tiles is not difficult to figure out and differs little from terracotta tiles, then used ubiquitously.

[96] Points made by Toynbee (1965) II: 632, and expanded by E. La Rocca, "Le tegole del tempio de Hera Lacinia ed it tempio della Fortuna Equestre: tra spoliazioni e restauri in età tardorepubblicana," in R. Spada, ed., *Il tesoro di Hera. Scoperte nel santuario di Hera Lacinia a Capo Colonna di Crotone* (Milan, 1996): 89–98. La Rocca sees the senatorial move as politically motivated and notes that Croton never really recovered (p. 93). Another possibility is that the outrage Livy attributes to the Senate was his own. See also the analysis of M. Jaeger in "Livy, Hannibal's Monument, and the Temple of Juno at Croton," *TAPA* 136 (2006): 389–414.

[97] A. Ruga, "La copertura dell'edificio A," in Spada (1996): 99–105. White island marble roofs were highly prestigious in the early fifth century BCE because the marble had to be brought from Paros or Naxos in the Cyclades. Most of the pieces from Croton are Parian, but among the finds are some repairs in Pentelic marble, from Athens. For the architecture of the temple, D. Mertens, "Aspetti dell'architettura crotoniate," in *Crotone, Atti del XXIII Convegno di Studi sulla Magna Grecia* (Taranto, 1983 [1984]): 189–230.

Hannibal.[98] A pertinent issue here is to what degree Hannibal, even though a Carthaginian, respected Greek sanctuaries and their contents. The Latin accounts of sacrilege in this era are often emphasized with the expression "not even Hannibal [did this]…," the same driven, unsentimental Hannibal who destroyed four hundred cities in Italy, waging war at some distance from Carthage, using mostly mercenaries, and therefore always in need of money and supplies.[99] That Hannibal would take the trouble to set up a bronze bilingual inscription (generally accepted as credible) lends credence also to the idea of pervasive respect for Greek sanctuaries and shows a clear awareness of the value of such monuments as publicity for his accomplishments. He must have been ambitious for a larger, Hellenistic intercultural reputation, not just Carthaginian glory.

Cicero recounts a story about Hannibal's actions at this sanctuary that he obtained from two sources he considered trustworthy: L. Coelius Antipater, who in turn used Silenos of Kaleacte, an historian who accompanied Hannibal on his campaigns (*Div.* 1. 49). Hannibal wanted to take a gold column from the sanctuary at Croton but first drilled into it to see whether it was merely plated or solid gold. When he found out it was solid, he decided to take it. That night, however, Hera appeared to him in a dream and threatened that she would make sure he lost his

---

[98] Polybius, 3.3.18, 3.56.4, mentions the sanctuary as once rich and full of offerings, 34.11.9; Livy, 28.46.16. Polybius was concerned that readers might think his precise figures for troops, cavalry, ships, and elephants were invented, so he cites the inscription as his source and says that he saw it himself. He does not mention the temple. Walbank states that the years of his internment in Italy (between 167 and 150 BCE) are the most likely occasion for his visit to the sanctuary (Walbank, *Commentary* I: 364–365). Livy adds the information that the inscription was in Greek and Punic, refers to it as an account of Hannibal's *res gestae* (i.e., what he had accomplished, a phrase and type of account used later by Augustus), and mentions the altar Hannibal dedicated.

[99] Destroyed four hundred cities: according to the bronze inscription per Appian, *Libyca* 134. Livy (implausibly) mentions Italians who had sought refuge in the sanctuary slaughtered in the precinct by Hannibal when they refused to go to Carthage with him (30.30). Hannibal did strip the Temple of Feronia (northeast of Rome, at Lucus Feroniae) of its treasures, and his soldiers left crude bronze bullion in expiation (Livy, 26.11.8–9).

FIGURE 7.   Temple of Hera, Croton. Photo credit: Author.

one remaining good eye if he did so. Instead of taking it, he ordered a statuette of a heifer to be made from the gold filings and set on top of the column. In this account, there is nothing inherently implausible about the dedication itself. The type is very much in keeping with known dedications in the Greek west and also the mainland, and possibly an actual gold column once in the sanctuary inspired the story, perhaps even bearing a gold heifer to represent the sacred herd of the sanctuary.[100]

In this story, we may find a parallel with Herodotus' scenario of the dream-troubled Persian Datis, searching the holds of his ships for a looted Greek statue and personally returning it for safekeeping to Delos, and the uneasy concern of Xerxes, who orders sacrifices to be made in front of the temples on the Athenian Akropolis he had burned down just the day before. Prominent invading foreigners of high rank are depicted by Greek and Roman historians as feeling they ought not to plunder or destroy these sanctuaries, ought even to make sacrifices or set up an altar. A dream is posited as the vehicle for a warning in all three cases. Thus a presumption of the normative ethics of respect for sanctuaries and their contents is extended even to hostile foreign leaders.

WEEPING ENVOYS: CRITICISM OF ROMAN PLUNDERING

Polybius is the earliest Greek author to voice criticism of Roman wartime plundering of art; Cato had complained still earlier of its decadent effects on Romans.[101] Already tensions had been mounting

---

[100] The gold column is noted also by Livy, who says that it was set up from the proceeds of the sacred cattle that were pastured but untended on land sacred to Hera, enclosed by a sacred grove (24.3.6). S. Lancel sees the story of the gold column as a literary reflection of Ennius' use of Euhemerus' account of a gold stele on an island in the Indian Ocean bearing an inscribed *res gestae* (S. Lancel, *Hannibal*, trans. A. Nevill [Oxford, 1998]: 156).

[101] Cato: Malcovati, *ORF*, fr. 224; Livy (in a different context, concerning the repeal of a sumptuary law) has him complain about statues from Syracuse in 34.4.4, dramatic date 195 BCE: translation given here in Appendix, no. 2. On Cato's role in escalating tensions over

among the Roman elite over each other's increasingly large hauls.[102] Here, again, Marcellus' siege and sack of Syracuse is the center point of the ancient discussion, and I discuss ancient authors' comments and supporting evidence in chronological order so as to show how the critique developed. Polybius' views are given explicitly in the course of his discussion of the siege in book 9 but, unfortunately, only fragments of this book are preserved so we do not have his full account, which likely would have included comments on why the Romans plundered and details about how they did it and what they took. Because he was writing his account only about sixty or so years after the event, such details would have been especially valuable. In the extant passage, he explicitly directs his comments not only to the immediate circumstances of the plundered Syracusan art but also to all future conquerors.

His strong disapproval rings throughout his comments and focuses on the seizure of Syracusan art (9.10). His points are practical, even if moralizing in a fairly standard way. The chapter begins, "A city is not adorned by external splendors, but by the virtue of its inhabitants...." and then the text breaks off.[103] In what follows, he excuses the taking of gold and silver because it is taken to reduce the strength of the enemy and increase that of Rome. He offers two primary arguments against taking art as plunder, buttressed by two subsidiary rhetorical arguments: (1) art contributes nothing to the power and expansion of the city; (1a) the victors became great while living simply, so why should they imitate the weaker people they defeated? (2) Seeing the art in its new context excites strong jealousy and hatred among the defeated and reminds them of their past calamities (i.e., it does not promote a peaceful

booty, see E. Gruen, *Studies in Greek Culture and Roman Policy* (Berkeley and London, 1990): 136–137.

[102] Gruen (1990): 129–137; Gruen (1992): 94–130.

[103] Polybius 9.10: for the extant passage in translation, see Appendix, no. 1. The following excerpt is translated by Paton [Loeb], modified slightly here with the suggestions of Walbank, *Commentary* II: 135–136.

settlement); (2a) it would be better to adorn the city with dignity and magnanimity, not with paintings and sculpture. He then sums up with universal advice by saying: "At any rate these remarks will serve to teach all those who succeed to empire, that they should not strip cities under the idea that the misfortunes of another are an ornament to their own country." He concludes by remarking that the Romans "on the present occasion, after transferring all these objects to Rome, used such as came from private houses to embellish their own homes, and those that were state property for their public buildings."

Especially notable here is the careful avoidance of even an implication of sacrilege or impiety.[104] Religious concerns are not invoked or specifically mentioned, only implied. He refers to "state property" and "public buildings" in his dichotomy between the public and private uses of the plundered art. In fact, temples were the frequent (but not the only) public destination: specifically, Marcellus' Temple of Honos and Virtus, mentioned often by other authors as the repository of Marcellus' finest plunder from Syracuse, including Archimedes' orrery. Perhaps Polybius deliberately avoids mentioning Marcellus and the fruit of his victory or, by referring to "public buildings," he wishes to keep Roman reputation free of any sense of religious violation in obtaining booty in war, at least in this case, or possibly he sees no violation. Polybius is far more outspoken and vehement in his condemnation of other plunderers in his history: the most egregious are the Aetolians and Philip V, but Prusias II and Antiochus IV also seemingly perish because of their impieties.[105] According to Polybios, these people act far more viciously than

---

[104] Gruen sees Polybius' criticism of the taking of art from Syracuse as a "tactical error rather than a moral failure" (1992): 98; Ferrary emphasizes Polybius' insight as a hostage himself on the envy, jealousy, and hatred the art might inspire in Greeks (1988): 576–578.

[105] Antiochus IV Epiphanes (notorious for religious violations in Jerusalem) tried to plunder a temple of Artemis in Elamite territory and died of madness, "some say" because of the attempted sacrilege (Polyb. 31.91–4); see C. Habicht, *CAH*² 8: 346–353. Prusias II, King of Bithynia, sacked a sanctuary at Pergamon and carried off a statue of Asklepios by the noted Athenian sculptor Phyromachos after ostentatious sacrifices to the same god the previous

the Romans ever did and were deliberately destructive of sanctuaries and religious property.

Philip V of Macedon, as we saw previously, ravaged the sanctuary of Apollo at Thermon, sanctuaries in Athens and Attica, and at Pergamon, where he not only destroyed statues and burned down the sacred grove, but he even dug up foundations of temples so as to destroy them utterly (16.1). Polybius gives his fullest criticism of plundering and the behavior of the conqueror to the defeated in a discussion of the wiser behavior of Philip V's Macedonian predecessors. He points to the policy of Philip II, who did not take vengeance on Athens but rather was fairly generous to the city; to his son Alexander (the Great) who razed Thebes to the ground but took utmost care not to touch any temple or sacred precinct (or the house of Pindar, according to other authors); even in Persia, Alexander was careful not to damage property of the gods. Polybius then states the same reasoning discussed previously, that destroying the enemy's resources is acceptable as a necessity, but wanton damage to temples gives no advantage and is the mark of a frenzied mind (5.9.1–14.6). Further on in his account, he gives his judgment on Philip V, for his behavior at Thermon: "he was not only guilty of impiety to the gods by destroying the offerings consecrated to them, but he wronged men, transgressing the laws of war, and acted contrary to his own purposes by showing himself the implacable and cruel foe of his adversaries" (7.14.3). By implication, Roman behavior was not as bad as this because, for the most part, they did not destroy sanctuaries deliberately, even though they did plunder them of dedications and offerings.

Polybius' comments indicate that his primary concern is with the aftermath of battle and the need to rule humanely. Judging behavior in

day (Polyb. 32.15). Prusias then proceeded to despoil and burn several other sanctuaries and soon his army suffered from hunger and dysentery, so that "it seemed" to be instant divine vengeance. Walbank comments on the evidence for Polybius' inconsistent religious attitude and his distancing remarks about divine vengeance only "seeming" to be in effect (*Commentary*, III: 539–540). On Prusias II's attack, see Habicht, *CAH*[2] 8: 359–360.

war is done according to the *laws of war*. Polybius advocates restraint in warfare, with damage done only as necessary, and respect for religious property. The practical advantage of restraint comes afterward, in ruling the conquered people, who will be less resentful and presumably more tractable if they have been treated with some clemency. Humane considerations and the matter of magnanimous reputation are important too. These are early and powerful statements on the concept of "laws of war," foundational statements for international law. His views may seem standard but, in fact, they helped set the standard.[106]

One part of his reasoning that is less persuasive is the first point, that art contributes nothing to the power and expansion of the city. Here Polybius seems to regard art reductively, simply as a type of spoil, as decoration, a type of trophy potentially leading to decadence: simple, rustic tastes bring strength, and soft luxuries and art will weaken moral fiber. While this was fine for rhetorical purposes (and has Catonian overtones), he surely knew better. Distinctive architecture and a plethora of sculpture were long since the mark of a strong capital of an empire. Thucydides had already made famous the contrast between the fabric of the cities of Sparta and Athens relative to their power, in the eyes of the future, and, even though he adds that we should not judge cities by their appearance, in effect he acknowledges that we do (Thuc., 1.10.2–3).

Polybius was living in a Rome that was transforming herself, and the plundered art and new temples, new roads, and aqueducts funded by booty were a significant part of that. True sophistication in the urban expression of power through art and architecture is one of Rome's great achievements that set the archetype for future western capitals, and it

---

[106] Phillipson (1911) II: 246–250; on the development of international law in antiquity, D. J. Bederman, *International Law in Antiquity* (Cambridge, 2001b); on Grotius and his use of ancient sources, D. J. Bederman, *Classical Canons. Rhetoric, Classicism and Treaty Interpretation* (Aldershot, 2001a): 113–141.

was then just beginning. Such urban expression obviously inspires and contributes to future aggrandizement (the moralizers were correct that art has an impact but not necessarily one of weakness or decline). The audience for the transformation, as Polybius rightly notes, was not only Roman but also the representatives of the conquered foreigners, whose emotions upon seeing their plundered art so concerned him.

The concern for the audience of foreigners, especially visiting Greek dignitaries, was not Polybius' alone. By the third century BCE, the Roman Senate frequently received foreign visitors and wished to treat them appropriately. In a study of the development of the basilica and the reason for the term (derived from the Greek for "royal"), K. Welch has convincingly resolved this longstanding conundrum in the architectural history of Rome.[107] She has demonstrated that the type was inspired by Hellenistic royal reception halls and was brought into Rome in the third century BCE, when royal visitors from around the Mediterranean began to visit the city. The Atrium Regium, Rome's first basilica, and the Graecostasis ("Stand of the Greeks"), two well-known landmarks in the Forum, belonged to a period of increasing diplomatic activity well before Rome's hegemony was taken for granted.

Welch argues furthermore that two famous statues in front of the Curia representing Alcibiades and Pythagoras (probably gilded bronze and life-like in style) may have been brought to Rome as war booty, possibly during the wars with Pyrrhus from Croton, the home of Pythagoras and near Thurii, to which Alcibiades fled under indictment when he left the Athenian campaign in Sicily.[108] Subsequent basilicas, such as the one built by Cato (in 184 BCE) also near the Curia, served as

---

[107] K. Welch, "A New View of the Origins of the Basilica: The Atrium Regium, Graecostasis, and Roman diplomacy," *JRA* 16 (2003): 5–34.

[108] Welch (2003): 32, with earlier bibliography on the two statues and their possible origins. These statues were commonly explained as representing the wisest and bravest of the Greeks (Pliny, *HN* 34.26, who expresses surprise at the choice); see Gruen (1992): 91.

monumental reception areas for an increasing throng of visitors in the second century BCE.[109] The fact that substantial resources were spent on monumental diplomatic facilities illustrates the sincere and practical Roman interest in the image they presented to foreigners. Hence, Polybius' comments about foreign reaction to seeing in Rome artistic and religious *spolia* taken from them should be seen as genuine Roman concerns, not merely rhetorical points.

That same type of audience (but about a hundred years later) is vividly evoked by Cicero in his own comments about plundered art. In the course of the *Actio Secunda*, Cicero describes in detail Verres' plundering of art while he was serving as a legate in Asia Minor, before he became governor of Sicily. Some of it was on display during a festival in Rome, where it was seen and recognized by visitors as having come from their own temples and sanctuaries. Cicero says he himself saw their reaction, as follows:[110]

> *A large number of envoys from Asia and Achaia, who happened at the time to be in Rome serving on deputations, were paying worship to images of their gods that had been carried away from their own sanctuaries (and now) were in the Forum, and recognizing as well the other statues and works of art, some here and some there, would stand gazing at them with weeping eyes. What we then heard these people saying was always this, that the ruin of our allies and friends was certain beyond all question; for there in the Forum of Rome, in the place where once those who had wronged our allies used to be prosecuted and found guilty, now stood, openly exposed to view, the objects seized from those allies by criminals.*

(Verr. *2.1.59*)

---

[109] Welch cites Polybius 23.1.1, 9: so many missions from Greece came in 184 that it took three days just to introduce them and the Senate was overwhelmed (Welch 2003: 34).

[110] For the whole passage, see Appendix, no. 3, trans. by Greenwood [Loeb].

Cicero's purpose is to show Verres' plundering of art was worse than the plundering in wartime, because he plundered indiscriminately (taking cult images, not just ordinary statues of people) and from allies, not enemies. Cicero does not in the *Verrines* offer criticism of the customary Roman practice of plundering in war. On the contrary, he contrasts the abstemiousness of famous generals (e.g., Marcellus, Aemilius Paullus, Mummius), whose houses are empty of statues and pictures but who adorn every part of Italy with their spoils, with the avarice of Verres, whose house is packed with stolen art (*Verr.* 2.1.50–51, 55). Lest it seem old-fashioned to recall the heroes of the previous century, Cicero points to one of the jurors, Publius Servilius, who as noted previously returned from taking a pirate city in Lycia and properly entered a full accounting of every statue, and has his account-book read aloud.

Elsewhere, however, Cicero is more revealing of his personal reactions to plundering and plundered art. In the context of discussing a "just war" in his essay *De Officiis* (On Obligations), he twice laments the sack of Corinth. First, he offers a (feeble) excuse: "I would not have sanctioned the destruction of Corinth, but I believe that there was a particular reason for it, notably its favorable location and the danger that this might at some time be an incitement to war" (I.35); later in the essay, he says more forcefully, "Wrongs are very often committed in the public sphere through choice of what is ostensibly useful, as when we perpetrated the destruction of Corinth" (3.46).[111] In the same essay, Cicero quotes Panaetius (the Stoic philosopher whose work he uses in the essay and who had been a teacher and house guest of Scipio Aemilianus), in praise of Scipio for his incorruptibility. Cicero notes again that Scipio Aemilianus, Aemilius Paullus, and L. Mummius all brought into Rome massive booty but brought to their houses nothing

---

[111] Trans. P. G. Walsh. See further A. Dyck, *A Commentary on Cicero, De Officiis* (Ann Arbor, 1996): 139–140.

except lasting memories of their fame. Cicero also uses the two Scipios (conquerors of Carthage in 202 and 146 BCE) as the interlocutors in the philosophical *Dream of Scipio* that would be so widely read and admired in the Middle Ages.[112]

In another philosophical essay written near the end of his life, Cicero expounds on the virtues of austere living (*Tusc.* 5.35.102). He says that among those who like statues and paintings, those who are not wealthy are actually better off, because they can see huge quantities of them in every public place in Rome. But those who rely on a private collection have fewer examples and see them less often, only when they are in the country: "and even then they feel somehow stung (by remorse), when they remember how they got them." Here, Cicero suggests that the uneasiness of taking other people's art will persist if it is exhibited privately, but if it is on display in public, it loses the stigma and becomes, presumably, part of a collective war commemorative.

The historian Sallust, writing about 42 BCE, takes up the theme of Roman decline in his short monograph on the Catilinarian conspiracy. In the preface, he gives a capsule history of Rome and sees the fall of Carthage in 146 as a turning point in Roman taste and morality. This was intensified, he says, during Sulla's warfare in Asia, when his soldiers acquired a taste for looting. There, they first learned "to cultivate a taste for statues, pictures, and embossed plate, which they stole from private houses and public buildings, plundering temples and profaning everything sacred and secular alike. When victory was won, as might be expected of such troops, they stripped their enemy bare" (*Cat.* 11, trans. Handford). Sallust himself had served under Julius Caesar and was the first governor in Africa of the new Roman province Numidia. Afterward, he retired to write history and purchased in Rome

---

[112] The younger Scipio is also a primary, idealized interlocutor in *De Republica* and *De Senectute*; Cicero admired Scipio Aemilianus as a man of action who also had serious literary and cultural interests. For a (very lengthy) list of references in Cicero's works to Scipio Aemilianus, see M. Rambaud, *Cicéron et l'histoire romaine* (Paris, 1953): 31–32.

(apparently with the proceeds of his governorship) the extensive gardens named after him, the *horti Sallustiani*, that eventually became imperial property.[113] In the comments on plundering, he deals with stock themes of declining morality; however, the specification of neglect of sacred/profane distinctions and stripping the enemy bare have clear Ciceronian echoes from the *Verrines*. Inasmuch as Sallust was himself under indictment at one point for maladministration in his province, he certainly would have taken time to read the *Verrines*.

Livy, writing about two decades after Sallust, addresses the topic of plunder in several contexts, as in the early episode at Veii discussed previously. It is in his narrative about the siege of Syracuse, however, that Livy's views on the ethics of taking art as booty are most explicit. Livy criticizes Marcellus' plundering of art from Syracuse, and he sees it as a turning point that led to further, truly unscrupulous actions. He states that the art was a legitimate spoil of war (*hostium quidem illa spolia et parta belli iure*) but regrets that the precedent led to blurred distinctions between the spoliation of sacred and profane buildings. His comments are preceded with praise of Marcellus:

> *After the capture of Syracuse, Marcellus had made a general settlement*
> *of affairs in Sicily, and that too with such honorable integrity as could*
> *not but enhance the dignity of the Roman people as much as it added to*
> *his own reputation. This is undeniable: but at the same time he removed*
> *to Rome the beautiful statues and paintings which Syracuse possessed in*
> *such abundance. These were, one must admit, legitimate spoils, acquired*
> *by right of war; none the less their removal to Rome was the origin of*
> *our admiration of Greek art and started the universal and reckless*
> *spoliation of all buildings sacred and profane which prevails today, and*
> *which ultimately turned against our own Roman gods, beginning with*

---

[113] For Sallust and his purchase of gardens, see K. J. Hartswick, *The Gardens of Sallust* (Austin, 2004): 8–10.

the very temple which Marcellus so splendidly adorned. For time was
when foreigners used to visit the temples dedicated by Marcellus at the
Porta Capena, drawn thither by the magnificent examples of Greek art
which they contained; but hardly any of them are to be seen today.

(25.40.1–3, trans. A. de Sélincourt)

His emphasis on the distinction between sacred and profane (which is not made directly by Polybius) was likely inspired by the example of Cicero's *Verrines*, where the point is impressed on the reader again and again, and he also echoes Sallust's monograph on Catiline. The theme had existed at least as early as Herodotus' account of Xerxes in Athens. But it had immediacy for Livy: as a member of the generation just after Cicero, in the time of Augustus, he had ample opportunity to witness the far worse depredations that occurred in the late Republic. It was as though even Verres, the object of Cicero's strong fulminations, had been surpassed. Livy traces the origin of this covetousness for Greek art, a passion fully defined by Cicero, back to the art brought as booty from Syracuse.

Augustus himself was in a position to take, leave, or restore whatever he chose from Greek temples, and he did so. As we shall see, he clearly wanted to present himself as a benign restorer and rectifier of distressed temples and sacred property but, in fact, did take items from Greece that were later displayed in or around his Temple of Mars Ultor in the Forum Augustum. His plunder is discussed in a notable statement on the looting of temples in wartime given by Pausanias, who was writing his description of antiquities and sites of pilgrimage in Greece much later, in the reign of Antoninus Pius. He summarizes the history of wartime looting as far back as the Trojan War (8.46, see Appendix, no. 7). Augustus took the best, most treasured items from Tegea: the ivory cult image of Athena Alea, by the archaic Athenian sculptor Endoios, and the tusks of the Calydonian Boar.

Apparently, Pausanias saw these items himself in Rome because he locates them precisely within the Forum Augustum and comments that one of the tusks had been moved to the imperial gardens. Like the tusks that King Masinissa of Numidia restored to Malta (and were later seized by Verres), these tusks might have been from prehistoric elephants.[114] The Calydonian Boar had first been wounded by Atalanta, Pausanias explains, so she was awarded the head and hide; her exploits and the hunt were depicted in sculpture in the pediment of the temple. He was able to see the hide still in the temple, now aged, with all its bristles missing: Augustus evidently was not interested in this old piece of pigskin, however venerable it still seemed to the Tegeans, or any of the other antiques, trophies, and curiosities still there and mentioned by Pausanias.

Pausanias seemingly exculpates Augustus of plundering on the grounds that he was only following a long precedent. His attitudes toward Romans in general, and emperors in particular, have been much discussed: toward Augustus, he seems to be levelly neutral, perhaps adopting a style of unemotional reporting akin to Thucydides.[115] Certainly the plundering of art by Romans mattered to him, since he mentions it often and does make it clear that he disapproves of it. His anger at plundering is focused primarily on Sulla, the one who "worships the gods with other people's incense." Sulla plundered the sanctuaries at Delphi, Olympia, and Epidauros, as well as numerous smaller temples

---

[114] For Augustus' collection of fossils on the island Capri and in Rome, including these tusks, see A. Mayor, *The First Fossil Hunters. Paleontology in Greek and Roman Times* (Princeton, 2000): 142–144. Their presumed antiquity suggests that the Tegean tusks were prehistoric, although as K. Lapatin notes, there is no proof that they were: K. D. S. Lapatin, *Chryselephantine Statuary in the Ancient Mediterranean World* (Oxford, 2001): 9 (where other references to the tusks are also given).

[115] So suggests C. Habicht, *Pausanias' Guide to Ancient Greece* (Berkeley and London, 1995, 1998 ed.): 122–123. For Pausanias' attitudes to Augustus, see also Arafat (1996): 116–138; Swain (1996): 347–356; useful comments on the state of scholarship on Pausanias in C. P. Jones, "Editing and Understanding Pausanias," *JRA* 16 (2003): 673–676.

and shrines. As C. Habicht points out, he describes Sulla's cruelty in six separate passages. Finally, about Sulla's death, Pausanias says,

> Sulla's treatment of the Athenians was savage and alien to the Roman character, and his treatment of Thebes and Orchomenus was similar; he committed yet another outrage at Alalcomenae by carrying off the very [cult] image of Athena. But after perpetrating these mad outrages on Greek cities and Greek gods he was overtaken by the most loathsome of diseases: lice broke out over his body, and that was the miserable end of what the world had once esteemed his good fortune. Henceforth the sanctuary at Alalcomenae, bereft of its goddess, was neglected. A great strong ivy-tree growing on the walls loosened the jointing of the stones and was tearing them apart.
>
> (9.33.6–7, trans. Frazer)[116]

Here again, we see the familiar theme of fatal recompense for the immoral behavior of plundering temples, as in the case of the Phocian leaders who plundered Delphi, Q. Fulvius Flaccus who took the marble roof tiles from the Temple of Hera at Croton, Antiochus IV, Prusias II and others.

What the gods thought about Roman plundering seemed knowable to ancient observers. As we have seen, Roman custom anticipated and forestalled a negative response by offering an invitation, the *evocatio*, to the image of a captured deity, such as Veientine Juno, who was brought back to Rome. The college of pontiffs felt able to discern the difference between the sacred and the profane images, to be treated differently, both among those taken from Capua and those M. Fulvius Nobilior had taken from Ambracia. Within the Greek east, the practice of *aphidruma* (making a ritually exact copy of a statue, altar, or shrine) offered a neat solution to some types of potential conflict and was continued under

---

[116] Frazer's translation is slightly modified. Cruelty: Habicht (1985): 120–121; on Sulla in Greece and Sulla's death, see Arafat (1996): 97–105.

Roman rule. It presupposes a willingness on the part of the deity to be duplicated and extended; this must have been done with the assent of an oracle.[117]

In ancient texts, the gods could show their reactions to potential or actual plundering quite vividly: when Augustus was about to arrive in Athens, which had supported Marc Antony, a statue of Athena turned around from east to west (toward Rome) and spat blood.[118] The chryselephantine Zeus in the Temple of Zeus at Olympia burst into laughter when Caligula's workmen started forward to the pedestal to dismantle it and take it to Rome and laughed so hard that the scaffolding collapsed (Suetonius, *Calig.* 57.1). The project was abandoned. This sort of anecdote is familiar from Livy's history and was no doubt inspired by it, but Virgil makes the most effective literary use of divine displeasure. He has the Palladion's eyes glowing with flames, her body sweating and the statue leaping three times, with her spear trembling, after she was stolen from Troy and taken to the Greek camp (*Aeneid*, 2.162ff.). Seeing this, the Greeks felt doomed.

THE IMAGE OF THE HUMANE GENERAL

Carthage fell after a long siege and was completely destroyed, with a curse imprecated on anyone who tried to rebuild it. Just as the final torching was about to start, Polybius, standing with the commander on a hill overlooking the city, noticed that Scipio Aemilianus had tears in his eyes. They then talked about the turn of fate, whether Rome might fall someday too, and thought of Priam's Troy. After this pause, the practical business at hand demanded attention and the issue of

[117] On *aphidruma*, see L. Robert, Hellenica. *Recueil d'épigraphie de numismatique et d'antiquités grecques, 13, d'Aphrodisias à la Lycaonie* (Paris, 1965): 120–125; I. Malkin, "What Is an Aphidruma?" *ClAnt* 10 (1991): 77–96 (Malkin emphasizes the transfer of cult over copy of image); E. Perry, *The Aesthetics of Emulation in the Visual Arts of Ancient Rome* (Cambridge, 2005): 172–177.

[118] Cass. Dio, 54.7.3. For discussion of animated, guardian, and dangerous statues, see C. A. Faraone, *Talismans and Trojan Horses. Guardian Statues in Ancient Greek Myth and Ritual* (Oxford, 1992).

booty once more came to the fore. For himself and his household, Scipio refused any of it. A massive quantity of booty was processed in the Triumph held in 146, said to have outdone in magnificence any previous triumph. It included many statues and votive offerings that the Carthaginians had taken in previous campaigns over many years from many places.[119] Scipio was generous to the soldiers who had fought in the war, perhaps remembering the controversies surrounding his natural father L. Aemilius Paullus' distribution in Macedonia, perceived then as far too stingy. Scipio also organized sacrifices and games in Africa and Rome and built a temple to Virtus in Rome, probably after this victory. The familiar pattern was nonetheless exceptional because of what the victory represented, the final and utter defeat of Rome's greatest enemy. His modern biographer A. Astin says about Scipio's Triumph that "it conferred, or at least ratified, *gloria* such as no living man could hope to rival."[120]

The truly distinctive action taken by Scipio, one that showed imaginative insight, respect for Greek culture, and a thoughtful, far-reaching view of historical interconnections, was the restitution of revered and sacred images that had been taken by Carthaginians from Greeks in Sicily. He sent messages to the towns in Sicily, inviting them to send envoys to reclaim from Carthage the statues and other plunder that had been taken from their temples and sanctuaries so that they could take it back. They did this, and the items were set up in public places and temples all over Sicily, on new bases with inscriptions labeling them as returned and dedicated by Scipio.

The plundering by the Carthaginians had taken place much earlier, at intervals reaching back at least as far as the last decade of the

---

[119] The Carthaginian Punic libraries were given away to chieftains in Africa by the Roman Senate, but they first arranged for a commission of scholarly Romans to translate Mago's treatise on agriculture into Latin (Pliny, *HN* 18.22).

[120] Astin (1967): 79. For the scene on the hill, Astin, 77–78, app. 4, with sources in app. 2; Scipio's personal abstemiousness, see footnote 81 previously; on the Triumph, Pietilä-Castrén (1987): 134–138; Pape (1975): 19–21.

fifth century BCE, when Selinous, Akragas, and Himera had been thoroughly sacked and plundered. The Carthaginians under Hannibal (an earlier namesake of the more famous general defeated in 202) had sacked Himera in 409 in an especially brutal way, described in detail by Diodorus, her people tortured and slaughtered in reprisal for the Greek victory at Himera over Carthage and that of Hannibal's grandfather in 480 (13.59.5-62). The temples were burned to the ground and the city razed. Now Scipio restored to Thermae Himerae (modern Termini Imerese), the newer city founded adjacent to the destroyed one, some of the items that had been taken some 263 years earlier. A preserved marble base found near Termini Imerese attests to one such restoration, with Publius Cornelius Scipio's name and the occasion inscribed on it.[121]

He also returned the famous bronze Bull of Phalaris to Akragas, where it was seen by Diodorus in the first century BCE (13.90.5; Cic., *Verr.* 2.4.73). Other Sicilian cities known to have made successful identifications and claims at Carthage are Gela, Tyndaris, and Segesta. In addition, at Engyion, Scipio dedicated Corinthian bronze cuirasses and helmets and bronze hydriae (sacred vessels for water) in the sanctuary of Magna Mater, the Great Mother (Cic., *Verr.* 2.4.97). Verres took them all, presumably for his household, leaving behind only the inscription attesting to Scipio's dedication, read by Cicero.

Although Polybius' own eyewitness account of the restorations is lost, his statements were used and echoed by many later authors on the subject.[122] It is Cicero who truly appreciated the significance of Scipio's gesture, and he makes much of it in the *Verrines*, where he discusses the repatriations ten times, in some instances in quite lengthy passages.

---

[121] *IG* XIV.315; Syll.³, 677; *ILS*.8769; further bibliography in Ferrary (1988): 579, note 26. *ILLRP*.326, a dedication in Latin by Scipio of spoils from Carthage, was found in San Benedetto dei Marsi (Marruvium Marsorum) near the former Fucine Lake in central Italy; it is probably a later (imperial) copy of the Scipionic inscription.

[122] Astin (1967): 76, footnote 4; Ferrary (1988): 579, footnote 25; for sources on Scipio Aemilianus generally, Astin (1967): 3–11.

Because he had traveled around Sicily at least twice, once when he was quaestor and again when he was collecting evidence against Verres, he had opportunity to see the repatriated statues on the first visit and read the inscriptions; on the second visit, he must have felt deep anger to see the empty inscribed pedestals of those statues, now stolen by Verres. In one passage, he attributes such feelings to the people of Segesta, left with an empty pedestal bearing Scipio's name in large letters. When Verres realized the pedestal was arousing fierce resentment, he took that too; Cicero presents as evidence the contract for its removal (2.4.79). In the course of these descriptions, he gives five reasons why (we Romans) should care about Verres' theft of Scipio's restitutions and dedications: the statues marked Roman victory over Carthage; as such they were the property of Rome, even though they bore the name of Scipio; they were a record of Scipio's benefaction, a memorial of his character, which should not suffer such insult; they were evidence of local alliance with Rome and Greek participation in the victory over Carthage and were their share of the spoils; and they provided religious peace of mind to the people.[123]

Why did Scipio Aemilianus bother to do this? Speculation has included the idea that he was rewarding Sicilian cooperation in the war; that he wished to establish a client–patron relationship with Sicilians; that this was a "gesture" that illustrated the dramatic reversal of fortune in war, one that also served as self-advertisement.[124] The suggestion that Scipio had in mind Alexander (who is said to have returned the Tyrannicides to Athens) does not stand up under scrutiny, but a more general parallel between western Greek confrontation with Carthage, and mainland and eastern Greek confrontation with Persia,

[123] Cicero, *Verr.* 2.1.11; 2.2.3; 2.2.85–87; 2.4.73; 2.4.74, 78, 79–82; 2.4.84; 2.4.93; 2.4.97; 2.5.124, 125; 2.5.185, 186.
[124] So Astin (1967): 77.

might possibly have occurred to Scipio.[125] Valerius Maximus remembers Scipio Aemilianus as an exemplar of magnanimity and even adds to the repatriation of the statues an anecdote about a teenage nephew of King Masinissa, who fought against the Romans without his uncle's knowledge, was caught as a prisoner of war, but was returned nicely dressed and on horseback by Scipio to the uncle; thus, "he thought that the greatest rewards of victory lay in returning temple ornaments to the gods and their kith and kin to men."[126] Hence the range of interpretive opinion extends from attributing motives of self-interest to simple noble virtue. Posterity remembered the magnanimity no doubt because of Cicero's emphasis but in fact, there is no true equivalent for this restitution in all of antiquity. The repatriation of plundered art to Italy after Waterloo under the direction of the Duke of Wellington provides the sole (inexact and modern) parallel.

Cicero's positive treatment of Roman generals involved in Sicily extends also to Marcellus, the conqueror of Syracuse, whose actions Cicero repeatedly ameliorates, as we have seen. By the 70s BCE, however, it does seem clear that Marcellus was indeed remembered with respect if not affection in Sicily, where he had been given quasi-divine honors, with even a festival originally named for him (perhaps later

---

[125] Suggested by Ferrary, who does note the difficulties with an Alexandrian connection in view of the conflicting attributions of repatriation of the Tyrannicides and lack of evidence generally (1988: 582–585). Furthermore, P. Green already has shown that there is little evidence for Roman ideas of *imitatio* of Alexander before the mid-first century BCE ("Caesar and Alexander, Aemulatio, Imitatio, Comparatio" *AJAH* [1978]: 1–26, repr. in *Classical Bearings* [Berkeley and London, 1989]: 193–209). As Ferrary also observes, any intended parallelism of west–east Greeks vs. Carthage and Persia lost force in the coming months with the Roman destruction of Corinth: if Greeks thought Romans were like Alexander, they would think first of Alexander's destruction of Thebes, not returned statues.

[126] 5.1.7, trans. Shackleton Bailey [Loeb]. Valerius Maximus' anecdote probably inspired the representation of Scipio Aemilianus among the Roman heroes in medallions surrounding a frieze representing magnanimity in a fresco painted about 1337 in the Palazzo Pubblico in Siena.

for a descendant of the same name). Even L. Mummius gets praise for not taking consecrated images from Thespiae in Greece (2.4.4) and is described as decorating many Roman temples with Greek images – but fewer even than Verres took (2.3.9) and, unlike Verres, not having any in his house (2.1.55). Cicero's strategy obviously is to make Verres look all the worse because his looting was carried out as a magistrate in peace, not as a general in war. One effect of Cicero's complimentary treatment of Roman generals was to raise the bar in expectations of contemporary and future generals. Among his contemporaries, it was (ironically) Julius Caesar who with hindsight appears to have met the challenge.

Julius Caesar astutely makes use of the theme of respecting temples and their treasuries in his own writing, certainly before it was used by Livy about past history. In his account of the Civil War, Caesar twice gives himself credit for blocking an intended looting of the treasury of the venerable Temple of Artemis at Ephesos (*B Civ.* 3.33, 3.105). He probably wrote the commentary soon after the event in 47 BCE, while traveling with Cleopatra up the Nile.[127] But Caesar may be said to have expanded the role of the beneficent general, made possible in part because of his extensive *manubiae* from Gaul. He built or intended to build in Rome considerably more than just a manubial temple or two. His many farsighted plans were likely inspired by the elegant example of Alexandria: new marble buildings, including the basilica in the Forum; his new extension of the Forum with its Temple of Venus Genetrix; and some practical matters of infrastructure, such as the harbor at Ostia and drainage in the city. In Greece, he acted as a "restorer" by refounding Corinth, and he donated 50 talents to Athens, used eventually for the Agora of Caesar and Augustus, in its plan also inspired by Alexandria. These are just the most notable of a long list of actual or intended benefactions: euergetism was not new in the Greek east, but it was extensively practiced by Caesar. Again, in keeping with

---

[127] So suggests C. Meier, *Caesar, A Biography* (New York, 1982): 412.

the humane Scipionic model, Caesar earned above all a well-deserved reputation for clemency and magnanimity toward defeated opponents, including Cicero, who had been politically active against him.

After he defeated Pompey at Pharsalus in 48 BCE, Caesar's arrangements with cities in Asia Minor, where some had sided with Pompey, included the restoration of *asylia* (inviolate status) to many temples that had lost it earlier under Sulla.[128] In this, Caesar was participating in a longstanding tradition, dating back to the early Hellenistic era, of awarding honorific "sacred and inviolate" status to temples, that began optimistically as a hope of real protection from plundering and even for refugees. This civic honorary custom, initially awarded by one community to another, was then used rhetorically and diplomatically to include cities and territories.[129] An example of a Roman grant of *asylia* that continued and enlarged existing status is the one made by Julius Caesar to Sardis for the Temple of Artemis and other temples, just eleven days before he was assassinated in 44 BCE. In the marble inscription, he is called Dictator for Life (*dikator dia biou*).[130]

Augustus too makes use of the image of the "humane general," following the pattern set by Julius Caesar. His reign began after his defeat of Marc Antony and Cleopatra in Greek waters and extensive

[128] Cities whose temples were given restored or extended *asylia* by Julius Caesar include Ephesos, Miletos, Magnesia, Pergamon, Sardis, Stratoniceia, Aphrodisias, and possibly Apamea (Rigsby [1996]: s.v. Julius Caesar). In 48 BCE, the Ephesians found it expedient to set up a statue of Julius Caesar in the precinct of the Dea Roma, calling him a "manifest god" (*theos epiphanes*): *Syll.*³ 760, discussed in Weinstock (1971): 183, 296, 403.

[129] The inspiration for this designation may have been the attempted sack of Delphi by the Gauls in 279 BCE, even though the earliest historical precedent was a grant of immunity to the Plataeans for their contributions in the Persian War (so Rigsby [1996]: 25–27). The titles continue under Roman rule but were reviewed by the Roman Senate in CE 22, and the actual right of refuge seems to have been abolished, even though the honorary title does continue (Rigsby, 25–29). Appeals to the emperor, and even the emperor's statue, now could be attempted in desperate cases. This gradually ended one of the very ancient ideas associated with Greek temples as inviolable sanctuaries cut off from the ordinary world and shifted the locus of authority onto a (deified) emperor. On possible *asylia* in Rome, Rigsby, 574–579.

[130] Rigsby, no. 214.

maneuvering within Greece. His immediate policy in Greece after Actium seems, in fact, far from humane. He made arrangements that were more lenient toward those who had been loyal to him and punished loyalty to Marc Antony. To build Nikopolis at Actium, whole populations were uprooted and resettled, along with the cult images from their temples and many nonsacred statues. Aetolians were shifted to Nikopolis or Patras, but some fled to Amphissa, near Delphi.[131] For his own use in Rome, he did not hesitate to pluck items such as the ivory cult image from Tegea. Nevertheless, he was quite concerned with his image, and in the *Res gestae*, summing up his activities over forty-four years, he makes the following claims to posterity about sacred property:

> *After my victory, I replaced in the temples of all the cities of the province*
> *of Asia the ornaments which my late adversary, after despoiling the*
> *temples, had taken into his private possession. Some eighty silver statues*
> *of me, on foot, on horse and in chariots, had been set up in Rome; I*
> *myself removed them, and with the money that they realized I set*
> *golden offerings in the temple of Apollo, in my own name and in the*
> *names of those who had honored me with the statues.*
>
> (*RG 24*)[132]

Here he attributes spoliation to Marc Antony (whom he outlived by forty-four years) and credit for restitution to himself. This assertion

---

[131] For Augustan cult displacement in Aetolia, see Arafat (1996): 134–138; S. Alcock, *Archaeologies of the Greek Past. Landscape, Monuments, and Memories* (Cambridge, 2002): 46–48; for further bibliography and discussion of the founding of Nikopolis, see J. Isager, ed. *Foundation and Destruction: Nikopolis and Northwestern Greece* (Aarhus, 2001); useful comments and rev. by W. M. Murray, "Foundation and Destruction: Nikopolis and Northwestern Greece" *JRA* 16 (2003): 475–478.

[132] Translation in P. A. Brunt and J. M. Moore, *Res Gestae Divi Augusti* (Oxford, 1967): 31; this inscribed account records for posterity how he wanted to be viewed; after his death, one copy in bronze was set up by his mausoleum in Rome and many copies were distributed around the Mediterranean. Three of them preserved on stone in central Asia Minor provide the extant text. For a discussion, with earlier bibliography, see B. Bosworth, "Augustus, the Res Gestae and Hellenistic Theories of Apotheosis," *JRS* 89 (1999): 1–18.

seems to be supported by other authors: Pliny mentions a statue of Apollo by Myron, taken by Antony from Ephesos but returned by Augustus after he was warned in a dream that he ought to restore it. Strabo also supports the claim by stating that Augustus returned to the sanctuary of Hera on Samos two of three colossal statues from one base, representing Athena and Herakles and attributed to the sculptor Myron, that had been taken by Marc Antony. The third, of Zeus, was dedicated by Augustus in a small temple on the Capitoline he built for it.[133]

Additional pertinent statements in the *Res gestae* include several generous distributions of money from his *manubiae* (*RG* 15); the construction of ten temples in Rome (*RG* 19); the restoration of eighty-two temples in the city (*RG* 20.4); construction of the Temple of Mars Ultor and his Forum from *manubiae* (*RG* 21.1); gifts to temples from *manubiae*, costing him 100 million sesterces (*RG* 21.2); and recovery of Roman spoils and standards from the Parthians (*RG* 29.2). Other than the passage quoted previously, he says little about generosity to the provinces (and in fact, Cleopatra's treasury in Egypt probably financed many of the other entries), no doubt because the account was aimed primarily at a Roman audience. An inscription from Athens, however, does refer to restoration of temples in Athens and Attica, possibly to be dated to the reign of Augustus.[134] Furthermore, many new public buildings and temples were built all over Greece and Asia Minor during his reign, some of them financed locally. On balance, he contributed more than he plundered, although that cannot be said of Egypt. Surely his most important restitution to the east, but at the price of autocracy, was that

---

[133] Pliny, *HN* 34.58; Strabo, 14.1.14 [637]. Evidently, the return of two of them was deemed compensatory for the third that was kept in Rome. Strabo also states Augustus returned a statue of Ajax that Antony had taken from Rhoeteum in Egypt (13.1.30 [595]).

[134] *IG* II² 1035, *SEG* 26.121, 31.107, 48.116; recent dating ranges from the post-Sullan period to the Flavian period; the Augustan period seems the more likely. The bibliography on Augustan Athens is extensive. See P. Baldasssarri, *Sebastoi Soteri: Ediliza Monumentale ad Atene durante il Saeculum Augustum* (Rome, 1998).

of peace after so many decades of war, in which plundered Greece was the primary battlefield.

The years of continuous plundering of Greek dedications, images, and treasuries during wartime were now over, at least for a while, until the barbarians arrived, and Roman gifts, dedications, and patronage in Sicily, Greece, and Asia Minor accelerated. This peaceful, usually beneficent interlude was punctuated by the actions of two individuals, Caligula and Nero, who decided simply to take whatever they wanted. Their acquisitions were not in wartime but rather by *force majeure* with governmental authority; hence, they belong to the species "collector" analogous to Verres and are discussed in Chapter 4. Of all Roman rulers, Hadrian was the most generous to Greece, and his contributions may be met in nearly every major city.

Roman military plunder from Britain, the Danube regions, Germany, Judea, and the Near East flowed into the city in sporadic intervals and helped finance its embellishment. But "art" in the form of statues, temples, sculptured reliefs, paintings, decorated public and private buildings, precious smaller items, luxurious consumables, furniture, and illustrated books was now being made energetically for Roman patrons to suit their tastes and purposes. Public art, including centuries' worth of plundered antique Greek art, had become such a prominent feature and integral part of Rome that when Constantine decided to build a "new Rome" at Byzantium, he took with him not only some of the choice trophy art already in Rome but also sent agents to Delphi and elsewhere in Greece to take whatever worthy items were still there off to the new capital, a City of Victory like Augustus's but named after himself.

2 THE ROMAN CONTEXT OF CICERO'S PROSECUTION OF VERRES

◎▣◎

Sicily was the first of all foreign
nations to become the friend and loyal
ally of the Roman people. She was the
first of all to be called a province, the
first ornament of our imperial rule. She
was the first to teach our predecessors
how splendid it is to rule a foreign
people.

(Verr. 2.2.2)

CICERO'S SICILY

For Romans listening to Cicero, Sicily was not just a large island next to Italy but also "a foreign nation" that had become Rome's first province as part of the outcome of the wars with Carthage. Sicily's ancient Greek culture still flourished in Cicero's day. Wealthy and sophisticated, the island was considered an extension of Greece, prominent in Greek literature and history with a major role in stirring military events, and the birthplace of such salient Greek cultural features as gourmet cuisine and the art of persuasive rhetoric.

Only about a mile and a half separates Sicily from the toe of Italy at its closest approach (see Map 2). Yet Sicily has always had a somewhat separate character from southern Italy, despite many shared episodes in history. Partly this is due to geology: although the Appenine Mountains continue across Sicily from the Italian peninsula, the Messinian Strait that divides the island from the mainland fills a deep offset, and Sicily itself is surrounded by meeting points of the tectonic plates converging from north Africa and Eurasia. In antiquity, sailors often

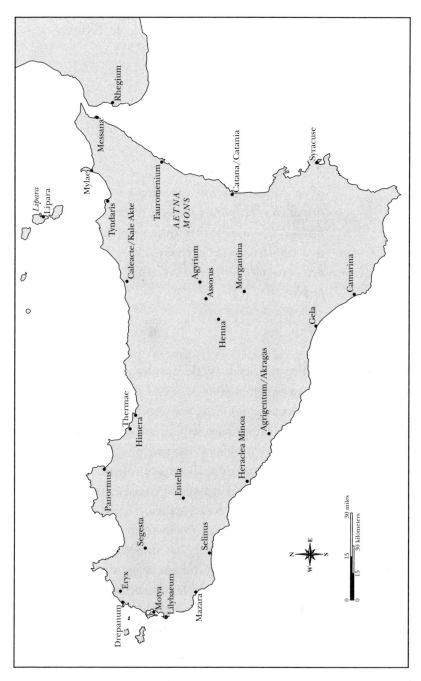

MAP 2. Sicily, first century BCE.

encountered fierce and erratic weather within the Strait – strong currents and whirlpools that gave rise to the legends about Charybdis – and they saw strange deep-sea creatures that were found nowhere else in the Mediterranean and that might have inspired the stories about Scylla. Mt. Etna dominates the northeastern corner of Sicily and, as one of the world's most active volcanoes, it was always a potential threat for humans as well as an awesome and great wonder. The fiery Aeolian (Lipari) Islands added to the "eschatological" geography of Sicily and its ancient reputation as an interface between this world and the underworld. Greek legend placed giants under the volcano and on its slopes, the Cyclopes, the one-eyed giants who proved so inhospitable to shipwrecked Odysseus.

Roman legend built onto the Homeric tradition but had the Trojan prince Aeneas visit the opposite, western side of the island, where for a while the fugitive Trojans settled and where Aeneas was said to have founded the famous sanctuary of Venus on Mt. Eryx. Even in Cicero's life-time, some Elymian cities in the west of Sicily had tax-free status because of their claim to share Trojan ancestry with the Romans. The constant north African (Punic) influence over the west and southwest of Sicily also distinguishes the island from southern Italy.[1] In addition to these reputedly Trojan descendants and the Carthaginian traders and settlers of Phoenician origin, Sicily's cultural heritage included early peoples of Italic origins (Sicels and Sicans) and Greeks from mainland Greece, Greek islands, and Greek cities in Asia Minor. Although all

---

[1] For the geomorphology of Sicily and its relationship to the Italian peninsula, see G. B. Vai and I. P. Martini, eds., *Anatomy of an Orogen: The Apennines and Adjacent Mediterranean Basins* (Dordrecht, Boston, and London, 2001), chapters 8, 9, 26. The geography of Sicily is discussed in E. Manni, *Geografia fisica e politica della Sicilia antica* (Rome, 1981); J. Bethemont and J. Pelletier, *Italy. A Geographical Introduction* (London and New York, 1983): 184–195; R. J. A. Wilson, *Sicily under the Roman Empire* (Warminster, 1990): 1–10; perceptions of "eschatological" geography in P. Horden and N. Purcell, *The Corrupting Sea. A Study of Mediterranean History* (London, 2000): 444–445; eruptions of Mt. Etna as a possible inspiration for Hesiod, Mott T. Greene, *Natural Knowledge in Preclassical Antiquity* (Baltimore and London, 1992): 46–88.

these people still retained distinctive qualities, Greek culture became dominant on the island.

Sicily was still thoroughly Greek early in the first century BCE. The major cities of Syracuse, Messina, and Agrigento were filled with sanctuaries and numerous temples dedicated to the whole array of Greek gods; public agoras with stoas, bouleuteria, altars, and markets; theaters, gymnasia, and libraries; and private houses ranging from the simple to luxurious palaces. Rich farmland was divided into small holdings but some larger private estates (*latifundia*), managed for mostly absent owners, were a clear signal of growing Roman ownership. The ports of Syracuse, Messina, Agrigento, and Lilybaeum (modern Marsala) bustled with trade from all over the Mediterranean. The island was still deeply green, well forested with ample rivers, and still seemed to visitors to merit the sobriquet, "Persephone's Island": so fertile and verdant that Zeus gave it to her as a wedding present. It was a major source of wheat to feed Rome. Deforestation had begun, but the serious environmental depredations Sicily would suffer lay many centuries ahead.[2]

Cicero (Fig. 8) had been elected quaestor and was assigned the post in Lilybaeum two years before Verres was governor.[3] When he arrived in Sicily in 75 BCE, it was culturally still Greek even though the western and central portions had become Rome's first province some 150 years

[2] For brief accounts of Sicily in the first century BCE, see Wilson, *Sicily under the Roman Empire*, 17–32, and *idem*, "Ciceronian Sicily: An Archaeological Perspective," in Christopher Smith and John Serrati, eds., *Sicily from Aeneas to Augustus* (Edinburgh, 2000): 134–160. The best general account of the history of ancient Sicily is still M. I. Finley, *A History of Sicily. Vol. I. Ancient Sicily to the Arab Conquest* (New York, 1968).

[3] There are many modern biographies of Cicero with a variety of approaches and understandings of his life; the most balanced account is Rawson's. All include discussions of the trial of Verres: M. Gelzer, *Cicero, ein biographischer Versuch* (Wiesbaden, 1969): 36–50; D. R. Shackleton Bailey, *Cicero* (London, 1971): 16–17; D. Stockton, *Cicero, A Political Biography* (Oxford, 1971): 41–49; E. Rawson, *Cicero, A Portrait* (London, 1975): 37–43; T. N. Mitchell, *Cicero, The Ascending Years* (New Haven and London, 1979): 107–149, and *idem*, *Cicero, The Senior Statesman* (New Haven and London, 1991); C. Habicht, *Cicero the Politician* (Baltimore and London, 1990): 25–27; M. Fuhrmann, *Cicero and the Roman Republic* (trans. W. E. Yuill, Oxford and Cambridge, 1992): 39–46.

FIGURE 8.

Marble bust of Marcus Tullius Cicero (104–43 BCE), first century BCE. Bought by the Duke of Wellington (1769–1852) in 1816. Apsley House (Wellington Museum), London. Photo credit: V&A Images / Victoria and Albert Museum, London.

earlier, as part of the settlement of the First Punic War (241 BCE), and the whole of the island was under Rome after Marcellus' siege of Syracuse in 211 BCE. Throughout the *Verrines*, Cicero recalls touring the island to see the major cities, and the temples, sanctuaries, monuments, and notable statuary set up in the course of the previous seven centuries as part of a great traditional religion, which was still very active. Later in his life, he recounted his discovery of Archimedes' tomb in Syracuse, which was quite overgrown with brambles and forgotten.[4]

Cicero was keenly aware of Sicily's past (he read Herodotus, Thucydides, Timaios, and Polybios, among others) and makes constant tactical

---

[4] For the significance, see M. Jaeger, "Cicero and Archimedes' Tomb," *JRS* 92(2002): 49–61.

and rhetorical use of his detailed knowledge of Sicily's earlier history in his speeches against Verres. While Cicero's narrative emphasizes Sicily's more recent past interactions with Rome, the "Greekness" of Sicily and the events of its specifically Greek past are presupposed as an integral part of Cicero's arguments about how Romans ought to rule Greek Sicily, a foreign nation and a loyal friend. For the events that occurred during Verres' term in the western cities of the island with non-Greek (Carthaginian or Elymian) ancestry, Cicero adds a further appeal for sympathy with references to their connections with Trojan legend. He implies that although they live now on a Greek island in a Greek cultural setting, they actually share ancestry with (us) Romans.

SICILY'S GREEK PAST

Starting in the mid-eighth century BCE, Greeks originally from Asia Minor, mainland Greece, and the Aegean islands began to settle widely throughout Sicily, except its far western edges, where the Carthaginians held on to their established trading bases. Sicans, Sikels, and Elymians, who preceded the Greeks in Sicily, were pushed toward the interior and western areas and, over the centuries, eventually blended into the prevailing Greek-style culture. The destinations of Greeks moving to the west included southern Italy and the Bay of Naples, northern Italy around the Po Valley on the Adriatic, the southern shore of France, and the northeastern shore of Spain. The western Greek cities competed and traded locally with Gauls, Etruscans, Carthaginians, and each other, and their longer trade routes included Britain, Egypt, and the Levant. They maintained close ties with eastern and mainland Greeks through trade, religious observances, and annual participation in the Panhellenic Festivals, especially at Olympia and Delphi.[5] From Selinous in

---

[5] Sentimental ties were also deeply felt in some cases: when Croton destroyed Sybaris in 510 BCE, the whole male population of Miletos, including boys, went into deep mourning and shaved their heads, according to Herodotus (6.21).

western Sicily, Athens was only about a nine-day sail for a merchant ship: these relatively short sailing distances meant communications could be frequent.

Sicilian wealth soon became proverbial and already in the sixth century BCE, many large stone temples were built in Syracuse, Agrigento, Gela, and Selinous. By the early fifth century BCE, the Greek cities in Sicily were regarded as among the most wealthy and powerful of all Greek cities anywhere, so much so that in anticipation of the war with Persia just before 480 BCE, Athenians and Spartans appealed for help to Gelon (master of eastern Sicily, including Syracuse and Gela), according to Herodotus' account (7.157–163). Herodotus gives us a neat parallel between mainland Greeks led by Athens and Sparta against Persia, and Sicilian Greeks led by Gelon against Carthaginians, who invaded Sicily on its north side at Himera. Crucial naval battles at Salamis and Himera on each front were said (by Sicilians) to have been waged and won on the same day. Thus, barbarians were defeated by Greeks, on land and sea, east and west.

Of the many temples built in the cities of Sicily after this victory, the most famous was the Temple of Athena at Syracuse, whose contents and gold and ivory doors were looted by Verres but described in detail by Cicero, who saw them before Verres took the dedications and tore off the gold bosses and ivory panels. The temples were physical reminders of Sicily's power and wealth in the sixth and fifth centuries BCE, just as the historic battles cited by Cicero recalled the Sicilians' ability to defend themselves against Carthaginian and Athenian aggression. This historical resiliency provides a foil for Cicero in his account of Verres' predatory behavior as a Roman governor.

Like the Greek cities in mainland Greece and Asia Minor, those in Sicily suffered loss of autonomy and economic decline in the fourth century BCE, a period punctuated by the rule of autocratic individuals and, for Sicilian Greeks, confrontations with Carthage. The most successful ruler in Sicily in this period was Dionysios I of Syracuse, who drove out most of the Carthaginians after they had pillaged Greek cities on the island at the end of the fifth century and even besieged and took over the Carthaginian city of Motya, their major base on the west side of the island. His personal reputation as a ruler fluctuated in antiquity, according to widely varying opinions of ancient authors.[6] Cicero calls Dionysios *crudelissimus tyrannos* and describes how Verres reused Dionysios' prison quarries to incarcerate innocent Roman citizens (*Verr.* 2.5.143).

In several respects, the regime of Dionysios I in Sicily anticipated those of later Hellenistic rulers not just for military effectiveness and personal ambition but also for his patronage of cultural institutions. He even wrote plays himself and entered them into competitions at Athens in the City Dionysia and Lenaia festivals. He was an admirer of Plato and invited him to Syracuse. Plato visited three times and cherished the belief for some years that he had found his ideal philosopher-king in Dionysios' son. Only proper training and education was needed, so Plato thought, but the son's character proved to be less resolute than Plato had hoped. After the death of Dionysios I, his son ruled briefly but eventually retired to Corinth, leaving Syracuse in disarray.[7]

In the aftermath of the chaos left by Dionysios' family, Greeks in Sicily invited Timoleon of Corinth to bring order and, in the ensuing events, the island was sufficiently calm to allow some economic recovery. After Timoleon's death, Agathocles rose to power as a mercenary, with ambitions to unite Sicily and southern Italy. He was the first to carry the ongoing struggle against Carthage to north Africa and Carthage itself, a tactic that would be used more successfully by Rome in the coming centuries. For a while, he ruled most of Sicily,

---

[6] For Dionysios I, see H. Berve, *Die Tyrannis bei den Griechen*, II (Munich, 1967): 637–656 (ancient sources); Sanders (1987); Caven (1990).

[7] L. J. Sanders, "Dionysius I of Syracuse and the Origins of the Ruler Cult in the Greek World," *Historia*, 40 (1991): 275–287; on Plato's visits to Sicily, Plato *Ep.* 7 (generally regarded as authentic since antiquity).

until he was assassinated in 289 BCE. He left behind a group of mercenaries from Campania, the Mamertines, who took over Messina and later precipitated the First Punic War by inviting both Carthage and Rome to their own defense against their Greek neighbors. The Molossian king Pyrrhus briefly intervened in Sicilian affairs in 278 BCE but soon retreated to Tarentum and, after inconclusive battles with Rome, back to Epirus.

Sicilians enjoyed a long period of stability and prosperity under the benevolent rule of Hieron II of Syracuse (269–215 BCE), who came to power through the military hierarchy and declared himself king but wisely negotiated a treaty of "peace and friendship" with Rome during the First Punic War (263 BCE).[8] Rome recognized his loyalty by renewing the treaty when it was due to expire in 248 BCE. Hieron II became a prominent Hellenistic prince, with far-flung connections in Carthage and Rhodes and with the Ptolemies in Egypt.

At home in Syracuse, he was a great sponsor of architectural projects, rebuilding Syracuse and nearby cities with stoas, gymnasia, altars, and theaters so as to make Syracuse a particular rival of Alexandria. Like Dionysios I in the previous century, Hieron II was a patron of intellectuals, such as Archimedes and the historian Timaios of Tauromenion and perhaps the poet Theokritos. Hieron II was also a generous benefactor to Rhodes, especially after an earthquake of 224 BCE (Polybius 5.80). Although immensely wealthy and powerful, he evidently was not corrupted by his circumstances and lived into his nineties. In the accounts of ancient historians, Hieron II's generosity at home and philanthropy abroad contrasted sharply with the ruthlessness and extreme

---

[8] Parts of Sicily had been taken by Rome, such as Catania; on that occasion, the consul Manius Valerius Messala is said to have taken Catania's sundial to Rome, where it was set up by the Rostra in the Forum but incorrectly oriented in the new location, and nonetheless was followed for ninety-nine years until a new one was made (M. Varro, cited by Pliny, *HN* 7.214). D. Roussel provides a succinct discussion of this period and a convenient collection of ancient epigraphical and literary sources in appendix 1 (*Les Siciliens entre les Romains et les Carthaginois a l'epoque de la premiere guerre punique* [Centre de recherches d'histoire ancienne, 3, Paris, 1970]: 141–147).

aggression so characteristic of previous Sicilian leaders. He is singled out for very high praise by Polybius.[9]

Hieron's personal wealth, based on the prosperity of Sicily, is exemplified by a famous luxury ship he had built. This ship was remembered and recalled by Athenaeus (fl. ca. 200 CE), who quotes an earlier author's description of the enormous *Syracusia* ("Lady of Syracuse"), commissioned by Hieron II and built under the supervision of Archimedes (206d–209e). The ship had dining rooms, a gymnasium, a library, promenades with garden beds fed by special watering systems, statuary, floor mosaics showing the entire story of the *Iliad*, and a shrine to Aphrodite with an agate floor and ivory doors. There were fish tanks, a huge freshwater tank, elaborate baths, stalls for horses, and various defensive schemes designed by Archimedes. For the woodwork and masts, rare timbers had to be sought on the slopes of Mt. Etna and in the Bruttii. According to the passage in Athenaeus, the ship was so large that it proved unwieldy in harbors, so Hieron II sent this ship (renamed the *Alexandris*, "Lady of Alexandria"), loaded with wheat, salted fish, and wool, as a gift to the Ptolemies in Egypt, at a time when they were suffering a shortage of grain.[10] The description of the ship gives us an idea of the level of luxury commanded by a Hellenistic prince and

---

[9] Polybios (7.8) says, in part: "Hieron is in the first place a more interesting subject [than his ill-reputed grandson] because he established himself as the ruler of Syracuse and her allies entirely through his own abilities, for he owed neither wealth, nor reputation nor anything else to Fortune. Most remarkable of all, he achieved his position by his own efforts, without killing, banishing or injuring a single citizen, and not only acquired but also maintained his power in the same fashion. . . . He not only conferred great benefits on the Greeks, but took trouble to win their good opinion, and at the end he left behind him a great personal reputation and a legacy of universal goodwill towards the Syracusans" (translation by Ian Scott-Kilvert). On Hieron II, H. Berve, *Koenig Hieron II* (Munich, 1956); for the nature of the "treaty" between Hieron II and Rome, see Gruen, *HWCR*: 67–68, with opposing views cited in footnote 69 on p. 67.

[10] Athenaeus describes other luxury ships in the passages preceding the one cited previously, and we may recall the ship outfitted by Cleopatra VII in Egypt for her trip to Tarsus, where she would seduce Marc Antony (Plutarch, *Vit. MA*, 26–27). Although such descriptions may seem fanciful, the remains of a similar luxury ship built for Caligula were found in Lake Nemi.

the wealth Hieron II derived from taxes and tithes in eastern Sicily: potential wealth later to be exploited by Verres.

Perhaps Hieron II's most enduring legacy was his system of tithes, regarded as fair and efficient and adopted as the "*lex Hieronica*" by the Romans throughout Sicily after the fall of Syracuse as a crucial source of their grain supply.[11] (Our primary knowledge of this system is from the *Verrines*.) The tithes were collected in the form of grain, which was then sold; additional obligations under Roman rule included the providing of ships, with their equipment, for defense of Sicily, and some conscription for manning the naval vessels. After his death in 215 BCE, Hieron II was succeeded by his grandson Hieronymous, still young and under the pressure of advisors. After a series of diplomatic and military maneuvers described by Polybius, Hieronymous sided with Carthage and then was assassinated within thirteen months of his accession; once again, Syracuse fell into chaos, riven by internal dissent. Because of Sicily's geographical position between north Africa and southern Italy, Sicily was the natural bridge between Rome and Carthage and, therefore, became a major battleground between those two competing powers.

SICILY AS A ROMAN PROVINCE

The Romans sent their best general, M. Claudius Marcellus, to take charge in Syracuse in 213 BCE. Marcellus and his siege of Syracuse – a turning point in the war with Hannibal – is a favored Roman topic discussed by many ancient authors, as noted previously in Chapter 1.

---

[11] Further comments on the Hieron's "treaty" with Rome and the nature of the tithe in J. Serrati, "Garrisons and Grain: Sicily between the Punic Wars," in C. Smith and J. Serrati, eds., *Sicily from Aeneas to Augustus* (Edinburgh, 2000): 115–133. For details of the tithe, R. T. Pritchard, "Cicero and the *Lex Hieronica*," *Historia* 19 (1970): 352–368; "Gaius Verres and the Sicilian Farmers," *Historia* 20 (1971): 229–238; "Some Aspects of First-Century Sicilian Agriculture," *Historia* 21 (1972): 646–660. The basic principle was a tithe of one tenth of the yield from each individual farmer, of grain, wine, oil, and fruit, to be collected and sold at a fixed price. For tax collection, E. Badian, *Publicans and Sinners* (Ithaca and London, 1983).

Cicero holds up Marcellus rhetorically as a shining model of proper behavior for a conquering general, the antithesis of Verres' behavior as governor. (As we have seen, other ancient authors give a more complex picture of Marcellus' actions in Sicily.) Polybius (8.3–7), Livy (24.30–34, 25. 23–31), and Plutarch (*Vit. Mar.*) provide vivid descriptions of the prolonged siege and especially Archimedes' ingenious devices that delayed the Roman victory, won eventually through blockade, plague, and treachery. For Plutarch, the capture of Syracuse marks the beginning of Greek education among the Romans.[12]

Sicily became a "province" of Rome only gradually, in stages over nearly six decades. With the fall of Syracuse, all Sicilian cities were now under Roman rule, although some had won a measure of self-administration or other special privileges. The whole of Sicily was a province of Rome, administered by a praetor (primary governor) and two quaestors (assistant governors), one posted at Lilybaeum (the office there had existed since 227), the other at Syracuse, which became the capital of the province. With the *lex Hieronica* now in effect throughout the island, Sicily would remain an important source of grain for Rome, until gradually superseded by Egypt after Augustus' defeat of Cleopatra and the absorption of Egypt into the Roman Empire.

Gaius Verres was posted to Sicily in 73 BCE as a peregrine propraetor (governor of a province) after a year as urban praetor in Rome. Second in rank only to the two consuls, the office of praetor in the Roman magistracy had developed gradually as Rome found it necessary to expand authoritative offices that included military powers, especially overseas; by the time of Verres, there were eight praetorships.[13] The

[12] J. Briscoe, *CAH²* 8, 53–55, 61–2, with references.
[13] For all aspects of the praetorship, see T. C. Brennan, *The Praetorship in the Roman Republic* (Oxford, 2000) (henceforth "Praetors"). Verres had served as (urban) praetor in Rome in 74, so technically he was propraetor in Sicily; see Brennan's discussion of Verres' time in office: 446–448, 482–492.

office could be lucrative for the holder and some personal profit was considered normal; however, the establishment of a permanent court to try cases of extortion from about the mid second century BCE onward shows that abuses and attempts to redress them were ongoing.[14]

Holders of the praetorship were elected annually, had judicial and military authority, and could be assigned by sortition (a type of formal lottery) either to the city (*praetor urbanus*) or to a province (*praetor peregrinus*). They could be formally requested by the Senate to serve a second or, in the case of Verres, even a third term in a particular assignment. Despite some knowledge about Verres' unscrupulous activities and formal complaints from Sicilians, Verres was allowed to keep his post in Sicily for three years, apparently because Rome was preoccupied with the slave insurrection led by Spartacus that started in 73 BCE. Verres' designated successor after his first year in office, Q. Arrius, was sent instead to help the consul L. Gellius put down Spartacus' slave revolt. Verres was then relieved by L. Caecilius Metellus in 71 BCE.[15] The ongoing turbulence of Spartacus' slave revolt meant for Sicily that the Sicilians suffered Verres' extraordinarily extortionate rule for three long years, not just the more typical term of one year; hence, they were especially eager to prosecute him in Rome.

The fear that the slave revolt could have spread into Sicily figures in Cicero's prosecution, where he anticipates claims Hortensius (Verres' advocate) might make that Verres had helped in Sicily's defense against Spartacus and the slaves. Originally from Thrace, Spartacus was enslaved and sold to a gladiatorial school in Capua, owned by a particularly vicious master. More than seventy of the gladiators broke out and took refuge on Mt. Vesuvius, where they were soon joined by

[14] For the legitimate and illegitimate ways that praetors (and their staffs) could make money in the provinces, see I. Shatzman, *Senatorial Wealth and Roman Politics* (*Collection Latomus*, 142) (Brussels, 1975): 53–63; for the political use of extortion trials, see footnote 21 following.

[15] For Q. Arrius, Brennan, *Praetors*, 432–434, 486; L. Caecilius Metellus, 492–493.

thousands of other slaves from the whole area. Spartacus' leadership and his men were so effective against Roman troops that the slave war lasted two years and ranged throughout Italy. Toward the end of the war, Spartacus and his men were maneuvered deep into Bruttium, the region around Rhegion at the tip of the toe of Italy, and held in by a wall constructed by the Romans across the narrowest part. They hoped to escape by crossing over into Sicily and had negotiated with pirates to provide ships. This arrangement fell through and eventually Spartacus and his huge group of escaped slaves were defeated by M. Licinius Crassus, with the help of Cn. Pompeius Magnus (Pompey).[16] The two "victors" against Spartacus, Crassus and Pompey, were elected consuls in that year (70 BCE).

Sicily was considered especially vulnerable to the menace of insurrection because just one generation earlier, the Second Slave War took place there and the First Slave War one generation before that. Sicily was beginning to be transformed by *latifundia*, large estates worked mostly by gangs of slaves.[17] This intensive slave-based agriculture yielded a surplus harvest that could be sent to Rome and high profits for the owners, but the harsh conditions led to the First Slave War (135–133 BCE) when the charismatic leader Eunus, a slave from Syria, led a massive armed revolt that eventually included free common people, posing a serious threat to the stability (and productivity) of the island. The Second Slave War (104–100 BCE) arose under similar conditions, but those slaves too were

---

[16] For the Slave War led by Spartacus, see K. R. Bradley, *Slavery and Rebellion in the Roman World, 140 B.C.–70 B.C.* (Bloomington and Indianapolis, 1989): 83–101; R. Seager, *CAH* 92 (1994): 211–223; B. D. Shaw, *Spartacus and the Slave Wars. A Brief History with Documents* (Boston and New York, 2001). For an overview of Roman slavery, K. R. Bradley, *Slavery and Society at Rome* (Cambridge, 1994), with extensive bibliography; also valuable on ancient slavery: J. Vogt, *Ancient Slavery and the Ideal of Man*, trans. R. Wiedemann (Cambridge, MA, 1975).

[17] Wilson notes that there is some archaeological evidence for small and moderate-sized farms in the first century BCE, around Heraklea Minoa and the territory of Himera; for latifundia, around Monreale and Alcamo; he observes further that Verres evidently preyed more on the owners of moderate farms rather than the (generally absent) owners of the latifundia, probably because the small landholders were more vulnerable (Wilson [2000]: 157–160).

finally defeated by Roman legions led by Manius Aquillius. Writing about these events some fifty years later, Diodorus Siculus reports that Sicily was chaotic and extremely dangerous during the war because not only slaves but also free peasants murdered, stole, and destroyed anyone and anything they encountered. Evidently, longstanding class resentment as well as the fury of newly enslaved men kept the insurrection going for four years.[18]

Although hostile to the leaders of the slaves, preserved ancient accounts of these three wars make clear the extraordinary organizational skill, ingenuity, courage, and endurance necessary to fend off Roman troops for so long. Spartacus' war in particular has lived on in history as the most successful slave rebellion ever, until that of 1791 in St. Dominigue (Haiti).[19] In his speeches against Verres, Cicero does not mention Spartacus by name (significantly), but he does refer to this most recent war, the two earlier Slave Wars, and the whole issue of maintaining control over slaves as one of his charges against Verres. At the time of Verres' trial in Rome, the repercussions of the slave war led by Spartacus were still urgent, and Roman troops would be "mopping up" pockets of resisting slaves in southern Italy for the next ten years.

VERRES' TRIAL IN ROME: LOGISTICS

The problem of corrupt Roman magistrates abroad was not new. In his prosecution of Verres, Cicero could draw on references to a longstanding problem with various attempted solutions. Some seventy years before Verres' trial, a permanent court had been established in which foreigners ruled by Roman magistrates could seek compensation in cases of extortion (by the *lex Calpurnia repetundarum*, 149 BCE). Before this, only Roman citizens could take action in cases of extortion, although aliens could appeal to the Senate, which might send

---

[18] 36.3.1–10.2 = Photios, *Library*, 387–390.
[19] For a recent account, Laurent Dubois, *Avengers of the New World. The Story of the Haitian Revolution* (Cambridge, MA, 2004).

a committee to investigate. The new law originally set into place a civil procedure, with only a refund of the monies taken as recompense. The extortion court was then radically reformed in 123 or 122 BCE by a law (*lex Acilia*) sponsored by C. Sempronius Gracchus. Many of this law's provisions are preserved on fragments of bronze tablets, discovered in Urbino (*CIL* I² 583).[20] Under the reformed law, the charges were now criminal rather than civil, with penalties of double repayment and loss of civil standing for the offending magistrate; cases were to be tried in Rome with a jury of fifty, drawn from the equestrian rank rather than the Senate.

The judicial procedure was modified during the following decades, most extensively by Sulla (*lex Cornelia*), ten years before Verres' trial. The jury was to be composed of senators – and an alleged malefactor would be judged by his peers, who themselves might have held or would hold in the future the very same position. In the volatile political setting of the 70s BCE, this seemingly straightforward procedure was manipulated in at least four ways: the bringing of a charge to begin with, then the choice of prosecutor, the composition of the jury, and the bribing of the jury.[21]

What began as a procedure to redress grievances of foreigners under Roman rule could also be used as a way of targeting political opponents who had served abroad or as a way of covering up legitimate grievances while making immense profits. Between the passage of the *lex Acilia*

---

[20] The fragments were first displayed in the library of Federico da Montefeltro, the Duke of Urbino, c. 1500: history of the inscription, text, translation, and commentary in A. W. Lintott, *Judicial Reform and Land Reform in the Roman Republic* (Cambridge, 1992); the identity of the law on the bronze fragments as a law of C. Gracchus and as likely to be the *lex Acilia* is discussed 166–169. Further revisions in M. H. Crawford (ed.), *Roman Statutes* (*BICS* Supp. 64), Vol. I (London, 1996): 35–112.

[21] For a thorough discussion of the political maneuvering that manipulated the judicial system, E. Gruen, *Roman Politics and the Criminal Courts, 149–78 B.C.* (Cambridge, MA, 1968): interpersonal politics (and other factors) made the courts and their composition a "political football" (p. 284); further discussion of trials as a mode of political engagement in Gruen, *LGRR, passim.*

(ca. 122 BCE) and Verres' trial in 70 BCE, some twenty-eight cases of extortion in the provinces are specifically attested, four of them for activities in Sicily.[22] In the last decades of the Republic after the prosecution of Verres, other trials are recorded for extortion in other provinces, but none for Sicily.

In the same year of Verres' trial, cumulative abuses by senators in the courts were prompting still further reform, including a proposal to return to the older custom of juries composed of men of equestrian rank. Senators were fighting this threatened loss of their exclusive privilege for jury duty. Cicero makes much of these pressing political issues in his prosecution, claiming that the senators on Verres' jury were themselves on trial for whether they could continue as jurors. In fact, reforming legislation was already under way and, by the end of the year, after Verres' trial, the *lex Aurelia iudiciaria* provided for juries with one third chosen by lot from the senate and two thirds from non-senators.[23] The new provisions in the *lex Aurelia* were passed after Verres went into exile but before Cicero completed the publication of his speeches, since he refers to the new law near the end of the *Verrines* (2.5.178.) Still, Cicero says in the speech he delivered in the Forum, Verres used to tell his friends openly that it was not just for himself that he was making money but that in his three-year praetorship, the profits of the first

---

[22] M. C. Alexander, *Trials in the Late Roman Republic, 149 B.C. to 50 B.C.* (*Phoenix* Supp. 26) (Toronto, 1990): for Sicily, nos. 46, 69, 70, 131; not all of the twenty-eight trials are certain: there are doubts about their dates, the charges, and other details. Cicero comments that "a number of praetors of that province [Sicily] have been convicted and only two acquitted" (2.2.155).

[23] For a detailed discussion of the political aspects of the trial (which Cicero exaggerates) and of the reforms in the composition of the jury, see Mitchell, *Cicero, Ascending Years*, 108–138, with criticisms of S. Butler, *The Hand of Cicero* (London and New York, 2002): 78. For subsequent modifications to the judicial procedure in the *lex Aurelia*, Lintott, *Judicial Reform*, 27–29. The regulations on extortion abroad were tightened further by Julius Caesar under the *lex Iulia de repetundis* of 59 BCE (Gruen, *LGRR*, 239–244; sources in Crawford, *Roman Statutes*, Vol. 2: 769–772). Because the complexity of these cases made successful prosecution difficult, in 4 BCE a simple procedure for compensation was reinstated to redress illegal exactions abroad. For a general account of the extortion courts, see A. Lintott, *Imperium Romanum. Politics and Administration* (London and New York, 1993): 97–107.

year were for himself, of the second for his advocates and defenders, and of the third (the richest) for his jurors (1.40).

Roman citizens prosecuted the cases of extortion in Rome on behalf of the alien plaintiffs. The selection of the Roman prosecutor was determined by a jury in a preliminary hearing called *divinatio*, in which competing speeches were given by prospective prosecutors showing their suitability to prosecute: the legal term hints at sortition, but the jury decided between them. Cicero's speech given in mid-January for the *divinatio* in Verres' case (*In Q. Caecilium divinatio*) sets forth the reasons why he rather than Q. Caecilius Niger, who had been Verres' quaestor in Sicily, ought to be chosen to prosecute Verres. This speech is the only *divinatio* preserved and, in it, Cicero has to praise himself, belittle Caecilius, and remind the jury of Verres' alleged crimes.

He was the prosecutor the Sicilians wanted, Cicero says, largely because they knew him from his term in Lilybaeum as *quaestor*. He professes not to have wanted this case, primarily because he preferred defense cases, not prosecutions (this would be Cicero's first prosecution), and he even asserts that he suggested Caecilius to the Sicilians. But they did not want Caecilius to represent them, since they knew he was in collusion with Verres. Cicero then goes on to elaborate Caecilius' lack of experience, with parenthetical excursions into Verres' nefarious activities and some reference to the skill of Verres' defender, Q. Hortensius Hortalus. Modern commentators on the trial have noted that Cicero agreed to take the case because it offered him a chance to compete with Hortensius, then the foremost orator in Rome, and because it was a prominent case that would garner lots of attention; they also concede that the requests of the Sicilians may have been a factor.[24] It

---

[24] L. R. Taylor discusses the political benefits Cicero gained from the trial (*Party Politics in the Age of Caesar* [Berkeley and Los Angeles, 1966]: 101–118). W. Stroh argues that Q. Caecilius Niger was not as ineffective and malleable as Cicero depicts him (*Taxis und Taktik: Ciceros Gerichtsreden* [Stuttgart, 1975]: 174–87).

seems that Verres and his supporters had hoped to quash the trial by having a sham prosecutor but, that January, Cicero won the *divinatio*.

Cicero then obtained an adjournment of 110 days so that he could go to Sicily to gather evidence against Verres. As Shane Butler has demonstrated in an original and important study of Cicero's use of written documents, the evidence he collected on his trip consisted of vast numbers of documents of all types: account ledgers, letters, treaties and other legal documents, inscriptions, edicts, wills, and more.[25] Cicero had the legal authority to inspect even private accounts, including those kept by Verres in Rome. He went around Sicily counterclockwise and visited all the major cities, where he listened to complaints about Verres and gathered evidence, marked it with a seal, and packed it up to be read at the trial. In later life, Cicero said he even interviewed Sicilian farmers at the plow.

In Butler's picture of the opening day of the trial in August, Cicero makes his way to the Forum accompanied by a retinue of bearers carrying a great many large chests of these documents (written on a variety of materials but especially waxed tablets).[26] There were also many witnesses, including Sicilians, who would give oral testimony in person at the trial (Fig. 9). Cicero then followed an unusual procedure, as he

[25] Butler (2002). Butler's demonstration of the amount and many kinds of evidence makes all the more remarkable the speed of Cicero's trip, for Cicero states he took only fifty days (1.6). E. Badian also emphasizes the evidence of documents kept by the *publicani* (tax collectors) that was then used by Cicero to prosecute Verres (*Publicans and Sinners*, 73–81). M. C. Alexander notes the importance of the fifty-six witnesses used and named by Cicero and provides a chart of witnesses and documents for the trial: *The Case for the Prosecution in the Ciceronian Era* (Ann Arbor, 2002): 26–28, 255–262. For the nature and use of documents more generally, see J. P. Small, *Wax Tablets of the Mind. Cognitive Studies of Memory and Literacy in Classical Antiquity* (London and New York, 1997): 53–71.

[26] Butler (2002): 63–64. The only painted representation of the trial known to me is that of Eugene Delacroix (1798–1863), in a spandrel of the Library of the Bourbon Palace, Paris, part of a thematic cycle representing "Law," a subset of a larger cycle for the library (Fig. 9). See M. Sérullaz, *Les peintures murales de Delacroix* (Paris, 1963): 49–77 and pl. 40; and N. Bryson, *Tradition and Desire. From David to Delacroix* (Cambridge, 1984): 176–212.

FIGURE 9. Eugene Delacroix (1798–1863), *Cicero Accuses Verres*, Fresco from the spandrels of the main hall, Library, Assemblée Nationale (Palais-Bourbon), Paris. Photo credit: Erich Lessing / Art Resource, NY.

124

himself tells us: rather than giving the customary lengthy speech with flourishes, which could have lasted many days, he gave a shorter speech to lay out the documentary evidence, having it read aloud with his commentary interspersed along with the witnesses' testimony – but even that procedure took nine days. The short speech is preserved in its published version as the first *Verrine* oration (*actio prima*), delivered before the jury in the Forum at the tribunal, probably located near the Temple of Castor and Pollux (see Plan 2).

The major reason for this strategy was that Verres' associates had managed to schedule another trial for extortion while Cicero was away, thereby delaying the beginning of this case until August. The defendant's supporters hoped that because of the late date, the trial would be delayed still further through the interruptions of Pompey's celebratory games and other events on the religious calendar – perhaps even stretched until the next year, when new consuls and praetors would take office, including supporters of Verres; one of the consuls-elect was Hortensius, Verres' own advocate. They all underestimated Cicero's determination and vigor. The mountain of documentary evidence and Cicero's strategy (which required him to forego the opportunity to display his own rhetorical powers) were overwhelming.

Verres left Rome for exile in Massilia (Marseilles) in August after the *actio prima* and, although it seems likely his advocate Hortensius spoke on his behalf, the evidence is not conclusive.[27] Quintilian refers to a speech of Hortensius' on this case, but it could have been a literary exercise, composed after Cicero's publications, or even a forgery. At the time of Verres' trial, Hortensius was regarded as the foremost barrister and orator in Rome, noted for his "Asiatic" style of speaking (filled

---

[27] M. C. Alexander argues that Hortensius did, in fact, give and then published a speech: "Hortensius' Speech in Defense of Verres," *Phoenix* 30 (1976): 46–53 (with a full review of modern discussions and the evidence in Cicero, Quintilian, and Ps.-Asconius). H. Malcovati, *Oratorum Romanorum Fragmenta*⁴ (Turin, 1976): 318, n. ix, believes that the speech by Hortensius (mentioned by Quintilian, 10.1.22–23) was a forgery. On Hortensius and his career, see F. von der Mühll *RE* VIII, 2, s.v. *Hortensius* (13), col. 2470–2481 [1913].

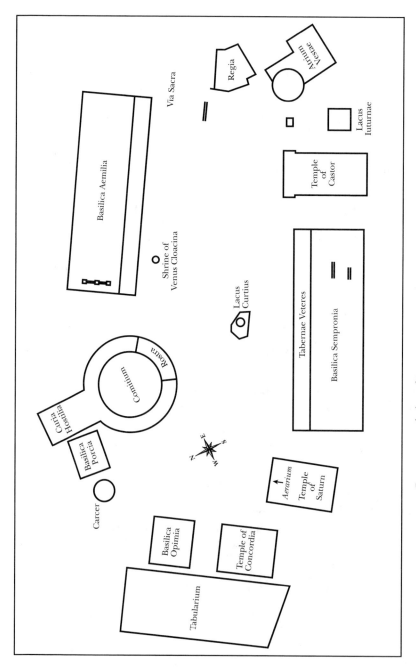

PLAN 2. Reconstructed plan of Roman Forum at the time of Verres' trial, 70 BCE.

with flowery abundance). His family was moderately well connected and, as a distinguished lawyer, he had no shortage of prominent friends who found it useful to cultivate his acquaintance. Some years after the trial of Verres, Cicero and Hortensius would work together on the same side, both forensically and politically. Later in life, Cicero wrote about Hortensius with high regard and included him as a character in a philosophical dialogue named after him.[28] Much of recent scholarship on the *Verrines* has been devoted to parsing out what the speeches tell us about the politics and political alliances of the period, and one question that is asked is why Hortensius took this case.

Cicero insinuates several times that Hortensius was to benefit financially from defending Verres. As noted previously, in the *actio prima*, actually delivered in the Forum, Cicero asserts that Verres talked openly about making money to pay advocates and judges and bribes for jurors. There was also the matter of reciprocity: in 75 BCE, Hortensius was aedile and in charge of public games. Verres loaned him many paintings and statues to decorate the city and the Forum, which helped make the games successful. While this pleased the Roman populace, its display, according to Cicero, caused visiting dignitaries from Greece and Asia Minor to weep upon seeing the sacred images of gods that had been taken from their own sanctuaries, as we have seen (2.1.59). In addition to the loan of art, Verres might have supported Hortensius in the following year, as the presiding urban praetor in a trial.[29] Furthermore, Hortensius' own interest in art may have made him sympathetic to Verres. He was so fond of a small sphinx Verres gave

---

[28] At the beginning of his essay *Brutus* (written in 46 BCE), Cicero speaks eloquently of his deep sense of loss on Hortensius' death. On *amicitia* between Cicero and Hortensius, see P. A. Brunt, *The Fall of the Roman Republic* (Oxford, 1988): 375–376.

[29] Hortensius may have felt obligated to Verres for assistance in 74 at the trial of Q. Opimius (Alexander, *Trials*, no. 157), over which Verres presided as urban praetor, when Hortensius was one of the prosecutors (Mitchell, *Cicero, The Ascending Years*, 139, with references to other comments by ancient authors about Hortensius in footnote 88). P. A. Brunt concludes Hortensius' motive was financial ("Patronage and Politics in the 'Verrines'," *Chiron* 10 (1980): 273–289, esp. 280).

him that he used to carry it around with him. This sphinx (variously described as bronze, ivory, or silver) is mentioned by Pliny, Plutarch, and Quintilian.[30]

VERRES' FAMILY

Who was this notorious Gaius Verres, Roman governor of Sicily for three years? Nearly everything we think we know about him comes from Cicero's speeches prosecuting him.[31] Even his family name ("boar") is not attested elsewhere, although there has been speculation that it might be Etruscan. His father was a senator, possibly with a distant family connection to the Metelli, and was perhaps nominated to the Senate when it was expanded under Sulla in the 80s BCE. He sent a warning to his son during his first year in Sicily that his activities there were becoming dangerous because one of his victims had arrived in Rome and was making quite a stir (2.4.41). Later, another victim arrived in Rome whose distress at Verres' hands was so acute that the Senate became involved, despite the father's pleas (2.2.95, 100). The father evidently died before Verres' trial because Cicero comments that he had inspected the account books of both father and son, the father's kept until his death (2.1.60). Verres and his wife Vettia (sister of P. Vettius Chilo, an *eques*[32]) had a daughter, who was married at the time

[30] Sphinxes were represented in Greek art as well as Egyptian art, usually as a lion's body with a female human head. Pliny, *NH* 34.48 (cites Hortensius as an example of how owners of "Corinthian" [a type of bronze work] figurines are so enamored of them that they carry them around with them); Plutarch *Cic.* 7; Quintilian 6.3.98. During Edmund Burke's prosecution of Warren Hastings (1788–93), Burke rhetorically imagines Hastings as owning such a sphinx (thus conflating Hortensius with Verres, Burke's negative model for Hastings).

[31] On Verres, see H. Habermehl, *RE* VIII A/2 [1958], s.v. *C. Verres* (1), col. 1561–1633; F. H. Cowles, *Gaius Verres; An Historical Study. Cornell Studies in Classical Philology*, 20 (Ithaca, NY: 1917). His father, C. Verres: *RE* VIII A/2 [1958], s.v. *C. Verres* (2), col. 1633–1634; no. 479 in T. P. Wiseman, *New Men in the Roman Senate, 139 B.C.–A.D. 14* (Oxford, 1971): 272.

[32] P. Vettius Chilo, Vettia's brother, is called as a witness in the trial, and one of his letters, discovered by Cicero in a corporate file in Syracuse, is read out loud; Cicero characterizes him respectfully as an honest and trustworthy man (II.3.166–168). A second brother served as Verres' quaestor.

of the trial, and a young son, who accompanied Verres in Sicily. Verres' son-in-law also was with him in Sicily.

In Rome just before Verres' trial, evidently Vettia was following her husband's situation closely enough that Verres sent slaves to inform her of urgent political news that would affect him. Shortly before the trial, Verres was warmly congratulated by friends upon the news that M. Metellus, a praetor-elect for the following year, had won the sortition for the extortion courts. His congratulators assumed that Verres would now escape conviction, and he immediately sent slaves to inform his wife about the results of the sortition (1.21).

Cicero had firsthand familiarity with Verres' house, an important part of the public "face" of politicians in Rome. Verres' house was filled with Greek art taken earlier in his career, with statues looted from the venerable sanctuary of Hera on Samos featured prominently in the atrium and peristyle garden. Cicero states that he saw the Samian statues when he went to Verres' house to seal evidence for the trial (2.1.50–51).

THE CHARGES AGAINST VERRES

The formal charge against Verres in the trial of 70 BCE was that he had extorted forty million sesterces from the Sicilians, and Cicero demands the return of one hundred million sesterces (i.e., repayment of two and a half times the extorted amount). But there are many other accusations of malfeasance and criminality advanced and demonstrated, even though Verres was not formally charged for them, such as the theft of art, judicial abuses, and the killing of innocent persons. In the speeches published after the trial, Cicero lays out Verres' earlier trajectory through the *cursus honorum* in detail as a way of establishing Verres' illegal and unethical behavior from the very beginning of holding public offices.[33] In 84 BCE, Verres was sent to Cisalpine Gaul as legate

---

[33] The best recent discussion of Verres' official career is in Brennan, *Praetors*, 446–448, 482–492.

for Cn. Papirius Carbo and already began to embezzle funds, alleges Cicero, referring to the absurdly brief financial ledgers from that time. He was named legate again in 80 BCE by Cn. Cornelius Dolabella, who was assigned as proconsul for the province of Cilicia. Cicero describes the path of destruction and looting left by Verres on his way to Asia Minor. In Greece, Verres tortured a local magistrate in Sicyon who was reluctant to hand over some money by confining him in a compact space filled with smoke from green wood. He stopped in Athens and removed gold from the Parthenon, a charge that came up later at Dolabella's trial for extortion, with the weight of the gold noted, says Cicero. While crossing the Aegean Sea, Verres stopped at the sanctuary of Apollo on Delos and removed several ancient and revered statues, a sanctuary that not even the Persians had violated during the Persian invasion of Greece. Then a huge storm came up and drove the loaded ship back onto the shore, where the statues were found lying on the beach in the wreckage. At that point, Dolabella intervened and ordered that the statues be returned (2.1.34–46).

Verres went on to pillage statues from sanctuaries on Samos, Tenedos, and Chios, and at Erythrae, Halicarnassus, Aspendos, and Perga. As legate, he manipulated inheritances and sold privately to pirates a ship supplied by Miletos (2.1.49–102). After Dolabella's term was up in 78 BCE, Dolabella was prosecuted in Rome and found guilty of extortion as governor of Cilicia, with Verres as the star witness for the prosecution, now betraying the man who had selected him.[34]

When Verres' urban praetorship started in 74 BCE, he had even more scope for illegal schemes, fraud, and peculation. One set of accusations is centered on his mistress Chelidon ("Swallow" in Greek), who ran a brisk business in bribes as a go-between for petitioners to Verres.

---

[34] Cicero, 1. I.11; fullest description at 2.1.95–100; complete references in Alexander, *Trials*, no. 135. During the following four years, Verres apparently kept a low profile, although Cicero says he was not forgotten but was the subject of constant remark (2.1.101).

Another set of accusations focuses on Verres' use of his judicial authority to arrange for large inheritances to come to himself, often through edict. He squeezed still more money from his administrative authority over contracts for public buildings, temples, and roads in Rome, by fraudulent bidding of contracts, neglect, or unreasonable zealousness.[35] In one instance, Verres declared the columns of the Temple of Castor to have been set imperfectly vertical and required that they be reset, at a cost six times the amount of the contract, with the profit, taken from the inheritance of a minor, for himself (2.1.130–152).

The specific examples Cicero provides of each type of abuse, complete with documentary evidence, foreshadow what was to come during Verres' term as governor in Sicily. In the *actio prima*, the published version of the speech of prosecution actually delivered in the Forum, Cicero first describes countermoves against himself that he believes Verres was attempting to take and then he declares his own intent to forego the usual lengthy speech of denunciation in favor of moving right to the evidence, so as to save time. He then demonstrates how Verres was able to accumulate such a sum in his dealings as governor by supporting the allegations with extensive documentary evidence and the testimony of witnesses. This was enough to make Verres leave Rome.

In the additional five speeches of the *actiones secundae*, Cicero published what he would have said if the trial had continued and he lays out in great detail the basic charges summarized in the *divinatio* and the first speech (*actio prima*): I have mentioned here just a few of them. In his focus on Verres' abuse of office while he was an urban praetor, Cicero supports with witnesses and documentary evidence Verres' violation of private property rights by judicial corruption and manipulation of inheritances and contracts. In Sicily as governor, Verres violated civic

---

[35] Verres' term as praetor urbanus is described most fully in 2.1.103–154; see comments of Brennan, *Praetors*, 445–448.

property rights by manipulation and profiteering in the grain supply, an especially serious charge at a time when grain shortages in Rome were not uncommon. This was the aspect of maladministration that was most lucrative for Verres and was thoroughly documented by Cicero. The *lex Hieronica* (Sicily's system of collecting tithes that dated back to the reign of Hieron II) was considered fair and efficient, so that extortion through contravening its provisions is made to seem particularly egregious.[36]

The sacrilegious theft of art, including consecrated images from temples, is the primary topic of the fourth speech, which I discuss in Chapter 3, but references to stolen art occur throughout all the speeches. In the fifth speech, Cicero discusses Verres' ineptness as an administrator. He first describes Verres' lack of military fitness in dealing with potential slave rebellion, a deficiency heightened by Cicero's amusing satirical descriptions. For example, far from taking any appropriate military actions, Cicero claims, Verres did not travel by horseback on marches but would have himself carried on a litter borne by eight men and provisioned with a delicate Maltese cushion stuffed with rose petals, wearing garlands around his neck and head, and carrying a fine linen mesh bag stuffed with petals that he kept at his nose (2.5.27). In fact, Cicero says, Verres spent most of his time in Syracuse because the weather was best there, carousing with the wives of townsmen in tents by the sea near the Arethusa spring on Ortygia, which overlooks the famous harbor where the Athenian fleet was defeated.[37]

His confiscation of ships (to transport his own plunder [*praeda*] from the island) and treachery in dealings with pirates imperiled both merchant shipping and the Roman fleet in the area, and he put to death innocent people involved in these episodes. Finally, he violated criminal law and procedure by imprisoning, torturing, and beheading Roman

---

[36] Verres' new edicts on the grain tithes promulgated as governor in Sicily (which then had force of law) were immediately overturned by his successor in office, L. Caecilius Metellus.

[37] 2.5.80–81: This passage was greatly admired by Quintilian for its vivid color.

citizens. The culminating atrocity was the fate of Publius Gavius of Consa, who escaped prison in Syracuse and fled to Messana but was recaptured, then stripped naked and flogged in the Forum, tortured with hot plates, and, finally, crucified – a punishment usually reserved for rebellious slaves. Gavius kept repeating "civis Romanus sum" (I am a Roman citizen!) while he was being flogged (2.5.158–163).[38]

THE OUTCOME OF THE TRIAL

No commentator doubts Verres' guilt: his early departure for exile must be construed as an admission of guilt and, while in the published speeches Cicero certainly used rhetorical flourishes in his depiction of Verres' earlier career and term as governor in Sicily, he could not have exaggerated too much about the actual circumstances because these were known events with contemporary witnesses, and Cicero's own credibility was at stake too.[39] Butler's observations (in *Hand of Cicero*) about Cicero's pivotal use of large quantities of documentary evidence also underscore Verres' guilt. Cicero uses Verres' flight to good effect in the speeches published after the fact, referring to it as an eventuality for which Verres surely must be planning: in the last *Verrine*, Cicero remarks that he himself saw Verres' ship docked at Velia, a city south

[38] Cicero says he knows this story sounds unbelievable, but he supplies as witnesses a Roman citizen who saw the crucifixion, fellow townsmen of Gavius, and the evidence of the ledger of prisoners from Syracuse with P. Gavius' name. He also (perhaps fictitiously) describes the presiding praetor at the trial, M'. Glabrio, abruptly adjourning the case when the episode is mentioned earlier in the trial because of the public outcry and even potential lynching of Verres (2.5.158, 163).

[39] In the effort to discern evidence for actual historical events of the period, modern scholars have taken up various aspects of Cicero's presentation of the case for historical consideration, but Verres' guilt has not been challenged: Rawson comments that in the published speeches, Cicero may have covered up for some friends who collaborated with Verres (*Cicero*, 42–43); Gruen discusses evidence for judicial reform in the speeches, rejecting the idea that the case had an impact (*LGRR*, 32–36); Mitchell is particularly interested in the political sympathies and allegiances of prominent people depicted in the speeches, especially Cicero's own alliances (*Ascending Years*, 138–149); Brunt discusses the limitations of patronage and of the case as a source for political events (1980: 286–289); Brennan sees some circumstantial weaknesses in an otherwise overwhelming case (*Praetors*, 482–483); Butler (2002) highlights the huge quantity of devastating documentary evidence presented by Cicero.

of Naples, loaded with the choicest art and other goods taken – as was the ship itself – from Sicilians, as though he expected to go into exile and was preparing for flight (2.5.44).[40] Cicero comments that when he went to Verres' house in Rome to collect and seal evidence, some of the statues formerly there (taken from sanctuaries in Asia Minor and the island Samos) had been moved after the first part of the trial (*actio prima*), suggesting that Verres was already packing up to leave (2.1.51).

Verres was condemned in absentia and expected to pay a fine the amount of which is uncertain. Plutarch states that the amount was about three million sesterces and that because it was so low, Cicero was accused of bribery to reduce it (*Vit. Cic.* 8). Plutarch's biography of Cicero has been found inaccurate in other details, and it may be that he cites the figure actually given back to the Sicilians.[41] In any case, Plutarch goes on to say (in refutation of the charge of bribery) that the Sicilians tried to reward Cicero lavishly after the case when he was aedile, but that Cicero used their gift of grain and produce to lower the market prices in Rome, without any profit for himself. Plutarch inserts his account of the trial of Verres into a description of Cicero's attitude toward money as an illustration, stating that he did not accept fees or

[40] Cicero says, "At the time when he was himself leaving the country, this ship, loaded with the plunder [*praeda*] of Sicily, and indeed itself a part of that plunder, put in at Velia with its large cargo, including the objects that he would not send direct to Rome, because of their great value and his special attachment to them. I saw this ship myself at Velia not long ago, and many others besides have seen it; a splendid vessel, gentlemen, and most completely fitted out; and I may add that all who saw it felt that it was anticipating its owner's banishment and preparing the way for his flight into exile" (2.5.44, trans. Greenwood [Loeb]).

[41] So suggests R. C. G. Levens, *Cicero, Verrine V* (Bristol, 1946 [repr. 1980]): xxxv, footnote 14. B. Perrin, translator of the Loeb edition of Plutarch's *Life of Cicero*, suggests that Plutarch's sum, given in drachmas, reflects confusion between denarii and sestercii, worth only one-fourth as much (pp. 87, 101), but that would yield a sum still too low. E. Badian accepts the sum and assumes it represents Cicero's concern not to force Verres' associates to pay (*Publicans and Sinners*, p. 140, note 38). For Plutarch's biography of Cicero as an historical source and the difficulties in using this moralizing literary work as a "source," see J. L. Moles, *Plutarch. The Life of Cicero* (Warminster, 1988): 32–53. For recent views on the sources and composition of Plutarch's *Cicero*, see C. Pelling, *Plutarch and History. Eighteen Studies* (London, 2002): 1–4, 26–29.

gifts as an advocate.[42] It seems that the Sicilians did not recover much of what Verres extorted, but they did at least have the satisfaction of legal redress in Rome and the exile of Verres from Rome. Their suffering under Verres' regime, as described by their astute choice of prosecutor, won them lasting memory; their case is still being read and studied more than two millennia later.

The legal scholar Greenidge points out that in cases of extortion, "exile" is a frequent consequence of condemnation, but it is voluntary, due to inability or unwillingness to pay the restitution demanded.[43] Although exile was not legally imposed on Verres and it was his choice as an escape from the punishment of restitution and fines, exile ended not just his career in Rome but also his rights as a citizen of Rome. He became an *exul* from Rome and surrendered all rights and obligations. In effect, it ended his legal rights altogether because he could not have rights independently of being a citizen of a particular place. Even if he somehow were to acquire citizenship in Massilia, he still could not then return to Rome as a Massaliote because, annually, a law of interdiction was passed against such individuals, labeling them as "accursed," cut off from the community with no legal protection from assault.[44]

VERRES' LONG EXILE AND DEATH

Presumably, Verres went off to Massilia with much of the fine art, statues, luxury goods, and huge sums of money he had taken from Sicily, and he lived there for twenty-seven years.[45] Massilia at that time had a role in southern France similar to Naples in the Italian peninsula: an ancient, prosperous, sophisticated city, founded by Greeks from

---

[42] For a list of Cicero's properties, sources of income (mostly rents and legacies), expenditures, and fluctuations in income during the course of his life, see Shatzman, *Senatorial Wealth*: no. 211, 403–425.
[43] A. H. J. Greenidge, *The Legal Procedure of Cicero's Time* (Oxford, 1901, repr. Union, NJ, Ltd., 1999): 509, with further discussion of the legal implications of loss of rights, 509–513.
[44] Greenidge, *Legal Procedure*, 512–513.
[45] For a tabulation of Verres' wealth, see Shatzman, *Senatorial Wealth*, no. 218, 429–437.

Phocaea (in Asia Minor) about 600 BCE, it flourished as a center of maritime trade and as a conduit into Celtic Gaul. The archaic Greek city was wealthy enough to build and furnish a handsome marble treasury at Delphi, later used as a Roman treasury. The Greek Massaliotes dominated their region culturally for several centuries and had friendly relations with Rome, which occasionally gave them military assistance. In 125 BCE, they appealed to Rome for support against a neighboring hostile tribe. After that and subsequent appeals, the inevitable result of ongoing Roman intervention in this part of Gaul was that the territory surrounding the city and its own holdings eventually became part of a Roman province; Massilia itself was besieged by Julius Caesar in 49 BCE, during the Civil War.[46] Like Syracuse and Naples, Massilia retained its Greek character well into the period of Roman control, and some Romans went there for education as an alternative to Athens (Strabo, 4.1.4–5).

Massilia was an attractive choice for a certain type of exile: L. Sergius Catilina wrote a letter stating that he intended exile in Massilia, before his capture and execution when the Catilinarian crisis was exposed by Cicero (Sallust, BC, 34.2). T. Annius Milo went there in exile after being convicted of the murder of Clodius in 52 BCE. He had been defended unsuccessfully by Cicero, and when he received a copy of the published version of Cicero's speech on his behalf, he is said to have remarked that if Cicero had delivered as good a speech as this one, he would not now be enjoying the excellent mullets of Massilia.[47]

[46] S. Dyson, *The Creation of the Roman Frontier* (Princeton, 1985): 126–171; A. L. F. Rivet, *Gallia Narbonesis. Southern France in Roman Times* (London, 1988): 39–53, 219–225; A. Trevor Hodge, *Ancient Greek France* (London, 1998): 99–109. The exact date of the beginning of formal Roman administration of Gallia Transalpina has been in dispute: see Brennan, *Praetors*, 363–364; he puts the beginning of regular Roman rule in the mid-90s BCE.

[47] Cassius Dio 40.54.3–4. The trial of Milo was held under disturbing conditions that are said to have affected Cicero's delivery; Asconius read both a record of the spoken version and the final published version (Asconius, *Pro Milone*, 42 Clark). Other references in Alexander, *Trials*, no. 309, 151–152.

Nothing further of Verres is heard again, except for several anecdotes about the circumstances of his death in 43 BCE. Pliny says that Verres was so attached to his Corinthian bronzes that he refused to give them up when Marc Antony demanded them – hence, Antony had Verres proscribed and executed.[48] Verres is said to have met his death bravely[49] and was told before he died that Cicero too had been proscribed by Antony and had just been killed.[50] While there is no way of knowing whether these stories are true, the comments do show the continuing interest in the character of Verres, whose iniquities Cicero brilliantly describes.

THE PUBLICATION OF THE *VERRINES*

A public official who abuses the public trust and makes money illegally by manipulating contracts and profiteering in taxes, who imprisons and even tortures citizens in order to protect his own corruption: such figures are all too familiar in our own headlines, nationally and abroad. Of thousands of such cases that have stirred public outcry in the course of centuries, this famous ancient case in particular continues to be remembered because Cicero decided to publish his speeches and because his readers so admired them for their vivid drama, rhetoric, and intrinsic historical interest that they continued to be circulated.

In an era before the printing press, "publication" meant arranging for authorized copies to be handwritten by scribes and then distributing the copies to interested readers, who in turn may have had more copies made. The books themselves were written on rolls of papyrus made in

---

[48] *NH* 34.6; a similar accusation was made of Augustus (that he had men proscribed just to acquire their Corinthian bronzes: Suetonius, *Vit. Aug.* 70.2); for further discussion of this anecdote, see pp. 205–206.

[49] Asinius Pollio quoted by Seneca, *Suas.* 6.24.

[50] Lactantius (fl. ca. 300 CE), *Instit.* 2.4.37.

Egypt and normally on one side only. Although standards of scholarship, editing, and textual analysis had become sophisticated earlier in Alexandria, the physical technology remained cumbersome, and the codex would not replace the scroll until the second century CE.[51] The seemingly haphazard reliance on informal distribution of books among Romans, mostly by social network, nonetheless was effective because it supplied the fuel for an explosion of interest in the first century BCE in reading, writing, editing, and writing commentaries and learned treatises, for those able to take time for it. An interest in books became an integral part of the persona of the elite and those who aspired to it.[52]

Later in Cicero's life-time, a "book trade" was coming into being, but he complains about its quality in a letter written to his brother Quintus on October 24, 54 BCE: "As regards filling the gaps in your Greek library and exchanging books and acquiring Latin ones, I should very much like all this done, especially as I too stand to benefit. But I have nobody I can employ on such business, not even for myself. Books, at least such as one would like to have, are not on the market and they can't be obtained except through an expert who is willing to take trouble." A week or so later on the same topic, he writes again to his brother, "As for the Latin ones, I don't know where to turn, the copies are made and sold so full of errors."[53] Nonetheless, Cicero's life-time saw considerable improvement in the modes of distribution and the availability of texts; by the Augustan period, there were booksellers and book publishers with teams of professional scribes.

[51] For overviews, L. D. Reynolds and N. G. Wilson, *Scribes and Scholars, A Guide to the Transmission of Greek and Latin Literature* (Oxford, 1991): 1–43; E. J. Kenney and W. V. Clausen, *Cambridge History of Classical Literature*, II, *Latin Literature* (Cambridge, 1982): 3–32; also Raymond J. Starr, "The Circulation of Literary Texts in the Roman World," *CQ* 37 (1987): 213–223; detailed discussions by G. Cavallo and P. Fedeli in G. Cavallo, et al., eds., *Lo spazio letterario de Roma antica, II, La Circolazione del testo* (Rome, 1989): 307–378.

[52] The classic account of intellectual life in this period is that of E. Rawson, *Intellectual Life in the Late Roman Republic*, London, 1985; also useful is the summary, "The Intellectual Developments of the Ciceronian Age," by M. Griffin, *CAH²* 9 [1994]: 689–728.

[53] *Q.Fr.* 24 (3.4.5) and *Q.Fr.* 25 (3.5.6), trans. Shackleton-Bailey.

Cicero's friend T. Pomponius Atticus (they knew each other from boyhood) would become very helpful to him in editing, publishing, and acquiring books, but he took on that role some years after the trial of Verres.

Evidence for publication in Cicero's life-time has been carefully gathered both from stray comments in his own writings and from those of his contemporaries.[54] Publication of the *Verrines* was especially impressive because of their length (more than a century later, the historian Tacitus has a character in a dialogue on oratory comment on the length of the *Verrines* and wonder who can take time to sit through them today, clearly a more impatient age [*Dial.* 20]). But even more impressive is that Cicero published them at all, for there was only limited precedent for published speeches in Latin and, by doing so, Cicero created a new literary type.[55]

Why Cicero chose to publish the *Verrines*, including a full version of speeches he would have given had the trial not been cut off when Verres fled into exile, is a question that has been extensively investigated and discussed. A didactic motive is granted by most commentators, especially because other later publications of Cicero are explicitly didactic.[56] This was Cicero's most important case to date, and he had done an enormous amount of preparation and research for it. Because of the timing and logistics of the trial, he had had opportunity to give only a fairly brief speech and used only a small part of what he had prepared – and

[54] Internal evidence for publication of Cicero's speeches is gathered and discussed by James N. Settle, *The Publication of Cicero's Orations* (diss. University of North Carolina, Chapel Hill, 1962): 1–18, 26–27, 99–111; recent discussion, with earlier views, in Alexander (2002): 15–31.

[55] This point is emphasized by E. Narducci, *Cicerone e l'eloquenza romana: Retorica e progetto culturale* (Rome and Bari, 1997): 157–173.

[56] Stroh argues this forcefully (Stroh [1975]: 49–52); overview in C. J. Classen, *Recht – Rhetorik – Politik* (Darmstadt, 1985): 2–11; excellent analyses of Cicero's motives in Butler (2002): 71–84, with earlier bibliography; and A. Vasaly, "Cicero's Early Speeches," in J. M. May, ed., *Brill's Companion to Cicero* (Leiden, 2002): 90–93; Alexander (2002): 25–26 (on why anyone would want to read the speeches).

it was a major triumph! Presumably, he wanted to bring more attention to the case and his own efforts; hence, the decision to publish the speeches as though he had delivered all of them, at length. Ann Vasaly aptly calls the *Verrines* Cicero's *monumentum* (which in Latin can mean a literary work as well as a monument), an offering to Rome of his enormous effort, analogous to the "public works" such as games, festivals, and building projects he would undertake as aedile-elect.[57]

The publication of the Verrines may also be viewed as a carefully calculated part of Cicero's trajectory into the powerful, elite segment of Roman society, designed to show his own worthiness as a (new) senator while reaching out to a broad audience that included plebeians and the equestrian class as well.[58] Why Cicero chose to publish some but not all of his speeches has been assessed most fruitfully by Jane Crawford. She finds both practical and political reasons behind Cicero's decisions: his primary motives for publication were their didactic and aesthetic value and potential political benefits; his motives for suppression likely included his wish to avoid giving offense to powerful individuals, or a particular speech might have concerned an unpopular issue, or the political situation was rapidly changing. Over the course of his career, Cicero published slightly fewer than half (i.e., seventy-nine) of his known speeches.[59]

The text of the *Verrines* offers an opportunity to assess possible differences between a delivered speech (only if the text may be treated as a sort of transcript) and a composed speech presented as though it

---

[57] Vasaly (2002): 91–92.

[58] Butler (2002): 76, 79–81; J. Dugan, *Making a New Man. Ciceronian Self-fashioning in the Rhetorical Works* (Oxford, 2005): 8–15.

[59] Jane W. Crawford, *M. Tullius Cicero: The Lost and Unpublished Orations*, Göttingen, 1984 (*Hypomnemata*, 80): 3–21, her tallies updated in *idem*, "The Lost and Fragmentary Orations," in May (2002): 305–330, chart on p. 327. Of seventy-nine likely published speeches, there are fifty-eight extant, sixteen fragmentary, and five lost, while eighty-three unpublished speeches are known by title or inference. Of the unpublished speeches, Cicero gave four in Sicily (Crawford [1984], no. 3, 6, 8, 9), two of them in Greek, on issues relative to the trial of Verres.

had been given, which may give the speech a more literary character.[60] This is of special interest here because the fourth *Verrine* focuses on Verres' theft of art, depicted with a dramatic vividness especially suited to readers' or auditors' attention, although Verres was not charged with theft of art. This entire topic could be regarded as a "digression" (in ancient rhetoric, a *digressio* serves to amplify the charges and persuade listeners; in modern terms, it could also be said to represent a pattern of behavior). The theme of theft of art, however, does appear in many places in the two speeches that Cicero actually delivered in court and was supported with documentation and witnesses. This topic was more than just a literary flourish.

Quintilian, a teacher of rhetoric under the Flavian emperors, argues strenuously in his treatise on rhetoric that speaking well and writing well are one and the same thing, and that there should be no distinction between the written and the spoken speech (he cites Demosthenes and Cicero as primary exemplars [*Inst.* 12.10.49–56]). His reasoning has the stamp of didactic idealism, which may cover over the subtleties that interest modern students of literature. In a discussion of the literary qualities of the *Verrines*, R. Enos sees differences between the speeches delivered and the "literate mode" evident in the undelivered speeches. He concludes that the initial orations offered "paradigms of effective legal argument," whereas the later ones served as more literary models. He goes on to point out that many generations of teachers and scholars have used Cicero's speeches as models not just for eloquence but also

---

[60] This aspect is analyzed thoroughly by R. L. Enos, *The Literate Mode of Cicero's Legal Rhetoric* (Carbondale and Edwardsville, 1988): 59–77; also discussed in A. M. Riggsby, *Crime and Community in Ciceronian Rome* (Austin, 1999): 178–184; M. von Albrecht, *Cicero's Style. A Synopsis* (Leiden and Boston, 2003): 206–217, and *passim*; T. D. Frazel, "The Composition and Circulation of Cicero's *In Verrem*" *CQ* 54 (2004): 128–142. Frazel in particular argues that there is little difference in style between the sets of speeches and that Cicero must have written at least a draft of the *Actiones Secundae* even before the trial. On the literary aspects of oratory more generally, "Cicero and the Relationship of Oratory to Literature," in Kenney and Clausen (1982): 230–267, and G. B. Conte, *Latin Literature, A History* (Baltimore and London, 1994b): 180, 199–200.

for humanistic values, and in this, Cicero's larger intention of personal commentary on social situations and conditions is fulfilled.[61] Other scholars have not seen such a difference in style and, more probably, all the speeches were meant to represent Cicero's best efforts but with the clear necessity to present the case as closely as possible to what was argued; after all, many of his immediate reading audience may have heard the version given in the Forum. What emerges from these studies on the relationship between oral and written versions is how closely they are intertwined. A sophisticated public accustomed to appreciating polished oratory in person will best appreciate it in writing. It is through both oral and written eloquence that Cicero's views on the ethics of acquisition of art have had such an impact.

The earliest literary papyrus in Latin (*P. Ianda*, V 90), found in Egypt, bears part of the *Verrines* (2.2.3–4) and is dated by R. Cavenaile to 20 BCE.[62] Cavenaile also presents seven other papyri (Nos. 21–27) bearing speeches of Cicero, two of them opisthographic and four from the *Actiones Secundae* of the *Verrines*, mostly dated to the fourth and fifth centuries CE, and one to the sixth century CE. Two of the papyri have interlinear translations in Greek, not surprising because Latin seems not to have taken root in Egypt.[63] Cavenaile comments that these fragments

---

[61] Enos (1988): 77, 92–93. There is only one speech, *Pro Milone*, which was considered to be better in publication than in person: evidently Cicero was rattled by the presence of armed guards at the trial. That this would be noticed and remembered tends to support the argument that the delivered and published versions were usually close.

[62] R. Cavenaile, *Corpus Papyrorum Latinarum* (Wiesbaden, 1958): 70–71, no. 20. The same papyrus is dated to the first half of the first century CE by R. Seider (*non vidi*), cited in L. D. Reynolds, ed., *Texts and Transmissions, A Survey of the Latin Classics* (Oxford, 1983), footnote 6, p. 55, with the comment that it "is the oldest witness to any Latin text preserved in medieval manuscripts."

[63] J. Adams reports the estimate that only 1 percent of surviving documents (nonliterary, among those in Latin or Greek) of the Roman period in Egypt are in Latin, and even military texts are only 10 percent in Latin (*Bilingualism and the Latin Language* [Cambridge, 2003]: 527–529). With the notable exception of Latin graffiti recording the visits of elite tourists of the Roman period on the Colossus of Memnon, one of a pair of pharaonic statues

indicate that studious youth in Egypt demanded models for the art of oratory. These are unusual finds, but as the early papyrus *P. Ianda, V 90* shows, the informal mode of publication in the late Republic was effective: within two or three generations after the trial, a student in Egypt was reading Cicero's account of Verres and, just as Cicero had hoped, he had a widespread and enduring readership.

ROMAN AUDIENCES OF THE *VERRINES*

The most important initial audience for the *Verrines* was of course the jury that heard the case in the Forum. These men were selected and empanelled from members of the senatorial class. Cicero names twenty of them, of whom six were challenged by the defense and did not serve; he does not name the six he himself must have challenged, apparently not wishing to embarrass them further (the potential for bribery was a factor in the selection). Among the fourteen known men who did serve, there are two former consuls (P. Servilius Vatia Isauricus [cos. 79], and Q. Lutatius Catulus [cos. 78]) and one former governor of Sicily (C. Claudius Marcellus). Among those rejected by the defense are another former consul, C. Cassius Longinus (cos. 73), who did serve as a witness against Verres, and another former governor of Sicily, Sex. Peducaeus, who had a reputation as the most honest and conscientious governor of Sicily ever (*Verr.* 2.3.216). The jury must have been larger than the twenty-six inferred from the text, but the exact number of jurors is not certain: it was likely thirty-two.[64]

---

later associated with the Ethiopian hero who fought on the side of Troy, most graffiti in Egypt is in Greek, even when naming Roman visitors (546–555, 579–589).

[64] Cicero gives the number of jurors in the trial of Oppianicus (sued under a different law for attempted poisoning, not extortion abroad), held in 74 BCE and thus after the reforms of Sulla, as 32 (*Clu.* 27.74). The jury has been analyzed by W. C. McDermott, "The Verrine Jury," *RhM* 120 (1977): 64–75, estimate of total jurors: more than 40, p. 75; F. Millar, *The Crowd in Rome in the Late Republic* (Ann Arbor, 1998) gives the number as 32, p. 13. For the praetors (governors) who preceded Verres, see Brennan, *Praetors*: 483–486. On the role and behavior of jurors generally, see Alexander (2002): 36–38.

The jurors were under oath and, although their primary duty was to decide whether the defendant had violated the law, discussions of character were considered valid and appropriate for evaluating the plausibility of the charges. The character and reputation of the advocates were also very much under examination because the speakers' ability to persuade rested in part on their acquired *dignitas* and *auctoritas*.[65] A distinctive feature of Roman trials for extortion abroad is that all the major participants – the defendant, the advocates, the jurors – knew each other personally, or at least of each other; in this trial, they were all from the senatorial class. Cicero exploits this adroitly, even naming the jurors (e.g., recalling the deeds of C. Claudius Marcellus' famous ancestor [2.4.90]) and also addressing them as a representative body that stood for Rome and Roman administration. It was as though the inner workings of a private club, its hierarchies and competitions, were put on display in public as a dramatic enactment but for very high stakes in the participants' public careers.

As Cicero points out frequently, the senatorial class was on exhibit during this trial, to themselves and to onlookers (let alone posterity). An acute awareness of a larger audience is always implicit in the proceedings. The audience next in importance was the *corona*, the circle of bystanders who stood around the tribunal set up outdoors in front of the Temple of Castor. Although their reactions to what was said (groans, laughter, shouts) might have made some impression on the jurors, whether the "crowd" had any real influence at trials (or generally in political matters) is a matter of ongoing debate.[66] Probably the real influence was felt after the verdict in reactions to changing

[65] Alexander (2002): 36; on the importance of character (ethos), J. May, *Trials of Character. The Eloquence of Ciceronian Ethos* (Chapel Hill and London, 1988).

[66] For the view that the crowd played an important role in politics even earlier: F. Millar, "Politics, Persuasion and the People before the Social War (150–90BC)," *JRS* 76 (1986): 1–11, elaborated further and for this period, Millar (1998), esp. 13–16, 64–72; opposed, H. Mouritsen, *Plebs and Politics in the Late Roman Republic* (Cambridge, 2001): 132–133;

reputations – that is, in the political standing of the various major participants. F. Millar points out, however, that Cicero frequently mentions a vociferous crowd in the course of the *Verrines*: popular opinion is represented as quite hostile to Verres and a significant element of the trial.[67]

Today's readers of the *Verrines* should keep in mind the outdoor, performative aspect of these speeches because Cicero frequently and skillfully invokes this atmosphere of a smaller group of men under a forensic spotlight, and a much larger crowd as an audience for that audience, within the venerable setting of the Forum.[68] The timing of the trial meant that Rome was then filling up with people from outside the city for the elections and census being held and the upcoming games to be given by Pompey; Cicero remarks that he wants this trial finished before these "multitudes" go home (1.54). While the jurors are responsible for the impact of their verdict and he himself is responsible for the hard work and anxiety of the trial, he says, "everyone" (all listeners) should know and remember what took place and what was said by each person.

Within Rome, the trial was likely to have been discussed for some time afterward. Once they were written, Cicero would have circulated his speeches first to his friends and associates among the senatorial and equestrian classes.[69] In effect, they were for Cicero the most important target audience, especially for the five speeches not delivered that gave

---

deeper scrutiny of the issue in R. Morstein-Marx, *Mass Oratory and Political Power in the Late Roman Republic* (Cambridge, 2004). For the level of knowledge and education of the "crowd," N. Horsfall, *The Culture of the Roman Plebs* (London, 2003), ch. 4, 7.

[67] F. Millar, "Popular Politics at Rome in the Late Republic," in F. Millar, ed., *Rome, the Greek World, and the East*, H. M. Cotton and G. M. Rogers, eds. (Chapel Hill and London, 2002): 169–170.

[68] A. Vasaly, *Representations. Images of the World in Ciceronian Oratory* (Berkeley and London, 1993): 104–108, 129–130.

[69] See T. Murphy, "Cicero's First Readers: Epistolary Evidence for the Dissemination of His Works," *CQ* 48 (1998): 492–505, for an instructive account of the circulation of Cicero's later philosophical writings.

a full accounting of what Verres had done. Copies were likely sent to Sicily and to his associates in the Greek cities of Greece and Asia Minor, where other victims would have welcomed news of the successful trial and Verres' forced exile. How wide the readership might have become is linked to the vexed question of the extent of literacy in the Roman world.

A scholarly consensus holds that oral communication and orality is a salient cultural feature for Romans, directly through *contiones* (public meetings often anticipatory of legislation), assemblies, trials, the theater, and so on or implicitly in texts (usually read aloud),[70] but its implications and variations are still debated. W. Harris's book on literacy (1989), with a very low estimate of 20 to 30 percent male literacy in Italy, has triggered much further discussion and extensive counterargument.[71] The many kinds of documentary evidence attested to in the *Verrines* and explicated by Butler (2002) certainly support his view of the deep significance of writing within Roman culture, even if literary literacy may have been limited in comparison with modern cultures. At the trial, much of this documentary evidence (letters, wills, receipts, records of inscriptions, edicts, and accounts) was read aloud. That Verres took the trouble to alter and forge documents suggests that he anticipated facing trial.

The didactic aspect of Cicero's speeches would remain a significant part of his legacy and even today the *Catilinarians* and the *Verrines* are staples in Latin language courses. In antiquity, their most obvious

---

[70] For discussion of reading aloud vs. reading to oneself, see A. K. Gavrilov, "Techniques of Reading in Classical Antiquity," *CQ* 47 (1997): 56–76, and N. Horsfall, "Rome without Spectacles," *G&R* 42 (1995): 49–56.

[71] W. V. Harris, *Ancient Literacy* (Cambridge, MA, and London, 1989): 259; responses in M. Beard et al., *Literacy in the Roman World* (*JRA* Supp. 3) (Ann Arbor, 1991); A. K. Bowman and G. Woolf, eds., *Literacy and Power in the Ancient World* (Cambridge, 1994); H. Solin, O. Salomies, and U.-M. Liertz, eds., *Acta colloquii epigraphici Latini, Helsingiae, 3.-6. Sept. 1991 habiti* (Helsinki, 1995); Horsfall (2003).

utility was as models for effective oratory for students of rhetoric and were read and studied as such: Cicero quickly became a canonical prose author, either to admire and emulate or to repudiate and denounce. In a renewal of interest in oratory in the late first century CE, Cicero's work is frequently cited by others writing about oratory, such as Tacitus, Pliny the Younger, and especially their teacher Quintilian, who quotes the *Verrines* fifty-eight times. Quintilian explicitly sets out to reestablish Ciceronian rhetoric as a proper model and hopes to reverse what he saw as a decline in morals generally, through a focus on education in rhetoric and oratory.[72] Later antiquarians, such as Aulus Gellius (who wrote in the Antonine period ca. 170 CE), admired Cicero and quotes from the *Verrines*. Gellius even believed he had seen a manuscript of them in the handwriting of Cicero's secretary Tiro.[73] Among late antique authors, Lactantius ("the Christian Cicero") and Jerome became particularly well known as devotees of Cicero.

Cicero's work also received scholarly treatment within just a few generations. The first preserved commentator on Cicero's speeches is Quintus Asconius Pedianus, who wrote a commentary on at least five of Cicero's speeches in 54–57 CE, in the early years of the reign of Nero. He wrote them for his sons, whom he hoped would have a public career, and he provides much valuable information and even some quotations from otherwise lost speeches of Cicero. Copied along with his commentary into the medieval manuscript discovered at St. Gall by Poggio Bracciolini in the summer of 1416 was another commentary, this one on the *Verrines*. Initially, it was also believed to have been Asconius' but was later found to have been written by a different,

---

[72] For Cicero's impact on Quintilian and the Silver Age, see M. Winterbottom, "Cicero and the Silver Age," in W. Ludwig, ed., *Éloquence et rhétorique chez Cicéron* (*Entretiens sur l'Antiquité classique*, 28) (Geneva, 1982): 237–266, discussion 267–274.

[73] 1.7.1,13.21.15; discussed by J. E. G. Zetzel, "*Emendari ad Tironem:* Some Notes on Scholarship in the Second Century AD," *HSCP* 77 (1973): 225–243.

nameless author who lived in the fifth century CE, now referred to as Pseudo-Asconius. Despite his late date, he also provides useful explanations and grammatical glosses.[74] Ps.-Asconius himself seems to have compiled his comments on the *Verrines* from other sources; thus, other commentaries in anquity may be posited.

Also in the first century CE, the cultural attitudes and ethical ideals Cicero so powerfully conveys were taken up for their own sake in a new type of publication: a sort of handbook of ethical anecdotes culled from several authors but especially Cicero and Livy, entitled *Memorable Deeds and Sayings*, by Valerius Maximus. He wrote ca. 30 CE in the reign of Tiberius, to whom he dedicated his book. Long viewed with scorn by modern scholars as a simplistic and unliterary "source" of only dubious historical value, this book was very popular both in antiquity and during the Middle Ages and early Renaissance, until the greater power of Cicero and Livy in the original caused Valerius Maximus to begin to fade into the background. Valerius is undergoing a scholarly revival, however, and his texts have been subject to new scrutiny and appreciation. The didactic purpose of his collection had long been recognized because it provides material for *declamationes*, a kind of practice-round for students of oratory who are given set topics or legal conundrums to explicate or defend. *Exempla*, paradigmatic stories that illustrate stellar or fatally poor reactions and behavior in difficult situations, were the fundamental basis for Roman ethical training and appear in many kinds of literature, especially history and oratory. Valerius condenses them and arranges them according to thematic categories, many of them domestic.

---

[74] B. A. Marshall, *A Historical Commentary on Asconius* (Columbia, MS, 1985): 1–2, 26–38; M. D. Reeve in Reynolds (1983): 24–25. On Poggio's discovery, L. D. Reynolds and N. G. Wilson, *Scribes and Scholars. A Guide to the Transmission of Greek and Latin* Literature[3] (Oxford, 1991): 136–140. On Ps.-Asconius, T. Stangl, *Ciceronis orationum scholiastae*, II (Paterborn, 1909).

Recently, Valerius' purposes and his intended audiences have been more tightly framed: W. M. Bloomer has located this book as aimed at an emerging class of aspiring administrators (including those in the provinces and Italy) who needed to learn true aristocratic values and ethics, and references to Roman Republican history that would be familiar to the well-educated. C. Skidmore insists that Valerius wrote for an audience including the elite, who might have appreciated clear ethical precepts but, in general, were too busy for longer texts.[75] In Valerius, it appears we have a distant ancestor of two very popular modern forms of publication: self-help/self-improvement books and collections of quotations and pithy sayings.

Among Valerius' anecdotes are numerous stories about sanctuaries and statues of gods and their treatment and the repercussions of bad behavior. Typically, he gives examples from Roman history (and, in this way, establishes what is appropriate for a Roman), with parallel "external" examples in which the protagonists are foreign, who sometimes behave virtuously. One of his *exempla* (1.1 *ext.* 2) focuses on King Masinissa of Numidia (modern Algeria), who initially sided with Carthage but then recognized Roman power, fought alongside Romans at Zama in 202 BCE, and was rewarded with the return of his kingdom; he died at age ninety in 148. Valerius refers to an incident described in detail by Cicero (*Verr.* 2.4.103), about Masinissa's reaction when his admiral brought home enormous ivory tusks from the sanctuary of Juno on Malta (a sanctuary that had not been violated during the Punic Wars or by pirates, says Cicero). When Masinissa learned of

---

[75] W. M. Bloomer, *Valerius Maximus & the Rhetoric of the New Nobility* (Chapel Hill and London, 1992); C. Skidmore, *Practical Ethics for Roman Gentlemen. The Work of Valerius Maximus* (Exeter, 1996); D. Wardle and H. Walker seem to agree with Bloomer's class distinctions among the intended audience, although Wardle points out that there is no clear evidence of class distinctions: D. Wardle, *Valerius Maximus. Memorable Deeds and Sayings*, Book I (Oxford, 1998): 12–13; H. J. Walker, *Valerius Maximus. Memorable Deeds and Sayings. One Thousand Tales from Ancient Rome* (Indianapolis and Cambridge, 2004): xxiii.

their origin, he had an apologetic inscription carved on them in Punic and sent them back in a quinquereme to be rededicated. Some 130 years later, Verres stole them, along with many other ivory statues from the temple.[76] Valerius comments that Masinissa's good character contrasted with his barbarian origin and that one should not judge character by origin.

I have included Valerius' handbook of ethical precepts in my discussion as a way of illustrating how diffuse was the influence of Cicero's *Verrines*, within just a century of their composition. Of course, Cicero's reputation has been based on a wide range of writings, not just the *Verrines*: his output was enormous and his philosophical treatises also have had major impact. During the Middle Ages and through the early modern period, probably the most widely read texts were initially *Somnium Scipionis* (*Dream of Scipio*) and then *De Officiis* (*On Duties*), the first book to be printed after the bible. In antiquity, however, from Quintilian's day onward, the most popular texts were his speeches – above all, the *Catilinarians* and *Verrines*.[77] Many ancient authors quote him directly but the impact of Cicero's ethical delineations is even more widespread in the authors' choices of *exempla* to illustrate their own points, their assumptions, and what they choose to highlight. Here, I am concerned with his views on the treatment of statues, dedications in sanctuaries, and other art. As we have seen, Cicero's influence on this topic may be traced in Julius Caesar's account of the war with Pompey,

---

[76] In another *exemplum* borrowed from Cicero, Valerius comments on the Persian respect for the sanctuary of Apollo on Delos because they did not plunder it (1.1.*ext*. 6). Here Valerius is using Cicero's *Verrines* 2.1.48, where Cicero contrasts Verres' nighttime theft of statues at Delos with the more restrained behavior of the Persians, even though they were on their way to invade Greece: Wardle (1998): 127–128, 134.

[77] Conte (1994b): 204–207. For summaries of Cicero's impact, see M. L. Clarke, "'*Non Hominis Nomen, sed Eloquentiae*'," in T. A. Dorey, ed., *Cicero* (London, 1965): 81–107; G. A. Kennedy, "Cicero's Oratorical and Rhetorical Legacy," in May (2002): 481–501; and still useful for the Renaissance and later, T. Zielinski, *Cicero im Wandel der Jahrhunderte*[5] (1912, repr. Stuttgart, 1967).

in Livy's account of the expansion of Roman power into southern Italy, and even in Augustus' *Res gestae.* Cicero's views on art were a formative influence on Pliny the Elder's chapters about the uses of art in his *Natural History* and, through Pliny, many subsequent discussions of art well into our own era.

3 CICERO'S VIEWS ON THE SOCIAL PLACE OF ART

◎▣◎

I come now to what he himself
speaks of as his favorite pursuit, his
friends as a foolish weakness, Sicily
as piracy. . . . Even more exactly: in
no man's house, even if he had been
his host; in no public place, even
though it was a sanctuary; in the
possession of no one, whether Sicilian
or Roman citizen; whether public or
private property, whether consecrated
or not consecrated, nowhere in all of
Sicily has he left anything that he saw
and wanted.

(Verr. 2.4.1–2)

THE METHODS AND MEANS VERRES USED TO ACQUIRE ART WERE illegal and coercive and now, in Cicero's fourth speech, the focus in the legal case is on the evidence for his seizure of art, both from temples and shrines and from private persons. Cicero includes the criminal acquisition of art in the speeches as a formidable buttressing argument and as a way to show that Verres' financial extortions were part of a whole set of violations of the normative ethics surrounding religion, patron–client customs, guest-friendship, and foreign relations. Verres did not face trial in Rome on art theft, but his thievery of art supported the extortion case against him and became the most memorable part of Cicero's literary indictment. Here, I address Cicero's commentary on art and what can be inferred about Roman attitudes to Greek art: his own, Verres', and those of his immediate audience.

Of course, Cicero's purpose in the *Verrines* was not to provide a commentary on art but to prosecute and condemn. Verres' guilt on the formal charge of extortion is established beyond any doubt. The details of his financial dealings, manipulation of inheritances and contracts, his conniving with pirates, and the physical reprisals, including torture, flogging, and crucifixion of innocent Roman citizens, make for sickening reading. Cicero must have felt it was not sufficient to establish that Verres was a criminal and cruel man, and wanted to show also that his behavior was un-Roman in his constant violation of temples and shrines, and of long-established customs of patronage, guest-friendship, and hospitality. This behavior demonstrated an absence of respect for tradition, for ancestors and predecessors, and certainly for Rome's reputation and image among foreigners. For Verres, the normative ethics developed over many centuries that were supposed to be ingrained in men of his social standing and official position were simply irrelevant to him, largely because of his obsession with art. The skill with which Cicero presents the ample evidence and witnesses has been extensively commented on by others (beginning in antiquity with Quintilian).[1]

A distinctive aspect of the more prestigious kinds of Greek art (statuary and painting, ritual vessels) is that their context and purpose were primarily religious: either gods were represented or housed or invoked, or an item was dedicated to the gods in thanks or in a vow, or the item was used to perform rituals in honor of a god. This is not to say that politics, propaganda, or self-advertisement were not present, for they were – in abundance – but always somehow within a divine penumbra. In

---

[1] For modern commentary on Cicero's skill, see especially Vasaly (1993, 2002). Some of the ideas in this chapter are published in M. M. Miles, "Cicero's Prosecution of Gaius Verres: A Roman View of the Ethics of Acquisition of Art," *IJCP* 11 (2002): 28–49.

antiquity, art served these purposes best in public, not private, because Greek and Roman religions typically were communal in ritual and observance. Over time, with the relaxing of social taboos against the private use of art, increasing personal wealth, and an ever greater abundance of public and personal visual objects, the distinctions between art in a public or a private sphere became increasingly defined. When ancient Greek art was taken out of its original context, either through warfare, purchase, or the *force majeure* exercised by Verres, and set in a new Roman context, the art took on new meanings to its new owners. Part of the value of Cicero's indirect social commentary lies in what it reveals about the implicit assumptions behind these distinctions. He frequently expresses the sense of outrage (we) Romans should feel that Verres illicitly took religious objects intended for communal use from others for use in his own house or villa. This twofold violation is the primary topic of the fourth speech.

The immediate audiences of the *Verrines* (the jurors, the crowd of onlookers in the Forum for the first two speeches, contemporary readers for all the speeches) were certainly familiar with Greek art and Greek artists. Roman knowledge of Greek art began early, at least by the sixth century BCE, as B. Ridgway has pointed out, and intensified with the art booty brought to Rome through conquest and through commissions in Rome.[2] As we have seen, even though some ancient authors disapprovingly traced Roman enthusiasm for Greek art back to Marcellus' booty from Syracuse, Romans already had a longstanding interest in Greek art: hence the positive reception of his art booty remarked upon by the moralizing critics. Apart from other ancient references (cited by Ridgway), just the *Verrines* alone provide ample evidence to illustrate the familiarity with Greek art Cicero could assume of his audience in 70 BCE.

---

[2] Ridgway (1984): 19–24. See also the comments of Rawson on Roman understanding of art in the late Republic (1985): 193–214.

Cicero refers to a few of the public exhibits of Rome, notably in the Portico of Metellus, and in temples such as the Temple of Honos and Virtus where Marcellus dedicated items from Syracuse. Greek art was still distinctive enough to warrant special efforts on the part of aediles to find excellent pieces for public display in the Forum during festivals (their elective office included the duty of mounting festivals and public games). Cicero assumes that his audiences will recall statues taken by Verres from the Greek east that he loaned to his advocate Hortensius, an aedile a few years before the trial, and recalls the more ethical example of Claudius Pulcher, aedile in 99 BCE, who borrowed a famous statue of Eros (Cupid) by Praxiteles from a Greek friend in Sicily, Gaius Heius. Specific statues were considered worth a visit for Romans traveling abroad: Heius' collection in his household shrine in Sicily was open daily to visitors. In mainland Greece, people went to Thespiae just to see another version of Eros by Praxiteles, and Cicero lists the famous works of art associated with nine other cities, in a context that assumes his audience likely knew about them and may have seen them. Cicero also speaks of professional guides in Syracuse, the *mystagogoi*, who took visitors around to see the sights. When he went to Segesta, the first thing his hosts took him to see was a famous statue of Diana (Artemis). Appreciating famous works of Greek art, whether in Rome through capture or loan or still *in situ* for Roman tourists abroad, was taken for granted by Cicero.[3]

Besides firsthand experience of seeing many statues and other works of art on display in public, some degree of knowledge about Greek art and artists was acquired as a part of basic rhetorical education. Well-known artists and their work were used as a didactic paradigm,

---

[3] On Roman tourism of ancient displays of art abroad, see L. Casson, *Travel in the Ancient World* (Baltimore and London, 1994 [1974]): 238–252; for later Roman travel and pilgrimage, see the essays in S. Alcock, et al., eds., *Pausanias. Travel and Memory in Roman Greece* (Oxford, 2001).

considered a useful analogy for developments in rhetoric, so that educated people would be expected to be conversant with a range of artists and their work. Such paradigms were reductive of detail and not scholarly, rather they were part of a general fund of knowledge that could be put to good effect. Earlier Greek "art historical" treatises, now lost, are mentioned by Pliny as his own sources, such as those by Xenocrates, Antigonus, and Duris (*NH* 1, index for 34).[4] Such treatises seem to have been intended either as historical commentary or for practitioners, and at least some were written by artists (Xenocrates was a sculptor); it seems likely that at least a few Romans (besides Pliny) read them. Hence a good general knowledge of art and artists could be assumed of Cicero's audiences, gained from firsthand experience of a wealth of art and from basic education, but only a few would have had technical or scholarly knowledge.

Private ownership of statuary and paintings quite likely began in the second century BCE. Items not dedicated by generals could be purchased from booty, and no doubt the beginning of an art market from Sicily, Greece, and Asia Minor was under way at the latest after Mummius' sack of Corinth in 146 BCE. This is attested further in finds from shipwrecks that include sculpture, such as the Mahdia wreck found near Tunisia in 1907. Here, the issue becomes more complex since such cargoes include not only older sculpture but new sculpture as well; not only was there older, almost "antique" Greek art but also contemporary art made for contemporary Roman clientele, more properly termed *Roman* art.[5] Romans were already interested and knowledgeable consumers of

[4] J. J. Pollitt, *The Ancient View of Greek Art. Criticism, History, and Terminology* (New Haven and London, 1974): 73–78; for thorough discussion of early "art history" and how it was distinct from our present-day art history, see J. Tanner, *The Invention of Art History in Ancient Greece. Religion, Society and Artisitic Rationalism* (Cambridge, 2006), especially 212–254.

[5] For accounts of the "market" for Greek art in earlier periods, see A. F. Stewart, *Greek Sculpture, An Exploration* (New Haven and London, 1990): 56–64; in the later Roman Republic, J. J. Pollitt, *Art in the Hellenistic Age* (Cambridge, 1986): 150–163. That the cargo of the Mahdia wreck was destined for Italian customers is widely accepted; Ridgway emphasizes

antique Greek art and contemporary (Roman) art by the time of Verres' trial. Nonetheless, much of the evidence for art-dealing discussed in recent scholarship – including letters of Cicero – actually belongs to later decades, after Verres' trial and exile.

Art continued to enter Rome as military plunder in the first century BCE. When Verres began his term as governor in Sicily in 73 BCE, only thirteen years had passed since Sulla had sacked Athens and acquired a large haul of artistic booty, although some of it had been lost at sea in transit to Rome. Sulla's campaigns in the east brought so much of it that one author, Sallust, moved the trope of Romans acquiring a fresh taste for art (also attributed to the aftermath of Syracuse, Pydna, or Corinth) to this later date (*Cat.* 11); military plundering of art from the Greek east would continue for several decades. Of the three major occasions that plunder was brought to Rome, Sulla's triumph in 81, Lucullus' in 63, and Pompey's triumph in 61, it was the latter's display of a remarkable haul of luxurious items that excited considerable comment.

Verres was a collector of a peculiar sort because he would stop at nothing to acquire Greek art. He had such a passion to own it that he broke several different kinds of property laws in getting it, doing so with outrageously unethical behavior. The extraordinary portrait of Verres given by Cicero is often used in discussions of Roman interest in Greek art as an (admittedly extreme) example, but his uniqueness in his era should be better acknowledged. There really is no recorded parallel for Verres until we look further into future history for other obsessive individuals.[6] His behavior should not be taken as an indicator of how

---

the significance of Greek production being directed to Rome (B. Ridgway, *Hellenistic Sculpture III* [Madison, 2002]): 10–11, *passim*.

[6] For the psychological view and numerous later examples of obsessive collectors, see W. Muensterberger, *Collecting, An Unruly Passion. Psychological Perspectives* (Princeton, 1994). On the idea of "collecting" in the Roman period, see R. Chevallier, *L'Artiste, le collectionneur & le faussaire. Pour une sociologie de l'art romain* (Paris, 1991); for a thorough study of Verres as a collector, see A. Bounia, *The Nature of Classical Collecting. Collectors and Collections, 100 BCE–100 CE* (Aldershot, 2004): 269–306.

his contemporaries behaved: there were others who extorted monies from provinces, others who collected art and who committed Verres' other crimes too, but the deeds of none compare in scale and intensity. Cicero makes this very clear.

THE LEGAL VIEW

Overall, the speeches show Cicero to be more interested in how Verres acquired the artistic items and intended to use them, and how they were appropriately used by their proper owners, rather than the full details of what they were. (To establish their value, however, he does describe them and I discuss the criteria he uses in the next section.) Although the legal charge is extortion, not theft, accusations against Verres of theft, pillaging, spoliation, and piracy abound in the text: some of this could be considered normal insults and invective used in Roman legal cases, but the actual legal thinking and terminology in use at the time of the trial surrounding concepts of property are worth considering. They show how Romans of Cicero's time viewed the intersection between religion and law and provide some context for how his immediate audiences would have perceived the accusations about the theft of art.

The composite legal authority closest in date to Verres' trial is the *Institutes* of Gaius, a legal teacher who wrote his elementary textbook on Roman law about 160 CE. On religion and property (*res* in Latin), Gaius says, "The principal division of things is into two classes: for some are subject to divine law, others to human law. [3] Subject to divine law are *res sacrae* and *res religiosae*. [4] *Res sacrae* are those consecrated to the gods above, *res religiosae* are those dedicated to the gods of the underworld."[7]

---

[7] Gaius 2.2–4, translated and discussed by A. Watson, *The State, Law and Religion. Pagan Rome* (Athens, GA, and London, 1992): 55; discussed also by F. de Zulueta, *The Institutes of Gaius*, 2, *Commentary* (Oxford, 1946[1953]): 55–57; A. Watson, *The Law of Property in the Later Roman Republic* (Oxford, 1968): 1–15.

This classification, some 230 years after Verres' trial, shows a clear bifurcation in the category of property (divine and human) that in the time of Cicero may have been more complex and not exactly as Gaius prescribes. M. Crawford has shown that epigraphical evidence, together with evidence from Cicero himself and other contemporaries, provides an additional way of thinking about these divisions.

A more accurate model emerges if we start with the concept of property, together with how its illegal removal is described. Property could be described as sacred, public, or private: *res sacrae, res publicae,* or *res privatae*. The theft of private property is *furtum* (theft); the theft of public property is *peculatus* (embezzlement of public monies or other public property); the theft of sacred property is *sacrilegium* (sacrilege). Crawford finds that the classification of these terms in the late Republic, although imperfect, shows that the essential boundary is not between divine and human (as Gaius has it ca. 160 CE) but rather between the sacred and the public together, and the private.[8] A. Watson, however, stresses that Gaius was correct even for this earlier period because there was absolute public control of the boundaries between both public and private and private and sacred.[9]

Part of the evidence for the dual boundaries is the word *profanus*, used by Cicero not as we sometimes use the English derivative to describe something defiled or irreverent or that used to be set aside for religious reasons but is now used commonly, but rather to describe everything that is not sacred. Cicero uses the word this way in the *Verrines*, saying that Verres literally took everything from Sicily, left nothing behind, "neither private nor public, neither consecrated (*sacri*) nor unconsecrated (*profani*)" (2.4.2). In describing Marcellus' actions as general when he conquered Syracuse, Cicero says he spared all buildings, public and

[8] M. Crawford, "Aut sacrom aut poublicom," in P. Birks, ed., *New Perspectives in the Roman Law of Property* (Oxford, 1989): 93–98.
[9] Watson (1992): 56, and n. 11, 117–118.

private, consecrated and unconsecrated (2.4.120).[10] These conceptual divisions and their juridical use underscore the legal perspective on Verres' violations: he not only transgressed normative ethics and behaved in a way offensive to religious propriety and feeling, but also he was actually and specifically guilty of three kinds of property violations. By removing something *sacra* and putting it into his private house, he is not only committing sacrilege, he is also violating (both Greek and Roman) public rights to it: an obvious deduction, but one with legal force in the late Republic.

Gaius also acknowledges distinctions between Rome and the provinces, saying "[7a] Again, though a thing consecrated in the province otherwise than under the authority of the Roman people is not strictly *sacrum*, it is nevertheless considered as such."[11] Hence the temples and shrines in Sicily, according to this usage and custom, were regarded legally as *sacrum*.

Yet another charge evoked in Cicero's choice of language and descriptions is that of *latrocinium* (banditry or piracy). As de Souza has shown, piracy is a major theme that runs throughout the speeches and it is evident in Cicero's choice of words.[12] Cicero describes the Mamertines in Messana as pirates, in collusion with Verres, and as analogous to the people of the city Phaselis that harbored the pirates of Cilicia (2.4.23, 2.5.59). Verres himself is frequently described as a *praedo* or *pirata*, in one case even worse than the pirates, who had respected the sanctity of the ivory tusks in the Temple of Juno on Malta (2.4.103). Piracy had become a significant problem in the Mediterranean in the two decades preceding the trial, so that in his use of piratical vocabulary, Cicero was tapping into a much-discussed topic of considerable concern to anyone

---

[10] Crawford (1989): 96–67; Cicero repeats the two antitheses in 2.5.1, saying that Verres plundered everything: *sacra profanaque omnia et privatim et publice spoliarit.*
[11] 2.7a, *The Institutes of Gaius*, 1, translated by F. de Zulueta (1946[1953]).
[12] de Souza (1999): 150–157.

even remotely involved in business, shipping, military affairs abroad, or wishing to travel. Julius Caesar had been kidnapped and ransomed by pirates as recently as 75/4 BCE, just before Verres' term as governor began. So serious had this problem become that just three years after the trial, in 67 BCE, Pompey was given *imperium* to rid the Mediterranean of pirates. Afterward he displayed the beaks from captured pirate ships in the atrium of his house.[13]

In building his legal case, Cicero emphasizes violations of property rights of several different kinds: public and private, sacred and ordinary. The insulting language he uses for the accused is drawn from the vocabulary associated with those infractions surrounding the charges, with the addition of sexual innuendo. Cicero observes a certain *decorum* (propriety) in the kinds of accusations he refrains from making, however. He does not insult Verres' wife or children: the young son is mentioned as present at the seaside feasts in Syracuse, as the subject of an honorary statue, and again when Cicero chastises Verres for exposing the boy to unseemly transactions (2.3.159–162), but we do not learn the boy's name. While Verres is depicted as effeminate, lazy and self-indulgent, and derelict in his duty as *praetor*, Cicero does not take up overt laments about *luxuria* in the consumption of food or other personal habits. True, his parties were raucous, but Cicero does not say Verres himself was carried away dead drunk, only that his guests were (as though the battle at Cannae had just been fought; 2.5.28). Cicero does not accuse Verres of any sort of violation of tombs or graves or their statuary or other decoration, even though Greek cemeteries in Sicily and abroad were full of the sort of antique statuary that might have appealed to Verres. Verres was responsible for putting people to death unjustly but evidently he was not a tomb robber.

---

[13] Cic. *Phil.* 2.26.68. For a history and interpretation of displays of booty in Roman domestic contexts, see K. Welch, "*Domi Militiaeque*: Roman Domestic Aesthetics and War Booty in the Republic," in Dillon and Welch (2006): 91–161.

DESCRIPTIONS OF ART

The social aspects of the Roman house, its decoration, and furnishings have received a great deal of recent scholarly attention, focused on Campania, where the evidence was best preserved by the eruption of Mt. Vesuvius in 79 BCE. The excavations of Herculaneum, Pompeii, and nearby villas have yielded a vast quantity of artifacts that illustrate Roman taste in this part of Italy. The last century or so of Pompeii's existence, from the Augustan era onward, is also a period when ancient authors commented often about changing social conditions, so that we have both individual voices as well as artifacts for interpretation. Thanks to this recent research, social practice reflected in the use of art during the very end of the Republic and the early empire has been well documented and analyzed. Cicero's comments on Verres stand at the beginning of a lengthy cultural discourse on the ownership and use of art: in his life-time Cicero would see and participate in great changes in the public and private consumption and display of art. The *Verrines* offer a detailed view of what was considered appropriate (and what was not) in one year, 70 BCE, in relation to events in Sicily over the preceding three years.

Cicero's speech devoted to Verres' unlawful acquisition of art builds on the additional instances of his thefts abroad in mainland Greece and Asia Minor already noted in the previous speeches. The foremost category of art discussed by Cicero is statuary, the most prestigious type of ancient representation, and the one that kept famous people, heroes and gods in the visual topography of cities. Other categories subject to collection include panel paintings, highly esteemed both for narrative content and skillful, lifelike representation; elaborate vessels, whose workmanship and material made them highly sought after; other types of domestic consumer goods such as tapestries and furniture; and other collectibles, including cameos, gems, seals, and rings. Of particular interest were their symbolic qualities, above all religious associations:

this aspect is the source of their highest value. The descriptions Cicero uses for making the art vivid to his audience, and where and how he thinks it should be used or placed, is interwoven with his scathing criticism of Verres' collecting activities in Sicily.

In the *Verrines*, Cicero approaches art in the art-historical mode familiar today that includes age, monetary value, attribution, previous ownership or historical association, and some aesthetic consideration. In addition he focuses particularly on the criterion of sanctity – that is, how the item functioned within its intended religious context (from which Verres uproots it). Cicero sought ways to convey the value attached to these items by the Sicilians that would elicit empathy in his audience of Romans, who would realize that the possessions meant far more to their owners than just comfortable goods. The presupposition of "shared values" between Greeks and Romans is striking. These critical judgments, even the familiar ones, should be examined more closely. I begin with the obvious ones, then proceed to the more complex criteria, all of which form an interlocking web.

Age

The age of a statue was an added value, assuming that other desirable qualities were present. Verres leaves behind a wooden image of Bona Fortuna (Agatha Tyche) in the private shrine of Gaius Heius that does not interest him, presumably because it is wooden. But the cult image of Herakles in the Temple of Herakles at Agrigento interests him very much; it is clearly both old and venerable, with its chin and beard partly worn away, smoothed by devotion. The image of Ceres at Henna is *antiquissima* (most ancient) as well as *religiosissima*.

Monetary Value

The monetary value of the art is discussed in refutation of Verres' presumed defense, that he bought rather than looted them. Cicero again has gathered extensive documentary evidence, showing absurdly low prices. He cites the normal prices for such items – some twenty-five times higher than what Verres paid. These prices may be compared with those paid by his contemporaries such as Caesar, Metellus Scipio, Lucullus, or Hortensius for paintings and statues: they do not seem exaggerated.[14] The more important point for Cicero, however, is that no individual or city would willingly part with their famous works of art for any sum. Would Knidos sell the Aphrodite (by Praxiteles) or the Thespians their Eros? He names nine Greek cities and their famous works of art that contribute to their civic identity; the statues and paintings clearly had not yet been taken as plunder (2.4.135). Some of them, such as the Aphrodite, were actually cult images.

Artist

The attribution of a work to a famous artist clearly adds value and makes it more significant, important, and desirable. Plutarch pictures Romans first becoming aware of this from Marcellus' booty from Syracuse, with social critics complaining that people were spending too much time talking about artists and aesthetics (see Appendix, no. 5). While the influx of art surely excited comment and interest, as I have noted previously, it is quite unlikely that Romans were so unsophisticated before then, as Plutarch (an educated Greek himself) probably enjoyed imagining. Awareness of "famous" artists would have begun much earlier, at least in the sixth century BCE. Pliny gives names of Etruscan sculptors such as Vulca of Veii, who made the terra-cotta statues for the roof of the Temple of Jupiter Optimus Maximus on the Capitoline; named Greek artists were brought to Etruria; the Roman aristocrat C. Fabius Pictor signed his paintings and perhaps

---

[14] Pritchett provides a convenient table of citations from Pliny of a selection of prices for works of art paid by noted collectors (*Greek State at War* 5: 107).

made painting respectable, for a while, among the elite (ca. 300 BCE). Pliny says he saw the paintings himself before they perished in a fire and provides many other nuggets of information about early named artists.[15] By Pliny's life-time, the list of Greek sculpture and painting by named artists known to have been displayed in Rome is lengthy.[16]

For Cicero, however, the recitation of Greek artists' names and the qualities and achievements of their output was something he would have learned as a young student, since it had already become a common trope in the repertoire of imagery for teaching and using rhetoric. In his handbook of rhetoric, Quintilian provides our fullest discussion: theories of rhetorical skills considered the art histories (actually the trajectory of sculptors and painters) useful analogies for the development of rhetorical styles. In his pathbreaking study of Greek and Latin terminology and explicit ancient art criticism, J. J. Pollitt subjects the Greek and Latin authors who mention the qualities of art to intensive and authoritative analysis in his *Ancient View of Greek Art* (1974). He thoroughly investigates the rhetoricians' use of mini-art histories as illustrations of the "evolution" of types of art, following a biological model from a less mature state to perfection, then decline, and suggests that both Cicero and Quintilian probably used the same earlier source, possibly Poseidonius (at least as an intermediary).[17] In a scheme given by Cicero in the *Brutus* (70), for example, the sculpture of archaic Greek artists such as Kalamis or Kanachos seem stiff, Myron's work is not completely natural but is "beautiful," and Polykleitos' work is perfect.

[15] For the pertinent ancient passages, see J. J. Pollitt, *The Art of Rome c.753 B.C.–A.D. 337. Sources and Documents* (Cambridge, 1983): 6, 8, 26; Ridgway (1984): 19–24.
[16] See the lists in J. J. Pollitt, "The Impact of Greek Art on Rome," *TAPA* 108 (1978): 170–174; and Ridgway (1994): 109–111. The accuracy (by modern standards) of such stated attributions by ancient authors, including Cicero in his speeches on Verres, is difficult to assess.
[17] Pollitt, *Ancient View* (1974): 61–62, 81–84; see also Tanner (2006): 292–295.

He gives a similar cycle for painting, with Apelles at the apex.[18] Pheidias is regarded as the greatest artist – the peak of perfection – by most authors, including Cicero in another context (*Orat.* 8–9).[19]

Because Cicero was surely quite well versed in all this, modern commentators on the speeches have pointed to two passages (2.4.4, 2.4.5) in which Cicero seems to fumble for a name as instances of blatant hypocrisy or at least disingenuousness, pretending not to know what he certainly did know. In explaining to his audience why the Sicilian Greeks cared so much about the loss of statuary and other art, he seems to distance Romans, saying that we, of course, would regard these things as trifles: a seeming condescension to Greeks (2.4.132). In many other passages, however, he speaks quite fluently and learnedly about art, naming other extant versions by the same artist (e.g., the marble Eros by Praxiteles) and where they may be found, and assumes his audience is also sophisticated enough to appreciate these facts.

The modern commentators have assumed that he pretended not to know or care much about "art" either because supposed neo-Catonian reactionaries among the jury would disapprove, or such knowledge was considered inappropriate or déclassé among his peers, or because he did not want to be identified with Verres, who cared passionately about art. These assumptions have no supporting evidence and should be discarded. In fact, they may be traced back to presuppositions about the supposed vast superiority of Greek art over Roman art and Roman unoriginal copying of Greek art that are rooted in the late eighteenth century. On the contrary, Cicero, presupposing a sophisticated audience, makes fun of what he presents as Verres' pretensions to connoisseurship

---

[18] These and other pertinent texts are given conveniently in J. J. Pollitt, *The Art of Ancient Greece. Sources and Documents* (Cambridge, 1990): 221–234.

[19] For the influence of this rhetorical scheme (a sort of "hall of fame" of artists) on J. J. Winckelmann and the subsequent development of art history, see the essential discussion of A. A. Donohue, "Winckelmann's History of Art and Polyclitus," in W. G. Moon, ed., *Polykleitos, the Doryphoros, and Tradition* (Madison, WI, 1995): 327–353.

by posing briefly as the opposite. Anne Weis demonstrates that his tone is meant as a sort of burlesque of an ignorant person, in opposition to Verres, whom he sarcastically posits as the true connoisseur who alone among Romans appreciates Greek art, and is ironically intended in those few passages.[20] Further, he assumes the whole audience is well informed and could (and would) prompt him if really necessary: we are meant to imagine the "crowd" in the Forum calling out the famous names, in a form of audience participation in the speeches. That is the atmosphere he deliberately evokes.

Provenance

Previous associations with Romans are emphasized over Sicilian owners except when the item has a very particular link to Sicilian history that adds piquancy or interest to the item. Cicero uses the previous ownership or historical association to invoke the generosity and humaneness of Scipio Aemilianus, who repatriated items that had been taken as booty to Carthage, as we have seen. One of the items returned by Scipio, the Bull of Phalaris, was important to the people of Agrigento because of its previous owner Phalaris, who was said to have used it terribly; they survived his cruelty and tyrannic rule (see Appendix, no. 6). Evidently, Verres did not want the bull. Marcellus and his restraint in war are invoked by what he did not take in the siege of Syracuse, including dedications in the Temple of Athena at Syracuse and its gold and ivory doors, and a significant statue of Zeus from the Temple of Zeus removed by Verres. Other items Verres removed from the Temple of Athena, now the Duomo of Syracuse, included a set of paintings representing a cavalry battle of Agathocles and more than twenty-seven

---

[20] A. Weis, "Gaius Verres and the Roman Art Market: Consumption and connoisseurship in Verrine II.4," in A. Haltenhoff et al., eds., *O tempora, o mores! Römische Werte und römische Literatur in den letzten Jahrzehnten der Republik* (Leipzig, 2003): 359–365, with discussion of earlier views. The nineteenth-century interpretations of Cicero's "feigned" ignorance are discussed by Cowles (1917): 127–135.

FIGURE 10. Temple of Athena (Duomo), Syracuse. Photo credit: Author.

paintings of past rulers of Syracuse, valuable not only for artistic merit but also as educational documents, says Cicero (2.4.123)[21] (Fig. 10).

Aesthetic Quality

For the criterion of aesthetic quality, Cicero sometimes resorts to generalities such as to call it "beautiful" (e.g., an extremely "beautiful" [*pulcherrimus*] statue of Apollo, on whose thigh was Myron's signature in small silver letters, which had been returned by Scipio [2.4.93]). The Canephorae of Polykleitos are vividly beautiful (*venustas*) (2.4.5). He also uses more precise evaluative terms. He says the Diana (Artemis) of Segesta was a work of extremely fine workmanship, of great size and

---

[21] On these interesting historical paintings, evidently forming two cycles, see F. Coarelli, "La *Pugna Equestris* di Agatocle nell'Athenaion di Siracusa," in *Revixit Ars. Arte e ideologia a Roma* (Rome, 1996 [1982]): 85–101.

height, but nonetheless had the youthful grace one would expect of a maiden; he then describes her attributes, the quiver on her shoulder, bow in her left hand, and a torch in her right hand (2.4.74). From a temple on Malta, Verres took several ivory Victories, made with "ancient workmanship, the highest skill" (*perfectus*) (2.4.103). An image of Sappho by Silanion also wins his praise: it is perfect, elegant, elaborate (*perfectus, elegans, elaboratus*) (2.4.126). Aesthetic qualities became well established in both Greek and Latin, and there is an extensive vocabulary that was used by rhetoricians and philosophers in technical treatises and by Cicero, Vitruvius, Pliny, and Quintilian, in particular.[22] Among Latin authors, Cicero was a pioneer in his *Verrines* for finding the Latin vocabulary for aesthetic qualities applicable to art.

These descriptive and evaluative categories, some precise and others less so, are quite familiar because we still use them.[23] They form the core of Pliny the Elder's (23–79 CE) descriptions of art in his encyclopedic treatise on nature and culture, placed within his discussion of metals and stone, earth and minerals. Pliny's purpose, as recent studies have emphasized, was to comment on the ethics of man's use of nature – hence the moralizing tone of many of his remarks.[24] Pliny's encyclopedia has never gone out of circulation, even though the motives of its audience

[22] Pollitt (1974) provides a glossary with commentary. Cicero's vocabulary is discussed by M.-L. Teyssier, "Cicéron et les arts plastiques, peinture et sculpture," in R. Chevallier, ed., *Présence de Cicéron* (Paris, 1984): 67–76, including the words *ordo* and *decentia* that Cicero uses in *Nat D* I.145 to explain how senses (the eyes) may lead to a refined aesthetic and moral perception, as in the visual arts.

[23] Current expectations have of course shifted, questioned, and expanded critical judgments; certain concerns such as "originality" of conception (or, at the least, novelty) were not important ancient criteria. The issue of searching for lost "originals" made by Greek artists by examining extant Roman emulations or versions of Greek prototypes is discussed later in this chapter.

[24] A. Wallace-Hadrill, "Pliny the Elder and Man's Unnatural History," *G & R* 37 (1990): 80–96; S. C. Marchetti, *Plinio il Vecchio e la tradizione del moralismo Romano* (Pisa, 1991); J. Isager, *The Elder Pliny's Chapters on the History of Art* (London and New York, 1991); M. Beagon, *Roman Nature: The Thought of Pliny the Elder* (Oxford, 1992); on the ideological and methodological structure of Pliny's work, V. Naas, *Le projet encyclopédique de Pline l'Ancien* (Paris, 2002);

for reading it and the choices of parts to read changed drastically. While for readers in the Middle Ages Pliny's text was authoritative for medicine and botany, for Renaissance artists and humanists it provided extensive information about ancient art and artists. When Lorenzo Ghiberti published the first commentary and Italian translation of the "art history" portion of Pliny's work (ca. 1450), he included himself and other fellow artists in his book.

Pliny's text was foundational for J. J. Winckelmann's more scholarly approach to art in the eighteenth century, in a shift in the way the ancient text was read from practical use to antiquarianism to art history. An example is the primacy given to the attribution of a work to a known artist, already explicit in Pliny's *Natural History*. Pliny feels it necessary to justify mentioning a statue whose artist is unknown and in one case, only special circumstances – that the statue's base had three inscriptions on it declaring the history of its placement – warranted its inclusion in his account (34.93). Through intermediaries, Pliny's schemata, terms, rubrics, and judgmental views are still part of art history. Pliny himself acknowledges his own debt to Cicero in several places, refers to him often, and to the case against Verres several times.[25]

In the Community

According to Cicero's presentation, what gives the art taken by Verres greatest value is its sacred associations: religion made images or other items truly important to the populace and to individual owners, more so than the criteria listed previously. Within the spectrum of what was "sacred," another distinction is articulated, that of "public" and "private," whose nuances are discussed further in this chapter. Publicly

on Pliny as an author and "collector" of facts, S. Carey, *Pliny's Catalogue of Culture. Art and Empire in the* Natural History (Oxford, 2003); on the authority and voice in the work as a whole, T. Murphy, *Pliny the Elder's* Natural History. *The Empire in the Encyclopedia* (Oxford, 2004).

[25] References to Verres: 34.6; 34.48; 36.22 (quoting *Verrines* 2.4.2).

sacred items were taken from temples, shrines, and agoras used by the whole community; Verres also took sacred items used in household shrines for domestic rituals. Cicero fulfills his objective of making all this matter to Roman audiences by showing that the violations of customary behavior not only indicated Verres' guilt but also were outrages against Roman gods that could bring down divine enmity on Rome as a whole because Verres as an official magistrate of Rome stood for the Roman populace as a whole. These actions were thus analogous to Q. Pleminius' theft of the treasury of Persephone at Locri (204 BCE) or Q. Fulvius Flaccus' theft of the roof of the Temple of Hera at Croton (173 BCE), two incidents considered serious enough that they were remedied by the Roman Senate, as noted in Chapter 1. Cicero's strategy includes linking each of the episodes in Sicily recounted here to the larger religious sphere that Romans shared with Sicilian Greeks. He draws on conventional ideas about respect for religious monuments that would seem persuasive to his immediate Roman audiences.[26]

CONSECRATED CULT IMAGES

Of everything stolen by Verres, whether from old Greece, the Cycladic islands, Asia Minor, or Sicily, Cicero considers nothing so egregious as his theft of the cult image of Ceres from her sanctuary at Henna in Sicily. Just before his description of this event, Cicero apologizes for the digression, saying that its magnitude did not allow him to summarize such a horrible crime (2.4.105).[27] Then follows the longest of all his descriptions of incidents concerning stolen art. He begins by

---

[26] For a general discussion of Roman religion in this period, see M. Beard, *CAH* 9² (1994): 729–768; *RoR*: 114–166. For a succinct account of Cicero's personal views, based on his later philosophical writings, see R. Schilling, "Cicero as Theologian," in Y. Bonnefoy, et al., eds., *Roman and European Mythologies* (Chicago, 1992): 123–125; of Cicero and others of the elite, A. Momigliano, "The Theological Efforts of the Roman Upper Classes in the First Century BC," in C. Ando, ed. *Roman Religion* (Edinburgh, 2003) (repr. *CPh* 79 [1984]: 19–211).

[27] On the use of *amplificatio* and other rhetorical aspects of Cicero's discussion of religion, see the useful remarks of U. Heibges, "Religion and Rhetoric in Cicero's Speeches," *Latomus*

saying the oldest Greek books and inscriptions indicate that the whole island is dedicated to Ceres and Libera (Demeter and Persephone) and that people believe they were born there. He recounts the rape of Persephone that occurred near Henna and alludes to Ceres' search for her daughter, using torches lit from Mt. Etna. There follows a lyrical evocation of the landscape, the festivals held to celebrate these events and the footprints (*vestigia*) or even the cradles (*incunabula*) of these divine persons. Because of the portents and numinous assistance she often gave, people believed that Ceres lived in Sicily and guarded it in person.

He comments that the intense devotion of the local populace to these goddesses extends to other people such as Athenians, who celebrate the Eleusinian Mysteries. Cicero links Ceres' sanctity to Rome, recalling that after Tiberius Sempronius Gracchus was murdered (133 BCE), prodigies indicated dangerous threats to Rome's general welfare. After consulting the Sibylline Books, the Roman Senate sent commissioners to Henna to perform expiatory rites. There was a beautiful, magnificent temple of Ceres in Rome, he explains, but the Sibylline Books ordered that the most ancient (*antiquissima*) Ceres (in Sicily) must be placated.[28] This very Ceres (*religiosissima*), the primary source for worship of the goddess among all peoples and nations, was taken from her own temple and seat by Gaius Verres.

Cicero then goes on to describe two other marble images in the two temples, of Ceres and Libera, of great size and notable beauty but not "old." The ancient bronze Ceres with her torches, of unique workmanship (*singulari opere*), he did take; two further statues of Ceres and Triptolemos were so large he did not take them, except for a Victory

---

28 (1968): 833–849. For Demeter (Ceres) at Henna, see V. Hinz, *Der Kult von Demeter und Kore auf Sizilien und in der Magna Graecia*, Palilia 4, 1998: 121–124.

[28] 2.4.106–108; the incident is discussed by B. Spaeth, *The Roman Goddess Ceres* (Austin, 1996): 73–79. The prodigies on this occasion (e.g., milk in a lake, owl, voice in a temple, birth of a hermaphrodite, and a girl with four feet) are collected and discussed in Rasmussen (2003): 154–156, Prodigy Table No. 94.

in the hand of Ceres, which he wrenched off, robbing one goddess of another goddess. Cicero says even retelling this makes him feel shaky and perturbed in spirit. He recounts his own visit to Henna, his reception by priests wearing fillets and carrying (suppliants') boughs, how the populace wept and groaned, complaining not of the financial extractions or the plundering of their private possessions, injustice in the courts under Verres, nor his many other outrages but of this atrocious violation, the theft of Ceres. It was as though the lord of the underworld had come again, this time to abduct Ceres herself.

He contrasts the behavior of the slaves who revolted in 132 BCE, who were besieged in Henna for two years but did not desecrate the sanctuary. He reminds the court that at stake here are the rights of allies, the authority of law, and the reputation and honor of the jurors (2.4.113). He then describes the religious terror in this area of Sicily, where everyone attributed anything that went wrong to Verres' sacrilege. He asks the jurors to restore the Sicilian's religious peace of mind and preserve their own (i.e., by finding Verres guilty). He sums up with the further point that this religion (worship of Ceres and Libera, Demeter, and Persephone) is shared by all and its rites performed by Roman forebears: How can we treat this with indifference? A. Vasaly has pointed out the sexual imagery in this episode and elsewhere concerning statues of young goddesses taken by Verres: the episode stands as an allegory for Verres' rape of Sicily.[29]

This event illustrates the power of the cult image, an effective stand-in for the goddess. In Latin texts, often the word for "image" (*signa, simulacrum, statua, imago*) is omitted, which makes the sense of identity

---

[29] Vasaly (1993): 120–124. The image of Ceres/Demeter described by Cicero, with Nike in hand until stolen by Verres, may be represented in bronze coinage of the Hellenistic period (after 258 BCE), suggests A. Giuliano, "Signum Cereris," in *Scritte Minori. Xenia Antiqua*, 9, 2001: 203–214. Examples of ill treatment of cult images and their consequences in the Archaic and Classical periods are collected and discussed by T. Scheer, *Die Gottheit und ihr Bild. Untersuchungen zur Funktion griechischer Kultbilder in Religion und Politik* (*Zetemata*, 105), 2000: 152–200.

between the statue and the deity even closer.[30] We see this in Cicero's suggestion that in his theft of the cult image, Verres was like a second coming of the lord of the underworld (*alter Orcus*). The close study of texts for the relationship between image and ritual has only begun, but so far it is clear that the devotee often posited an identity between a deity and the image. This is not a naïve identification but rather a way of making ritual feasible, focused, repeatable, and vivid. A representation of a deity in the form of a statue brings the god firmly into the community as a participant, especially when devotees behave toward the statue as a respected person. A recent study by J. Elsner of Pausanias' treatment of statuary shows this unambiguously. Pausanias elaborates even more than Cicero the ritual role served by images, often giving precise, almost clinical details.[31] Pausanias was writing about 250 years after Cicero and with a much different purpose. Yet his attitudes and criteria for evaluation in his descriptions of the sanctuaries in Greece follow well established conventions, even though his account is distinctive in other ways.

Verres was not always successful in his depredations. In two instances, both by proxy through gangs of thugs, he tried to take off cult images; in both cases, however, the townspeople managed to defend their sacred property. The townspeople of Agrigento are on the alert and react vigorously because Verres has just taken off a statue of Apollo (the one with Myron's signature in silver on the thigh) that had been returned to the city by Scipio and rededicated in the Temple of Asklepios. Much distressed, civic authorities arrange for a nightwatch over sacred temples. Verres did not dare to remove items openly, Cicero says,

---

[30] For a full discussion of terminology and its implications, see P. Stewart, *Statues in Roman Society. Representation and Response* (Oxford, 2003): 20–45; valuable comments in R. Gordon, "The Real and the Imaginary: Production and Religion in the Graeco-Roman World," *Art History* 2 (1979): 5–34.

[31] J. Elsner, "Image and Ritual: Reflection on the Religious Appreciation of Classical Art," *CQ* 46 (1996): 515–531.

because so many Roman citizens lived there. So he sent a body of armed slaves, led by his freedman Timarchides, to the Temple of Herakles to pry off its pedestal a venerable, ancient image, the one with the chin worn away with so many prayers and caressing pats.[32] The guards and watchmen try to defend the statue, but the thugs use clubs and cudgels against them and drive them away, and then break into the temple and begin applying crowbars to the statue. The guards raise the alarm in the town, and even the most elderly men get out of bed, grab whatever could be used as a weapon, and surge in a crowd to the temple. The thugs were having trouble prying off the statue and used ropes and levers but could not move it. Now the crowd started forward with stones to drive the thugs off, and they flee, taking two small statuettes as their booty (*praeda*). Cicero says the Agrigentines humorously gave credit to Herakles for driving away the monstrous hog (*verres* = boar) as yet another Labor (2.4.93–95).

The next episode takes place at Assorus, a small interior town in Sicily just northeast of Henna; Cicero says the local people copied the courage of the Agrigentines. A river that flowed nearby, the Chrysas, was revered by them as a numinous part of the landscape. On the road between Henna and Assorus, a country temple housed a distinguished (*praeclarus*) marble image of the personified Chrysas, featured on coins minted at Assorus.[33] Here, because of the exceptional sanctity of the temple, Cicero says, Verres used his Cibyratan "Finders" Tlepolemus and Hieron, two Greek brothers from Asia Minor who were accused of temple-robbery in their own town and were hired as art advisers and agents by Verres (one was a wax-modeler and the other was a painter).

---

[32] This would be similar to the medieval image of St. Peter in St. Peter's basilica in Rome, whose feet are partly worn off from touches over the centuries.

[33] B. V. Head, *Historia Numorum. A Manual of Greek Numismatics* (1911, repr. Chicago, 1967): 127; illustrated in R. Calciati, *Corpus Nummorum Siculorum* III. *La monetazione di bronzo* (Novara, 1987): 259, nos. 1, 2: said to be minted "after 212 BC" (i.e., during the period of Roman domination of Sicily).

They brought a band of armed men and broke down the door of the country temple to Chrysas. On the alert, guards gave a signal by cow horn, and all the nearby farmers converged to drive Verres' men off. The robbers succeeded in taking only one small bronze statuette (2.4.96).

The effective impact of Cicero's narration of these two incidents is that we see the Sicilians are not totally helpless in defending their sanctuaries, at least when Verres' *force majeure* as the Roman governor is reduced to the level of gangs of slaves and thugs, operating at night or in a sneaky raid out in the remote countryside. More tellingly, these events also provide the starkest contrast to the Roman custom of acquisition of art as booty through military conquest, heightened by Cicero's use of military terms in the Latin text. Actual warfare would be even more cruel to inhabitants but conducted through the laws of war, in daylight, in open confrontation, and against a declared enemy, not local farmers in peacetime. Furthermore, Roman wars were not waged with the specific object of acquiring the enemy's cult images.

DEDICATIONS

Many of the noted objects taken by Verres would be considered dedications – that is, statues (often representing gods) or other items set up by a community or individual in a sanctuary or temple in honor of the presiding deity as consecrated to him or her. They are viewed by both Greeks and Romans as the property of the god and thus have sanctity, although not to the same degree as the cult images themselves. The evidence for this view of the sanctity of a deity's possession for the Classical period is considerable. Extant financial inscriptions for various sanctuaries in mainland Greece (e.g., inventories for the Parthenon, construction accounts for the Eleusinion in Athens and in Eleusis, for the sanctuary of Zeus in Lebadia near Thebes) include rubrics for broken arrowheads, coils of rope, roof tiles, dismembered building parts, old baskets, and so forth that show the idea extended even to the deity's cluttered debris: this was a legal concern, not a matter of sentiment or belief. Whether these legal strictures could be maintained so vigorously in Greek sanctuaries of the first century BCE is less clear, but it seems still to have been the prevailing view. As we just saw in the episode at Henna, Verres took a statuette of Victory from the hand of an image of Ceres outside her temple, thus "robbing one goddess of another goddess."

The list of specific thefts of dedications begins back in the first speech of the *Actiones Secundae*, as Cicero lays out the pattern of Verres' earlier career as a *legatus* of Dolabella (2.1.44–54). As they move eastward toward Cilicia, Verres takes statues from Achaia, gold from the Parthenon, tries to take statues from Delos, and succeeds in taking the revered image of Tenes, the founder-hero of the city. Later he loaned the Tenes to a Roman aedile for a festival display when it was set up in the Comitium. The Roman party continued on to Samos, where Verres took statues from the Temple of Juno (Hera) from her famous sanctuary. At Aspendos in Pamphylia, he takes "all" the statues; while at Perga, he strips a statue of Artemis of its gold. Cicero uses this trail of thefts of dedications from Greek sanctuaries as a way of describing Verres' earlier career in public office before he became governor of Sicily.

Among the thefts of dedications within Sicily, Cicero highlights episodes that represent different geographical areas of the island: Segesta in the far west (see Fig. 11), Tyndaris on the north coast, Engyion in the interior, and the largest city Syracuse in the southeast coast, thus illustrating the geographical thoroughness of Verres' activities. The theft of the ivory tusks from Malta represents the outlying islands of Sicily. The thefts occur in differing contexts, showing variety, and the towns also represent the various people of differing backgrounds and histories in Sicily. Although in general Cicero generally characterizes Sicilians as "Greeks" in opposition to Romans, he was well aware of

FIGURE 11. Temple at Segesta, Sicily. Photo credit: Author.

ethnic distinctions and makes use of them in this account: (we) Romans should feel particularly empathetic to the people of Segesta because they share (our) ancestry as descendants of refugee Trojans.

The Diana (Artemis) of Segesta, whose aesthetic qualities Cicero particularly admired, was one of the items returned from Carthage by Scipio, as proclaimed on an inscribed pedestal Cicero saw. Some of the very oldest people even remembered the occasion when it was brought back, when she was greeted with great rejoicing. After serious financial reprisals and threats of total ruin both to the town and to its individuals, the community, in great grief, agreed to give up the statue to Verres (2.4.75–76). None of them would themselves agree to carry out the actual removal, so workmen were hired from Lilybaeum, whose contract Cicero collected as evidence. All of the women and girls of Segesta anointed the statue with perfumes, decorated her with flowers, and with incense escorted her as she is removed by Verres. Alluding to

Scipio Aemilianus, Cicero says, "Then, the commander of the Roman armies, a most honorable man, was returning ancestral gods to Segesta, recovered from an enemy city; now, from a city of allies the praetor, a most filthy and impure man, was carrying off those gods in an execrable desecration" (2.4.77).

In his initial description of the Diana of Segesta (he had seen it himself as quaestor in 74 BCE), Cicero asserts that its capture by Carthaginians and removal was only a change of people, for its original religious quality was preserved: the statue was so unusually beautiful that even a hostile people recognized that it was worthy of the greatest veneration (2.3.72). This comment is interesting for the positive spin Cicero gives to Carthaginian reception of Greek art as booty. Another incident seems to support his expectation that they intended to respect it; but, under duress, they are said to have worried about it. In this story, told by Diodorus and repeated by Curtius Rufus and Plutarch, a colossal bronze image of Apollo was set up in response to an oracle at Gela, east of Agrigento on the southern coast of Sicily. When Gela was sacked in 406 BCE, the Carthaginians plundered it thoroughly and transported this statue to their mother-city of Tyre in Phoenicia as a gift, where it was received with all due reverence and respect. Seventy-five years later, when Alexander besieged Tyre, the people of Tyre were worried that the Apollo might be on Alexander's side, so they bound the statue with gold chains (or ropes, in another version) and attached the Apollo either to its base or to an altar of Herakles, their own patron deity, in the hope of keeping Apollo with them. When Tyre fell, Alexander said the statue should be called Apollo Philalexander – but he did not return it to Gela.[34] These stories suggest a view that includes reverence but also presumes primary allegiance of the image (and deity) to the

[34] Diod. 13.108.4, 17.41.8, 17.46.6; Q. Curt. 4.22 (where the statue is from Syracuse); Plut. *Alex.* 24.4 (where the statue is reviled for supporting Alexander and nailed to the pedestal). Apollo Philalexander could be translated as the "Alexander-loving Apollo."

original owners – or at least the original ethnic group, broadly defined, that made it. It also sets apart the anxious Phoenicians from Greeks and Macedonians, probably the intention behind the story.

At Tyndaris, once again Verres covets another of the ancient statues returned by Scipio, an image of Mercury (Hermes), which people honored with an annual festival and depicted on coins minted at Tyndaris.[35] He peremptorily commands that it be removed and forcibly coerces a chief magistrate, Sopater, an elderly and distinguished town leader. When Sopater is obdurate and refuses the demand for its removal, Verres has him stripped naked in icy rain, tied to a bronze equestrian statue that represented one of the Marcelli family, and exposed there in the agora. When he was half dead and nearly frozen, the townspeople were moved by pity and forced the local senate to yield the statue. Sopater himself appeared as a witness in Verres' trial (2.4.92). The keeper of the gymnasium where the statue had stood was on hand as well, although Verres had tried to make a deal whereby the statue would be returned if he received in return all the written evidence against him.

At Thermae (the former Himera) on the north coast of Sicily, Verres coveted other bronze statues that had been returned from Carthage by Scipio, including a bronze personification of Himera (Dawn); a statue of the Archaic Greek poet Stesichoros, who had lived there, represented as a old man holding a book; and a statue of a she-goat (2.287). Each of the three statues is depicted individually on coins minted at Thermae.[36] He was blocked from taking these by the actions of a prominent businessman, Sthenius of Thermae, who had been his host and whose

---

[35] Head, *Historia Numorum*: 190; illustrated in Calciati, I: 81, no. 13, dated 254–214 BCE.

[36] Head, *Historia Numorum*: 147; illustrated in Calciati, I; 120–121, no. 16 (goat); no. 19, 20 (female, perhaps Himera or Dawn); no. 18 (Stesichorus, leaning on a staff and reading a book; dated ca. 345–275 BCE in *British Museum Catalogue*). C. Michelini takes a cautious view of whether the statues (returned by Scipio Aemilianus) are actually represented on coins ("Il patrimonio artistico de alcune *poleis* siceliote nel *de Signis* ciceroniano," in *Terze gionate internazionali di studi sull'area elima* (*Gibellina-Erice-Contessa Entellina*), 2000: 791–793). The Sicilian bronze coinage of this era has been difficult to date precisely, but some types are clearly continued

household furnishings and collection of antique bronze vessels Verres had already forcibly removed. Sthenius fled to Rome, however, where he had powerful connections, and complained to the Senate. This was the occasion when Verres' father tried to warn him that this case was causing a stir in Rome, but Verres ignored the warning and continued to prosecute Sthenius on a trumped-up capital charge *in absentia*, and confiscated all the rest of his property. In the end, Verres did not get the Himeran statues because of the support Sthenius had in Rome, and Sthenius is said to have testified against him at the trial (2.2.83–119).

In the cases of the theft of Corinthian bronze helmets, cuirasses, and hydriae dedicated by Scipio to the Magna Mater (Great Mother) from her temple at Engyion and of the elegant statue of Sappho from the prytanion at Syracuse, Cicero excoriates Verres' pretensions at connoisseurship. Did Scipio have so little taste that he did not know what he was dedicating, Cicero asks. Are spoils taken from the enemy now to become just household items of furniture in that man's house (2.4.97)? As for the Sappho, Cicero says sarcastically, such an accomplished and erudite person as Verres must have it – and we, the rest of us, if we want to see fine works such as this, we can go to the temples of Felicitas or Fortuna or the Portico of Metellus (all in Rome, places of display of art booty), or we can apply to visit the Tuscan villas of one of Verres' friends (2.4.126). Cicero wonders how long the jurors will tolerate this from someone so uncouth, better suited for hauling statues than collecting them. He notes further that the pedestal for the Sappho Verres left behind had a notable Greek inscription, which Verres would have taken if he could have read it. With those insults, he moves on to another theft of a consecrated cult image of Paean Apollo from the Temple of Asklepios at Syracuse and several more statues from other temples. The result is that the *mystagogoi*, the guides who take visitors

from earlier periods. On abused citizens of Thermae (Himera), see L. Bivonia, *Iscrizioni latine lapidarie del Museo Civico di Termini Imerese* (*Kokalos*, Supp. 9, 1994): 68–72.

around Syracuse, now reverse their explanations and describe what has been taken away (2.4.132).

COMMEMORATIVES

I have already commented on Cicero's emphasis on the repatriation of art by Scipio Aemilianus as an illustration of Scipio's magnanimity, but the repatriation had a significant political dimension as well. The body of dedications formed a special commemorative to Scipio, to the victory in the third Carthaginian war, and to Rome's claim to a more beneficent role toward Sicilians. Because they had been restored some seven decades earlier under extraordinary circumstances and were antiques, they acquired a political aura along with intensified sanctity. Cicero makes use of these themes by addressing a descendant of Scipio who is empanelled on the jury, P. Scipio Nasica, and requesting that he find a way to return the image of Diana of Segesta and the commemorative pedestal with his ancestor's name. He invokes the strong power of family tradition and reverence for ancestors, a primary cultural theme in Roman society. Cicero then offers to step in and take up the role of defender of this Scipio Nasica's ancestry, thus crossing a class boundary since Cicero himself is a "new man" (meaning that he cannot claim noble ancestry and centuries of politically prominent forebears but must demonstrate his own *virtus*). He will gladly do this to honor the memory of Scipio, such a great Roman that (we) all may claim him as our own.

This is one of several self-reflective passages in the *Verrines* on issues of class and status and the genuine political power that ancestors bring when invoked by their descendants.[37] A descendant of C. Marcellus, conqueror of Syracuse, is similarly addressed in an aside about the incident at Tyndaris, where the magistrate Sopater was tied up on a statue representing one of his family. Does not the current Marcellus

---

[37] The topic of the practical uses of ancestry is explored fully by H. Flower, *Ancestor Masks and Aristocratic Power in Roman Culture* (Oxford, 1996); on this aspect, 60–70.

feel his family has been tarnished by this terrible use of their statue? (2.4.89). Implicit is the symbolic but very real contemporary power of these commemorative inscriptions, dedications, and statues. The art restored by Scipio was in its original location once again but now had intensified and increased significance for both the Sicilian Greeks and the Romans: the emblems of the Sicilian past, even in their proper, original location, are grafted on to Rome's past and present.

Verres manipulated the custom of honorary portraiture that had started in the Greek east but had long since arrived in Etruria, Rome and Italy generally. Pliny states that the first commemorative statues of individuals set up officially were the portraits of the deceased Tyrannicides Harmodios and Aristogeiton, in the Agora of Athens in 510 BCE (and then taken by Xerxes off to Persia as booty, but soon replaced and eventually returned, as we saw in Chapter 1 [Fig. 3]).[38] Greeks felt then that portraits of individuals should be reserved for the dead or for victorious athletes in Panhellenic festivals. In the course of the Classical period, however, the social restrictions began to weaken and honorary portraits of living people were occasionally set up with institutional authority. By the Hellenistic period, individuals (including women) were often honored with painted or statuary portraits. In Rome, portraits of individuals set up in public had to be approved by the Senate or People (unless in the home, in a cemetery, or in a temple, where the statue would belong to the deity); they were usually specifically honorary.[39]

By the time of Verres' governorship, a set of expectations was implied by the financing and setting up of an honorary portrait, most

---

[38] 34.17; for the archaeological evidence, C. Mattusch, *Greek Bronze Statuary, From the Beginnings through the Fifth Century B.C.* (Ithaca, 1988): 119–127.

[39] Good overview in J. Tanner, "Portraits, Power and Patronage in the Late Roman Republic," *JRS* 90 (2000): for Rome, 25–30, for provinces, 30–36 (with the *Verrines* as important evidence). For discussion of the literary sources on the development of Roman honorary portraits, see M. Sehlmeyer, *Stadtrömische Ehrenstatuen der republikanischen Zeit, Historia,* Einzelsch. 130 (Stuttgart, 1999): 27–44; for the contexts of honorary portraits in the empire, see P. Stewart (2003): 79–117.

importantly involving the patron–client relationship so fundamental to the workings of Roman society and their relations with foreigners.[40] In a perversion of the concept, Verres exacted money for such statues, even coerced financial contributions from people holding minor offices or from other specific groups of individuals and from towns throughout Sicily, with the threat of violence as a reprisal for noncompliance. In Syracuse, for example, the city paid for statues of Verres, his father, and his son. But he demanded one for the agora, one for the bouleuterion (senate house), one to be set up in Rome, and subscriptions for others from other groups such as the wheat farmers.

The embassies from Sicily finally submitted a petition in Rome requesting that they not have to promise portrait statues to a Roman official until he has left the province (2.2.146). In effect, not only was Verres demanding the honor but he was making money from it as well because his own freedmen handled the contracts. As a result, in Rome, two gilded equestrian statues of Verres were set up near the Temple of Vulcan, one of them inscribed ostensibly as from the wheat farmers of Sicily.[41] Representatives of these same farmers gave testimony against Verres in the trial, an embarrassing inconsistency Cicero elaborates to the detriment of the defendant. In any case, as soon as Verres left Sicily, nearly all the portrait statues were immediately attacked and thrown down by crowds: Cicero says he would not believe it (because it is shocking behavior) had he not seen them wrenched off the pedestals – he saw an empty pedestal at Tauromenium and a riderless horse at

[40] On this generally, E. Badian, *Foreign Clientelae* (264–70 B.C.) (Oxford, 1958): on Verres in particular, 282–284; somewhat different views in P. A. Brunt, "Clientela," in *The Fall of the Roman Republic and Related Essays* (Oxford, 1988): 382–442; overview in A. Wallace-Hadrill, "Patronage in Roman Society: From Republic to Empire," in A. Wallace-Hadrill, ed., *Patronage in Ancient Society* (London and New York, 1989): 63–87. Sehlmeyer (1999) provides a detailed analysis of the Roman custom of erecting honorary statues during the Republic.

[41] For the location of the Temple of Vulcan (*Volcanus*) in Rome, see Ziolkowski (1992): 179–183; if the association of C. Aurelius Cotta, conqueror of Lipara, with this temple is correct, then Verres' choice of location suggests a gathering of commemoratives with a Sicilian theme, in keeping with the two islands' volcanic features; see further Sehlmeyer (1999): 214.

Tyndaris. He notes that even the Rhodians did not overthrow statues of Mithradates VI, although they hated him; he found that Greeks have a tradition of sanctity attached to such honors (2.2.159). Yet, so strong was the revulsion against Verres that the people of Tauromenium, Tyndaris, and Leontini threw down his statues and huge mobs assaulted others at Syracuse (2.2.160). The local council at Centuripe also passed a decree calling for his statues there to be removed.[42]

All this had happened before Cicero arrived in Sicily to collect evidence against Verres. When Cicero saw statues of Verres and his son in the bouleuterion at Syracuse, he assumed the Syracusans would not give evidence against him, since they must have a patron–client relationship.[43] They groaned when they heard this and offered much evidence for the prosecution (2.4.138–139). Apart from the money extorted for their manufacture, Cicero suggests that the reason Verres had all these statues made – especially those in Rome – was to protect himself against prosecution: he could point to them as evidence of the honor and affection of the Sicilians toward him (2.2.167–168).[44] Thus, we see that in the case of newly created statues, even of himself, Verres does not follow customary behavior; he distorts and disrupts the expected Roman customs surrounding the patron–client relationship with foreigners and the Greek customs of honoring foreign benefactors.

AT HOME

While touring a Roman *domus* in Pompeii, the modern visitor is likely to be struck by how different the houses seem from modern

---

[42] Verres successor as governor, L. Caecilius Metellus (a supporter of Verres), required them to put the statues back, although they did not rescind the decree. Metellus stopped the overthrow of some statues; otherwise, no vestige of the statues would have remained in all Sicily, says Cicero (2.2.160–162). On Metellus' damage-control, see Brennan, *Praetors*: 492–493.

[43] Discussed further by Tanner (2000): 32–35.

[44] Sehlmeyer (1999: 213–214) and Brennan (*Praetors*: 488) suggest that Verres had them made with political goals in mind, to enhance his chances in a future consular election.

private houses. Although there is a clear progression of spaces and rooms, the shapes of the spaces and their architectural decoration resemble the areas of the Forum, but on a smaller scale: a true microcosm of the larger civic world, which also has its own coherent architectural language. What was "private" for a Roman was not the same as what we generally intend by the term two thousand years later. A sense of seclusion, of withdrawal from the world behind a barrier to it where we are free to behave however we wish is a quality we cherish (and for which we have legal protections), but Romans would not have wanted it on a daily basis. Romans with political ambitions even felt they must always behave as though they were in the public eye.[45]

Recent studies of the *domus* have illuminated the central importance of the house as a location for political and publicly oriented activities. In effect, the Roman *domus* served the functions of an office and reception area, as well as a place of hospitality and dining that often had business purposes and larger social connotations: thus, *negotium* was in effect combined with *otium* (business and relaxation).[46] The *domus* was a point of intersection of a smaller, chosen public and the family. These aspects are discussed and codified by Vitruvius, writing in the generation after Cicero (ca. 30–20 BCE) in his prescriptions for the construction of the

[45] Discussed by C. Edwards, *The Politics of Immorality in Ancient Rome* (Cambridge, 1993): 150–151. She cites the example of Livius Drusus, elected tribune of the plebs in 91 BCE, who when offered by an architect a design for a house on the Palatine that would prevent all spying, asked instead for a plan that would make him constantly visible (Vell. Pat. 2.14.2–4). See also A. M. Riggsby, "'Public' and 'Private' in Roman Culture: The Case of the Cubiculum," *JRA* 10 (1997): 36–56 for detailed discussion of gradations of "privacy," with specific references to the *Verrines*.

[46] Essential studies include E. Gazda, ed., *Roman Art in the Private Sphere* (Ann Arbor, 1991); J. Clarke, *The Houses of Roman Italy 100 B.C.–A.D. 250: Ritual, Space, and Decoration* (Berkeley and Oxford, 1991); A. Wallace-Hadrill, *Houses and Society in Pompeii and Herculaneum* (Princeton, 1994); J. Elsner, *Art and the Roman Viewer: The Transformation of Art from the Pagan World to Christianity* (Cambridge, 1995): 49–87; S. Hales, *The Roman House and Social Identity* (Cambridge, 2003). On the Roman concept of privacy, see Gazda: 4–6; on the origins of the aesthetic traditions (linked to the display of war booty), see the discussion in Welch (2006).

Roman house. In his treatise on architecture, he devotes one entire book to a discussion of the principles of design for houses and their decoration, including proportions for the atrium and the division of public and private spaces (book 6).[47]

Although they were on constant exhibit and open to the concerns and importuning of dependents in the *domus*, the Roman elite could retreat to villas in the countryside that had a more leisurely atmosphere. The rules of hospitality and social display were still maintained; at a distance from Rome, however, and with fewer visitors, it was possible to read and write, go for walks, think about new acquisitions and improvements to the property, and entertain friends. This is the picture we get from Cicero's letters to his brother and friends, preserved from the decades after Verres' trial, and comments in many other authors. Romans began building country villas in Campania soon after the defeat of Hannibal, and villas were also built closer to Rome at Sperlonga, Terracina, Praeneste, Primaporta, and Tivoli, and farther south at Velia, as attested to both by literary comments and excavations.[48] By the late first century BCE, Strabo could remark that the coast along the Bay of Naples appeared to be one long single city made up of villas (5.4.8 [C 247]).

Within a well-established set of architectural conventions, Roman owners expressed "individuality" in their town houses through the display of family history and ancestry, in the level of display of *luxuria*, and in matters of taste. Traditionally, the atrium was the most accessible of the rooms, usually positioned near the entrance, and the place where masks of ancestors (*imagines*), housed in wooden cupboards, and other items recalling past histories of the families were likely to be displayed. These might include ancestral trophies, *spolia*, paintings, and distinctive

---

[47] For translation and commentary, see Vitruvius, *Ten Books on Architecture*, trans. I. D. Rowland (Cambridge, 1999).

[48] On the history of Roman villas in Campania, see J. D'Arms, *Romans on the Bay of Naples* (Cambridge, MA, 1970); on Cicero's comments about social life there, 48–61.

or historical armor.[49] The atrium, according to Vitruvius, was a part of the house accessible even to uninvited guests.[50] With increased personal wealth in the course of the second century and early first century BCE, those who could afford it began to use more costly materials for the atrium. Eventually, this characteristically Roman feature was even adopted into houses in Sicily.[51]

Speaking of the accelerating competition in ever more lavish furnishings for houses, Pliny says, "The most accurate authors agree that in the consulship of Marcus [Aemilius] Lepidus and Quintus Catulus [78 BCE] there was no more beautiful a house in Rome than that of Lepidus himself, but, by god, within 35 years the same house was not among the first hundred" (36.109). Lepidus' house was the first to have a doorsill made of Numidian marble, a yellow stone quarried at Chemtou (in Tunisia), for which he was criticized, claims Pliny (36.49) – the criticism seeming to focus on the use of exotic marble as a threshold block. Cicero's references to Verres' house in Rome and villa(s) should be seen in this context: not yet had imported marble become commonplace in the *domus*, and the lavish villas with fishponds and long colonnades were still to come. The atrium of a senator was expected to be a place of austere family ancestry on display, contributing to a sober atmosphere by highlighting the traditional value of individual achievement in public service to Rome.

[49] See discussion in Flower (1996): 185–222; Welch (2006). For actual arms and armor on display, see E. Rawson, "The Antiquarian Tradition: Spoils and Representations of Foreign Armor," in *Roman Culture and Society. Collected Papers* (Oxford, 1991): 582–598 [repr. from *Staat und Staatlichkeit in der frühen römischen Republik* (Stuttgart, 1990): 157–173].

[50] 6.5.1; Varro (*Ling.* 5.161) also defines *atrium* as for common use of all (definitions discussed by Flower [1996]: 187–203). For wall decoration, especially First Style, see Flower's brief account, and R. Ling, *Roman Painting* (Cambridge, 1991): 12–22.

[51] L. Nevett, "Continuity and Change in Greek Households under Roman Rule: The Role of Women in the Domestic Context," in E. N. Ostenfeld, ed., *Greek Romans and Roman Greeks* (Aarhus, 2002): 81–97.

Cicero comments on the stolen art from the sanctuary of Hera on Samos he saw himself featured in the atrium of Verres' house in Rome:

> *What paintings, what statues he lifted from that place! I recognized them myself when I went to his house just recently, in order to seal up the evidence. Where are the statues now, Verres? I'm asking about those I saw just now, by all the columns, even in the spaces between columns, and in the greenery arranged in the open air.* (2.1.50–51)

Evidently, Verres' domus in Rome was up-to-date with a peristyle courtyard surrounding a garden, a feature adapted to Roman houses that was borrowed originally from the Hellenistic east as seen notably in excavated houses on Delos. Verres had recently sold off or given away much of his loot, Cicero suggests, in anticipation of having them sold off to pay his fines after being found guilty in the trial, but he kept the pair of statues from Samos. Cicero goes on to recall the testimony of Charidemos of Chios, who had been assigned patrol duty in a warship that accompanied Verres on a tour of the islands. Charidemos was later prosecuted by the Samians for robbing their sanctuary of Hera, but he was found innocent when he proved that it was Verres who had pillaged the sanctuary.

Then Cicero mentions the statue of a cithara-player taken from Aspendos – so famous it had become the subject of proverbs – also in Verres' house. Cicero comments that

> *You went to those cities with the rights and rank of* legatus, *but if you had invaded them by force with the rank of commanding general* (imperium)*, then, I believe, that any statues or art you would have taken from those cities you would transport not to your own house nor the suburban houses of your friends, but to Rome, for the public.* (2.1.54)

Cicero returns to this point later, in the fourth speech, when he wonders why Verres should be the one to own the Syracusan statue of Sappho by the artist Silanion, taken from the prytaneion (civic magistrates' building) at Syracuse and destined for a country villa (2.4.126).

Cicero builds on the military imagery of Verres' looting in the third speech (primarily concerned with the manipulation of the grain supply). He chastises the members of the jury who consider themselves friends of Verres and asks: Why should we who work hard for the Roman people and earn merit through our public service tolerate this robber who has too much of everything?

> *Should Verres decorate your villas with manubiae? Is it Verres who*
> *competes with L. Mummius [destroyer of Corinth], so that he is seen*
> *plundering more cities of our allies than Mummius plundered cities of*
> *our enemies, that he decorates more villas with art taken from temples*
> *than Mummius decorated temples with spoils from enemies? (2.3.9)*

Given the abundance and prominence of Mummius' dedications, this barbed criticism of Verres' friends must have struck its targets. Cicero continues on with theme of Verres "gifts" to friends, now in Sicily, not Rome, but again invoking military terms:

> *What spolia taken from the enemy, after what victory, from what*
> *praeda or manubiae is comprised the means for your gifts? (2.3.136)*

Apparently Verres gave as gifts gold rings to subordinates and friends, using his illicitly acquired funds to have them made.

Verres also evidently violated notions of appropriate use of space within the *domus* by carrying out business activities at home in the *cubiculum* (usually used for reclining or sleeping, as a "bedroom"). A. Riggsby has analyzed a range of testimonia that suggests Verres did not follow the usual customs in the way he made judicial decisions, awarded tax-contracts in the *cubiculum*, and permitted certain individuals entry that Cicero expected would be regarded as unseemly by the Roman jury.[52]

With reference to Verres' house in Rome as a place of business and his domestic arrangements, Cicero brings up repeatedly his mistress Chelidon. In the year before he became praetor in Sicily, Verres was a *praetor urbanus* in Rome and in that capacity had considerable authority over contracts and inheritances. According to Cicero, the legal specialists whose authority in such matters was customarily sought by petitioners found their houses standing empty, but Chelidon's house in Rome was always packed, thronged with petitioners. She served as an intermediary for Verres, and people soon realized that if they wanted anything accomplished, they should go through her (2.1.137).[53] Cicero says directly of Verres that far from excluding Chelidon from his house after he won election, he transferred to the *domus* of Chelidon his whole praetorship (2.5.38). Cicero refrains from denigrating Chelidon herself (other than to say that she is "that sort" of woman: *ut meretrix, non inhumaniter*) and refers to her as good-natured, even while accepting bribes.

In Sicily (after Chelidon had died), Verres found other mistresses to play that role, named Pipa and Tertia, who became the conduits for petitioners wanting relief from exorbitant grain tithes (2.3.78). Pipa's role became so well known that ribald graffiti were written repeatedly on the governor's tribunal (2.3.77). But Cicero still recalls Chelidon for his Roman audience with several references to the inheritance she passed on to Verres. After Verres wrests away a bejeweled gold candelabrum from prince Antiochus of Syria that had been destined to be dedicated in Rome in the Temple of Jupiter Optimus Maximus, Cicero wonders,

---

[52] Riggsby (1997): 47–48; *Verr.* 2.2.133; 2.3.56; 2.3.79; 2.5.27.

[53] The resulting situation was much like the scandal in England in 1809 that surrounded the Duke of York (Frederick Augustus, second son of George III), commander in chief of the Army, whose mistress was said to have supervised the awarding of promotions and assignments; the Duke of York had to resign but was reinstated in 1811.

should this candelabrum, promised to Jupiter himself, now stand in his *domus* and illuminate his orgies and debaucheries? Should the sacred candelabrum stand among art given to him by Chelidon? (2.4.71). A similar complaint is made on another ground about the Corinthian bronze helmets, cuirasses, and hydriae that Scipio Aemilianus had dedicated to the Great Mother at Engyion: spoils from the enemy, memorials of great generals, had now become just the household goods (*supellex*) of Verres (2.4.97).

In addition to the criminal mode of acquisition, the other Roman principle Verres violates by using this stolen art in his house, or giving it to others for their houses or villa, is that of *decor*, of what is appropriate, seemly or fitting in the aesthetic sense.[54] This Roman value lay behind many cultural aspects of Roman life, especially any contingent to public life; both aesthetic and moral (*decorum*), it underlies the deep Roman respect for ancestors, continuity from the past, and comprises a sort of authority for social and cultural matters. In an important study of the principle of *decor* in artistic choices, E. Perry demonstrates that it is crucial to understanding Roman styles and types of art that loosely recall earlier Greek styles. She points out that *decor*, always to be interpreted by someone with knowledgeable authority, validated tradition and helped to create a formulaic visual culture; it also left room for new interpretations because of the necessity to suit various contexts.[55] In the *Verrines*, the aesthetic principle of *decor* and its ethical equivalent *decorum* are conspicuously missing in that Roman governor's use of Greek art.

Cicero's complaints about the furnishing of Verres' house with his "booty" illustrate how Verres contravenes this principle, and he presumes this will outrage the jurors and his larger audiences – hence the lengthy and recurring discussion. What might be suitable for

---

[54] For a full discussion of these terms, see Pollitt (1974): 341–347.
[55] E. Perry, *The Aesthetics of Emulation in the Visual Arts of Ancient Rome* (Cambridge, 2005): 31–49.

conquering generals is not suitable for Verres (although the best of them, as we saw, did *not* use booty to decorate their houses); antique dedications from sanctuaries are *not* decorous additions to peristyle gardens; an elaborate bejeweled lamp-stand, previously dedicated to Jupiter, should *not* be used to illuminate Verres' dinner parties. A theme of complaint about *luxuria* runs in both Latin prose and poetry (especially typical of the Augustan period and later); in the passages I have just discussed, however, that is not the main concern. Cicero is angered first about the illicit acquisition of art, an offense then compounded by its indecorous use by Verres.

The Inner Sanctum

The Roman *domus* had provision for household religious observances. Most houses at Pompeii have *lararia* (shrines for the household deities, the *lares*) either on built-in altars, with miniature architectural framing, or on wooden altars that also resemble miniature temple-like enclosures. The *lares* and *penates*, and the *genius* (vital spirit) received daily offerings and were particularly important for rites of passage within the household. Western Greek houses also had household shrines, typically using small portable altars (well-preserved examples are in the museums of Syracuse, Agrigento, Palermo, and Reggio).[56] Some larger Greek houses of the Hellenistic period had fixed *sacraria* with images of deities installed, attested in excavations on Delos.

Cicero describes in detail one such private shrine, in the house of Gaius Heius of Messana, in a famous passage of the fourth *Verrine*, already much studied and discussed (2.4.1–18).[57] Heius was a successful

---

[56] For discussion of features (usually not permanent or architectural) in Greek houses for domestic offerings, see M. Jameson, "Private Space and the Greek City," in O. Murray and S. Price, eds., *The Greek City from Homer to Alexander* (Oxford, 1990): 171–195.

[57] On the skill of Cicero's presentation of this topic, Vasaly (1993): 111–114; discussed by Weis (2003): 359–365; fullest discussion with excavated comparanda in G. Zimmer, "Das Sacrarium des C. Heius. Kunstraub und Kunstgeschmack in der späten Republik," *Gymnasium* 96 (1989): 493–531 (with earlier bibliography).

Sicilian businessman with close ties to the international market on Delos and was very highly regarded within his community. He also had social ties of guest-friendship with prominent Romans. His *sacrarium* (chapel or shrine) was a special room set apart in the house and had several statues that had been in his family for generations: the two consecrated images that received offerings were a marble Eros by Praxiteles, similar to his famous Eros at Thespiae, and a bronze Herakles by Myron. They had altars in front of them. There were two other bronze images of young women holding baskets on their heads (Canephorae) by Polykleitos. Cicero says all Romans passing through Messana (the first stop in Sicily if one crosses from the Italian peninsula) would visit this shrine and that it was open daily for anyone who wished to visit – it was for all to enjoy, not just the owner.

Gaius Claudius Pulcher (*aedile* in 99, cos. 92 BCE) had borrowed this Eros when he had responsibility, as *aedile*, to provide suitably impressive furnishings for festivals and games in Rome; because he was a guest-friend of Heius' family, they lent it, and he returned the famous statue. Cicero comments parenthetically that until very recently (referring to Verres' loans of his art booty), such statuary displayed in festivals in Rome was typically on loan from friends, not plundered from friends and then carried off to one's *domus* or villa. In this instance, Verres took everything from Heius' private *sacrarium*, except for the wooden Bona Dea, and alleged that he had purchased them, but at ridiculously low prices, as we have seen. Cicero wonders how Verres has no sense of shame; he had stayed at Heius' house as a guest and had witnessed him performing offerings to those gods in his *sacrarium* (2.4.18). Heius came to Rome and provided testimony at the trial: he was supposed to give a "eulogy" of Verres on behalf of Messana, a community that supported Verres in return for reprieve on the expected tithes. Heius (who had also been bilked in other financial transactions by Verres) gave more than the eulogy, however, and the details about the statuary and other transgressions came out in public. Heius said all he wanted back were his ancestral images: Verres could keep the Canephorae.

Verres' now familiar pattern of violating sanctuaries and shrines thus extended into people's private houses. Cicero gives other examples by citing the confiscation of items associated with ritual: Verres was eagerly interested in collecting fine old silver and gold vessels. His interest seemed to be in their ancient and aesthetic qualities because after he obtained the vessels, he would pry off attached decoration and remount it on newer vessels, disregarding the original settings. Typically he would send his agents, the Cibyratan "Finders" Tlepolemus and Hieron, to gather up such items in each town. Many of these vessels were originally made and used for ritual purposes, in sanctuaries or in household shrines.

Cicero states that when Sicily was flourishing, the island was a substantial and major producer of this sort of art, so much so that most households, even those unable to afford entire services of silver, would at least have *patellae* (bowls), *paterae* (dishes for libations), and a *turibulum* (thurible, a vessel for burning incense).[58] These were used by the women of the household for rituals in the house (2.4.46). He remarks parenthetically that this equipment was of the highest craftsmanship and that once everything in Sicily must have been equally excellent; although her misfortunes deprived her of such treasures, the people still had managed to keep those that truly mattered because of their religious use. "I said, jurors, that there were once many of these among

---

[58] Weis (2003, 373–374, note 59) refers to several existing examples of Sicilian silver, including the Morgantina hoard (now in the Metropolitan Museum in New York, on loan from the Republic of Italy, and almost certainly taken illegally from Morgantina in Sicily). Malcolm Bell III, who reexcavated the robbers' trench at Morgantina, suggests that the hoard was taken to Morgantina and buried there just before Marcellus' sack of Syracuse ("La provenienza ritrovata: cercando il contesto di antichità trafugate," *BdA* Suppl. to n. 101, 1997 [2000]: 31–41 *apud* Weis, *non vidi*). Arrangements are being made for the return of the hoard to Italy.

all Sicilians," he says, "but I affirm that now there is not one" (2.4.47). He says we should imagine the tears and lamentations of the women and their bitter distress, as they had used these vessels for their daily rituals after inheriting them through generations and now they were snatched away.

Dining

Verres' covetousness of gold and silver vessels extended to dinner services as well. Here his un-Roman behavior violated another essential Roman value, that of hospitality and guest-friendship expressed through the customs surrounding dining. These social customs, the archaeological evidence for their setting, and dining as a theme in literature (especially Trimalchio's dinner in Petronius' *Satyricon*) have been much discussed in recent years. It is now well established that Roman dining was an almost choreographed ritual that enacted social status, display of wealth, hierarchy, and family structures. The Latin word for a dinner party, *convivium* ("living together"), was acknowledged in antiquity as emphasizing a unifying aspect in dining with family or associates.

Extending hospitality to foreigners or receiving it while traveling abroad included implications of potential political support or other social reciprocity.[59] These customs had earlier Greek versions as antecedents and parallels; a primary difference between the Greek and Roman spheres was that women usually did not participate in the Greek symposia, except as entertainers or sexual partners, and in the symposia more attention and time was spent in prolonged drinking. Verres' associates violated these Greek customs in an episode at Lampsacus in Asia

[59] Useful discussion of recent research in K. M. D. Dunbabin, *The Roman Banquet. Images of Conviviality* (Cambridge, 2003); J. F. Donahue, *The Roman Community at Table, During the Principate* (Ann Arbor, 2004); see also essays in W. J. Slater, ed., *Dining in a Classical Context* (Ann Arbor, 1991); for Greek dining, O. Murray, ed., *Sympotica. A Symposium on the symposium* (Oxford, 1990).

Minor, when they insisted that the unmarried daughter of the host be present at a dinner gathering.[60] The enjoyment of excellent and exotic foods and gastronomy as a special pursuit began in Sicily by the late fifth century BCE, and interest accelerated in the Hellenistic period. Romans continued and expanded this aspect of dining.[61]

Cicero says we should not expect him to make a house-to-house enumeration of everything taken but describes instead the basic pattern, with an emphasis on the Roman connections of the victims, so as to emphasize the violation of Roman norms. When Verres would arrive at a dinner party, a frequent event because he was governor, as soon as he saw any piece of service with embossed decoration, he would simply take it. Verres sometimes sent back the vessel after prying off the embossing, as in the case of a vessel owned by Cn. Pompeius Philo of Tyndaris, a Roman citizen. At the house of Eupolemos of Kaleacte, who was a friend of the socially prominent general Lucullus (and served in the Roman army with Lucullus in Asia Minor), Verres actually pulled off the decoration from two cups right in front of the other guests (2.4.49).

Another technique of acquisition, when Verres made the rounds of the island, was to summon a local magistrate and order all gold and silver vessels to be collected and sent to him at Syracuse.[62] The silver plate of Centuripe and the Corinthian bronzes of Agyrium were gathered this way, but at Haluntium, the ascent to the town was too steep for Verres,

---

[60] 2.1.63–67; analyzed by C. Steel, "Being Economical with the Truth: What Really Happened at Lampsacus?" in J. Powell and J. Paterson, eds., *Cicero the Advocate* (Oxford, 2004): 233–251.

[61] See A. Dalby, *Siren Feasts. A History of Food and Gastronomy in Greece* (London and New York, 1996), and A. Dalby, *Empire of Pleasures. Luxury and Indulgence in the Roman World* (London and New York, 2000).

[62] For the importance of silver and gold plate in Roman life, see D. E. Strong, *Greek and Roman Gold and Silver Plate* (London, 1966): 123–125; on its value and status, M. Vickers and D. Gill, *Artful Crafts, Ancient Greek Silverware and Pottery* (Oxford, 1994). It came into general use by about 200 BCE, after the second Punic War, when the silver mines from Spain were taken over by Rome, and the booty from Syracuse and Tarentum came into Rome. Shatzman discusses evidence for the escalating use of silver plate from the second century onward, including occasional sumptuary laws (1975: 96–97).

so he sent for the magistrate to attend him below and waited for the loot as he reclined on a litter by the seashore. Cicero pictures the scene in the town, everyone running to and fro, as if the Trojan Horse had entered, with vessels being torn from weeping women's hands, just as in a captured city (2.4.52). Cicero brings his audience back to Rome by saying he collected statements from the abused magistrates that were read at the trial.

Among the violations of hospitality, Cicero describes at length the circumstances of the offense to prince Antiochus of Syria (then a wealthy and powerful kingdom) because he sees it not merely as sacrilege and injurious to the reputation of Rome but also seriously harmful in foreign relations. The prince had come with his brother to Rome quite recently – Cicero expects the jurors to remember the two-year visit – to solidify his claim to his father's throne and lodge a claim for the throne of Egypt, held by the Ptolemies.[63] They were unable to present their claim to the Senate (Cicero says the state of public affairs in Rome prevented this)[64] and so decided to return home. As a gesture of goodwill, they had brought the lavish decorated candelabrum referred to earlier but could not dedicate it properly or with the appropriate public ceremony and attention because the temple of Jupiter Optimus Maximus on the Capitoline was still under repair after the fire of 83 BCE. They decided to take the golden, jeweled candelabrum back home and send it to Rome later for the reconsecration ceremony when the temple was completed.

The return trip took them through Syracuse, where Verres invited them to dinner. They prepared a banquet for him in return, using their own best plate, and a wine-ladle carved from a single precious stone with

---

[63] The prince's mother was a daughter of Ptolemy VIII Euergetes "Physcon," hence the claim, made in opposition to Ptolemy XII Neos Dionysos "Auletes," father of Cleopatra VII.

[64] At the time, Romans were fighting Mithradates VI, Sertorius in Spain, the Slave War (Spartacus), Dalmatians, and Thracians and were trying to deal with the pirates so prevalent in the Mediterranean.

a gold handle. Verres then asked the prince to "loan" him these items, which he did and thereby lost them. Not content, Verres implored the prince to let him "see" the candelabrum: the prince sent it to the governor, who was thrilled by its quality, huge size (because it was for a temple), and magnificence. Days passed, and Verres refused to allow the prince's men to take it back. Eventually there was a confrontation and Verres told the prince to leave the island; the prince went to the agora and made a public speech on the matter, declaring the candelabrum to have been a dedication for Jupiter. At this point in the speech, Cicero calls on Q. Lutatius Catulus, one of the jurors, who was responsible for the reconstruction of the temple on the Capitoline, to seek vengeance and satisfaction in this matter, emphasizing that Verres prevented a royal prince from making a dedication in that temple.

Cicero also makes use of the issue of dining and hospitality in his depiction of Verres in Syracuse, now in a sort of summer camp of linen tents set up by the shore near the spring of Arethusa on the island Ortygia, the oldest part of Syracuse. Although other governors would regard this as the peak time to inspect the island and attacks by pirates were still a constant threat, Verres was on vacation. There he is said to have held daily dinner parties for women, the wives of the Syracusans, including Pipa (who had replaced Chelidon). No other men were present, only Verres' young son and occasionally his freedman Timarchides, says Cicero. The whole episode reads like an inversion of a typical Roman convivium: it is outdoors, no or few male guests are present, it lasts many days.

The feasting had serious repercussions. To lure one very comely matron to the party, Verres put her husband Cleomenes of Syracuse (who was not a Roman citizen) in charge of the small fleet that was supposed to protect Sicilian ports from pirates. The fleet was deliberately underequipped and undermanned, and Cleomenes' courage was not a match for the pirates, who chased the little fleet into a port, captured some, and burned the rest of the ships. Meanwhile, the music and feasting went on near the shore by the spring of Arethusa. At least one captured captain was ransomed, another one killed, and the crews presumably sold into slavery. When the news was learned at Syracuse, the people came to the governor's palace and at last roused him out of bed, but it was too late: the pirates were able to enter into the Syracusan harbor – never before entered by an enemy – and after sailing around, waving trophies and mocking the townspeople, they left. To conceal any testimony that might be given by the remaining captains, Verres had them beheaded. So ended the series of summer dinner parties on the seashore (2.5.80–125).

After relating this episode, in the next passage Cicero sums up his criticism of the unethical mode of acquiring art. Now near the emotional culmination of the speeches, he says the people of Sicily are not asking back their gold, silver, tapestries, slaves, treasures, and the statues that once were in their temples; they want only justice. Cicero then asks whether any statue or painting that adorns Rome was not brought here from an enemy defeated in war. But, in contrast, the country-houses of these men (Verres and his friends) are overflowing with the most beautiful *spolia* they have robbed from our most loyal allies. "Where would you suppose is the wealth of the foreign nations who now are so poor, when you see Athens, Pergamon, Cyzicus, Miletos, Chios, Samos, in fact all Asia, Achaea, Greece and Sicily now contained within a few villas?" he asks (2.5.127). Cicero concludes the speeches with lengthy prayers and invokes the deities, enumerating as he names every god or goddess the major offenses committed against each by Verres: a brilliant summary of the whole charge.

Consumers and Traders of Luxury

Verres gathered up equipment and furniture that would allow him to play host on a large scale: he had bronze couches and bronze candelabra made and set up textile factories in various towns in Sicily where cloth is woven and dyed purple. In his defense, it was remarked that Verres supplied the dye and his friends supplied the (slave) labor. He collected Delphic tables (tripods) in great number and especially looked for citrus-wood tables, long favored by the elite.[65] He was also interested in tapestries, both embroidered and "Attalic," a style developed in Pergamon that includes gold threading, and coerced Heius to send him his Attalic tapestries (2.4.27). He also collected from people's private possession personal items such as *phalerae*, or "bosses" – that is, silver or bronze decorated chest plates for men, sometimes with horses' heads, based on the original custom of military use and then military decoration. He looked for *rhyta*, vessels used for drinking or libations in the shape of the forepart of animals, often horses; one victim of this theft, Calidus, complained at Rome over this. In an investigation of one part of Verres' accounts, Cicero says he is willing to overlook the four hundred amphoras of honey, but why so much Maltese cloth and so many bronze dining couches? Did he want to equip all his friends' villas? So large are the quantities of these luxury items that Cicero wonders several times whether (we) Romans have given *imperium*, the power of independent rule, to a merchant (*mercator*) so that he can go about his business unfettered.

Modern commentators have assumed that Verres was a collector of art, moved by passionate interest in the objects and the desire to own them and a desire for the prestige owning such objects would bring. A. Weis argues that he was an art-dealer, with analogies in eighteenth-century Paris but also familiar in the contemporary world, which would explain his peculiar rapacity.[66] Presumably, monetary gain would have

---

[65] The first mention of citrus-wood tables in Latin literature is in a fragment of a speech by Cato, complaining about people using ivory and citrus-wood; a citrus-wood table was considered a manly but luxurious possession. Pliny says tables of citrus-wood, grown in north Africa, are cited by ladies to counter criticism (by men) that they are overly fond of pearls, and comments further that Cicero himself purchased a very costly citrus-wood table that "still exists" (13.91–92).

[66] Weis (2003): 378–382, 387–388. Verres as a collector is presented well in F. Cowles' early study, *Gaius Verres: An Historical Study* (Ithaca, 1917); discussed further by Bounia (2004): 269–306.

been his main motive in that case. It is true that Cicero labels him as a *mercator*, but the tone and context show the label is meant as a stunning insult. Other studies of the sources of senatorial wealth in this period of Roman history make the idea of Verres openly engaged in dealing art seem unlikely. To be sure, there is no doubt that senators had extensive business dealings, as J. D'Arms has demonstrated in detail. An old law of 218 BCE (*lex Claudia*) prohibited senators from owning ships of merchant size because, Livy says, such profit-seeking other than agricultural appeared unseemly (*indecorus*) for senators (21.63.4). Such laws (and social customs) could be observed in appearance if not in fact: Senators' business affairs were conducted at a remove, behind representatives and middlemen. Senators were backers, not dealers, and when they did engage in trade openly, it had to be on a truly large scale to be respectable.[67]

Cicero's tones of disparagement are far from unique, and the tone continues in writings of others into the imperial period.[68] Within the context of D'Arms' detailed picture of financial dealings in the late Republic, Verres' activities seem much more those of a collector, not a dealer; to be sure, he could use his art and luxurious commodities to further his political career but not as merchant. He could be generous to friends and associates and give memorable parties and lavish gifts. Verres' evidently sincere appreciation of excellent workmanship or a fine statue makes it unlikely he would part with it easily unless there was a specific political motive: in Cicero's portrait, we do not see him selling art or other commodities.

[67] J. D'Arms, *Commerce and Social Standing in Ancient Rome* (Cambridge, MA, 1981): 3–4, 20–47. On ownership, capital, and capitalism, see also W. V. Harris, "Between Archaic and Modern: Problems in Roman Economic History," in W. V. Harris, ed., *The Inscribed Economy*, *JRA* Supp. 6 (Ann Arbor, 1993): 20–25.

[68] Cicero gives his son an explanation of the social scale of various occupations and means of acquiring wealth in a famous passage, *Off.* 1.50–151; see commentary in Dyck (1996): 336–338, with comparative ancient references and modern discussions.

This is shown additionally by his rejection of many of the settings of embossed plate and other marks of connoisseurship: the motive was collecting fine specimens, not simply making money by engaging in a lucrative trade. Cicero mocks Verres for his intense interest in the settings for the gold *emblemata* he had removed from other people's plate. In this scenario, Cicero depicts Verres in a workshop, set up in Hieron's old palace in Syracuse. He gave orders that all skilled metalworkers should assemble, and he had additional skilled men in his own retinue. They worked for eight months without a break, just on gold items. The *emblemata* torn from servers, thuribles, and other vessels he now had set into new vessels but so skillfully that "you would say they were made that way" (2.4.54). Verres himself would sit there much of each day, wearing a Greek workman's clothing.

All modern commentators have noted the incongruous picture Cicero presents of a Roman governor in a smock, supervising goldsmiths. This passage has been variously interpreted; Weis in particular notes that Cicero shows this as one aspect of Verres' tyrannical *superbia* (arrogance) and disrespect for others' social status by appropriating these items and refashioning them. It also indicates, as Cowles pointed out long ago, that Verres must have had knowledge and interest in the technical aspects of these vessels: he was a connoisseur.[69] He did this because he was interested in refining his collection. The historical integrity of the pieces, the (modern) archaeological idea of "context" or "original setting," was not an aspect he cared about for any of the art he took.

Cicero immediately follows his description of Verres' palace workshop with the story of Lucius Piso Frugi, of the previous generation. While he was praetor in Spain, his gold ring broke into pieces during a military exercise. He summoned a goldsmith to him in public in Cordoba and, in the open, weighed out the gold and had the man make

---

[69] Weis (2003): 373–377, with full citation of earlier discussions; Cowles (1917): 110–11.

a new ring right there. Cicero suggests he had this degree of scrupu-
losity because his own father had brought forth the first extortion law
(2.4.56–57). He then contrasts their names, Frugi (frugal) and Verres
(boar), saying they both lived up to them. This parallel anecdote establishes another level of criticism: that it is not the possession or use or
wearing of gold that is at fault, but rather the attitudes surrounding
its use. Frugi is straightforward, quick, and open in his dealings, but
Verres sets up a closed shop for months, lingering over his stolen goods.

Verres also shows his interest as a collector in taking curiosities, such
as the giant bamboo spears from the Temple of Athena at Syracuse
and the large tusks from the Temple of Juno at Malta that had King
Masinissa's Punic inscription on them. Cicero remarks parenthetically
that he noticed the jury was quite interested in the bamboo but, really,
it was enough to hear about them and more than enough to see them
once (2.4.125).[70] Yet such curios of natural history were of interest also
to Augustus, and much later to collectors in early modern Europe and
England.

Cicero himself is quite aware of Verres' connoisseurship because he
denigrates it in various ways. In a scenario that maintains the idea that
the trial is still ongoing and that Verres has not yet fled Rome, he
says Verres is eager to have the reputation as a connoisseur, but was
so stupid that just the other day at a banquet in the house of L. Sissena, Verres went up to the silver to inspect it in a leisurely way, piece
by piece. He was immediately the target of gossip, as people marveled
that he would confirm the very behavior of which he was accused!
Cicero then speculates that the servants were keeping a close watch on
him and remarks that if Verres' could not keep his passion in check
even during his trial, how could he refrain from taking Sicilian silver

---

[70] Pliny says that Indian bamboo could grow to the size of tree trunks and could be seen
commonly in temples (16.162).

while he was praetor (2.4.33)? Cicero's jibes at Verres' supposed deficiency in Greek include not only the ignored pedestal for the statue of Sappho, inscribed with a fine epigram, but also reference to ribald graffiti about Pipa, said to have been written above his head on the governor's tribunal, as though he could not read it and object to it. And there is the occasional comment, in sarcastic burlesque, that, of course, the rest of us are ignorant of such things, whereas Verres is the great expert to whom we should defer in matters of taste.

Where Verres does demonstrate expertise, Cicero transfers it to his servants, the "Finders," Tlepolemus and Hieron. Cicero says he wondered how Verres could seem to be an expert in anything but then discovered that the "Finders" were like hunting dogs who would seek out art: they were his eyes. Verres was avidly interested in Corinthian bronzes, a rubric that denotes both a style of vessel and a type of alloy, which were the object of a kind of craze among the elite in the first century BCE.[71] Besides those dedicated by Scipio at Engyion, Verres made a particular effort to scour the whole island to find other examples. He sent the "Finders" as agents to obtain them from anyone rumored to own such things; these men could be bribed, however (thus showing Verres' misplaced trust). Verres acquired from Pamphilus of Lilybaeum a large hydria by the master metalworker Boethos that had been in his family for generations and was used for feast-days and special guests (2.4.32). Later the governor sent slaves to demand a pair of antique, carefully worked cups as well, but once Pamphilus arrived at the praetor's residence, he was able to bribe the "Finders" to say that they were worthless.

Pliny has several tart comments about the enthusiasm of some Romans for Corinthian bronzes, especially valued by his contemporaries. He observes that Corinthian bronzes led to Verres' death because

---

[71] For discussion of the actual alloys used and Pliny's belief that gold and silver were used, see Mattusch (1996): 26, 95–96.

during the proscriptions of 43 BCE, Marc Antony had him put to death, when Verres (then living in Massilia) refused to give over his collection of Corinthian bronzes to Antony (34.6). This is one of several instances of a story told by Pliny that appears transparently descriptive but in fact maligns Marc Antony; by illustrating Verres' attachment to Corinthian bronzes, made famous by Cicero, he implies that Antony was just like Verres, who would stop at nothing to acquire art. Pliny remarks acerbically that the majority of these manic fanciers of Corinthian bronzes (of whom Verres and Antony are prime examples) are not true connoisseurs but only poseurs and do not have exceptional knowledge of the subject (which he himself does).

By far the largest profits Verres made in his time in office were from the manipulation of the grain supply: that outweighed any other profit.[72] He apparently anticipated high expenses that would ensue as a result of the trial, if we may believe Cicero that Verres told his friends openly about his three-year profits intended for a judicial proceeding. In addition to that income, the large quantities of luxury goods would prove useful to furnish his various houses and estates, and serve as gifts, in ways that could be politically useful. Verres is known to have had estates in Italy, including more than one at Beneventum acquired during the proscriptions of Sulla. Verres was a dealer in swindles, favors, bribes, and the power of his office, not art.

Verres crossed paths with three men who could perhaps be called art dealers, or at least dealers in luxury goods. The prosopographical evidence for them illustrates significant contrasts with Verres – they were businessmen, of different social and ethnic backgrounds, with no claims or ambitions for public office in Rome. Two were Sicilians, Sthenius of Thermae (Himera) and Gaius Heius of Messana, whose

---

[72] For a tabulation of Verres' property and profits as governor, see Shatzman, *Senatorial Wealth*: 429–437; references to his property and estates, *Verr.* 2.1.38; 2.4.36, 58, 126.

unfortunate encounters with Verres are described previously in this chapter. The third, P. Granius, was based in Puteoli. All three men also had connections with Delos, which even after the sack of 88 BCE by a general of Mithradates VI had recovered somewhat as an international emporium, rebuilt with Roman assistance. The prosperous markets on the island ended abruptly when it was subsequently sacked by pirates in 69 BCE. The sack was so thorough and vicious that it effectively ended Delos' significance as an emporium.[73]

Gaius Heius of Messana, whose *sacrarium* Verres robbed, is identified at Delos with an inscription naming C. Heius T. f. Libo, who was a *magister* in one of the prominent associations (collegia) of merchants, called the Hermaistai, Apolloniastai, and Poseidoniastai (HAP).[74] This association built a large, elaborate colonnaded building within the Agora of the Italians on Delos. While Heius' primary income may have come from dealing in slaves (Delos was a major slave market before it was sacked), N. Rauh suggests he also may have dealt in art and crafts made in Asia Minor but sold through Delos.[75] In addition to the statues by Praxiteles, Myron, and Polykleitos in his household shrine that were taken by Verres, he also had gold-embroidered Attalic tapestries (taken by Verres) that were likely also imported from Asia Minor, even from Pergamon itself.

Sthenius of Thermae was a connoisseur of both Delian and Corinthian bronze vessels and had a large collection (taken by Verres). Cicero says he was a knowledgeable collector, studious of these items since his youth, and had besides the especially elegant bronzes, many

---

[73] On Roman trade in this period, see J. Paterson, "Trade and Traders in the Roman World: Scale, Structure, and Organisation," in H. Parkins and C. Smith, eds., *Trade, Traders and the Ancient City* (London and New York, 1998): 149–167, and G. K. Young, *Rome's Eastern Trade. International Commerce and Imperial Policy, 31 BC–AD 305* (London and New York, 2001).

[74] *ID* 4, 1754, line 1; 5, 2612, line 18. The evidence for C. Heius at Delos is discussed by N. Rauh, *The Sacred Bonds of Commerce* (Amsterdam, 1993): 56–57.

[75] Rauh (1993): 67.

paintings, and finely made silver. He had collected them in Asia Minor and used them to receive guests and offer hospitality, adds Cicero. His honesty and forthright behavior saved his life at a dangerous time of reprisals for siding against Sulla. He was pardoned for opposing Sulla after he approached Pompey, saying that only the guilty in the town of Thermae should be punished, not the innocent. When Pompey asked who was guilty, he said it was himself, and he had persuaded the others to take the wrong side. So impressed was Pompey that after granting the pardon, they became guest-friends (Plutarch, *Pomp.* 10.5). His other Roman guests came to include the senators C. Claudius Marcellus and L. Cornelius Sissena. Later, when persecuted and prosecuted by Verres, he relied on his Roman *hospites* (guest-friends) and was able to get the two consuls Gellius and Lentulus to act in his favor and the tribune M. Lollius Palicanus.[76] Sthenius is also listed as a *magister* in the same collegium (HAP) as Heius, about 113 BCE. He too was probably involved in the slave trade, with an interest in art and antiquities on the side.

The third businessman who got entangled with Verres was P. Granius, an Italian merchant based in Puteoli (described by Cicero as "an honored man of substance" [2.5.154]). On Delos, Granius' family had been very prominent since 166 BCE and, by the time of Publius Granius, their network had expanded within the Aegean to Athens, Kos, Samos, Chalcis, and Mitylene and to Antioch in Syria.[77] P. Granius had several agents documented in the slave trade on Delos.[78] He is depicted by Cicero as testifying in the trial in Rome that Verres had beheaded his freedmen (in the plural, number not specified) who were captains of his ships. Verres had wanted to confiscate the cargo, comprised of luxury

---

[76] Badian, *FC*: 155, 282.

[77] Rauh (1993): 55; *ID* 2180.

[78] J. Hatzfeld, "Les italiens résident à Délos" *BCH* 36 (1912): 40–41; Rauh states that P. Granius' name was also found on a seal stamp in a banker's archive in one of the houses on Delos, Rauh (1993): 56 and n. 151.

goods from all over the Mediterranean, and alleged that the men were rebels allied with Sertorius in Spain. They protested this accusation and offered their cargo and manifests as proof that they were merchantmen: they had Tyrian purple dye, incense, perfumes, linen fabric, jewels and pearls, Greek wine, and slaves from Asia Minor, cargoes whose disparate origins proved they were merchantmen. But Verres accused them of dealing with pirates, put them in the dreaded Quarries of Syracuse, confiscated the cargo, and then killed them (he did this also to Roman citizens [2.5.146–154]). The cargo listed by Cicero illustrates the ongoing luxury trade that interested Verres. The inscriptions attesting to these three men on Delos, all victims of Verres, should provide a shock of historicity to what may have begun to seem like a novelistic account of his crimes. The documented events also illustrate the overlapping circles of businessmen who dealt in slaves, luxury goods, and art, and the elite in Rome.

Spectacular evidence for the luxury trade is provided by shipwrecks, such as the Antikythera wreck (80–50 BCE), discovered in 1900 between Crete and Kythera, that yielded a large quantity of marble and bronze sculpture dating from the fourth century BCE onward.[79] Of great interest too is the Mahdia wreck, whose cargo of durable luxury goods also shows disparate origins, like that of P. Granius' ships. The shipwreck (discovered off the east coast of Tunisia in 1907) likely had Athens as her last port of call and was en route to Italy before being blown off course, probably about 80–70 BCE.[80] The cargo includes about seventy marble columns, capitals, and other architectural pieces, apparently

---

[79] The sculptural finds from the Antikythera wreck are discussed by Mattusch (1998): 87–94.

[80] The cargo is discussed in essays by a large international team of scholars in G. Hellenkemper Salies, ed., *Das Wrack. Der antike Schiffsfund von Mahdia*, 2 vols. (Köln, 1994). The date of the ceramics from the wreck that provide the likely range for the time of her last voyage is established by S. Rotroff, "The Pottery," 133–152. For a gazetteer of other shipwrecks of this period, some with durable luxury goods, see A. J. Parker, *Ancient Shipwrecks of the Mediterranean & the Roman Provinces, BAR*, 580 (Oxford, 1992).

from Athens; numerous statuary of varying sizes, including the now well-known Herm of Dionysos signed by Boethos; bronze furniture such as klinai (couches or beds) and lamp-stands; marble candelabra; marble and bronze vessels; bronze decorative attachments; and many other items – even a few stray Athenian inscriptions that seem to have gotten in by chance. The cargo effectively illustrates the kinds of items enumerated by Cicero as the object of Verres' collecting.[81] One of the hydriae taken by Verres, noted earlier, was signed by Boethos, who was active in the mid-second century BCE.[82] Although the cargo appears to include looted items, possibly from Athens (plundered by Sulla, earlier in the 80s) or from Delos (looted by pirates, in 69), much of it was new.[83] Customers in Italy are unlikely to have worried about purchasing pirates' loot, since they readily purchased people who were captured for sale into slavery by pirates.

Art for Cicero

My discussion so far has focused on Verres' ruthless and criminal modes of acquisition of art and Cicero's view of the distasteful ways he meant to use it. I conclude here with a brief examination of what Cicero thought was the appropriate way of using art, in keeping with the principle of *decor*.[84] For the public sphere, we have seen already that

---

[81] The connections are discussed by G. Zimmer, "Republikanisches kunstverständnis: Cicero gegen Verres," in Hellenkemper Salies (1994) 2: 867–874, and H. Galsterer, "Kunstraub und Kunsthandel im republikanischen Rom," in Hellenkemper Salies (1994), 2: 857–866.

[82] On the artist Boethos, see C. Mattusch, "Bronze Herm of Dionysos," in Hellenkemper Salies (1994), 1: 431–450; also A. Linfert, "Boethoi," in Hellenkemper Salies (1994), 2: 831–848.

[83] The evidence of looted items is gathered and discussed by B. Barr-Sharrar, "Some Observations Concerning Late Hellenistic Bronze Production on Delos," in O. Palagia and W. Coulson, eds., *Regional Schools in Hellenistic Sculpture* (Oxford, 1998): 185–198. She suggests that the bronzes were likely manufactured on Delos and plundered from there.

[84] Cicero's taste has been much studied; see A. Demouliez, *Cicèron et son goût: Essai sur une définition d'une aesthetique romaine à la fin de la République* (Brussels, 1976); M. Marvin, "Copying in Roman Sculpture: The Replica Series," in *Retaining the Original. Multiple Originals, Copies, and Reproductions*, Vol. 20, *Studies in the History of Art* (Washington, DC,

Cicero expresses some ambivalence about art as military plunder: the emotional reaction of foreign visitors to seeing their consecrated images in the Roman Forum is vividly portrayed. Yet he is not rigorously critical of the practice and admits only near the end of his life that it was not a good thing to have destroyed Corinth. No comments are made by him (or others, as far as I know, except for one man noted for hating Romans) expressing ambivalence over the presence in Rome of older Etruscan statuary, at least some of which was plunder, such as the two thousand statues brought from Volsinii.[85] The military acquisition of quantities of Greek art from defeated Greek cities was more recent and more memorable, since Rome had both Etruscan and Greek artists creating art in Rome from the Archaic period onward.

Although the Greek art taken from Syracuse by Marcellus is not described in detail, it seems likely that much of it was in styles of the Hellenistic period, full of drama, vitality, and emotion; extremely life-like; and made of marble and bronze rather than terra-cotta – therefore, its impact on an urban audience was all the greater. Cicero objects to Verres' looted art on public display in the Forum (loans to his friends who were serving in office as aediles) because of the way it was acquired, and because it would be returned after display to Verres and thus be associated with him in popular memory. As long as it is accessible to all, however, Cicero has no strong criticism of such art in public: in the case of Metellus' displays in Rome, Mummius' dedications in Italy, or Scipio's in Sicily, he views them as appropriate memorials of Roman military achievement. As dedications in temples or in public areas, the statuary continued in the same status in which it was created. These

---

1989): 29–25 [repr. in E. D'Ambra, *Roman Art in Context* (Englewood Cliffs, NJ, 1993): 161–188]; Leen (1991); Bounia (2004).

[85] Pliny says that a man named Metrodorus Misoromaios (the "Roman hater") alleged that the storming of Volsinii (in 264 BCE) was for the sake of its two thousand statues (*HN* 34.34). Many of them were apparently small in scale: see McDonnell (2006): 72–75.

ideas about the legitimate display of captured art in public were taken up and carried a step further by Julius Caesar and Pompey, as we shall see in Chapter 4.

Cicero makes a more general point about appropriate expenditure in private and in public. In a defense speech given in 62 BCE, *Pro Murena*, Cicero recalls an incident just after the death of Scipio Aemilianus in 129. Scipio's two nephews were making arrangements for a public funeral banquet to honor him, and one asked the other, a Stoic philosopher named Tubero, to provide the couches for the funeral banquet. But Tubero (son of Scipio's sister) arranged for mangy goatskins to cover wooden benches and, for the feast, only cheap Samian pottery, as though a Cynic philosopher were being honored rather than the great hero. As a result, people thought he was far too stingy and, despite sterling credentials and his distinguished family, he lost the election for praetorship, all because of the goatskins! Cicero then says, "The Roman people hate private luxury, they prize public magnificence" (*Mur.* 76).[86]

For the private sphere, Cicero's preserved private letters and a speech for a legal case about his own house provide some evidence for his own houses and villas.[87] This evidence dates to the decade after the case prosecuting Verres. Cicero was interested in purchasing art for his houses; he plainly was not a "collector" in the same sense that Verres was but rather wished to furnish his house appropriately. His preserved correspondence with his childhood acquaintance T. Pomponius Atticus, who became a close friend, begins with a few letters in the 60s, in which he seeks Atticus' help with the selection and purchase from Athens of suitable art for his villa in Tusculum. M. Marvin has studied these letters thoroughly for their implications for Cicero's

[86] This point is the subject of a poem written in the next generation by Horace, *Carm.* 2.15.
[87] For a discussion of his personal feelings about his residences, see S. Treggiari, "Home and Forum: Cicero between 'Public' and 'Private,'" *TAPA* 128(1998): 1–23; on memories of Greece deliberately evoked, see E. Narducci, "La memoria dell grecità nell'immaginario delle ville ciceroniane," in M. Citroni, ed. *Memoria e identità. La cultura romana costuisce la sua immagine. Studi e testi*, 21 (Firenze, 2003): 119–148.

taste and expectations, and her analysis offers considerable insight into what this one Roman considered desirable and appropriate.[88] Although Cicero was knowledgeable and sophisticated about provenance, artists, materials, and so forth, as we have seen, none of those criteria is even mentioned to Atticus. Instead, Cicero wanted suitable sculpture that would be appropriate for a part of his villa he calls the "Academy," meaning that it was meant to evoke his student days in Athens and warm memories of conversations and relaxation in the right ambience. Marble statuary should represent styles and content that would contribute to the atmosphere of study and reflection: it could shape memory and recall a specific place. One arrival from Greece that pleases him greatly, for example, is a herm with a head of Athena. Cicero clearly trusts Atticus' knowledge and good taste and gives him complete choice in the selection.

In contrast, for another project twenty years later (46 BCE), Cicero is politely upset with M. Fabius Gallus who sent not only Bacchantes (female followers of Dionysos), strangely comparing them with Metellus' Muses, but also a statue of Mars for Cicero's lecture hall. Cicero says (referring to the Mars), "What can I, as an advocate of peace, do with that?" What is clear from the letters and Marvin's discussion of other examples is that Roman patrons were looking for sculpture that would fit the concept of *decor* (grace or elegance) and be appropriate for specific settings. He is concerned also with *utilitas* (usefulness): he wants to create a particular setting and expression and, in that sense, the pieces are functional. The letters to Atticus, written only a few years after Verres' trial, show Cicero eager to purchase Greek art then being made (not necessarily antiques) but caring about quality and suitability. As

---

[88] Marvin (1989). The ten letters to Atticus Marvin studies are 1.7, 2.2 (both Nov. 68 BCE), 3, 4.2 (both Feb. 67), 5.2 (March or April, 67), 6.3–4 (May 67), 7.3 (Aug. 67), 8.2 (end 67), 9.3 (first half, 66), 10.5 (before July 17, 65); and one letter to M. Fabius Gallus, dealer, no. 209 (Dec. 46 BCE); numbers follow D. S. Shackleton Bailey, *Cicero's Letters to Atticus*, vol. 1 (Cambridge, 1965) and idem, *Cicero: Epistulae ad familiares*, 2 vols. (Cambridge, 1977). The letters are also discussed usefully by Leen (1991) and Bounia (2004).

Marvin notes, this is different from collections and replicas of classical art assembled in eighteenth-century neoclassical country houses, such as Syon House by Robert Adams, where a more general "ancient" atmosphere is evoked without regard to the actual content of the statuary.[89] For Cicero, the content of the images and the styles were still living: the statues are not artifacts from the past.

Marvin (writing in 1989) concluded in her study that a major correction was needed in the study of Roman art, especially that of mythological and decorative statuary (*Idealplastik*, to use the common German term). Formerly, this type of Roman art created for Romans was regarded as a weak derivative of Greek art, and mostly studied for what it might yield about the earlier, presumed Greek prototypes. We should focus instead on the Roman purpose and context of Roman "ideal sculpture" and study it for what it indicates about its Roman audiences. Such a correction has been under way ever since, and Roman expectations and choices in art have received new, more nuanced interpretations. It is now recognized that Roman artistic choices are best understood as deeply inflected by rhetorical principles, with *decor* as fundamental.[90]

Cicero's villa at Tusculum that Atticus helped him furnish was formerly owned by Sulla, probably purchased in 68 BCE, just two years

---

[89] Marvin (1989): 167.

[90] As Marvin notes in her own clarion call, revisions were suggested by P. Zanker, "Zur Funktion und Bedeutung griechischer Skulptur in der Römerzeit," in *Le classicisme à Rome aux I^{rs} siécles avant et après J.C.*, *Entretiens Hardt* 25 (1978): 283–306, and B. Ridgway, *Roman Copies of Greek Sculpture: The Problem of the Originals* (Ann Arbor, 1984). Along with Marvin's article, conceptual studies by T. Hölscher, *The Language of Images in Roman Art* [trans. from original German ed., 1987] (Cambridge, 2004); the essays in E. Gazda, ed., *The Ancient Art of Emulation* (Ann Arbor, 2002); and, more recently, E. Perry (2005) have moved the subject forward, assisted by many individual and more technical studies of specific bodies of Roman sculpture and painting. On issues of historiography, see especially P. Stewart (2003); the essays in A. Donohue and M. Fullerton, eds., *Ancient Art and Its Historiography* (Cambridge, 2003); Perry (2005); and the review article by C. H. Hallett, "Emulation versus Replication: Redefining Roman Copying," *JRA* 18(2005): 419–435. See also B. Ridgway, *Hellenistic Sculpture III. The Styles of ca. 100–31 B.C.* (Madison, 2002).

after Verres' trial.[91] In addition to the purchases of suitable art from Athens mentioned in his correspondence with Atticus, the villa had a painting showing the army presenting Sulla with a grass-crown (a high honor) at Nola, apparently left in the house (Pliny, *HN* 22.12). Panel painting especially pleased Cicero, who comments in the letter to Gallus mentioned above that he added some sitting areas to a small portico in the villa at Tusculum so as to include paintings "for, if anything of that sort delights me, a painting delights me" (*Fam.* 209). The villa had a library, a gymnasium, porticoes, and an exedra and also was a working agricultural unit, with a large garden that was rented out.[92]

Cicero was forced into exile in 58 BCE by his political enemy Clodius, and his house on the Palatine in Rome was looted and destroyed; on that occasion, his villas at Tusculum and Formiae were also looted. The speech he gave on his return the next year persuaded the Senate to return the property, provide money for its rebuilding, and compensate him for the looting of both his house and his villas. That speech, *De Domo Sua*, gives an emotional accounting of the significance of his house to him personally and to his public image. He was able to rebuild on the Palatine and to refurnish the house and villas.[93]

Of all of his properties, his villas at Tusculum, Cumae, and Puteoli, the latter acquired through inheritance, were the ones he furnished most comfortably, but even they were productive and profitable

[91] In the course of his life-time, Cicero owned at least twenty houses and estates, including two houses in Rome, small wayside travel lodges, and numerous rental properties in Rome and in the country. The details with expenses and income are listed by Shatzman (1975): 403–425. All of his country properties had agricultural land attached. In a comparative evaluation, Shatzman notes that Cicero was prosperous, but not unusually so, and had fluctuations in his income due to political crises, 424–425.

[92] For Cicero's library at Tusculum, see T. K. Dix, "A Survey of Ancient Libraries," (review article), *JRA* 15 (2002): 473–475.

[93] On the social aspects of the speech, S. Hales, "At Home with Cicero," *G&R* 47 (2000): 44–55; on its logistical and legal aspects, W. Stroh, "De Domo Sua: *Legal Problem and Structure*," in Powell and Paterson (2004): 313–370. For the importance of villas as a type of monument to individuals, see J. Bodel, "Monumental Villas and Villa Monuments," *JRA* 10 (1997): 5–35.

agriculturally; they were not merely luxurious residences.[94] In a letter to his brother Quintus, written in September 54 BCE, Cicero tells him that he has looked at a property at Laterium that Quintus was planning to refurbish and says that he approved of his ideas for additions; true, he says, it is now like a villa *philosopha* (tasteful and conducive to study) and rebukes those built with insane extravagance, but still the additions would be pleasant . . . and the Greek statues in their cloaks between the columns look as though they are doing some gardening (*QFr* 21). The same letter has a lengthy commentary showing Cicero's interests in the architectural arrangements and decorative details of his own and Quintus' other properties. When Cicero was at his villa at Cumae, Julius Caesar came to visit with a retinue of two thousand, whom Cicero could not accommodate, but his neighbor L. Marcius Philippus was easily able to house them.[95] Above all, D'Arms, in his study of Roman villas in Campania, singles out the quality of *amoenitas* (delightfulness) as the salient desired feature: they should be sighted with good views, in a pleasant setting, and be lovely to look upon. These are the positive qualities that Cicero mentions about villas in his correspondence and are consistent with his views on Greek art in the *Verrines*: a statue or a building should be aesthetically pleasing but its context is also very important.

In his essay *De Officiis* (On Obligations), Cicero gives advice to his son about the appropriate size and decoration for a house, stressing the importance of the house to one's image and *dignitas*. He mentions M. Aemilius Scaurus, who tore down an earlier house that had belonged to Cn. Octavius, first of his family to be consul, on the Palatine for an elaborate addition to his own (with imported marble columns), but

---

[94] D'Arms comments on the relative modesty of Cicero's villas (*RBN* 45) and notes that Plutarch denies they were large (*Cic.* 8.2).

[95] *Att.* 353 (13.52); D'Arms, *RBN* 45, 189–191.

who was later disgraced and forced into exile (in 53 BCE). Cicero says, "The fact is, though a person's standing (*dignitas*) can be enhanced by a house, it should not be wholly sought from it. An owner cannot be ennobled by his house, but a house can be ennobled by its owner."[96]

Cicero left a deep and positive impression on his households, according to Pliny. After he was murdered as a result of Antony's proscription in 43 BCE, his villa at Cumae was purchased by a C. Antistius Vetus, probably the consul of 30, who was allied with the triumvirate since 37 BCE.[97] This Cumaean villa also had a portico and grove that Cicero called Academia, naming it after the one in Athens, and he is said to have composed his books *Academia* there. Soon after Cicero's death, Pliny says, and while Vetus was the owner, hot springs burst out of the ground near the front of the estate that proved to be salubrious for eye complaints. The healthful hot springs were celebrated by one of Cicero's freedman, Tullius Laurea, who wrote a poem on the springs and on Cicero, cited in full by Pliny (*HN* 31.6–8). The last lines of the poem read, "Surely this place itself gave this gift to honor its own Cicero, when it brought to light springs with this power. Since he is read throughout the whole world without end, thus there may be more waters good for the eyes."

---

[96] *Off.* 1.138, trans. P. G. Walsh; see Dyck (1996): 317. Imported columns, of Lucullan marble, used first in a temporary theater built by Scaurus, then in his house: Pliny, *HN* 36.5–6.

[97] Shatzman (1975): 295; for discussion of the acquisition by Vetus, D'Arms, *RBN*: 69–70, 172. For Cicero's freedmen, S. Treggiari, *Roman Freedmen during the Late* Republic (Oxford, 1969): 252–264.

4 ROMAN DISPLAY OF ART: FROM LUCULLUS TO LAUSOS

⊚🔲⊚

Then after he saw many of the sights,
deeply moved with amazement, the
emperor complained about reputation
as weak or malicious, that while
describing everything else it constantly
exaggerates, but as for what is at Rome,
it becomes feeble....
Amm. Marc., 16.10.17, on Constantius'
reaction to Rome (357 CE)

CICERO'S PUBLICATION OF THE *VERRINES* AND THE DAMNING PORTRAIT of Verres as a collector must have dampened the ardor to collect antique Greek art among Cicero's peers, at least a bit. Who would want to risk appearing to behave like Verres with a great many acquisitions? Yet, Greek art was already woven into the fabric of Roman culture and (except for acknowledged antiques, now taking on new meanings in new settings) was already a part of "Roman" art. Shipwrecks such as the Mahdia wreck and Antikythera wreck show that at least a few antiques continued to be sent off from the Greek east to Italian customers. In comments by ancient authors about how the elite were living in the decades after the trial, however, we see a distinct shift in the focus of luxury and consumption away from accumulating antique statuary and into different forms of status display.

Because Cicero's speeches on Verres were widely distributed and read in his own life-time, they must have had some impact on his contemporaries, and not only as a textual rhetorical model. Verres, now in exile, must have become a negative social exemplar, a warning figure. Not until some 150 years later in the first century CE is he mentioned by name (by Pliny the Elder): whether this is by happenstance in the preservation of texts, or a sort of informal *damnatio memoriae* is unknown. Cicero's style of oratory had definitely gone out of fashion in the course of the first century CE, and perhaps the *Verrines* were not read much then, at least not until Quintilian brought back Cicero as a "classic" and the *Verrines* as an esteemed model of rhetoric. By the early second century CE, Juvenal uses Verres several times as a byword for greed and corruption: he was not forgotten but had become part of the cultural vocabulary.

It is worth considering whether in choices surrounding the use of art and luxury the Verrine model was avoided by men who were in a position to choose how well they lived. Cicero's contemporaries seem to have disdained the Verrine model for private uses of art. Here I examine the impact of the *Verrines* in the decades after the trial and later in the first century. The *Verrines* are frequently cited in modern scholarship as indicative, even if an extreme example, of (Republican) Roman passion for Greek "originals." What I hope to show is a more nuanced picture of the acquisition and use of art in the late Republic, following the trial of Verres.

In the public sphere, the successful generals Pompey and Julius Caesar in the decades following Cicero's publication of the *Verrines* continued and expanded the earlier Republican model of using plundered art and manubial funds for public displays in Rome. During the Principate, such public displays of captured art as war trophies became an integral part of the image of the imperial city. Augustus created a new type of triumphal monument that featured Egyptian obelisks and this would be imitated persistently as an urban symbol of power through the nineteenth century. When private collecting of art again became respectable in the late first century CE, the image of a "connoisseur" of art was commemorated in poetry. At the same time, the idea of "compassionate returns" of significant statues was not entirely forgotten.

With the advent of Constantine as sole ruler, however, and his support of Christianity as his own religion, once again the plundering of art and its repositioning into a new context becomes a prism through which we see far-reaching social and political shifts. For the decoration and adornment of his new city, Constantinople, Constantine removed more than a hundred statues from many cities, including Athens and Rome: apparently, antique statuary was considered necessary to give the new city instant status as an authoritative urban center. As late as the fifth century CE, Lausos, the Grand Chamberlain of Theodosius II, assembled a remarkable collection in Constantinople gathered from the famous, but closed, sanctuaries of Greece.

PISCINARII

After Verres' trial, patterns in public life and fashions in luxurious living among the Roman elite were set by three men in particular: Q. Lutatius Catulus (cos. 78, a juror in Verres' trial), his brother-in law Q. Hortensius Hortalus (cos. 69, Verres' advocate), and L. Licinius Lucullus (cos. 74). They were prominent *optimates* (aristocrats) and influential in the politics of the 60s BCE. Catulus opened the decade in 69 with lavish games to celebrate the rededication of the now completed Temple of Jupiter Optimus Maximus (which had burned down in 83) and the dedication of the Tabularium, both on the Capitoline, which he had sponsored.[1] Hortensius was beginning to be eclipsed as an orator by Cicero after Cicero's victory in Verres' trial, but after his consulship of 69 he was still active in politics and public life. Lucullus held *imperium* (sole command) in the war against Mithradates VI for seven years, starting in 74 BCE, until he was superseded by Pompey in 66, after political maneuvering by his rivals. He then had to wait three years, outside the

---

[1] For the dedicatory inscriptions, *ILLRP* 367, 368; on the roles and prominence of the three men, see Gruen, *LGRR*: 50–58.

pomerium of Rome, before he was awarded a Triumph for his accomplishments in the east. By 60 BCE, Catulus had died, and Lucullus and Hortensius were participating much less in the politics of public life.[2] Hortensius took on some defense cases, but both men became increasingly interested in building and equipping their villas for luxurious living. They and some of their like-minded friends became famous for their intense interest in pisciculture: they were nicknamed "*piscinarii*" (fish-fanciers) and "Tritons of the fish-ponds" by Cicero.[3]

Cicero uses the nickname with a derogatory tone because he felt annoyed and anxious that these men were not taking sufficient interest in public affairs and instead were just sitting on the sidelines in semi-retirement. He complains in a letter to Atticus written about June 3, 60 BCE, "Our leading men think they have transcended the summit of human ambition if the bearded mullet in their fish ponds feed out of their hands, and let all else go hang."[4] All sorts of anecdotes were told later about the *piscinarii*: the fish were pets, wore jewels, and had special names; the owners would not eat them; Hortensius is said to have wept when his beloved moray eel died; and the subsequent owner of his villa at Bauli, Antonia (daughter of Marc Antony and Octavia, and wife of Drusus), put gold earrings on a favorite eel, which made the villa a tourist attraction.[5] The fish ponds were expensive to build and

---

[2] On Lucullus' reasons for withdrawal from public life, see A. Keaveney, *Lucullus. A Life* (London, 1992): 129–144. For details of his Triumph, see Pape (1975): 22–24.

[3] Cicero, *Att.* 19.6, 20.3; fishponds mentioned at 18.6, 21.7; Tritons of the fishponds: *Att.* 29.1; Macrobius (*Sat.* 3.15.6), writing in the early fifth century CE, attributes the term to Cicero, and names Lucullus, Hortensius, and Philippus (apparently the Philippus who was Cicero's neighbor at Cumae) as the prime fanciers. (The phrase "fish-fancier" is used by D. Shackleton Bailey in his translations of Cicero.)

[4] *Att.* 21.7, trans. Shackleton Bailey. For a thorough study of the extensive archaeological remains of the fishponds, see J. Higginbotham, *Piscinae. Artificial Fishponds in Roman Italy* (Chapel Hill and London, 1997). The evidence shows that most fishponds were built around the mid-first century BCE, until the first quarter of the first century CE; the later ones were farther inland and on a much smaller scale (such as those in Pompeii), showing that people of more modest income were continuing the fashion set earlier by Lucullus and his friends (pp. 58–59).

[5] Pliny, 9.172; Varro, *Rust.* 3.3.10, 3.17.2–9.

maintain even using freshwater, but Lucullus went one step further: at one of his villas near Naples, he dug an extensive canal opening out into the Bay of Naples so that he could keep saltwater fish. His construction caused him to be called (by either Pompey or the philosopher Tubero) "Xerxes in a toga," a reference to Xerxes' canal through Mt. Athos.[6]

The same aristocratic coterie is said to have established wild-game preserves, aviaries, and snail ponds with different varieties of snails, and to have kept peacocks; oysterbeds had been laid near Baiae earlier about 90 BCE.[7] And naturally they were interested in fine wines: Hortensius is said to have left to his heirs ten thousand jars of Chian wine.[8] Lucullus, who was rich even before his campaigns in Asia Minor but became even more so with the *manubiae* from it, gained a reputation as a gourmand who gave lavish dinners with exotic foods served on jeweled plate. When once he was dining alone, his butler served him only one modest course, thinking it sufficient since no one else was invited, but Lucullus reprimanded him, saying (famously), "Did you not know that today Lucullus dines with Lucullus?" (Plut. *Luc.* 41) The gastronomic interests taken up by the fish-fanciers really were a continuation of passions rooted in earlier Sicilian cuisine and Hellenistic royal luxury. The author of a cookbook in verse, Archestratos of Gela (mid-fourth century BCE), gives directions for preparing fish in a verse gazetteer of the fishes of the Mediterranean, even prescribing what time of year certain species must be caught. It truly would take the resources of a Lucullus to follow such directions.[9]

[6] Plut., *Luc.* 39.3 (Tubero); Pliny, *HN* 9.170 (Pompey). Keaveney comments on the roles taken by Pompey and Lucullus in such anecdotes: they had been political rivals, and in these stories Pompey is shown as the man of action and Lucullus as devoted to leisure (Keaveney 1992: 150–151).
[7] Pliny, *HN* 8.211; 9.168, 173; 10.45.
[8] Pliny, *HN* 14.96, quoting Varro on the wines that were the most highly regarded in his day.
[9] On Sicilian gastronomy and Archestratos, see Dalby (1996): 113–129. Archestratos' cookbook is known primarily through extensive quotations given by Athenaeus. For Lucullus' wealth and holdings, see Shatzman (1975): 378–381.

Apart from the stories surrounding fish ponds, food, and dining, Lucullus was particularly remembered as a builder: he seems to have been genuinely interested in architecture and imported a special black marble from Teos (or Melos or Chios) in the Aegean, which came to be known as "Lucullan" marble.[10] A more general interest in imported marble for architectural features at this time is supported archaeologically by the extensive number (about seventy) of marble architectural members in the Mahdia wreck: the bulk and weight of those pieces was far greater than that of the sculpture, which might have been add-ons in the cargo.[11] Lucullus purchased extensive gardens in Rome on the Pincian Hill, the *horti Luculli*, which later passed into imperial possession, and had his main residence in the city on the Pincian Hill, with porticoes and a library. His interest in plants and gardening (and in food) inspired him to import the cherry tree from Asia Minor into Italy, according to Pliny (*HN* 15.102). He took on building and refurbishing several villas outside of Rome, those near Naples and also at Tusculum, where he had another good library used by Cicero.[12] For the villas in the Bay of Naples, he is said to have built artificial hills and buildings on platforms out into the sea (of the type illustrated in Pompeian wall paintings), in addition to the fresh- and saltwater *piscinae*.[13]

[10] On the introduction of marble in this period, see J. Clayton Fant, "A Distribution Model for the Roman Imperial Marbles," in Harris (1993): 146–147.

[11] H. von Hesberg, "Die Architekturteile," in Hellenkemper Salies (1994) 1: 175–194; N. Ferchiou, "Recherches sur les éléments architecturaux," in Hellenkemper Salies (1994)1: 195–207; H. Heinrich, "Die Chimärenkapitelle," in Hellenkemper Salies (1994) 1: 209–237.

[12] For details of the library, see T. K. Dix, "The Library of Lucullus," *Athenaeum* 88 (2000): 441–464.

[13] For his building projects in Campania, see V. Jolivet, "*Xerxes togatus*: Lucullus en Campanie," *MEFRA* 99 (1987): 823–846; for the theme of landscapes and building as a form of status through the first century CE, see B. Bergmann, "Painted Perspectives of a Villa Visit: Landscape and Status and Metaphor," in Gazda (1991): 49–70. A well-illustrated conspectus of maritime villas is now provided by X. Lafon, *Villa Maritima. Recherches sur les villas littorales de l'Italie romaine (IIIᵉ siècle av. J.-C.(IIIᵉ siècle ap. J.-C.)* BEFAR 307 (Rome, 2001), with the *piscinarii* discussed at 196–225.

The *piscinarii* had certainly not lost interest in art, however. I have already mentioned Hortensius' fondness for the small sphinx Verres gave him, made of either bronze, silver, or ivory – a fondness so intense that he would carry it around with him. He is said to have paid an exorbitant price for a painting of the Argonauts by Kydias, a Greek painter of the fourth century BCE, which he put in a special temple-like enclosure in his villa at Tusculum (Pliny, *HN* 35.130). Lucullus also was willing to pay a high price (two talents) for a copy (*anagraphon*, in Greek) made by Dionysios of Athens of a fourth-century-BCE painting by Pausias of Sicyon (Pliny, *NH* 35.125). This anecdote is especially interesting because we are told specifically that the high price was for a copy of an original by a famous painter who lived about three hundred years earlier, and the contemporary copier is named, thus illustrating one aspect of the art production in Athens in Lucullus' life-time. Lucullus was personally friendly with the contemporary sculptor Arcesilaos, in an example of unusual (for Roman patrons) fraternizing with an artist. In a passage commenting on the great number of bronze statues in Rome, both Lucullus and his brother are said by Pliny simply to have imported "many" statues.[14]

Out of his *manubiae*, Lucullus dedicated a bronze statue of Herakles wearing the poisoned tunic that killed him, a sculpture greatly admired for the expression of agony on the hero's face. The artist is not known (presumably Hellenistic), says Pliny, who saw it in the Forum next to the Rostra and says he mentions it because of the history of its three dedications, which he quotes.[15] Because it was not in the inscription, apparently the artist's name was unknown to Lucullus, or not significant enough to include, or deliberately suppressed. Evidently he made the

[14] Pliny, *HN* 35.155 (Arcesilaos); *HN* 34.36 (bronze statues). On the issue of "copies" (of statuary rather than paintings), see Perry (2005) for discussion of recent scholarship.

[15] Pliny, *HN* 34.93; Pliny quotes the three inscriptions; the first was the dedication *de manubiis*; the second, by Lucullus' son according to a decree of the Senate; the third, by T. Septimium Sabinum, who as aedile restored it to the public after it had been in private hands.

choice of statue to dedicate in public based on its quality, not the name of the artist.

Lucullus' indulgence in luxury did not escape criticism, even though he was very generous in public donatives and with distributions of his *manubiae* after the campaigns in Asia Minor. Pliny says his villas fell under the category of having more floor to sweep than land to plow (*HN* 18.32). Cicero more specifically upbraids Lucullus (posthumously) in his essay *De legibus*, composed some twenty years after Verres' trial, for not setting the proper model (of restraint) for others to follow. He recalls that Lucullus is said to have defended his *luxuria* on the grounds that his two neighbors, a Roman *eques* on a hill above him and a freedman below, owned luxurious houses – so why shouldn't he also? Cicero says in reply that their greed was inspired by him, Lucullus. Returning to a theme of the *Verrines*, Cicero continues, "Who would tolerate such people, on seeing their houses crammed with statues and pictures, some of which are public property and others are of a sacred and holy kind? We would all put a stop to their acquisitiveness if it weren't for the fact that those who ought to do so are guilty of the same greed. The vices of the leading citizen are not so serious an evil (though in themselves they *are* a serious evil) as the fact that those men beget a host of imitators."[16] This type of criticism of *luxuria* was continued by Sallust and Horace, Pliny and Suetonius, and, as C. Edwards points out, was a way of commenting on the socially disruptive consequences of what was perceived as an improper distribution of wealth.[17]

The *piscinarii*, then, found avenues for connoisseurship that were exclusive and indulgent and enjoyable for them, and perfectly legal, even though they excited some criticism. They also set new fashions: their passions can be seen reflected on a smaller scale in the small *piscinae*

---

[16] *Leg.* 3.30–31, trans. N. Rudd. On criticism of *luxuria* in building as a literary topos, see Edwards (1993): 137–163.

[17] Edwards (1993): 140.

and mosaics that lovingly depict many varieties of fish, found in houses of Pompeii and Herculaneum.[18] Lucullus himself seems more interested in architecture and building than art, but he was quite willing to pay handsomely for suitable art – even a fine copy of a painting – for his villas. In sum, the *piscinarii* took conspicuous consumption into new channels, away from the Verrine model.

T. POMPONIUS ATTICUS

The Verres we know through Cicero's detailed rhetorical portrait has an antithesis, that of his friend Titus Pomponius Atticus (c.110–32 BCE). He is known to us through Cicero's preserved letters to him, dating from the mid-60s to 44 BCE, and from an encomiastic *Life of Atticus* by Cornelius Nepos, also a friend.[19] Nepos' biography of Atticus provides a portrait of an educated, urbane Roman, deliberately delineated, I believe, as an opposite to Verres. In the selection of details in the biography of Atticus, we see the impact of Cicero's rhetorical Verrine model on the (then rather new) genre of Latin biography. Here, I briefly remark on some of the salient features of Nepos' *Life of Atticus* so as to illustrate the continuing significance of a man's relationship to art and Greek culture as a part of Roman characterization.

Nepos' biography is unusual for three reasons: first, the subject was a Roman *eques* (but of an old, wealthy family that traced ancestors back to Numa, the second king of Rome), not of senatorial rank. Atticus was an unusual subject because he did not follow the usual *cursus honorum* at all but instead left Rome during the 80s for Athens, where he lived for about twenty years (hence the nickname "Atticus") and escaped the political conflicts of that decade. Furthermore, Nepos wrote most of the account while Atticus was still alive, so it is the first preserved

---

[18] For the connotations of status and privilege represented by the fish mosaics, see C. Kondoleon, "Signs of Privilege and Pleasure: Roman Domestic Mosaics," in Gazda (1991): 105–115.

[19] Best account of Atticus and his friendship with Cicero in D. R. Shackleton Bailey, *Cicero's Letters to Atticus* I (Cambridge, 1965): 3–59; also Rawson (1985): 100–104; for Nepos, N. Horsfall, *Cornelius Nepos. A Selection, including the Lives of Cato and Atticus* (Oxford, 1989).

contemporary biography from antiquity. Atticus' own interests were literary and antiquarian, and he wrote family histories for friends. Not only was he helpful to Cicero with selections of sculptural furnishings for his villas but also with his manuscripts, offering criticism, editing, and the copying services of his trained staff, and promoting the distribution of Cicero's books.

Atticus' taste in art was considered elegant and knowledgeable so that Pompey was happy to have him arrange his art collection, presumably the exhibition in the portico attached to his theater in Rome.[20] He built a shrine to the nymph Amalthea on his estate in Epirus with dedicatory epigrams.[21] When in Rome Atticus lived modestly in a house on the Quirinal, which he maintained in the style of the previous generation, only making necessary repairs. His philanthropy was notably generous and unobtrusive: he gave grain and loans at low rates rather than buildings to Athens and tried to avoid being the subject of the Athenians' honorary statues. His quiet generosity extended to friends in peril, a frequent event in these decades. Remarkably, he was able to maintain at the same time friendship with people who were sometimes at odds: Cicero and his rival orator the *piscinarius* Hortensius, and later Antony and Octavian. His daughter married Marcus Vipsanius Agrippa, and their daughter Vipsania was the first and beloved wife of the future emperor Tiberius.

Atticus and his life's history as presented by Nepos form a striking contrast to many of his more famous contemporaries. Nepos stresses his neutrality in politics, his abstention from public honors, and his unusual ability to be a sincere and valued friend to many disparate, competing people.[22] In an essay on Nepos' portrait of Atticus, F. Millar

---

[20] Cicero, *Att.* 85.1, dated April 27, 55 BCE, before the dedication of the theater-temple.
[21] Cicero, *Att.* 13.1; 16.15,18.
[22] H. Lindsay thinks the neutrality in politics Nepos attributes to Atticus must be exaggerated: "The Biography of Atticus: Cornelius Nepos on the Philosophical and Ethical Background of Pomponius Atticus," *Latomus* 57.2 (1998): 324–336.

has drawn attention to the ways that Atticus' way of life and intellectual interests anticipated the changed social realities for men of his class under the Principate. Neutrality in politics, philanthropy without self-advertisement, tending one's garden, family, and friends were just the qualities Augustus would later encourage among the elite. The documentation of antiquarianism and its implicit reverence for past were deployed by Augustus in such monuments as the *fasti triumphales* in the Forum Romanum and the display of ancestors and Roman heroes, with inscribed capsule biographies, in the Forum of Augustus.[23]

The *Life of Atticus* is notable as the first contemporary political biography, but Nepos also took on a much larger project that included parallel Greek and Roman lives; in this, he helped establish a new genre that would be refined later by Plutarch. Although Nepos has been severely criticized as an author by some commentators (disappointed by his restricted purposes and stylistic shortcomings), recent scholarship is rehabilitating him, with a better appreciation of his goals as a biographer, working in a new genre.[24] Nepos, Atticus himself, and Varro all were interested in researching and writing brief (even epigrammatic) biographies of famous people, Roman and non-Roman, divided into types (generals, historians, kings).[25] Since these mini-biographies were in effect *exempla* with a didactic message, the subjects were selected for their prominence, eminence, accomplishments, or stellar personal qualities, and they drew on many different sources and previous literary categories.[26] Their principles of selection and juxtaposition borrowed

[23] F. Millar, "Cornelius Nepos, 'Atticus,' and the Roman Revolution," in Millar (2002): 183–199 [repr. from *G & R* 35(1988): 40–55].

[24] An issue summed up by F. Titchener, "Cornelius Nepos and the Biographical Tradition," *G & R* 50 (2003): 85–99.

[25] Rawson (1985): 228–232; J. Geiger, *Cornelius Nepos and Ancient Political Biography, Historia Einzelschr*, 47 (Stuttgart, 1985). Varro's were illustrated with portraits inserted into the text (Pliny, *HN* 35.11).

[26] For a summary on ancient biography, with an emphasis on developments in the imperial period, see S. Swain, "Biography and Biographic in the Literature of the Roman Empire,"

from the rhetorical ideas of thesis and antithesis, and parallelism. For examples of ancient "biographies" of persons of ill-repute and the criminally minded, we must look to historians (who offer brief sketches), prosecutorial speeches, and other forms of invective that provide indirect biographies.

Pertinent here is Nepos' use of themes from the *Verrines* as a way of characterizing Atticus. N. Horsfall comments on Nepos' use of Cicero's essay on friendship, *De amicitia*, for themes and descriptions of what constitutes the ideal friend (Atticus apparently was exemplary). Cicero's *Verrines*, as we have seen, draw a vivid portrait of Verres, with details of his life, character, and behavior all inventoried. I suggest that Nepos also made careful and extensive use of the *Verrines* to help him construct the biography of his opposite, Atticus, using antithetical parallels.

At issue is not the historicity of Nepos' biography or who the "real" Atticus was (or the "real" Verres) but rather how Nepos selected details about a man with whom he was acquainted and who was still living for a brief but surprisingly vivid biography. Here are a few examples of many of these antitheses: Verres' father consorted with bribery agents, but Atticus' father loved literature; Verres was detested by the foreign peoples he visits, whom he extorts and robs, but Atticus was beloved by the Athenians and loaned them money at favorable rates; Verres manipulated the grain supply in Sicily, but Atticus donated grain to hungry Athens. Verres demands and extorts honorary statues, and they are thrown down after he leaves, whereas Atticus refuses offered statues, but after he leaves the Athenians put them up anyway. Verres manipulated inheritances of strangers to his benefit, but Atticus was so pleasant to a crusty elderly uncle that he surprised him with an unexpected inheritance. Verres' knowledge of Greek is deemed uncertain and mocked, but Atticus spoke Greek like an Athenian and

in M. J. Edwards and S. Swain, eds., *Portraits. Biographical Representation in the Greek and Latin Literature of the Roman Empire* (Oxford, 1997): 1–38.

was a grammatical critic in both Greek and Latin. Verres took lucrative posts abroad, abused them, and was always under suspicion, but Atticus was offered such posts abroad and refused them to avoid any suspicion. Verres' house in Rome was stuffed with looted art and he hoarded gold and silver plate, but Atticus maintained his old house as it was, with modest furnishings and tableware. Verres used dubious foreign freedmen and slaves to do his dirty business, but Atticus had an excellent slave household, with slaves born there and trained by him, all of them literate. Verres held banquets with carousing and excess, attended by other men's wives, but at Atticus', one dined with friends while a reader read aloud from literary works. Verres went into ignominious exile and was proscribed by Antony, but Atticus survived the proscriptions and eventually died surrounded by friends.

In Nepos' biography, Atticus' character and life are constructed as an antithesis of Verres'. These vignettes illustrate what was considered admirable at the time and the selective skill shown by Nepos, following principles of rhetorical training (and using Cicero's speeches as a model, I believe) for this new genre of biography. Plutarch's more developed and much longer biographies written more than a century later provide some degree of psychological insight into his subjects and ultimately are far more complex and successful. Nepos is a representative of a pioneering stage in Roman biography and produced an essay that may recall a traditional encomium or funeral eulogy but does not seem merely laudatory (and after all, Atticus was still alive when he wrote most of it). His selection of rhetorical features for the biography contributes to the inevitable dichotomy between "good" and "bad" aspects of character that still continues in authors writing biography after him, such as Suetonius. The strength of this early stage of Roman biography is its vividness, engendered from rhetorical training.

Atticus himself regretted that Cicero wrote no history of Rome, and as the *Verrines* illustrate his powerful representational skill, we should regret also that he wrote no direct biographies. In Cicero's hands, and in his follower Nepos, one's houses, furnishings, servants, friends, art, Greek language and literature, even Greek Sicily or Athens itself are expertly crafted into expressions of Roman character and Roman lives.

Public Displays of Art

When Pompey returned from the east and staged his third Triumph in 61 BCE, the celebration took two days, September 28 and 29, the second one his birthday. Plutarch comments that some observers thought he was like Alexander the Great because his three Triumphs were awarded for victories in three continents at a young age; but in fact, he was older than Alexander (forty-five). Plutarch adds that it would have been better for him to have died at this peak of glory, considering what happened to him later (*Pomp.* 46). He was celebrating victories over the pirates and Mithradates VI of Pontus primarily, but the conquered territories included Pontus, Armenia, Cappadocia, Paphlagonia, Media, Colchis, Iberia, Albania, Syria, Cilicia, Mesopotamia, Phoenicia, Palestine, Judaea, and Arabia. There was more than enough to display for two Triumphs, and not all that had been prepared could be included in the procession. There were huge quantities of coined gold and silver and gold plate (twenty thousand talents) but, even more interesting, placards promising a huge increase in tax revenue from the conquered territories (Plut. *Pomp.* 45).

Pliny says that Pompey's victory made pearls and gems very fashionable. Out of the spoils, Pompey dedicated on the Capitoline a ring-cabinet that had belonged to Mithradates VI – and later Julius Caesar dedicated six of them in the Temple of Venus Genetrix (Pliny, *HN* 37.11). He brought to Rome (for the first time, says Pliny) and dedicated to Jupiter on the Capitoline crystal vessels ("myrrhine" ware or fluorspar crystal, colored, or clear) and immediately there was a fashionable demand for them (*HN* 37.18). Quoting from the triumphal records of

Pompey, Pliny says that the items included a gaming table, 3 feet by 4 feet, made out of two gems; enough gold vessels inlaid with gems to fill nine sideboards (*abaci*); gold statues of Minerva, Mars, and Apollo; a square mountain (probably an elaborate, large epergne for a dining table) in gold, with deer, lions, and golden vines, and a grotto of pearls with a sundial on top; a portrait of Pompey made out pearls; and silver statues of Pharnaces I and Mithradates. It was austerity that was defeated, says Pliny, and luxury that triumphed.[27]

Plutarch reports that Pompey was very selective about what he brought back from Asia Minor and, for example, allowed Stratonike, Mithradates' favorite concubine, to keep a great deal of what Mithradates had given her, taking only what might be dedicated in temples in Rome or make an impression in his Triumph. The King of the Iberians sent a gold bed, table, and throne, which Pompey handed over to the Aerarium (*Pomp.* 36). Mithradates had committed suicide, but representations (in wax?) of him and of Tigranes were processed, along with their living relatives, now Roman prisoners.

It is striking that what was listed and recalled by ancient authors were private, domestic "luxury" items such as gems and crystal and gold furniture rather than antique statuary or painting. *Spolia* from the east perhaps were expected to be fabulously luxurious and indulgent and in the category of private "consumables" rather than the traditionally publicly oriented (Greek) arts of sculpture and painting. Assuming that the accounts are factual, they indicate Pompey's taste and what he selected to take from the east (which surely did have a great deal of sculpture and painting). Triumphs were meant to impress deeply and, in the reports of Pompey's selection, there is an implicit presentation

---

[27] Pliny, *HN* 33.151; 37.12–14. On the Triumph, also Plutarch, *Pomp.* 36, 45–46; App., *Mith.* 17,116–117. Myrrhine cups continued to be cherished: Augustus is said to have kept for himself only one myrrhine cup out of the royal treasure captured at Alexandria (Suetonius, *Aug.* 71).

of Mithradates as a personal enemy and an enemy of Rome, finally conquered after a long struggle, so that displaying his captured private luxury and household effects would illustrate his complete and final defeat. There is also the implicit warning that such luxury leads to defeat, one of Pliny's themes.

Pompey undertook a new building project in Rome, paid for out of his manubial funds. He was inspired by the architecture he had seen at Pergamon and Mytilene and wanted something grander than a new temple, the offering favored in the previous century.[28] He built the first permanent stone theater in Rome and made it acceptable with the inclusion of a temple to Venus Victrix on the top of the *cavea* (theatral seats).[29] Attached to the front, open side of the theater was a large rectangular portico that enclosed a spacious garden-park, planted with trees exotic to Italy that Pompey had brought back, rivaling Lucullus' introduction of the cherry tree. There was also a Curia built into the portico for meetings of the Senate, where a painting by Polygnotos hung, noted for its ambiguity in representing motion.[30] A. Kuttner emphasizes the use of landscape elements as a form of appropriation of the conquered countries; she also provides extensive exegesis of the programmatic and antique statuary and painting known to have been

[28] He may have built a temple to Minerva at this time, in which he made the manubial dedications noted by Pliny (*HN* 7.97, Diod., 40.4) or the dedications could have been made in an existing temple: nothing further is known of the temple mentioned by Pliny; see L. Richardson, *A New Topographical Dictionary of Ancient Rome* (Baltimore, 1992), s.v. Minerva, Delubrum. Vitruvius mentions a temple of Hercules Pompeianus near the Circus Maximus, 3.3.5.

[29] Because of the association of unruly people with the theater, only temporary ones had been allowed in the city up to this point. The idea of combining a temple with steps arranged for a theatrical area was likely based on examples elsewhere in Italy, such as at the Sanctuary of Fortuna Primigenia at Praeneste. For the project, see D. Favro, *The Urban Image of Augustan Rome* (Cambridge, 1996): 57–60; *LTUR*, s.v. Porticus Pompei, Theatrum Pompei, Venus Victrix; summary and bibliography in Haselberger, *MAR*, s.v. Porticus Pompeianae, Theatrum Pompeium.

[30] Pliny, *HN* 35.59.

placed in the porticoes.[31] One of the programs was a series of female personifications of the fourteen Nations (conquered by Pompey) made by the sculptor Coponius, according to Varro, says Pliny, and another group featured *mirabilia*, including birth-prodigies.[32]

With the new portico filled with manubial artistic displays, Pompey was following Q. Caecilius Metellus Macedonicus' precedent (after his victory in 146 BCE) that extended display for sculpture from a temple itself to a surrounding enclosure, the portico referred to by Cicero in the *Verrines* as a place we (Romans) can go to see sculpture in public. Metellus built the portico around a Temple of Jupiter Stator, next to a restored Temple of Juno Regina. The most famous group exhibited there was Lysippos' Granikos monument, featuring statues of Alexander the Great and twenty-five of his companions, all on horseback at the battle of Granikos – hence, an exceptionally impressive display. Metellus had transported this whole bronze group from Macedonia to Rome.[33] Because of the size and unified theme of the display, the idea for programmatic grouping was thus already established in Rome.

Pompey's splendid new complex, dedicated in 55 BCE, became a noted landmark in the city and an expanded precedent for what was possible as a form of museum-like display of both antique art and contemporary art for the public. The complex was renovated several times in antiquity, with statuary added; as an important artistic landmark and garden-park, it is featured in poetry evocative of Rome. It is also remembered as the site of the assassination of Julius Caesar only nine years after

---

[31] For living trees in the Triumphal procession, Pliny, *HN* 12.111. On Pompey's theater complex, especially its garden, the art displayed in the porticoes, and Pergamene antecedents, see A. Kuttner, "Republican Rome Looks at Pergamon," *HSCP* 97 (1995): 157–178; and "Culture and History at Pompey's Museum," *TAPA* 129 (1999): 343–373. One of the items said to have been displayed there is the Sappho by Silanion, presumably the one taken by Verres from Syracuse.

[32] Pliny, *HN* 36.41, 7.34; discussion of the Nations in Carey (2003): 62–63.

[33] *Verr.* 4.4.126; Pliny, *HN* 34.64; for Metellus' triumph, Pape (1975): 15–16; Metellus' portico, Haselberger, *MAR*, s.v. Porticus Octaviae (renamed after renovation in the Augustan period); discussion of art collection, Isager (1991): 160.

its dedication (in 44 BCE), in the Curia located within the portico. Augustus was the first to renovate the complex (even though Pompey was an opponent of Julius Caesar), in part because of the Republican values associated with Pompey, and because the complex had already become a popular gathering place in the city. He states in the *Res gestae* that he restored it at great expense without inscribing his name on it (*RG* 20.1).

Plutarch comments that Pompey's new house was built next to the theater complex, like a small boat tethered to a ship. Earlier he had lived in a modest house (the one decorated with rostra from pirates' ships), but even this one was not large. A later owner of the house is said to have been puzzled by its modest size, wondering where Pompey the Great held his dinner parties (*Pomp.* 40.5). Although the theater complex has left its footprint on the modern city of Rome, and parts of its brick and concrete vaulted substructure can be visited in two restaurants where they serve as wine cellars, the foundations of the house have not yet been identified. After the third Triumph, Pompey also built near the lake at Albano a villa that later passed into imperial hands and was rebuilt by Domitian; the Pope's residence at Castel Gandolfo now sits over the remains of the villa.[34]

Even before Pompey's new complex, Julius Caesar had appreciated the value and potency of architectural patronage as an expression of political power. He was keenly aware of the superior sophistication and grace of Alexandria and Pergamon, Antioch and Rhodes, and hoped to rebuild Rome with similar elegance. Of concern to him too were practical amenities: he wanted to alleviate the constant problem of flooding from the Tiber with better drainage and canals and to improve the harbor at Ostia, and he had road and drainage projects in mind for sites elsewhere in Italy. He was also mindful of the usefulness of public

[34] For Pompey's various houses, estates, and personal wealth, see Shatzman (1975): 389–393; for the villa at the Alban lake, see F. Coarelli, *Dintorni de Roma* (Rome, 1993): 68–69, 72–76.

entertainment and expanded and refurbished the Circus Maximus. He set up temporary venues for spectacular shows such as scaled "sea-battles" (*naumachiae*) using small boats in a large tank of water. His vision for a grander city was partly realized in his life-time but because of his death, many of his plans were only carried out later by Augustus. He was able to change the calendar by pontifical fiat (the basis for the one we now use), but conquering space took longer than mastering the reckoning of time.

Of interest here is his broader, more comprehensive view of the possibilities of the manubial purse: not content with spectacular games and displays – he had already arranged them when he was aedile in 65 BCE, with gladiators using silver equipment – and not content with manubial temples and statuary, he wanted to rebuild the public areas of the city. In effect, he was inventing for Rome the new role of *princeps* as a patron that extended far beyond the conquering general of the Republic. Those older manubial dedications were agglutinative within the city and, in contrast, he wanted to replace what was there with marble buildings and expand the public spaces of the city.

In a letter written about July 1, 54 BCE, Cicero tells Atticus about L. Aemilius Paullus' reconstruction of the old Basilica Aemilia in the Forum, using antique marble columns, and how Caesar's friends (meaning himself and C. Oppius, he explains) have spent large sums on his behalf to widen the Forum with a *monumentum* (the Forum Iulium) and how they intend to extend the Saepta (voting precinct) in the Campus Martius with a colonnade a "mile" in perimeter. In this letter, at least, it seems that Julius Caesar's plans were well received by at least some of his contemporaries, who were willing to act as agents on his behalf. Two of his buildings stand out today as impressive even in ruinous condition: his Basilica Julia in the Forum Romanum, begun in 54 according to Cicero's letter, and paid for by spoils from the Gallic wars, was 101 m by 49 m, with at least two stories and fronted in white marble. The Forum Iulium was also started in 54 BCE, in the form of a rectangular enclosure framed with porticoes, and a temple of Venus Genetrix at the end on the long axis. In a twist on Pompey's dedication of a temple to Venus Victrix, here Caesar was emphasizing the descent of his family from the goddess herself, through Iulus, the son of Aeneas.[35] The purchase price for the land alone for the Forum Iulium was formidable because the land had to be bought up from various owners, and it was prime real estate adjacent to the Forum Romanum. Pliny and Suetonius claim it cost a hundred million sesterces, and Suetonius says specifically the funds came from his *manubiae*.[36]

Julius Caesar dedicated in the temple of Venus Genetrix the six cabinets of gems and rings noted previously and two paintings by Timomachus, a contemporary painter, of Ajax and of Medea that cost him eighty talents, mentioned by Pliny three times. He also dedicated there a breastplate made of British pearls, apparently an inferior variety.[37] Suetonius states that Caesar was personally very interested in gems and pearls, collected them, and would weigh them knowledgeably with his hand. He also collected antique statues and paintings; unbelievably, he even claims that Caesar went to Britain in the hope of acquiring pearls! (*Iul.* 47). Notable in these comments by authors writing more than a hundred years after his death is that they do not mention by artist or subject any sculpture or painting that was in his private collection, only those he dedicated in temples.[38] Quite likely he appreciated such art, but actual ownership and private display was not his primary objective, since he had more important ambitions and little leisure.

---

[35] He was said to have vowed a temple to Venus Victrix on the eve of the battle at Pharsalus, but later changed the epithet to Venus Genetrix (Appian, *B Civ.* 2.68). For the cult, see Weinstock (1971): 80–90.

[36] Pliny, *HN* 36.103; Suet., *Iul.* 26.2. For details of the basilica and forum, see Richardson (1992) and *LTUR* s.v. Basilica Iulia and Forum Iulium; Favro (1996): 60–78.

[37] Pliny, *HN* 7.126, 35.26, 35.136; pearls: 9.116.

[38] The painting by Apelles and Protogenes described by Pliny (*HN* 35.82–83) and destroyed by fire on the Palatine was owned by Augustus, not Julius Caesar, *pace* Bounia (2004): 190. For J. Caesar's houses in Rome (not on the Palatine) and villas, see Shatzman (1975): 356.

Another project for public benefit that Julius Caesar had in mind was a public library, what would be the first public library in Rome: Suetonius says that he planned libraries of Greek and Latin authors, to be accessible to the largest possible public, and he even had selected Marcus Varro to be their manager and head (*Iul.* 44). This project too was cut short by his death, but the idea was taken up by C. Asinius Pollio (76 BCE–4 CE), another correspondent of Cicero, who achieved the consulship in 40 and, after a victory over the Parthini in Illyria in 39, was awarded a Triumph.[39] From the *manubiae*, he built the first library in Rome (the first in the world to be built *ex manubiis*, Pliny emphasizes), with separate areas for Greek and Latin texts. The library had statuary of authors, and only one living author was represented, Marcus Varro, a special honor for the scholar.[40] After his Triumph, Pollio seems to have retired from public life and taken up scholarly pursuits. He was a respected critic and grammarian and wrote a *History* of the recent civil war that featured his eyewitness testimonia.

Asinius Pollio also established a famous public art collection, whose holdings are described by Pliny in some detail. It included a few antique (fourth century BCE) Greek sculptures, but the emphasis in it seems to have been contemporary pieces, perhaps favoring marble over bronze; it seems that Pollio used manubial funds to commission art.[41] The location of what must have been a very sizable collection is uncertain. The combined literary references suggest but do not state that the art collection was in the Atrium Libertatis (together with the libraries

[39] On Pollio and his treatment by other ancient authors, especially contemporary poets, see L. Morgan, "The Autopsy of C. Asinius Pollio," *JHS* 90(2000): 51–69.

[40] Pliny, *HN* 7.115, 35.10; Isidore, *Orig.* 6.5.2.

[41] Pliny, *HN* 36.23–25; 36.33; listed by Ridgway (1984): 110. The collection has been extensively discussed; see, e.g., G. Becatti, "Letture Pliniane: Le opere d'arte nei monumenta Asini Pollionis e negli Horti Serviliani," in *Studi in Onore di Calderini e Paribeni*, 3 (Milan 1956): 199–210; P. Gros, *Aurea Templa: Recherches sur l'architecture religieuse de Rome à l'époque d'Auguste*, *BEFAR* 231 (Rome, 1976): 163–165; Isager (1991): 163–167; Bounia (2004): 188–190.

and an archive), a building also used by the censors. The location of
the Atrium Libertatis, however, is also much disputed: an attractive
solution is that it was northwest of the Forum Iulium, later built over by
Trajan's Basilica Ulpia and two libraries, which would have replaced the
Republican library.[42] E. La Rocca has suggested that the art collection
itself was not in the Atrium Libertatis but rather in his gardens, the
horti Asiniani, in the area later occupied by the Baths of Caracalla.
The Farnese Bull (a complex, large-scale statue-group representing the
Punishment of Dirce), found in the Baths, may be a link to Asinius
Pollio's collection because Pliny states that he had an apparently large
and impressive piece of that subject.[43]

If La Rocca's suggestion is correct, Asinius Pollio combined a garden-
park with a display of sculpture, much like the porticoes attached to
Pompey's theater complex, and given the scale and number of the sculptures, a garden would be an attractive setting for them (within an architectural frame, as was typical of the period). Especially significant in
these projects, the libraries and the public art collection, is the emphasis
on access to these cultural works for everyone. Pliny specifically states
that Asinius Pollio wanted spectators for his "*monumenta*," referring
to the collection of sculpture (*HN* 36.33). Here again, we see the astute
use of public displays to enhance reputation; Pollio no longer wanted
to follow the traditional trajectory of a public career (or more likely
saw that he could not pursue one in the political climate). With the
manubial offerings of the public library and public art collection, he

---

[42] For a summary with bibliography, see Haselberger, *MAR*, s.v. Atrium Libertatis.

[43] E. La Rocca, "Artisti rodii negli *horti* romani," in M. Cima and E. La Rocca, eds., *Horti romani: atti del convegno internazionale*, Roma, 4–6 maggio 1995 [1998]: 203–274. La Rocca argues that the literary references do not specifically name the Atrium Libertatis as the site of the collection, and the Farnese Bull, discovered in the Baths of Caracalla, provides at least a thematic connection, possibly an actual holdover. The Farnese Bull is usually thought to be a later Antonine or Severan version of the subject; see D. Kleiner, *Roman Sculpture* (New Haven, 1992): 338–339.

won lasting remembrance (paid for by military success) for his cultural interests and public generosity. Even though the presumed objectives for public access might have been in part self-serving, and the displayed items were acquired in war or paid for by war booty, nonetheless the first ideas for public libraries and public museums are firmly rooted in the cultural currents of the first century BCE in Rome.

Many of Julius Caesar's projects were cut short, but the ideas were there and enough had been put into motion so that after the battle at Actium, Augustus together with Marcus Agrippa were in a position to take over the projects and expand some (such as the Temple of Mars and the Saepta) and abandon others (the canals). Like Julius Caesar, Augustus was acutely aware of the programmatic and even propagandistic value of architectural patronage, a subject by now much discussed and thoroughly studied.[44] In his *Res gestae*, he states that he completed Julius Caesar's buildings, constructed new temples and other buildings (twenty are listed), and refurbished and restored eighty-two temples, aqueducts, roads, and Pompey's theater. His additions to Rome's magnificence were especially remarkable in three separate regions of the city. The Forum of Augustus expanded the public space of the old Forum Romanum and complemented the new Forum Iulium, to which it was attached; the Campus Martius now became a place for dynastic monuments, starting with his mausoleum and the Ara Pacis; and on the Palatine, where the family's private houses were modest, Augustus built a Temple of Apollo adjacent to his house, with long porticoes attached, decorated with sculpture, and Rome's second library. He thereby retained an image of modesty in private living, but under the shade of Apollo and with suitable amenities.

Three times in the *Res gestae*, the source of the funds spent is noted as "*ex manubiis*": Augustus used booty to give a generous cash donative

---

[44] Essential on this topic are P. Zanker, *The Power of Images in the Age of Augustus* (Ann Arbor, 1990); the essays in K. A. Raaflaub and M. Toher, eds., *Between Republic and Empire* (Berkeley, 1990); K. Galinski, *Augustan Culture* (Princeton, 1996); Favro (1996).

to the people of Rome individually (15.1); for the construction of the Temple of Mars Ultor (the Avenger) and the Forum of Augustus around it on ground he purchased (21.1); and for dedications on the Capitoline, the Temple of Divus Julius, of Apollo, of Vesta, and of Mars Ultor, costing one hundred million sesterces (21.2).[45] The manubial funds from Cleopatra VII's treasury in Egypt must have funded most of this.

The emphasis in the *Res gestae* on the use of *manubiae* for the Temple of Mars Ultor and the new Forum is supported by the clearly triumphal nature of its sculptural program and some of the dedications it housed.[46] Within the large rectangular space (ca. 90 × 125 m), framed by two-story porticoes on the two long sides, was the Temple of Mars Ultor, in the Corinthian order with an octastyle façade and built of white Luna marble. The second story of the porticoes featured three-quarter-scale replicas of the Caryatids on the Erechtheum in Athens. Inside the temple were statues of Mars the Avenger, Venus, and Divus Julius (the deified Julius Caesar). In the back wall of the porticoes and along the two hemicycles that break out from the back wall were some 108 niches for statuary. Among the people represented were early Roman historical figures, the stars of the Julian clan back to Aeneas, and the *summi viri* (great men) of the Roman Republic, with brief biographies inscribed on their pedestals.[47]

Works of art placed there by Augustus included two paintings by Apelles, of Castor and Pollux, and War and the Triumph of Alexander. The ancient ivory cult statue of Athena Alea taken by Augustus from her temple at Tegea in Greece was there, along with an ivory Apollo and goblets made of iron. Four tent-supports that had belonged to Alexander

---

[45] The dedicated gifts in the Temple of Jupiter included sixteen thousand pounds of gold, pearls, and precious stones, according to Suetonius (Aug. 30).

[46] Zanker (1990): 193–215, *passim*; Galinsky (1996): 197–213.

[47] For the Forum Augustum and Temple of Mars, see Richardson (1992), *LTUR*, and Haselberger, *MAR*: s.v. Forum Augustum; for the sculptural program, Zanker (1990): 114–115, 193–201; on the *summi viri* and how the selection may relate to Livy's history, T. J. Luce, "Livy, Augustus, and the Forum Augustum," in Raaflaub and Toher (1990): 123–138.

the Great were brought to Rome; Augustus set up two in front of the Temple of Mars Ultor and two in front of the Regia in the Forum Romanum, thus linking the two complexes.[48] Items associated with Alexander had added value because of their provenance: in the Temple of Apollo on the Palatine, Augustus dedicated a lamp-stand shaped like an apple tree that Alexander had taken as booty from Thebes and dedicated at Kyme.[49] In Pausanias' description of Tegea, the removal of the ancient ivory statue of Athena Alea along with the tusks of the Calydonian Boar was the point at which he includes a long excursus about plundered art, discussed previously in Chapter 1, with a plea to excuse Augustus, since others had similarly looted art from conquered people (see Appendix, no. 7).

Between the Forum Iulium and the Forum Romanum was the Curia Julia (Senate House), where Augustus dedicated a statue of Victory that he took from Tarentum in southern Italy, apparently on the occasion of his own victory. This statue became a point of contention later in the fourth century CE, when it was removed by Constantius, returned by Julian, and removed again by Gratian in 382. The Tarentine statue of Victory was decorated with spoils from Egypt, and other Egyptian spoils were dedicated in the temples of Jupiter Capitolinus, Juno and Minerva, Divus Julius, and Venus, according to Cassius Dio (writing in the third century CE). He goes on to comment that Cleopatra was thus glorified because her possessions were dedicated in Rome's temples, and that there was a gold statue of her in the Temple of Venus (Genetrix).[50] Another carefully orchestrated program of display was located in the

---

[48] Paintings: Pliny, *HN* 35.27, 93–94; Pliny says the emperor Claudius cut out the face of Alexander and substituted that of Augustus. Ivory Apollo: *HN* 7.183; iron goblets: *HN* 34.141; tent supports: *HN* 34.48; ivory from Tegea: Pausanias, 8.46.4–5.

[49] Pliny, *HN* 35.151.

[50] Cass. Dio, 51.22. The statue of Cleopatra is mentioned also by Appian, *B Civ.* 2.102, who states that Julius Caesar put it there.

Temple of Concordia Augusta in the Forum Romanum, just below the Tabularium. It contained many works of art, a few of them Greek antiques but most of them contemporary, in an arrangement that had cosmological and zodiacal significance.[51]

Two of Augustus' many projects deserve special notice since they feature plunder as primary focal points. Augustus was the first to take obelisks outside of Egypt and make new, triumphal monuments with them.[52] Two obelisks were brought from Heliopolis (now a suburb of Cairo) in 10 BCE and used in open areas in two different sectors of the city where they would be highly visible. Their identical inscriptions carved on supporting pedestals proclaimed them as dedications to the Sun and commemorations of the conquest of Egypt.[53] One of them was quarried originally in the Nineteenth Dynasty, by Seti I (with hieroglyphs added by his son Ramses II [1304–1237 BCE]) from red Aswan granite and was placed by Augustus in the Circus Maximus on the *spina* (central divider) on the south edge of the Palatine Hill. It was excavated and moved a considerable distance in the sixteenth century and now stands in the Piazza del Popolo, north of the Campus Martius. The obelisk became such a well-known feature of the Circus Maximus that it is represented in several later depictions of the circus (such as the mosaic in the apodyterium to the baths at Piazza Armerina), and it inspired Theodosius I to import an obelisk from Egypt to Constantinople for the Hippodrome there. In placing the Egyptian obelisk in the Circus Maximus,

[51] For exegesis of the sculptural program, see B. Kellum, "The City Adorned: Programmatic Display at the *Aedes Concordiae Augustae*," in Raaflaub and Toher (1990): 276–307.

[52] Pliny, *HN* 36.71. On obelisks in Rome, see C. D'Onofrio, *Gli obelischi di Roma* (Rome, 1965); E. Iversen, *Obelisks in Exile*, I (Copenhagen, 1968); A. Roullet, *The Egyptian and Egyptianizing Monuments of Imperial Rome* (Leiden, 1972); Richardson (1992): 272–276.

[53] *CIL* 6.701 (formerly in Circus Maximus) and 702 (Campus Martius): IMP. CAESAR DIVI. F. AUGUSTUS PONTIFEX MAXIMUS IMP. XII COS XI TRIB. POT XIV AEGUPTO IN POTESTATEM POPULI ROMANI REDACTA SOLI DONUM DEDIT: Imperial Caesar, son of Divus (Julius), Augustus, chief priest, in 10 BCE, Egypt having been brought under the will of the Roman People, gave this as a gift to Sol (the Sun).

Augustus was also linking himself to Julius Caesar, who had expanded the circus earlier, and to Romulus, credited with its initial construction.

The second obelisk was given a special setting in the Campus Martius, where it became the pivot of a set of dynastic monuments (Fig. 12). Originally quarried by Psammetichus II (595–589 BCE), it was also of red Aswan granite and was placed on a stepped base so as to stand 100 Roman feet (ca. 30m) high. It served as the gnomon of an enormous sundial (*horologium*) marked with bronze lines and labels set into travertine pavement. The pavement and a few of the Greek labels were discovered by E. Buchner in excavations of 1979–80, carried out in the basement of an apartment building now over the original site of the horologium. Pliny remarks that Novius Facundus, a mathematician, worked out the arrangement so that the length of the shadow cast by the obelisk-gnomon on the winter solstice fell on the whole width (radius) of the circular pavement surrounding it. In addition, the shadow pointed to the nearby Ara Pacis on September 23, Augustus' birthday. At different times of day and year, it could point north to the Mausoleum of Augustus and south to Agrippa's Pantheon, thus encompassing Augustus, his family, and all the gods. There was an additional play with geometry: the Mausoleum is circular in plan, as was Agrippa's Pantheon (predecessor to the current Pantheon built by Hadrian), and the pavement for the horologium was also circular. Two smaller red granite Egyptian obelisks framed the entry to Augustus' mausoleum and the bronze tablets with the text of the *Res gestae*, making the connection among the tomb, Augustus' achievements, and the horologium all the more explicit.[54]

Novius Facundus tipped the obelisk with a gilt ball so as to focus its shadow. But, for the previous thirty years, Pliny says, the gnomon and pavement were out of adjustment; the pavement was subsequently

[54] The pair of smaller obelisks for the Mausoleum was quarried of red Aswan granite in the Roman period and left uninscribed. The pair is not mentioned by Pliny. One stands behind Sta. Maria Maggiore, the other is in the Piazza del Quirinale.

FIGURE 12. Egyptian obelisk from Augustus' Horologium, now in Piazza di Montecitorio, Rome. Photo credit: Author.

raised and restored under Domitian, and Buchner's excavations revealed a part of that rebuilding.[55] The problem of flooding from the Tiber over the Campus Martius would not be resolved until the later nineteenth century, and flooding or subsidence under the heavy obelisk must have contributed to the misalignment. This second Egyptian obelisk not only brought together Augustus' dynastic monuments on the Campus Martius but also, together with its brother obelisk in the Circus Maximus, linked two regions of the city where large numbers of people could gather with plundered memorials of the triumph over Egypt. The scale of the huge, authentic monuments from Egypt and their dedicatory Latin inscriptions beneath the Egyptian hieroglyphs on the faces of the obelisks were constant reminders of Rome's dominion over the Mediterranean. The two plundered obelisks were Augustus' most impressive and dramatic trophies over Cleopatra VII and indirectly, Marc Antony.

Later Roman emperors brought more obelisks from Egypt, some of them ancient and others newly quarried (left blank or carved with rather garbled, uncertain new hieroglyphs). The last, oldest, and largest obelisk brought to Rome from Egypt was a gift to the city from Constantius II (r. 337–361), who was dazzled by his first visit there. An account of the gift is provided by Ammianus Marcellinus, writing in the late fourth century CE, in which he sets forth the issue of the ethics of its acquisition. His retinue urged Constantius to move it, saying that Augustus had been reluctant to try because of its huge size. Ammianus corrects their assertion, saying that Augustus knew it was dedicated to the Sun, and that because it was set inside the sacred precinct of a temple with forbidden entry, this was the reason he left it untouched (17.4; see Appendix, no. 8).[56] It was in the Temple of Ammon (Karnak) at

---

[55] Pliny, *HN* 36.72–73; E. Buchner, *Die Sonnenuhr des Augustus* (Mainz, 1982); Haselberger, *MAR*: s.v. Horologium Augusti.

[56] For an evaluation of Ammianus Marcellinus as a source, see Conte (1994b): 647–650; D. Rohrbacher, *The Historians of Late Antiquity* (London, 2002): 14–41.

Thebes, and the obelisk had been quarried and set up by the Eighteenth Dynasty Pharaoh Tutmoses III, 1504–1450. Constantine I, earlier in the fourth century CE, decided to move it – Ammianus says that he dismissed the idea of sacrilege and believed it would not be sacrilegious to move it from one temple to another because he rightly regarded Rome as the temple of the whole world. (Actually Constantine seems to have intended it for Constantinople, not Rome.) But when Constantine died, the obelisk simply lay at Alexandria. Twenty years later, it was sent by Constantius II to Rome as a gift, where it was set up on the *spina* in the Circus Maximus along with Augustus' obelisk from Heliopolis. Today it stands in front of St. John in Lateran.[57] The imperial image of the Circus Maximus with *two* obelisks was later imitated in the Hippodrome at Constantinople (Fig. 13).

In total, forty-eight obelisks are known to have existed in Rome, of which twenty-six are accounted for and twenty-two are missing. Fragments exist within the pavements and steps of various churches in Rome. Because of the image and reputation of Augustus, and because many of the obelisks had later histories and new uses in early modern Rome, plundered obelisks shaped the very image of the imperial city well into the nineteenth century. Only one authentic Egyptian obelisk exists in the United States, quarried by Tutmoses III and moved by Cleopatra VII to Alexandria for a monument to Julius Caesar; its twin from Alexandria is in London.[58] In many smaller cities and towns in the United States, United Kingdom, and western Europe, however, one can

---

[57] *CIL* 6.1163, 31249-*ILS* 736; D'Onofrio (1965): 160–172; Iversen (1968), 1: 55–64. It was moved from the Circus Maximus to its present position by Pope Sixtus V, in 1587, with D. Fontana as architect.

[58] The obelisk in Central Park, New York, was offered to the United States by the khedive of Egypt Ismail Pasha in 1869 as a gesture of friendship. The first of the pair from Alexandria, now in London, was given to the United Kingdom out of gratitude for the defeat of Napoleon in 1801, but it was not moved from Egypt until 1877. See M. D'Alton, *The New York Obelisk, or How Cleopatra's Needle Came to New York and What Happened When It Got Here* (New York, 1993).

FIGURE 13. Obelisk of Theodosius I, Hippodrome, Istanbul. Photo credit: Vanni / Art Resource, NY.

FIGURE 14. Pedimental sculpture representing the Amazonomachy of Theseus, attributed to the Temple of Apollo Sosianus in Rome, originally Greek, perhaps from Eretria, mid fifth century BCE, Capitoline Museums, Rome. Photo credit: Author.

find small imitation obelisks set up in central squares. The Washington Monument in Washington, DC, built larger and hollow with stairs and elevators, evokes the visual imagery of a capital city with its obelisk-shape on an even larger scale. Augustus' use of plundered obelisks as trophies was transformed into an expression of imperial might and eventually into local civic pride. Obelisks have become such a familiar part of the urban vocabulary that it is almost forgotten that the first pair originally taken by Augustus, for the Circus Maximus and the Campus Martius, was war booty.

Augustus kept mostly for himself the prerogative of grand imperial projects, but he did allow Marcus Agrippa to take on the improvement of the infrastructure of Rome and the construction of the original Pantheon. He encouraged public donatives of various sorts and allowed

C. Sosius (cos. 32 BCE) to start the rebuilding of the temple of Apollo Medicus (Sosianus) near the Theater of Marcellus, in white Luna marble. The pediments were probably decorated with the early fifth-century BCE original pedimental sculpture taken from the Temple of Apollo Daphnephoros at Etretria in Euboea, apparently as art booty; many pieces of it have been preserved in Rome, found around the foundations of the temple[59] (Fig. 14).

In addition to the ancient Greek pedimental sculpture (nearly five hundred years old by then), an antique Phoenician cedar-wood image of Apollo was brought from Seleucia by Sosius, apparently as art booty and perhaps used as the cult image in the Roman temple. This temple became another showcase for famous antique art, and new friezes were carved for its interior, lavish with colored-marble floors and columns. Other sculpture set up in the temple related to Apollo: Niobids by Scopas or Praxiteles; an Apollo by Philiscus of Rhodes; Apollo with a lyre by Timarchides; Apollo, and his sister Diana and mother Latona, and the nine Muses.[60] Despite Sosius' contributions that the name of the temple commemorates, it seems likely that Augustus either completed the temple or took over the project: the triumphal imagery of the friezes suggests victory over northern barbarians rather than easterners, where Sosius had won victories (in Judaea), celebrated in a Triumph of 34 BCE.[61] If this suggestion is correct, we see in one temple the transformation from manubial dedications made by a *triumphator* of the Republic to the imperial prerogative for such constructions by the emperor.

By the time of these elaborate programs of Augustan display, a few Greek antiques and *spolia* were included, but by far the majority of the sculpture and the buildings themselves were new creations. Those

---

[59] E. La Rocca, *Amazzonomachia. Le sculture frontale del tempio di Apollo Sosiano* (Rome, 1985). The pedimental sculpture represents Theseus and the Amazons.
[60] Cedar-wood image: Pliny, *HN* 13.53; Niobids: 36.28; Apollo, other groups, 36.34.
[61] Kleiner (1992): 84–86.

that were ancient, including the ivory Athena Alea from Tegea and Myron's Zeus from Samos, were rededicated in Rome and might have been selected by Augustus not only for their quality but also because their content suited the intended new context.[62] Apart from the obelisks, dazzling and highly prized in their own right and because of the extraordinary difficulty of transporting them by sea, the Roman era of acquisition of art as plunder was drawing to an end.

Because of his position as emperor inaugurating a new age and a new political system, Augustus is naturally the main character in many anecdotes told by later authors as illustrations of cultural changes. One of them was used by Cassius Dio to illustrate approvingly Augustus' proper frugality and dislike of luxury. In this account, Augustus, in a seaside villa at Pausilypon on the Bay of Naples, was the guest of P. Vedius Pollio, an *eques*, son of a freedman and probably from Beneventum, who became quite rich and was famous for his cruelty.

In a throwback to the generation of the *piscinarii*, Vedius Pollio has kept up the *piscinae* but with man-eating eels he uses for punishment. When a slave accidentally broke a myrrhine cup (fluorspar crystal, the type made popular by Pompey), Vedius Pollio motioned to other slaves to throw the culprit into the pool with the eels. But the boy flung himself at the feet of Augustus and begged for mercy. Augustus did intervene, but Vedius Pollio refused to pay attention until Augustus ordered that all other crystal vessels be brought out and proceeded to break them, one by one. Finally, Vedius Pollio got the point, and the slave was not punished, or at least not thrown to the eels (Cass.

---

[62] The Tegean Athena Alea might have been intended to evoke Evander and the Arcadian past of Rome, suggested in Virgil and Livy (references in Gros [1975]: 157, footnote 18); this was in keeping with the sculptural program of the Forum of Augustus and the Temple of Mars Ultor with its emphasis on Rome's history. (Evander is depicted in Roman literature as a heroic émigré from Arcadia in Greece who introduced into early Rome a cluster of cultural features, including the alphabet.)

Dio, 54.23). When Vedius Pollio died (in that year, 15 BCE), he left to Augustus the villa at Pausilypon, a large amount of money, and his house in Rome. Augustus had the house in Rome razed so that Vedius Pollio would have no memorial (*monumentum*) and built the Porticus of Livia on the land. It became a recreational area for the public with extensive gardens.[63]

Pliny relates another unusual dining experience of Augustus (*HN* 33.82–83). Again as a guest, this time in Bologna, Augustus was dining with a veteran army officer known for his wit who had fought under Antony in the Parthian campaigns of 36 BCE. Augustus remembered that in that campaign, a famous, very ancient cult image made of solid gold, representing Anahita, a Persian fertility goddess, had been taken from the Temple of Anahita. He asked his host whether it was true that the man who took the statue as plunder was struck blind, became paralyzed, and died. The host replied that Augustus was right then eating his dinner off one of the goddess's legs, that he himself had taken the statue and owed his whole fortune to the plunder. (After plundering the statue, he apparently had no hesitation in melting it down and turning part of the goddess into a dinner service!)

VERRINE EMPERORS

Two of the Julio-Claudian emperors, Caligula (r. 37–41) and Nero (r. 54–68), are depicted by ancient authors (especially Pliny, Suetonius, Josephus, and Cassius Dio) on the Verrine model. In these accounts, their passion, rapacity, and cruelty had little restraint and they expressed it in ingenious and novel ways. They need not have exercised the duplicity of Verres, for they were emperors, not accountable and not potentially

---

[63] For the porticus, Richardson (1992) and Haselberger, *MAR*: s.v. Porticus Liviae; for the villa Pausilypon and its *piscinae*, which have been excavated and accord well with the historical account, see Higginbotham (1997): 191–194. For Vedius Pollio, see R. Syme, "Who Was Vedius Pollio?" *JRS* 51 (1961): 24–30.

facing a trial in Rome. Both evidently delighted in Greek art, especially famous antiques, and plucked choice pieces from public displays in Rome for their private use. Not content with that, they reached into mainland Greece to requisition whatever caught their attention. Caligula is said to have wanted to insert an image of himself into the Temple at Jerusalem. Both fancied themselves as especially qualified connoisseurs of statuary: Caligula, taking on a guise of divinity, felt he knew his fellow deities best; and Nero, considering himself a great artist, felt he alone could truly appreciate masterpieces and therefore naturally deserved to own them. These portraits are built up by ancient authors out of anecdotes told about how each deviated from the normative ethics surrounding the use of art and architecture as egregious illustrations of their character. As in Nepos' *Life of Atticus* and Cicero's portrait of Verres in the *Verrines*, there is a clear dichotomy between "good" and "bad" associations with art and architecture that contribute to judgments about the men themselves.

In the second part of his biography of Caligula, where the "monstrous" side of his character is described, Suetonius draws on the abuse of statuary as one of the themes that illustrate Caligula's depravity.[64] In Rome, Augustus had moved many statues of prominent people from the Capitoline to the Campus Martius because the Capitoline had become overcrowded with statuary. In a mark of his envy and malice toward others, even the dead, Suetonius says Caligula had all these statues overturned and smashed so thoroughly that it was impossible to reconstruct them with their inscriptions (*Calig.* 34). Thus, Caligula tried to destroy memory itself by attacking the *monumenta* of others. He also is

---

[64] G. Suetonius Tranquillus (c. 70–130 CE), a friend of Pliny the Elder's nephew Pliny the Younger, probably wrote his *Lives of the Caesars* early in the second century, during the reign of Trajan. He held various administrative posts in the imperial bureaucracy, including a position as a secretary under Hadrian (and was fired, ca. 122, for an unknown reason). As an administrator, he had access to archival material and other primary evidence for his biographies.

said to have built an extension between his palace on the Palatine and the Temple of Castor and Pollux, making the temple of the twins his vestibule.

He ordered that all statues of gods in Greece that were notable for religious and artistic significance should be brought to Rome so that their heads could be removed and replaced with his own. To emphasize Caligula's rapacity and lack of scruple, here Suetonius inserts the story about the laughing chryselephantine image of Zeus at Olympia, made by Pheidias nearly five hundred years earlier. This happened near the end of the emperor's life, at age twenty-nine, and the laughter and collapsing scaffolding was seen as an omen of his assassination (*Calig.* 22, 57).

From Greece, Caligula succeeded in removing the famous Eros by Praxiteles at Thespiae, the one Cicero mentioned in the course of his description of Gaius Heius' private shrine at Messana, from which Verres took another Eros by Praxiteles. The one looted by Caligula was returned to Thespiae by Claudius, Caligula's successor. Then it was stolen again from Thespiae by Nero, Claudius' successor, who put it in the Porticus of Octavia (the replacement for the Porticus of Metellus) and it eventually was burned in the fire of 80 CE.[65] So important was the statue to the people of Thespiae, however, that they commissioned a copy by the Athenian sculptor Menodorus. This copy was celebrated in a verse dedication written by a Roman woman, Herennia Procula, probably in the Flavian period, and carved in stone, perhaps on the pedestal of the copy.[66] Clearly Menodorus' "copy" of the Praxitelean original was sufficiently evocative and impressive to sustain the interest of visitors to the sanctuary.

---

[65] Cicero, *Verr.* 2.4.4, 2.4.135; Strabo, 9.2.25; Pausanias, 9.27.3; Pliny, 36.22. Praxiteles evidently sculpted several versions of Eros. Pausanias (I.22) tells the story of how Phryne, Praxiteles' mistress, tricked him into revealing that an Eros in his workshop was one of the two of his works he valued most highly; he then gave it to her. It is possible that the one at Thespiae was once Phryne's because a statue of her was also set up in the sanctuary.

[66] K. Gutzwiller, "Gender and Inscribed Epigram: Herennia Procula and the Thespian Eros," *TAPA* 134 (2004): 383–418.

Caligula also took statues from Athens that were later returned by Claudius. Preserved today are parts of seven statue bases, with inscriptions thanking Claudius for returning the statues.[67] On one of the fragmentary bases, the original dedicatory inscription reveals that the base originally held a statue honoring Sempronia Atratina Paulla, daughter of L. Sempronius Atratinus and wife of L. Gellius Publicola (cos. 36 BCE). Such an honorary statue would seem to be an odd choice to loot and take off to Rome: perhaps the Athenians filled a Caligulan quota in this way.[68] Cassius Dio makes a broad statement about Claudius, that he returned to cities the statues that Gaius (Caligula) had taken from them, and gave back to the Dioscouri (Castor and Pollux) their temple, and to Pompey his theater – Caligula had obliterated the inscription with Pompey's name.[69] Claudius, then, was in the mold of his great-grandfather T. Pomponius Atticus with this gesture to Athens and reminds us of Scipio Aemilianus' *humanitas* with these restorations. In this instance of the looting and restoration of statuary, we have not only the statements of ancient authors but also the actual inscriptions in Athens thanking Claudius for the return of statues. Claudius is also credited by Josephus with returning to Jews the ritual vestments and crown of the high priest that had been under Roman control.[70]

Nero, however, not only took again the Eros from Thespiae but also is said to have taken five hundred bronze statues from the sanctuary

---

[67] *IG* II² 5173–5179, with additional fragments, listed and discussed by M. C. Hoff, "The So-called Agoranomion and the Imperial Cult in Julio-Claudian Athens," *AA* 93(1994): 116, and footnote 126.

[68] *IG* II² 5179, *SEG* XL.124; P. Graindor suggests that Caligula was collecting more than just antiques (*Athènes de Tibère a Trajan* [Cairo, 1931]: 9–10). It is also possible that the base used for the returned statue did not belong with it. The find-spot of this base was on the Akropolis; the others (where specified in *IG*) were found as follows: 5173: west of the Parthenon; 5174: north of the Propylaia; 5175: north side of the Akropolis; 5176: in the Theater of Dionysos, on the south slope of the Akropolis.

[69] Cass. Dio, 60.6.8; he does not state specifically which cities.

[70] Josephus, *AJ* 20.10–14. Josephus also mentions earlier restorations of sacred vessels to the Temple by Cyrus, Darius, Ptolemy Philadelphus, and Antiochus III: see Weitzman (2005): 93–95.

of Apollo at Delphi. The context of this accusation is found in Pausanias' account of the history of looting at Delphi. He begins with a discussion of the possible origins of names of topographical landmarks and places around Delphi, and then of the name "Pythian," an epithet of Apollo. He gives various versions of stories, legends, and genealogies to explain the name, but the stable feature in them is that Python was an opponent of the god or a monster whom the god defeated. The last, rationalizing version features Python as the son of a chieftain on Euboea who looted the sanctuary and stole from wealthy men. Pausanias quotes an oracle about Apollo protecting his sanctuary from looters:

> At close quarters Phoebus [Apollo] will shoot a grievous shaft at the man
> Who robs Parnassus; and men of Crete
> Shall cleanse his hands from blood; and the glory shall never die.
>
> (10.6.7. trans. Fraser)

Pausanias remarks that from the beginning, Delphi was the object of plotters, starting with Python, the Euboean pirate; then Pyrrhus, son of Achilles; then part of Xerxes' army; then the Phocians, who were the worst; followed by the Gauls; and after that, Delphi did not escape the infinite sacrilege of Nero, who robbed Apollo of five hundred bronze statues of gods and men (10.7.1). Nero's theft is viewed by Pausanias in an entirely different category and context from Augustus' removal of the ivory statue of Athena Alea at Tegea and the tusks of the Calydonian Boar; there, as we have seen, he excuses Augustus on the grounds that he followed earlier precedents. But Nero was not a conqueror, nor at war; rather, he was a pirate like Python himself – implicitly, like Python, Nero would eventually meet his demise at the hand of the gods he had offended. At Olympia, Pausanias simply points out a missing statue from a group and some missing dedications and says that Nero "is said to have taken" them to Rome (5.25.8; 5.26.3). The implication is that this is what guides at Olympia were telling visitors. At Delphi, however, Pausanias states the looting as fact, suggesting that he saw some evidence of it himself, but a fact welded onto a long legendary account, giving it rhetorical tinge.

We hear about Nero's misdeeds in Rome primarily from Pliny, his contemporary, and the later authors Suetonius, Tacitus, and Cassius Dio.[71] The principal cause of the indignation directed at him, and the target of much clever invective, was his construction of the Domus Aurea (Golden House) after the fire of 64 CE that devastated most of the city.[72] Ancient descriptions specify the features that made this house akin to maritime or countryside villas: size, scale, and the introduction of the "wild" (game parks, woods, and a lake) into the middle of the city, and this is not merely a facet of rhetorical denunciation or typical moralizing about the abuse of nature. It truly was inappropriate for a large imperial city with a large population, most of which had just been displaced by the fire. The tradition of suburban villas extended back to Scipio Africanus the Elder, some 250 years, and location was always their essential, defining aspect: away from the city and close to nature, even if "nature" was artificially contained or manipulated. The Domus Aurea as a whole was in the wrong place, not just for Rome but for any city, and no imagined reversal of Nero's posthumous reputation could change that.[73]

Pliny's repeated complaints about Nero's use of art and architecture stem from Nero's apparent fondness for gigantism and for gilding, not lilies, but their man-made equivalents. Nero set up a colossal statue of

[71] On their views of Nero, see T. Champlin, *Nero* (Cambridge, MA, 2003), ch. 2.

[72] For minifying interpretations of Nero's architectural transgressions, see, e.g., J. Elsner, "Constructing Decadence: The Representation of Nero as Imperial Builder," in J. Elsner and J. Masters, eds., *Reflections of Nero, Culture, History & Representation* (Chapel Hill, 1994): 112–127; Champlin (2003) 127–132, 200–206.

[73] This is true regardless of the brilliance of the design of the Esquiline wing of the Domus Aurea (by Severus and Celer).

himself, 106.5 feet high, made by Zenodorus.[74] Nero commissioned a colossal painting of himself, on linen, 120 feet high, that was struck by lightning and destroyed by fire, along with the gardens in which it was displayed. Nero covered the Theater of Pompey with gold for just one day, to impress the visiting Tiridates, King of Armenia – but the theater was small compared to the Domus Aurea, which filled the entire city! Nero was so pleased by a portrait of the young Alexander by Lysippos that he ordered it to be gilded. This turned out to diminish its aesthetic appeal, however, and so later the gold was removed; the statue was considered more valuable without the gold, even though the scars and incisions from the added gold still remained.[75] These specific illustrations of Nero's excess contribute to Pliny's overall theme of lament over luxury and declining moral standards.

In another large-scale attempt at intervention into nature, Nero planned and began a huge canal (wide enough for two ships with five banks of oars to pass) between Misenum and Lake Avernus in the Campania, and a canal between the lake and Ostia. But when he had used up all available funds for the project, he turned to Verrine-style manipulations of inheritances and false accusations to raise money (described in detail by Suetonius), and eventually he looted dedications from temples and melted down statues of gold and silver, including the Roman Penates, which were replaced later by Galba (*Ner.* 32). Tacitus describes an episode that presents the *topos* of Verrine behavior in reverse: an honest and diligent Roman governor of the province of Asia, Q. Marcius Barea Soranus, had ruled fairly and even improved the

---

[74] After its death, its features were changed to represent the Sun; its position adjacent to the Flavian Amphitheater later gave the name Colosseum to the amphitheater. The statue's features were changed again to represent various emperors in late antiquity.

[75] Colossus: Pliny, *HN* 34.45; colossal painting: 35.51; gilded theater: 33.54; gilded Alexander: 34.63. Pliny depicts Nero as ill-tempered and selfish right up to his death: when he knew the end was near, he deliberately smashed two extremely valuable myrrhine cups (of the type made popular by Pompey) so no one else could use them (37.29).

harbor at Ephesos. When the people of Pergamon forcibly prevented a former slave of Nero named Acratus from looting statues and paintings from the city, he did not punish them. As a result, Nero malevolently and falsely accused the honest governor of revolutionary intentions, and his conviction was timed so as to demonstrate Nero's supposed imperial strength to the visiting king Tiridates – or, says Tacitus, it was meant to divert attention from domestic abuses to foreign affairs (*Ann.* 16.23).

Another of Pliny's accusations against Nero is that he looted for himself the choicest sculpture by well-known artists that previously had been on public display and put them in the Domus Aurea. Earlier Tiberius is said to have done something similar: he moved the Apoxyomenos (athlete cleaning off after a workout) by Lysippos from the baths of Agrippa into his bedroom, but there was such an outcry from the public that he was forced to return it. The complaint against Nero is located at the end of a long list of distinguished sculptors and their work. Pliny continues by saying that the emperor Vespasian dedicated all those choice works that had been taken by Nero in his Temple of Peace and other public buildings.[76] Thus the theme of private use versus public displays of sculpture continued to exercise indignation. The negative portrait of Nero given by these authors (Pliny, Suetonius, Pausanias) is consistent in representing him as violating the norms surrounding the ownership of art (like Verres) and as self-indulgent and grandiose in his architectural projects.

THE TEMPLE OF PEACE

Vespasian (r. 69–79) is depicted in a positive light by Pliny, and his immediate successor and son Titus (r. 79–81) was the dedicatee of Pliny's book. Vespasian's legitimacy as a successor to the Julio-Claudians (after the brief rules of Galba, Otho, and Vitellius) must have been a concern,

---

[76] Pliny, *HN* 34.84 (Nero and Vespasian); 34.62 (Tiberius and the Apoxyomenos).

at least initially; in one quick stroke, he demonstrated that he was no Nero: he had the artificial lake for the Domus Aurea drained and on its location began the Flavian Amphitheater (Colosseum), thus turning a private folly into a much-admired public amenity that eventually became as emblematic of imperial Rome as the obelisks. Four very large inscriptions set around the interior proclaimed that the amphitheater was built *ex manubiis*, of which one is preserved.[77] This inscription linked the new building explicitly with the victory over Judea and the military campaign that was ongoing when Vespasian was acclaimed as the new emperor. Suetonius, also giving a positive portrait of Vespasian, presents him as discovering that Augustus had intended to construct such a building and so now he was fulfilling those plans.[78] In this and other ways, Vespasian deliberately recalled both the Republic and the reign of Augustus. He rebuilt the Capitoline temple that had been burned down in the confrontation with Vitellius, and restored many other temples; he also addressed the infrastructure of Rome and improved the city's amenities. The city was still under great duress from the fire of 64, even though Nero had begun the rebuilding, with wider streets and safer materials. Titus continued the breaking up of the Domus Aurea by building enormous public baths over its Esquiline wing, thereby turning that part of the Neronian palace into a filled-in basement. Centuries later it was explored by Renaissance artists as a "grotto."

Vespasian and Titus jointly staged a Triumph in 71, a celebration of the capture of Judea in 70. The siege of Jerusalem resulted in the complete destruction of the Jewish Temple. The eyewitness Josephus

[77] For the inscription, Alföldi (1995); discussed by A. J. Boyle, "Introduction: Reading Flavian Rome," in A. J. Boyle and W. J. Dominik, eds., *Flavian Rome. Culture, Image, Text* (Leiden, 2003): 60–67; for the Colosseum, E. Gunderson, "The Flavian Amphitheatre: All the World as Stage," in Boyle and Dominik (2003): 637–658.

[78] Suetonius, *Vesp.* 9. See also Levick's discussion of Vespasian's building and restorations in the city: B. Levick, *Vespasian* (London and New York, 1999): 124–134.

narrates the events of the siege, and depicts Titus as reluctant to destroy it and even attempting to save it. Josephus gives details of a debate among Titus' officers with their different views about the potential *sacrilegium* in the intended attack.[79] The Triumph held in Rome is also described in detail by Josephus, with a vivid picture of the precariously towering floats with painted illustrations of the battles; the huge number of precious stones; the statues of Roman gods and Victories, made of ivory and gold; and the sacred articles from the Temple at Jerusalem. This had been an important war that required extensive military resources, and the celebration of victory was a part of Vespasian's effort to establish legitimacy. Part of the procession is represented in symbolic form on the interior friezes of the Arch of Titus, dedicated in 81.[80] On one side, we see Titus in his quadriga, surrounded by allegorical figures; on the other, the sacred implements from the Jewish Temple at Jerusalem, including a gold Menorah, gold Table of Showbread, and silver trumpets, are carried in the triumphal procession by Roman soldiers. This is the best known and most frequently illustrated representation from antiquity of captured booty in the form of sacred objects from a temple (Fig. 15).

[79] Josephus, *BJ* 6.230–442; he also depicts Pompey as respecting the Temple and its contents earlier, 1.154–155. The destruction may have been accidental, as Josephus describes it, or a military necessity; in Josephus' narrative, it was discussed by Titus' staff, which was concerned about sacrilege, but also the use of the Temple as a fortification by the besieged (*BJ* 6.237–241). For a modern account of the siege with bibliography, see E. Cline (2004): 116–131. Tacitus' lost narrative, used by Sulpicius Severus in the fifth century CE, presents Titus as arguing the military necessity of destruction, discussed by T. D. Barnes, "The Sack of the Temple in Josephus and Tacitus," in J. Edmondson, S. Mason, and J. Rives, eds., *Flavius Josephus and Flavian Rome* (Oxford, 2005): 133–137; for an analysis of the intended religious implications of the destruction, J. Rives, "Flavian Religious Policy and the Destruction of the Jerusalem," *ibid.*: 145–166.

[80] On the Triumph, see Josephus, *BJ* 7.131–53; and for a discussion of his account, M. Beard, "The Triumph of Flavius Josephus," in Boyle and Dominik (2003): 543–558; F. Millar, "Last Year in Jerusalem: Monuments of the Jewish War in Rome," in Edmonson et al. (2005): 101–128; for useful comments on the Arch of Titus and other triumphal arches, see the review article by F. Kleiner, "The Study of Roman Triumphal and Honorary Arches 50 Years after Kähler," *JRA* 2 (1989): 196–206.

The sacred items were then dedicated in Vespasian's new Temple of Peace (*Templum Pacis*), a large porticoed complex with gardens and libraries, that recalled both Augustus' Palatine and the nearby Forum Augustum.[81] Josephus concludes his account of the Triumph by saying that Vespasian kept the Law (i.e., Torah) and the curtains from the Inner Sanctum of the Temple of Jerusalem not in the Temple of Peace but in his palace, for safekeeping. We hear of no effort to repatriate them.[82]

The triumphal Temple of Peace became a place of public display and, in addition to the trophies from the Judaean war, there was a large marble map of Rome (later replaced by the partially preserved Severan marble map of Rome). Here, publicly exhibited once again, were the sculptures taken by Nero from various places for his private enjoyment in the Domus Aurea. Josephus comments that so many paintings and statues were there that everything worth traveling the world to visit was brought together in that one place. Implicitly, Rome now owned the whole world, in the form of its best art. The Temple of Peace and its surrounding complex contained the first example of a museum-like display that offered "universal coverage," with obvious dynastic and political overtones. Many centuries later, the ideal of universal coverage became an ambition that helped fuel acquisitions by national museums in the nineteenth century, with similar overtones of triumphalist national power.

---

[81] For the details of its architecture and the other building projects of the Flavians, see J. Packer, "*Plurima et amplissima opera*: Parsing Flavian Rome," in Boyle and Dominik (2003): 167–198, with illustrations and earlier bibliography. The Temple of Peace itself is not completely excavated, but parts of its surroundings are visible today, and its plan is known from the Severan Marble Plan of Rome.

[82] Josephus, *BJ* 7.153. In the sack of Rome in 455 CE, the gold items were taken by the Vandals to north Africa, then retrieved and taken to Constantinople in 534; then they are said to have been moved to a church in Jerusalem, but after the seventh century, their fate is unknown. On legends about the temple implements and on efforts to rebuild the Temple by Julian and others, see Weitzman (2005): 101–114, 158–159.

FIGURE 15. Relief from the Arch of Titus, showing a scene from the Triumphal procession of the emperor Titus after the destruction of Jerusalem in 70 CE. Spoils from the Temple at Jerusalem are carried in procession. Rome. Photo credit: Werner Forman / Art Resource, NY.

TRUE CONNOISSEURS

The Flavian author much read through millennia is Pliny, whose notices of art have been so important both to artists and art historians. In the penultimate book of his encyclopedic account of man's use of nature, Pliny says that in Rome (our) buildings show that (we) have conquered the world; he imagines all the buildings of Rome piled in a heap so as to create another world (*mundus alius*) in one place. This seems to be a vision of validation of the autocratic, imperial regimes that built them (rather than a prescient glimpse of a post-modern city). In a list of outstanding Roman buildings, he includes the Forum of Augustus and the Temple of Peace among the most beautiful buildings in the world.[83] He also comments earlier on the Triumph of Vespasian and

[83] Pliny, *HN* 36.101–102; on the heap of buildings, see Carey (2003): 91–99; on the Temple of Peace, see Naas (2002): 438–447.

Titus, stating that living trees were carried in it, balsam from Judaea that now pay tribute to Rome, just like the conquered people of Judaea.[84] Thus nature itself could be transported and possessed by the victors, just as manubial funds could be used for the most beautiful buildings in the world.

Pliny's encyclopedia in thirty-seven books provides a glowing, triumphalist picture of the Roman world of the Flavians, despite the laments over moral decline. It is no mere "transparent" compendium of facts. As recent scholarship has demonstrated, Pliny has a definite agenda, uses rhetorical tropes, reflects his class and gender, his support of the Flavians and his triumphalist Roman point of view, and seems conservative but at the same time innovative. He was the first author to give a detailed table of contents and a bibliography, for example. The 1,900th anniversary of his death in 79 inspired a wave of new research that has provided a deeper, more complex, and more nuanced picture both of the work and of the author.[85] S. Carey convincingly presents and discusses Pliny as a "collector" of facts, who uses art and architecture as a mirror for his world-vision and represents the totality of the known world that when collected is also conquered.[86]

For his discussions of art, Pliny took up Cicero's basic paradigms for how art should be used and worked the paradigms throughout his text: public displays versus private uses, ambivalence over luxury, respect for the religious purposes of art, so that captured or looted statuary should be resanctified in Roman temples. Pliny is also a true connoisseur not of art but rather of interesting facts and especially of marvels. He is informed, passionate, and highly skilled in selecting and arranging his

---

[84] Pliny, *HN* 12.111–112; he says Pompey was the first to have living trees in his triumphal procession.

[85] Recently, Wallace-Hadrill (1990); S. C. Marchetti (1991); J. Isager (1991); M. Beagon (1992); V. Naas (2002); S. Carey (2003); T. Murphy (2004); J. Tanner (2006).

[86] Carey (2003), esp. 75–101.

facts. That it was possible for him to accomplish the writing of this encyclopedia is testimony to Roman wealth in books, libraries, and archives; social stability that afforded him support and time; and, of course, his own industry and dedication.

The conditions of the Flavian period, even in the narrowing, darker regime of Domitian (r. 81–96), permitted true connoisseurship of art, as we glimpse in the poetry of P. Papinius Statius (ca. 50–ca. 96). Statius was the son of a distinguished poet and teacher from Velia in southern Italy who had won victories in the Panhellenic festivals at Delphi, Nemea, and Isthmia and the Augustalia in Neapolis (Naples). Steeped in literary culture from his birth in Naples, Statius brings a new sensibility of the social potential of art (and poetry) and its enjoyment in the private sphere. His *Silvae* are written on a variety of topics, including the particular concerns of individuals, such as a marriage or the birth of a child.

In *Silvae* 4.6, published in 95, he presents a brilliant portrait of a connoisseur of art, Novius Vindex.[87] Vindex and his small statue of Herakles (Hercules) are also the subject of two epigrams by the poet Martial (9.43, 44), who is likely celebrating the same occasion marked by Statius' poem. Statius begins by saying he was in Rome, at the Saepta (Julia), when Novius Vindex, a generous man, invited him to dinner. Pleased by the memory of that evening at Vindex' house, Statius then recalls it for us.

The food was good but not overly exotic, and the focus instead was on conversation and Vindex' art collection. Statius learned from him about the beauties of ivories and bronzes and wax *imagines* that "seemed likely to speak. For who could anywhere rival the eye of Vindex in recognizing the stamp of the old masters and ascribing an artist to untitled statues? He will show you which bronzes skilled Myron spent sleepless hours

---

[87] He is generally assumed to be a real person, not merely a character; on his identity, see K. Coleman, *Statius. Silvae IV* (Oxford, 1988): 173.

fashioning, which marbles have come alive through painstaking Praxiteles' chisel, which ivory was smoothed by an Olympic thumb, what
statuary was bidden draw breath in Polycleitus' furnace, which outline
betrays from afar Apelles of old...."[88] Art is Vindex' *amor* (passion); a
poet himself, when he is not writing poetry, it is art that calls him away
from the Muses.

Statius then describes the Herakles Epitrapezios ("on the table"), a
statuette of the hero made by Lysippos, who captured Herakles' courage
and valor, even on a small scale, but at the same time planned a Herakles
on a colossal scale![89] The statue represented a seated Herakles, pausing
for a rest, looking slightly upward, and was meant to be placed on a
table (Fig. 16). Statius narrates the history of ownership of the statue:
first made for Alexander, he carried it with him all the way to India,
and used to tell the Herakles about that day's battles; right before he
died, he noticed the statue was sweating. Then Hannibal owned it, and
the Herakles hated being in his possession because of the lost Roman
blood and burnt Roman buildings and his temple defiled at Saguntum.
Next, Sulla owned the statue. Now in Vindex' house, the Herakles is
not surrounded by a royal palace but rather "the pure and innocent
outlook of a master of old-fashioned loyalty, whose pact of friendship
once begun is eternal ... so here ... bravest of the gods, you can enjoy
welcome peace and look not on wars and fierce battles, but on lyre and
chaplet and the bay clinging to the brow."[90] (Vindex was himself a poet
as well as an art connoisseur.)

Friendship and the role of the artist (and, by implication, the poet)
to patron are primary concerns in the poem, along with moral and
aesthetic values. In her exegesis of this poem, C. Newlands rightly
points out that one implication of Statius' use of the provenance of the

---

[88] Lines 20–30, translation by K. Coleman (1988): 35.
[89] A likely reference to the colossal seated Herakles taken by Fabius Maximus from Tarentum
and dedicated on the Capitoline.
[90] Lines 90–98, translation by K. Coleman (1988): 39.

FIGURE 16. Herakles Epitrapezios (Hercules on the table), Roman statue after small-scale type made famous by Lysippos in the late fourth century BCE. National Archaeological Museum, Naples. Photo credit: Erich Lessing / Art Resource, NY.

statue is the question of where the true center of cultural authority in Flavian Rome should be located: in the palace or a private mansion?[91] This poem makes a new statement about the possibilities of private ownership, and even luxury: with the expanding material wealth of a now stable empire, a domestic setting takes on a protective role for traditional Roman values of purity, loyalty, enduring friendship, and hospitality, away from the competition and rivalry of court life.[92] Now it seems that luxury, used correctly, could enable virtue rather than trigger decline: cultured, wealthy men like Vindex were the defenders of traditional virtues.[93]

As we saw previously, Cicero criticized Lucullus for his private display of wealth and urged that he should have been a model of restraint for his neighbors (*Leg.* 3.30–31). Lucullus too was cultured, a lover of the arts and a generous patron (and, like Vindex, he also had literary aspirations), but he was regarded as exceptional in his milieu in part because of his lavish expenditures. Especially notable is that connoisseurship of art should now, under Domitian, be the subject for short, elegant poems, sketches written as a gesture of friendship: not a target of invective, forensic speeches or historical diatribe. *Ekphrasis* (the literary description of art) had been used in poetry since Homer, but here the expert knowledge of art and the character of the connoisseur himself is the subject.

Like Verres, Novius Vindex understands and appreciates the value of antique art and has a "passion" for it; but, unlike Verres, Vindex collects art honestly, with careful discernment and knowledge and for aesthetic and intellectual enjoyment, not to further his ambitions and public career: Vindex' use of art fits the rhetorical strictures of *decor* (Verres simply grabbed whatever he happened to see that appealed to him in

---

[91] C. Newlands, *Statius' Silvae and the Poetics of Empire* (Cambridge, 2002): 82.

[92] Points made by Newlands in her excellent commentary on the poem (2002: 83).

[93] Newlands (2002): 6. See also the useful comments of N. K. Zeiner, *Nothing Ordinary Here. Statius as Creator of Distinction in the* Silvae (New York and London, 2005): 190–200.

Sicily and accumulated as much as possible, whereas Vindex is *selective*.) The antithetical difference in character between the two men is obvious, but the social and political environment also has changed drastically in 170 years. The intense competition of the late Republic led some to monstrous behavior, but under an autocratic regime, ambition had to be met with different sorts of compromises and withdrawals. Martial (ca. 40–ca. 102) also presents the royal and autocratic provenance of the statue and concludes his shorter epigram, "Vexed by the boastful threats of fickle courts, he is glad now to dwell beneath a private roof; and, as he was of old the guest of gentle Molorchus, so has he now chosen to be the god of learned Vindex."[94]

Vindex is portrayed as having in his collection works by artists in the "hall of fame" (Myron, Polykleitos, Pheidias ["Olympic thumb"], Praxiteles, Apelles) established by Hellenistic rhetoricians. Although the provenance of the statue is one of its important attributes and is celebrated by both Statius and Martial, whether it was truly owned by Alexander, Hannibal, and Sulla (all autocratic owners) is of course unknowable. But, Lysippos' Herakles Epitrapezios is so closely described by the poets that it has been identified in many extant versions (see Fig. 16). Lysippos set a new fashion in the late fourth century BCE by taking up the challenge of the small-scale image. As E. Bartman has argued, the miniature version was the original and later, the scale was expanded into larger versions.[95]

Statius dedicated Book 4 of his *Silvae* to his friend Vitorius Marcellus in a prose preface to the poems that shows the continuation of the

---

[94] Lines 11–14, trans. Walter Ker [Loeb].

[95] Bartman provides a full commentary and catalogue on twenty-one extant versions: E. Bartman, *Ancient Sculptural Copies in Miniature* (Leiden, 1992): 147–186; see also *idem*, "Sculptural Collecting and Display in the Private Realm," in Gazda (1991): 71–88, and *idem*, "Lysippos' Huge God in Small Shape," *Bulletin of the Cleveland Museum of Art* 73(1986): 298–311. For the view that the type may be a Roman invention, see B. Ridgway, *Fourth-Century Styles in Greek Sculpture* (Madison, 1997): 294–304. On the poets' use of artists, see W. J. Schneider, "Phidiae Putavi Martial und der Hercules Epitrapezios des Novius Vindex." *Mnemosyne* 54 (2001): 697–720.

social implications of literary exchanges, rooted in the late Republic. In Statius' poem, Novius Vindex represents a private connoisseur of art in an age when definitions of public and private were slowly shifting away from those formulated by Cicero, since the political circumstances and the nature of the "public" sphere were changing.

A younger friend and addressee of Martial, the poet Juvenal (ca. 50–ca. 130), recalls Verres three times in his *Satires*, a fitting reference for biting complaint about corruption and venality.[96] Juvenal seems to have been trained as a lawyer and had given *declamationes* earlier in his career. That rhetorical training proved to be a good foundation for his social commentary. In contrast to the long tradition in Roman literature of all genres of using positive *exempla*, Juvenal uses negative *exempla* in *Satire* 8, published about 121, in the reign of Hadrian (r. 117–138).[97]

The poem is addressed to Ponticus, who was apparently about to embark on a career post abroad, to whom Juvenal offers positive advice about how to be a governor of a province. The larger theme is an exploration of nobility – with or without good character, a familiar *topos* in Latin literature – and, later in the poem, Cicero himself is used as a positive model of courage in high office. Here, Juvenal adds a new twist to the theme and his exhortations for good behavior with the negative *exempla* that warn of the corruption in Roman life. In this excerpt, he addresses with irony, even cynicism, the issue of possible proceeds to be gained by a Roman administrator in a province:

> *Once, when our allies were newly conquered and still were thriving,*
> *things were different. To be sure, they groaned with pain at their losses;*
> *but their private houses were full of goods; masses of money*
> *remained untouched. They had Spartan cloaks and Coan purples.*
> *They had Phidias' ivories, with Myron's bronzes and Parrhasius'*

---

[96] 2.26; 3.53; 8.106.
[97] For analysis of this Satire, see S. H. Braund, *Beyond Anger: A Study of Juvenal's Third Book of Satires* (Cambridge, 1989): 72, 92–101.

pictures – wonderfully life-like; Polyclitus' marbles were all around;
There was hardly a table without its piece of Mentor's silver.
Then Dolabella and the greedy Antonius, then the unholy [sacrilegus]
Verres set about smuggling home in their tall-hulled ships
peace-time trophies which far exceeded the spoils of war.
Now we can steal no more from our allies, on taking a croft,
than a few yoke of oxen, a handful of mares along with the stallion,
and the actual gods of the hearth – if there's a decent statue,
or a single Lar in his little shrine.

(Lines 98–111, trans. N. Rudd)[98]

The people out in the provinces in past years are depicted nostalgically as wealthy and owning fine art. As S. Braund notes, Juvenal builds on Cicero's descriptions of Sicily before Verres arrived (e.g., in *Ver.* 2.4.46–7).[99] For Juvenal, Verres' governorship of Sicily has become almost proverbial and Verres was now a symbol of sacrilegious looting, a character in the Republic, swiftly becoming a distant era and no longer lamented. The possibilities for graft and corruption continued in the Principate but, because of Cicero's prosecution, Verres had become the warning figure, the negative exemplar, and ineluctably associated with the looting of art.

In contrast to Juvenal's sad and sour picture of the typical provincial citizen in Hadrian's reign, Edward Gibbon, in his *History of the Decline and Fall of the Roman Empire* (1776), famously judges the new, post-Flavian era as follows:

> *If a man were called to fix the period in the history of the world, during*
> *which the condition of the human race was most happy and prosperous,*
> *he would, without hesitation, name that which elapsed from the death*
> *of Domitian to the accession of Commodus. The vast extent of the*

---

[98] N. Rudd and W. Barr, *Juvenal. The Satires* (Oxford, 1991): 73–74.
[99] Braund (1989): 95.

> Roman empire was governed by absolute power, under the guidance of
> virtue and wisdom. The armies were restrained by the firm but gentle
> hand of four successive emperors, whose characters and authority
> commanded involuntary respect. The forms of the civil administration
> were carefully preserved by Nerva, Trajan, Hadrian, and the
> Antonines, who delighted in the image of liberty, and were pleased with
> considering themselves as the accountable ministers of the laws. Such
> princes deserved the honour of restoring the Republic, had the Romans
> of their days been capable of enjoying a rational freedom. (Ch. 3)

Throughout this period deemed happy by Gibbon (96–180 CE), at least
some large-scale imperial projects and civic amenities were funded with
manubiae, gained from gold and silver captured from the enemy, the sale
of slaves and agricultural lands, and other sources of revenue squeezed
from the defeated. Booty still flowed into Rome, especially after Trajan's
victories over the Dacians. The funds were used to help construct the
Forum and Markets of Trajan, and the victories were commemorated in
the sculptured reliefs on the Column of Trajan, located between the two
libraries in his Forum. But "art" taken as booty from the enemy was not
an issue that left a mark in the historical record, since the opponents of
Rome in this period (on or near the outer borders of the empire) were not
creating and owning items that Romans wanted as artistic objects. Captured arms and armor taken from the enemy are featured on the pedestal
of Trajan's Column, and, presumably, actual arms and armor were
dedicated in temples in accordance with longstanding tradition. The
statuary, paintings, furniture, luxurious domestic items, and scientific
curiosities that figure in earlier accounts of military triumphs, however, were now being created and collected for Roman patrons, in Rome
and across the empire. A confident Roman synthesis of art and architecture, with local variations and subtleties, may be seen in substantial
remains across Europe, north Africa, Anatolia, and the Near East.

CONSTANTINE AND THE NEW ROME

The next memorable appropriation of plundered art on a large scale took place during the reign of Constantine I (r. 306–337). This started in 324, and the purpose of his plundering was to reuse antique statuary in the decoration of his new city Constantinople. Initially in his reign, Rome was still Constantine's putative base and capital, even though he spent little time there, and he did plan and finance new construction for the city. After the battle of the Milvian Bridge and the defeat of Maxentius on October 28, 312, Constantine's victory was commemorated by an Arch dedicated by the Senate and People of Rome, set within the traditional triumphal route that had been used for centuries. It featured reused sculpture and architectural blocks scavenged from monuments set up in honor of previous emperors.[100] The Arch proclaimed his victory over Maxentius in imagery literally taken down from older monuments that would link him with Trajan, Hadrian, and Marcus Aurelius – hence, Gibbon's happiest era.

Soon after the battle, Constantine dedicated in fulfillment of a vow to Christ a piece of property within the walls of Rome, but away from the civic center, for a new church. Formerly, the barracks of the imperial horse guards had stood there, but all that was razed. Centuries earlier, Nero had requisitioned the nearby estates of the Laterani family, whose name nonetheless remained, so the new church, when it was built and consecrated probably six years later, became the Lateran cathedral (S. Giovanni in Laterano).[101]

---

[100] On the Arch of Constantine, see J. Elsner, "From the Culture of *spolia* to the Cult of Relics: The Arch of Constantine and the Genesis of Late Antique Forms," *PBSR* 68 (2000): 149–184; F. S. Kleiner, "Who Really Built the Arch of Constantine?" (review article), *JRA* 14 (2001): 661–663, with earlier bibliography.

[101] R. Krautheimer, *Rome, Profile of a City, 312–1308* (Princeton, 1980, 2000): 21–24, and *idem, Three Christian Capitals* (Berkeley, 1983): 1, 12–15: Krautheimer conjectures that the vow was fulfilled only thirteen days after the battle (p. 15). For more recent ideas about the

No martyr's grave caused the selection of the Lateran for the first Constantinian church; rather, the chosen site had the advantage of distance from the great imperial monuments and temples of the previous centuries. A distinctive architectural choice of Constantine was the selection of the basilica as a new type for the Lateran. In Rome, the basilicas first constructed in the Forum to receive foreign dignitaries (discussed in Chapter 1) had already inspired many subsequent uses as public facilities and had evolved into the standard type for audience halls of the emperor. That type seemed ideal for a large gathering with a focus on the altar and an enthroned bishop in the apsidal end. When the Lateran was being constructed, only private houses, converted into churches through donation or purchase, existed for Christian congregations. Constantine was rapidly transforming architectural expectations that would mirror the shift from small, private gatherings of Christians to larger, public groups.

In the construction of the Lateran cathedral, many marble architectural members were taken from older buildings and reused as *spolia*, so that the magnificence of exotic marbles traditionally associated with public buildings in Rome was transferred into his church.[102] This practice of using architectural spolia was continued by Constantine and members of his family for other churches constructed soon after the Lateran, over martyrs' graves around the outside of Rome, most of them located on imperial property. He set a precedent of deliberate spoliation and recycling that would persist through many centuries.

motivations and choices of sites for the new churches, see J. Curran, *Pagan City and Christian Capital. Rome in the Fourth Century* (Oxford, 2000).

[102] The term *spolia* is used by art historians for this period and later with reference to reused ancient pieces; it has no military implication but rather one of pillaging or simply scavenging costly materials for reuse (sometimes, but not necessarily, from dilapidated buildings), often with intentional associations with the past. Brenk points out that the Lateran cathedral is the first sacred structure built with extensive spolia. See B. Brenk, "Spolia from Constantine to Charlemagne: Aesthetics versus Ideology," *DOP* 41 (1987): 103–109; Kinney (1995); D. Kinney, "Spolia. Damnatio and renovatio memoriae," *MAAR* 42 (1997): 117–148; D. Kinney, "Roman Architectural Spolia," *ProcAPS* 145 (2001): 138–150.

The evidence is visible still today, and much of it has been thoroughly studied.[103]

Constantine nonetheless provided the traditional buildings expected of an emperor, such as his great new baths and new porticoes where antique sculpture was displayed, such as the bronze Terme Boxer, and the bronze "Hellenistic ruler" (currently in the Palazzo Massimo Museum, formerly in the Terme Museum in Rome) that were found on the Quirinal. Still, much of the construction of his reign was Christian in character, and the new buildings marked the start of a gradual transformation of Rome into a Christian city but within the ancient context and traditional social venues and rhythms of public life.[104]

In contrast, when Constantine dedicated new ground in 324 for his new city Constantinople, he had a far freer scope to build as he wished. The site itself was that of ancient Greek Byzantion, founded on the inner end of the Bosporus by Byzas of Megara perhaps as early as the seventh century BCE, and refounded by Septimius Severus in the late second century CE.[105] Constantine's new site was tied both with Greek antiquity and the recent Roman imperial past but less engaged in the complicated, firmly rooted, and ongoing social and religious traditions in Rome. (Tradition could evoke authority: R. Krautheimer pictures Constantine walking the perimeter with a dragging spear point to etch out the new boundary, in effect recalling Romulus setting the pomerium of Rome.) Embracing the framework of Severus' plan but much expanded, Constantine created a new urban center that featured imperial amenities, such as long colonnaded streets, a great bath complex, a Forum, a church

---

[103] See, e.g., the thorough documentation for both the fourth century and present St. Peter's in L. Bosman, *The Power of Tradition. Spolia in the Architecture of St. Peter's in the Vatican* (Hilversum, 2004); D. Kinney, "Spolia," in W. Tronzo, ed. *St. Peter's in the Vatican* (Cambridge, 2005): 16–47.

[104] For various ways the space (and calendar) of the city was appropriated, see M. Salzman, "The Christianization of Sacred Time and Sacred Space," in W. V. Harris, ed. *The Transformations of Urbs Roma in Late Antiquity, JRA* Supp. 33 (Portsmouth, RI, 1999): 123–134.

[105] For the pre-Constantinian Byzantion, see C. Mango, *Le développement urbain de Constantinople* (IVᵉ–VIIᵉ siècles) (Paris, 1990): 13–21.

(Hagia Eirene), and the palace with its accompanying Hippodrome, all in central locations. In a concession to traditional Roman expectations, there was even a Capitoline dedicated to Jupiter, Juno, and Minerva.[106]

Constantine took the proper ornamentation of his new city as a serious requirement and one that had to be met instantly, almost as though the credibility of the enterprise of founding a new city was at stake. The sculptural decoration in particular was clearly a priority. The centerpiece of the city was the new Forum, a circular space surrounded by porticoes, with its central focal point marked by a tall porphyry column that supported a statue of Constantine wearing a radiate crown and holding a lance and a globe. The rayed crown was associated with Helios (the Sun) and Apollo Helios, so that some ancient authors who saw it believed the statue to have been a reused image of Helios or Apollo. S. Bassett suggests it is more likely to have been a reused image of a Hellenistic ruler, who already came equipped with the radiate crown.[107] There was also some sculpture left in the city from the Severan refoundation, and new portraits were made of Constantine, his mother Helena, and his sons Constans and Constantine II.

Nonetheless, by far the bulk of the extensive statuary that adorned the refounded city in the course of many centuries to come was brought there by pillaging of other cities and sanctuaries.[108] In a superb new

---

[106] For the city and its administrative organization, see G. Dagron, *Naissance d'une capitale. Constantinople et ses institutions de 330 à 451* (Paris, 1974); on the city and its founding, see also Krautheimer (1983): 43, 45–61; Mango (1990): 23–36; P. Speck, "*Urbs quam Deo donavimus.* Konstantins des Grossen Konzept für Konstantinopel," *Boreas* 18 (1995): 143–173; S. Bassett, *The Urban Image of Late Antique Constantinople* (Cambridge, 2004): 18–33.

[107] Bassett collects and comments on all the testimonia and modern opinions (2004: 192–204, no. 109); on the significance of the association with Helios, see further Krautheimer (1983): 62–67; on Constantine's vision in the sun before the battle of the Milvian Bridge that later became iconic, see P. Weiss, "The Vision of Constantine," *JRA* 16 (2003): 237–259.

[108] An important initial exploration of this topic was set forth by C. Mango, "Antique Statuary and the Byzantine Beholder," *DOP* 17 (1963): 53–75, with much of the testimonia gathered in J. Overbeck, *Die antiken Schriftquellen zur Geschichte der bildenden Künste bei den Griechen* (Leipzig, 1868, repr. Hildesheim, 1959).

reconstruction of the whole project, Bassett has gathered together all the testimonia for the ancient sculpture and monuments, their new positions, and their ultimate fates. Only a few of them still exist: many survived multiple vicissitudes only to be melted down or taken in battles, especially the Fourth Crusade of 1204. Several inscribed statue bases also provide evidence for Bassett's reconstruction.

Constantine had no compunction whatsoever, it seems, at raiding the ancient sanctuaries of old Greece and the Greek cities of the eastern Mediterranean. Bassett counts twenty-two cities, in addition to Rome, that suffered loss of statuary to Constantinople, and she divides the acquisitions into three phases.[109] More than a hundred monuments were set up in time for the dedication ceremony of 330: hence, the plundered art was gathered up between 324 and 330, under the direction of Constantine himself. More was taken later either by Constantine or his son and immediate successor in the East, Constantius II. Bassett sees a second phase of pillage (about thirty monuments) that began under Theodosius I (r. 379–395) and continued into the early fifth century under the direction of Lausos (an aristocratic courtier, in a private initiative). The final phase took place during the reign of Justinian (r. 527–565), with the addition of a few more pieces. The cities and sanctuaries that supplied the art over these three periods included Athens, Sardis, Knidos, Delphi, Olympia, and Rome, and the removed statues represented earlier emperors, poets and philosophers, gods, heroes, and mythological creatures. In the first two phases of accumulation, Bassett notes a clear preference for Late Classical, Hellenistic, and Roman period sculpture, and the materials included bronze, marble, porphyry, and Egyptian stones. I mention here just a few examples from Bassett's catalogue.

In the Basilica at Constantinople sat the weary, much-traveled Herakles by Lysippos: attested in Byzantine sources, this seems to be the

---

[109] These and the following figures and descriptions are taken from Bassett (2004): 37–42.

seated Herakles who was originally at Tarentum, then taken by Fabius
Maximus to Rome in 209 BCE and set up on the Capitoline, and then
brought from Rome by Constantine for the Basilica. Later it was moved
to the Hippodrome. Its base was left behind in Rome and remains today
in the Capitoline Museums.[110]

In the Baths of Zeuxippos (originally a part of the Severan city), a pantheon of eleven gods was set up, representing Apollo and Aphrodite,
Hermaphroditos, and divine couples including Herakles and Auge,
Poseidon and Amymone; twenty-nine mythological and literary figures from Homeric epic; and at least two from Theban epic.[111] The
prominence of the Trojan cycle suggests a deliberate thematic statement
of connections with Troy. Several of the accounts and descriptions of
the porphyry column that supported the statue of Constantine claim
also that the Palladion had been secretly brought by him from Rome
and was hidden inside the column: the city was not only a new Rome
but also a new Troy, now protected by the Palladion. There are also
representations of Constantine holding the Palladion; hence, he may
actually have taken it from Rome to Constantinople.[112]

The Hippodrome in Constantinople was an important site of formal meeting between the emperor and the people of the city, and its
location was near the palace, on the model of the Palatine and Circus
Maximus in Rome. Especially notable among the monuments moved
to Constantinople for its decoration is the Serpent Column, which
once supported a gold tripod dedicated to Apollo at Delphi by the
collective Greeks who defeated Xerxes at Plataia, now standing in the
Hippodrome (Fig. 5). One of Augustus' victory monuments for Actium
at Nikopolis, a statue group of an Ass and its Keeper (representing an
omen of victory just before the battle) stood nearby; thus, together, the

[110] Overbeck (1868): no. 1468–1472; Bassett (2004): 152–154.
[111] Bassett (2004): 52–55.
[112] Bassett (2004): 68–71, 205–206, no. 114; Bassett points out that the legend and images are
consistent and fit with thematic aspects of the sculptural programs.

Greek and Roman monuments represented key victories of the past –
now for Constantine, Constantinople itself was a new Nikopolis, a
city of Victory. On the *spina* of the Hippodrome were set not only
the victory monuments but also gods, apotropaic animals, sphinxes,
bronze tripods from Delphi, at least two representations of Herakles,
and images of previous rulers including Alexander, Julius Caesar, and
Roman emperors.[113]

The effect of all this plundered statuary was a visual usurpation of the
cultural patrimony of the Greco-Roman world, and the new definition
of the city Constantinople as its center; because its own past was obscure
and limited, the whole past of the Mediterranean was taken over and
shifted to the new city. The plundered statues came with histories and
literary contexts and now would acquire a new set of meanings. To some
viewers, such as Eusebius, the plunder was a deliberate defilement of
pagan imagery; to others, the statues brought authority and prestige to
the new city, while stripping it from the old cities.[114] C. Mango discusses
the popular view of such statuary (that it was animated and could be
threatening, protective, apotropaic of vermin, oracular, or an indicator
of guilt or deception, depending on context and narrator) and contrasts
it with the "intellectual" view that saw it within the rhetorical tradition
of aesthetic qualities. Since his stimulating essay was published in 1963,
further research has shown a wide range of responses to ancient statuary,
both in Constantinople and in Rome.[115]

---

[113] Serpent Column, Ass and Keeper: Bassett (2004): 44 and catalogue no. 141, 122; for the
Serpent Column, see also Chapter 1. Suetonius and Plutarch describe Augustus' chance
encounter just before the battle at Actium with a man named Eutyches (Fortunate) and a
donkey named Nikon (Victor); Augustus commemorated the good omen with statues of
both in the temple precinct he built afterward at Nikopolis (Suet. *Aug.* 96, Plut. *Ant.* 65.3).

[114] Euseb., *Vit. Const.* 3.54; on reactions of contemporaries to statuary, see Bassett on possible
reasons for the extensive plundering of art by Constantine and its reception (2004: 45–49).

[115] Mango (1963): 59–70; R. L. Gordon (1979); H. Saradi-Mendelovici, "Christian Attitudes
toward Pagan Monuments in Late Antiquity and Their Legacy in Later Byzantine Centuries," *DOP* 44 (1990): 47–60; J. Curran, "Moving Statues in Late Antique Rome: Problems
of Perspective," *ArtHist* 17 (1994): 46–58; P. Stewart (2003): 267–299.

Especially notable is the response of Jerome (ca. 347–420) to Constantine's plundering. He says, *Dedicatur Constantinopolis omnium paene urbium nuditate* (*Chron*. 324): "Constantinople was dedicated by stripping nude nearly every city." This sums up the matter succinctly and with a negative tone of judgment. It seems that the saint's admiration of Cicero and his extensive reading of classical texts helped shape his perspective on this particular issue of the plundering of art.[116]

Later in the fourth century, Theodosius I added an Egyptian obelisk to the *spina* of the Hippodrome (see Fig. 13). The obelisk was originally quarried by Tutmoses III and set up in the Temple of Amon at Karnak, like the one taken by Constantius II to Rome (the two obelisks were not originally a pair, but both were moved from Thebes to Alexandria by Constantine I). In imitation of the two in the Circus Maximus at Rome – where the one set up by Constantius II complemented Augustus' obelisk from Heliopolis – at Constantinople, a "Built" obelisk, made of ashlar blocks instead of one piece of granite, was constructed to form a pair (visible in Fig. 13).[117] The Egyptian obelisk was taken not as a military trophy but rather as a way of rivaling Rome and equaling the accomplishments of previous emperors.

Over the starting gates of the Hippodrome, Constantine II's grandson Theodosius II (r. 408–450) set four gilded bronze horses, attested by the author Niketas Choniates. These are usually assumed to be the four horses taken by the Venetians as war booty after the Fourth Crusade to Venice and placed on the façade of San Marco (Fig. 17). They were then taken by Napoleon and placed on the Arc de Triomph in Paris

---

[116] Jerome relates that he had a dream in which he heard the words, *Ciceronianus es, non Christianus*: "You are a Ciceronian, not a Christian" (*Ep.* 22.30); Jerome's attitude toward Cicero is discussed by M. L. Clarke, "'*Non hominis nomen, sed eloquentiae*,'" in T. A. Dorey, ed., *Cicero* (London, 1965): 87.

[117] The date of the Built Obelisk is unknown and disputed, but Bassett plausibly suggests that it too was built under Theodosius (2004: 262, footnote 20, and catalogue no. 138).

FIGURE 17. Bronze Horses of San Marco, Venice. Greek, fourth to third century BCE, or Roman. Taken from Istanbul in 1204. San Marco, Venice, Italy. Photo credit: Cameraphoto Arte, Venice / Art Resource, NY.

but were returned to Venice after Waterloo. The place of origin of the four horses is unknown. Delphi seemed a likely possibility when they were believed to be of the early Classical period (and seemed associated with the Serpent Column), but the horses now have been redated to the Roman imperial period; therefore, they could have been taken from anywhere, including Rome.[118]

In the 390s, Theodosius I issued a series of decrees limiting the rituals that could be held in ancient sanctuaries, or anywhere, and actually

[118] They have been dated variously between the fourth century BCE and the fourth century CE; but a Roman imperial date now is most likely in view of more recent technical evaluations during conservation. The horses were gilded and contain an alloy to facilitate this, a technique used in the Roman imperial period: see the essays in *The Horses of San Marco* (trans. J. and V. Wilton-Ely) (London, 1979); Bassett (2004): 222.

closing many of the temples and sanctuaries.[119] Christianity became the official state religion, ending Constantine's policies of accommodation and continuity of traditional religions. At this point, the ownership of the land and the contents of the sanctuaries all became imperial property. Bassett notes that this is when cult statues began to be brought to Constantinople: other monuments, like the Serpent Column from Delphi, had been votive offerings confiscated from the property of Apollo. Evidently, the closures and confiscations offered a fresh opportunity to collectors with appropriate imperial connections and resources for moving statuary.

The person who recognized and exploited these opportunities was not an emperor but rather a private individual, the courtier and sometime Grand Chamberlain, Lausos (*praepositus sacri cubiculi*). Lausos held high office under Theodosius II and was the dedicatee of a book on holy renunciates. His magnificent collection of art was destroyed in a fire of 475, so we know it only through literary sources, although ancient versions of some of the most famous statues exist in various media elsewhere. The basic reliability of the Byzantine descriptions of the lost art collection was established by Mango.[120]

---

[119] Overview in G. Fowden, *CAH* 13 (1998): 548–554; F. R. Trombley, *Hellenic Religion and Christianization, c. 370–529* (Leiden, 1993) I: 10–34; see also S. Williams and G. Friell, *Theodosius, The Empire at Bay* (New Haven, 1994): 119–133, where they comment on the fourth law of Nov. 8, 392 (a comprehensive prohibition against all rituals and sacrifices): "In its assault on vernacular traditions it was as if today an authoritarian atheist regime were to criminalise Easter eggs, holly, Christmas cards, Halloween pumpkins, first-footings, and even such universal gestures as the drinking of toasts" (p. 123).

[120] For Lausos as a literary patron, grand chamberlain, and collector, see C. Mango, M. Vickers, and E. D. Francis, "The Palace of Lausos at Constantinople and Its Collection of Ancient Statues," *JournHistColl* 4 (1992): 89–98, where Mango discusses the Byzantine texts describing the collection; S. Guberti Bassett, "'Excellent Offerings': The Lausos Collection in Constantinople," *ArtB* 82 (2000): 6–25; Bassett (2004): 98–120, 232–238, catalogue nos. 151–157. The previous identification of the remains of Lausos' palace (accepted by Mango, Vickers, and Francis) is now considered problematic, and the most likely position for it is established by J. Bardill, "The Palace of Lausus and Nearby Monuments in Constantinople: A Topographical Study," *AJA* 101 (1997): 67–95.

Under Lausos' direction, especially fine statues that had stood in their sanctuaries for many centuries now were put into a new setting: the major pieces in the group were (1) an archaic image of Athena Lindia that had been dedicated by an Egyptian Pharaoh at Lindos, made of a hard green stone, perhaps green diorite, and was probably a votive, not a cult image, attributed to Skyllis and Dipoinos; (2) an archaic image of Hera, from the Temple of Hera at Samos and probably a votive, not a cult image, attributed to Bupalos; (3) the fourth Wonder of the World, the famous chryselephantine statue of Zeus made by Pheidias for the Temple of Zeus at Olympia, ca. 430 BCE; (4) the storied and much-admired Aphrodite of Knidos by Praxiteles;[121] (5) a statue of Eros by Lysippos taken from Myndos; (6) an image of Kairos (Opportunity), by Lysippos;[122] and (7) statues of wild animals and pans and centaurs (presumably Hellenistic or Roman).

As this list suggests, Lausos must have had in mind the "hall of fame" of artists, established by Hellenistic rhetoricians and repeated with variations by Cicero, Pliny, and at greater length by Quintilian. How apt that an archaic image made of Egyptian stone was included, to represent the "hard" quality spoken of in these authors' texts! Just as in other Hellenistic canonical lists, such as the Seven Wonders of the World, in Lausos' choices we see both a geographical spread and a chronological range. This showcase would have delighted Lausos'

---

[121] The loss of this statue must have seemed devastating to Knidos, which became famous for it: Pliny says that king Nicomedes of Bithynia offered to relieve them of all public debt if they allowed him to buy it, but they refused (*HN*7.127, 36.21); on the statue, see C. Havelock, *The Aphrodite of Knidos and Her Successors: A Historical Review of the Female Nude in Greek Art* (Ann Arbor, 1995).

[122] This personification (Kairos means the "perfect moment" or opportunity within time) was shown as a winged young man, bald at the back of his head and with a forelock of hair in front, because he must be grasped as he comes and cannot be caught after he leaves. A careful, precise, and somewhat didactic definition is given in the form of a dialogue in an epigram attributed to Poseidippos, ca. 270 BCE (*Anth Graec*. 2.49.13); see Pollitt (1990): 103–104, for translation and discussion; Pollitt notes that the personification of Kairos was a favorite ekphrasis for rhetoricians.

circle of the social elite, who – although Christian – were steeped in the old educational and rhetorical traditions and had access to Hellenistic rhetorical treatises. They may have felt that Lausos had "saved" or "rescued" the statues from oblivion (or from improper and illegal worship).

We have little personal information about Lausos, but his collection suggests that he was a connoisseur, like Novius Vindex. The collection obviously was created as an illustration of the aesthetics of art, for these statues were brought to Constantinople because they were beautiful. This final collection of plundered art in antiquity differs from previous collections in the mode and circumstances of acquisition: the statues were taken from sanctuaries forcibly closed; and the statues were seen simply as statues, with august literary and historical provenances to be sure, but no longer as living gods or as possessions of living gods. Vindex' Herakles would not sit tranquilly in this setting.

5 ART AS EUROPEAN PLUNDER

◎▣◎

*We have all in our early education
read the Verronean [sic] orations. We
read them not merely to instruct us,
as they ought to do, in the principles
of eloquence, to instruct us in the
manners, customs and Laws of the
ancient Romans, of which they are an
abundant repository, but we read them
for another motive for which the great
Author published them, namely that
he should leave to the world and the
latest posterity a monument by which
it should be shewn what course a great
public Accuser in a great cause ought
to follow, and as connected with it, is
what course Judges ought to pursue in
such a cause.*

*Edmund Burke, prosecution of W.
Hastings, June 16, 1794*[1]

DEBATES TODAY OVER "CULTURAL PROPERTY" AND "CULTURAL
heritage" assume a protected status for these categories, a status that is
supported by national and international laws. In this chapter, I briefly
trace the significant events that led to a change in thinking about art as
spoil of war and the emergence of the idea that "cultural property" is a

---

[1] P. J. Marshall, ed., *The Writings and Speeches of Edmund Burke, Vol. 7: India: The Hastings
Trial 1789–1794* (Oxford, 2000): 662–663.

special category that should be protected in both war and peace. Two social dynamics drove this development: the evolution of legal thought and public perceptions of ethical violations, both impelled by the advocacy of influential individuals in reaction to specific episodes of plunder. It was warfare itself (the European experience of the Napoleonic campaigns), however, that precipitated the shift in practice. Actual legal changes did not come until later in the mid-nineteenth century, discussed in the Epilogue.

The shift in legal thinking took place in spurts over a long period, but much of its genesis was in the mid-eighteenth century under the inspired influence of the Swiss jurist Emmerich de Vattel (1714–1767). Shifts in social views about art as plunder, so far as they can be documented, are various and meandering, but Sicily and the past travails of Sicilians under Verres played a surprisingly significant role. These two interlocking stories of evolving legal thinking and changing social reactions to art as plunder have as their common basis a pervasive cultural respect for Cicero as an authority, all the more authoritative *because* he was "ancient" and Roman. The cultural weight of classical antiquity, with Cicero as its primary spokesman on the topic of plunder, helped create new views in European societies that remained receptive to classical ideals despite historical distance. Since emulation and appropriation of the past already lent validation and support for new ideologies, ranging from the ideals of the French Revolution to British imperialism abroad, adopting Cicero's idealistic views about repatriating antiquities (with Scipio Aemilianus as the extraordinary hero) became all the more reasonable and the natural next step.

The Survival of the *Verrines*

In the post-antique periods, the manuscripts of Cicero's *Verrines* were never lost, but the speeches were not widely circulated until the sixteenth century, when again models of rhetoric were eagerly sought and

Cicero was established as a preeminent Latin author. The court library of Charlemagne of ca. 790, for example, had a text of the *Verrines*, along with Cicero's Catilinarian orations and many other Latin historical authors and poets.[2] School texts as early as the eleventh century included excerpts from Cicero's *De inventione* for pedagogy in rhetoric, and his ethical and philosophical essays such as *De officiis*, *De senectute*, and *De amicitia*, and especially Scipio's Dream (*Somnium Scipionis*), continued to be read, but his work was not yet of central importance.

Cicero began to become a prominent author again after Petrarch discovered Cicero's letters to Atticus (in 1345, at Verona), and more discoveries followed, including more of his letters. Then Poggio Bracciolini found the manuscripts of Cicero's speeches including Ps.-Asconius' commentary on the *Verrines* (at St. Gall, 1416), discoveries that launched fresh interest in Cicero and Latin prose. Cicero became "the greatest authority of the Latin language" both for school curricula and for Renaissance writing generally.[3] Just as there was a "backlash" against Cicero's style of oratory in the first century CE (propelled in part by Seneca), however, so too eventually the Dutch humanist Erasmus (ca. 1466–1536) led a movement to counterbalance what he saw as excessive imitation of Cicero. It seems that across millennia, Cicero's writing can inspire fervent admiration (as St. Jerome experienced) but also a negative response in people weary of his style or of what they perceive as overly adulatory reception and imitation by others.[4]

Apart from the excitement about Cicero as a literary author, there is no evidence that Cicero or the *Verrines* had any influence on ideas about booty or plundering in war, until the treatise of Grotius on the topic,

---

[2] Reynolds and Wilson (1991): 96; for the manuscript tradition of the *Verrines*, Reynolds (1983): 54–62, 68–73.

[3] P. F. Grendler, *Schooling in Renaissance Italy. Literacy and Learning, 1300–1600* (Baltimore, 1989): 121–124, quoting Guarino's letter to his son, 1452, p. 123.

[4] The classic account of the reception of Cicero is T. Zielinski, *Cicero im Wandel der Jahrhunderte*[5] (1912, repr. Darmstadt, 1967).

written in 1625. A recitation of major occasions of plundering of art is a grim reminder that the ancient idea of "to the victor go the spoils" that Xenophon attributed to King Cyrus of Persia (see the epigraph to Chapter 1) is the most common and persistent basis for these actions. Especially notable instances of such plundering include the crusade and sack of Constantinople led by the Venetians in 1204, the sack of Rome in 1527, the seizure of the Palatine library of Heidelberg in 1623 by Pope Gregory XV, and Queen Christina of Sweden's sack of Prague in 1648.[5]

SICILY AS A DESTINATION

In the Renaissance, growing scholarly interest in the geography, history, and antiquities of Sicily led to careful reading of ancient authors as a source of information on the island. This was an extension of the intense interest in classical antiquity more generally in Italy and renewed enthusiasm for ancient art from an archaeological perspective.[6] The Bolognese humanist and Dominican friar, Leandro Alberti (d. 1552), had projected a treatise on Sicily as part of his larger project for Italy, *Descrittione di tutta Italia* (published in 1550), but it was left unwritten. While Alberti was writing his book on Italy, he was unaware that another Dominican friar, the Sicilian Tomaso Fazello (1498–1570), was already at work on a description of his own island.[7] Fazello was born in Sciacca in Sicily; went to Palermo, Rome, and Padua for his studies; and,

---

[5] All of these episodes have been well studied. As entries into the topics, with particular relevance for art as plunder, see the following: G. de Villehardouin, "The Conquest of Constantinople," *Chronicles of the Crusades*, trans. M. R. B. Shaw (London, 1963): 29–160, and J. Phillips, *The Fourth Crusade and the Sack of Constantinople* (New York, 2004); A. Chastel, *The Sack of Rome, 1527* (Princeton, 1983); H. Trevor-Roper, *The Plunder of the Arts in the Seventeenth Century* (London, 1970); and the essays in K. Bussmann and H. Schilling, eds., *1648. War and Peace in Europe* II (Münster, 1998).

[6] See, e.g., two essential accounts on different aspects: F. Haskell and N. Penny, *Taste and the Antique. The Lure of Classical Sculpture, 1500–1900* (New Haven, 1981), and L. Barkan, *Unearthing the Past. Archaeology and Aesthetics in the Making of Renaissance Culture* (New Haven, 1999).

[7] A. Momigliano, "La riscoperta della Sicilia antica da T. Fazello a P. Orsi," in E. Gabba and G. Vallet, eds., *La Sicilia Antica* 1.3 (Naples, 1980): 767–780.

after returning to Palermo, balanced religious exercises with intense work on his history of Sicily. The result was *De Rebus Siculis decades duo*, published in Palermo in 1558.

As part of his research, he tells us in the preface, he walked around the island four times. He eagerly sought out the actual physical remains of the ancient cities that figured in his sources and made a significant contribution by correctly identifying the site of Selinous. In addition to his own observations from autopsy, Fazello steeped himself in the ancient authors who discuss Sicily or refer to the island: he cites more than a hundred of them and read all of the relevant sources except Pindar, whose poetry was not yet available. He says he felt like Asclepius, bringing back to life the dismembered parts of Hippolytus (p. 2 of preface).

His constant companion throughout his book is Cicero's *Verrines*, cited on most pages of the text of the first decade that concerns the topography of the island, and in the second decade on the island's history. Fazello also expects his readers to know the content of the *Verrines*; he alludes to the speeches and gives specific references but assumes a degree of familiarity with them. As A. Momigliano has pointed out, Fazello's book on Sicily is a hybrid between topographical, geographical, and antiquarian research, arranged geographically by site around the island, and a historical narrative of Sicily, recounted chronologically.[8] Fazello sees the history of Sicily as a series of invasions from outside, a historiographic model noted by Momigliano and astutely analyzed further by G. Ceserani, who finds a more complex relationship between Sicily's history as an island and early modern historians of the larger Mediterranean more generally.[9] Fazello's underlying view of Sicily as a crossroads and place of contention by outsiders was shaped by his use of the *Verrines* as his primary source and model. As we have

---

[8] A. Momigliano, *The Classical Foundations of Modern Historiography* (Berkeley, 1990): 71–73; on antiquarianism, see A. Schnapp, *The Discovery of the Past* (London, 1996): 179–219.

[9] Momigliano (1980): 768; G. Ceserani, "The Charm of the Siren: The Place of Classical Sicily in Historiography," in Smith and Serrati (2000): 174–193.

seen, Cicero presents Sicily and its history that way to his jurors and readers in order to make Verres' maladministration of the province all the more shameful in the light of Rome's triumphant control over a strategically important, historically much-contested, and very wealthy province.

Fazello's book on Sicily remained authoritative and in print well into the nineteenth century and was published and republished in many editions. The first to depend on him for another serious scholarly project was Philip Cluwer (Cluverius, 1580–1623), the geographer and humanist who settled in the Leiden Academy after personal vicissitudes and who published *Sicilia antiqua* (1619). Again, Cicero's *Verrines* and Fazello's topographical account were important sources. The significance of the books by Fazello and Cluverius went beyond scholarship, however, when Sicily began to be a destination for visitors from abroad (a more benign form of invasion). Those early visitors were eager to be informed about what they were seeing, and their travel accounts, published letters, and journals reflect their own research and reading: primarily Cicero's *Verrines* and then Fazello and Cluverius are the "authorities" they cite most often.

One early traveler who made the trip without Fazello's guidance was Sir Thomas Hoby (d. ca. 1566), whose autobiographical *Booke of the Travaile and Lief of me Thomas Hoby* was not published until 1902.[10] He traveled to Sicily in 1550, and when he arrived in Messina (home of Gaius Heius, whose Praxitelean Eros Verres had taken), he remarks, "Cicero maketh oft mention of this towne in his orations against Verres... abowt yt are verie auntient ruines."[11]

A traveler who read Fazello but was not content with merely seeing the sites of Sicily was a German, Georg Walther (G. Gualtherus).

---

[10] Discussed by E. Chaney, *The Evolution of the Grand Tour* (London, 1998): 6–7.
[11] Cited by Chaney (1998): 7.

He claimed to have collected twenty thousand inscriptions from Sicily or relevant to Sicily and published remarks about his collection in 1625. Both he and the collection were lost at sea. The huge number of inscriptions reveals how much documentary evidence for Sicily's history has been lost because of the actions of this one individual collector.[12]

Going to Sicily was a fairly unusual trip for outsiders such as Sir Thomas Hoby in the sixteenth century, but, by the eighteenth century, it became a natural extension of the Grand Tour.[13] Travelers from France, Germany, and England would first visit Rome, then Naples, with a side trip to Pompeii after 1748, when the excavations there started, and they then would sail by ferry to Palermo. By the later eighteenth century, travelers often brought painters or an architect with them to make illustrations of the sites of Sicily, a way of capturing and memorializing the trip, somewhat analogous to tourists' photography today. Richard Payne Knight (1751–1824), for example, who would later be involved in the controversy over the purchase of the Parthenon Marbles by the British Museum, made in 1777 what he calls an "Expedition into Sicily." He traveled in the company of Charles Gore and Philipp Hackert, who made watercolors and drawings, and Knight kept a diary that was translated into German by Goethe (who later made his own trip).[14] The young Knight shows his classical education with learned

[12] B. Lavagnini, "Sulle orme dell'epigrafista Georg Walther," *RömMittHist* 27 (1985): 339–355; W. Stenhouse, "Classical Inscriptions and Antiquarian Scholarship in Italy, 1600–1650," in A. E. Cooley, ed., *The Afterlife of Inscriptions. Reusing, Rediscovering, Reinventing & Revitalizing Ancient Inscriptions* (London, 2000): 82.

[13] H. Tuzet, *La Sicile au XVIIIe siècle vue par les voyageurs étrangers* (Strasbourg, 1955); she lists in an appendix all known trips to Sicily and published accounts by non-Sicilians in the eighteenth century, 515–520.

[14] Now published in English, with the watercolors of Hackert and Gore, and commentary by C. Stumpf, *Richard Payne Knight. Expedition into Sicily* (London, 1986). For Goethe's trip to Sicily (1787), see J. W. von Goethe, *Italian Journey, Goethe's Collected Works*, 6, trans. R. R. Heitner (New York, 1989): 183–254.

references to Cicero's *Verrines*, site by site, as he describes the groups'
travel around the island.

The more scholarly Baron Riedesel visited Sicily ten years before
in 1767 and published *Reise durch Sicilien und Gross Griechenland* (1771),
translated into English and French soon after. His account is in the form
of two letters to J. J. Winckelmann, whom he had met in Rome in 1762.
The travel narrative helped that scholar form his ideas about Greece, at
a time when travel to mainland Greece was still difficult, expensive, and
unusual. Riedesel's book on Sicily is short, but the itinerary he presents
became a standard one. He did eventually visit mainland Greece, but
without Winckelmann, despite several invitations to him for a joint
trip.[15]

Patrick Brydone, a scientifically minded author, made a similar
trip in 1770 and published in 1773 *A Tour through Sicily and Malta*, an
account in the form of thirty-eight letters to Mr. William Beckford
of Somerly Hall, who would himself become an author on Jamaican
topics and whose uncle with the same name was Lord Mayor of London.
Brydone had served as his tutor some years earlier. The light style, filled
with humor (and sprinkled with references to Cicero and the *Verrines*)
made it an international hit, after quick translations into German (1774),
French (1775), and even American editions. The author worries in the
preface about competition from Baron Riedesel's book on Sicily (then
available in translation), but thinks it won't "interfere" with his; he gives
a disclaimer, saying he was writing only for friends. Here is a sample
of his breezy style: [at Agrigento] "it was here that the famous statue
of Herakles stood, so much celebrated by Cicero; which the people of

---

[15] See Ceserani for comments on Riedesel's perceptions of Sicily and his influence on Winckelmann's view of Greek culture (2000: 188–191). Winckelmann himself did not go to Sicily
or to Greece when Riedesel invited him (intimating that he was too busy, too old, and it
was too dangerous). See further D. Constantine, *Early Greek Travellers and the Hellenic Ideal*
(Cambridge and New York, 1984): 124–146; on Winkelmann, A. Potts, *Flesh and the Ideal:
Winckelmann and the Origins of Art History* (New Haven, 1994); S. L. Marchand, *Down from
Olympus. Archaeology and Philhellenism in Germany, 1750–1970* (Princeton, 1996): 7–16.

Agrigento defended with such bravery, against Verres, who attempted to seize it. You will find the whole story in his pleadings against that infamous praetor," but then continues two pages later by saying, "I should be very tedious, were I to give you a minute description of every piece of antiquity. Indeed, little or nothing is to be learned from the greatest part of them."[16]

Before the trip to Sicily, Brydone had already accomplished numerous experiments with electricity, inspired by Benjamin Franklin, and he was interested in the vulcanology of Mt. Etna. His observations on electricity and vulcanology in his travel account earned him an invitation to join the Royal Society, but he also raised the ire of some divines who objected to his comments on the stratigraphy of the lava. Intrigued by the suggestions of a Sicilian priest, Signor Recupero, Brydone had noticed that the layers of deposition and correlations with Diodorus Siculus' accounts of eruptions during the second Punic War would lead one to conclude that some eruptions must have flowed at least fourteen thousand years ago – far more anciently than the presumed date of the creation of the world, according to biblical accounts (4004 BCE). The decisive rupture between calculations of geological chronology and assumptions based on the Bible would not come about until decades later, with Charles Lyell's *Principles of Geology* (1830–33), but Brydone's observations in Sicily and the ensuing fuss anticipated it.[17] The controversy made his travel narrative on Sicily all the more popular, and it went into nine editions during his life-time.

I mention these travelers here because their trips, accounts, and letters to people back home revived the story of Verres' misdeeds in Sicily as a general cultural reference, in an era when many educated

[16] P. Brydone, *A Tour through Sicily and Malta, in a Series of Letters to William Beckford, Esq. of Sommerly in Suffolk* (Greenfield, MA, 1798): 182, 184. For the addressee William Beckford, *ODNB* 4: 730–731 [R. B. Sheridan].

[17] This account of Brydone's scientific contributions is given in *ODNB* 8: 426–427 [K. Turner]; about other contributions to the discovery of stratigraphy, see Schapp (1996): 289–303.

people also could (and did) read the original Latin text of Cicero with ease. The participants on the Grand Tour were, for the most part, the elite of northern Europe and England who traveled as part of their extended education. Seeing Sicilian sites firsthand or reading travel accounts about them at home gave an impetus to read the Latin text, and a realism to the Greek and Roman past beyond the text.[18] Moreover, many travelers to Italy wanted to bring back authentic "souvenirs" in the form of ancient sculpture, so that the phenomenon of the Grand Tour also inspired a burgeoning impetus toward private collecting of art. These private collections of sculpture – and sometimes architectural fragments – were used as decoration in private houses and estates. A market for antiquities (and some forgeries) kept pace with the increasing volume of visitors.[19]

Scholarly Efforts on the *Verrines*

The antiquarian spirit of the eighteenth century is reflected in new dissections of the *Verrines* for information about art, with a focus on the fourth speech, now often referred to by the nickname *De signis* (On Statues). The first author to isolate and discuss this aspect of Cicero's speeches was the Abbé Fraguier, in an essay translated and published in

---

[18] The bibliography on the Grand Tour is extensive. See, e.g., J. Black, *The British Abroad. The Grand Tour in the Eighteenth Century* (New York, 1992); Chaney (1998); B. Dolan, *Ladies of the Grand Tour* (New York, 2001). For the role in the Grand Tour of Sir William Hamilton, British envoy to the Bourbon Court at Naples, see B. Fothergill, *Sir William Hamilton, Envoy Extraordinary* (New York, 1969); and I. Jenkins and K. Sloan, *Vases and Volcanoes. Sir William Hamilton and His Collection* (London, 1996). The numerous British and Irish travelers are gathered in John Ingamell's *A Dictionary of British and Irish Travellers in Italy, 1701–1800* (New Haven, 1997).

[19] For collecting during the Grand Tour, see, e.g., J. Scott, *The Pleasures of Antiquity* (New Haven, 2003): 53–84; social implications of collecting, see the essays in J. Elsner and R. Cardinal, eds., *The Cultures of Collecting* (Cambridge, MA, 1994); S. M. Pearce, *On Collecting. An Investigation into Collecting in the European Tradition* (London and New York 1995); for antiquarianism and collecting, see the essays in M. Myrone and L. Peltz, eds., *Producing the Past. Aspects of Antiquarian Culture and Practice, 1700–1850* (Aldershot, 1999).

London in 1740 from the French original of 1718.[20] The Abbé is careful to explain in his Preface,

> *The Design of the Discourse on the Gallery of Verres, is not to celebrate*
> *the infamous Verres, but the Masterpieces of ancient Art, which his*
> *Vanity and Avarice had amassed by Methods diametrically opposite to*
> *that generous and humane Temper which is the natural Concomitant of*
> *good Taste; and which, if the polite Arts do not produce, they indeed fall*
> *far short of Their principal Aim and best Effect: That noble Tendency to*
> *humanize the Mind, whence They anciently took their Name* (Literae
> humaniores) *to which I have often regretted there should be none for*
> *them in our Language strictly or adequately correspondent. (p. xvii)*

The Abbé begins by stating that Rome was ignorant of the arts until Marcellus, Scipio, Flamininus, Paulus Emilius [sic], and Mummius brought goods to the city. As for Verres, the governor took everything but it was probable that the best was in his renowned Gallery. He then goes on to list and describe all the major statues mentioned by Cicero, item by item, and other pieces such as the elephant tusks from Malta with Punic inscriptions and the horse trappings of King Hieron II. He notes the sculpture returned by Scipio, and he gives supporting quotations from other ancient authors, his own opinions and speculations, and comments about Cicero's own good taste. This early study contained many of the elements that authors would return to in future work, including this one.

Conyers Middleton's biography of Cicero (*The History of the Life of Cicero*, 1741) also brought the story of the prosecution of Verres into wide

---

[20] George Turnbull, trans., *Three Dissertations; One on the Character of Augustus, Horace and Agrippa ... Another on the Gallery of Verres by the Abbé Fraguier, in Which Many Excellent Pieces of Ancient Statuary, Sculpture and Painting are Described....* (London, 1740): preface, 68–86. This essay was originally composed for the Memoirs of the Academy of Belles-Lettres and Inscriptions at Paris, May 13, 1718 (p. 68).

readership. Middleton (1683–1750), a clergyman based in Cambridge and involved in ongoing unpleasant disputes with the tyrannical Richard Bentley, had taken a breather and traveled to Rome for several months in 1723–24. He was deeply influenced by his visit both in his classical scholarship and his theological views, which became quite controversial. His biography of Cicero was supported by 1,800 subscribers, some of whom ordered multiple copies (e.g., Sir Robert Walpole ordered five). It won a very large readership and became a standard reference for Cicero, until well after his death when he was accused (unjustly) of plagiarism. Even then, his work is a frequent reference for later authors writing about Cicero and Sicily.[21]

Middleton has much to say about corrupt public administration, and deals with the case of Verres extensively (I: 79–108). He describes and analyzes the charges against Verres in great detail and brings in comments from other writings of Cicero, Pliny, and Plutarch. Middleton severely condemns Verres' actions, and his views are presented in a vivid, rhetorically effective style, no doubt honed by his many polemical pamphlets and essays.

The fourth and fifth speeches of the *Actio Secunda* were translated into English by Charles Kelsall and published in 1812 with notes and illustrations, making these parts of the *Verrines* more accessible to readers in Great Britain.[22] He comments in the preface, "the *De signis* [fourth speech, on looted art] speaks to the imagination, the *De suppliciis* [fifth speech, on unjust punishments] to the heart" (p. vii). In his notes, he gives miscellaneous remarks on modern Sicily and acknowledges his

---

[21] The biography struck a chord with contemporary readers, some of whom might have seen possible parallels between Cicero as a faithful, long-term servant of the state and Walpole. For the details of his life, work, and the accusation of plagiarism, see *ODNB* 38: 51–56 [J. A. Dussinger]. In standard histories of classical scholarship in this era, Middleton is barely mentioned and usually only in connection with his opposition to Bentley; yet, at least into the first quarter of the nineteenth century, he appears in many footnotes.

[22] Charles Kelsall, trans., *The Two Last Pleadings of Marcus Tullius Cicero against Caius Verres; translated, and illustrated with notes* (London, 1812).

debt to Cluverius, Mirabella, Arezzo, Hoüel, and Wilkens for antiquities, and Brydone and Swinburne (authors of travel accounts) for descriptions of the modern state of the island. He then comments on natural products, manufactured goods, arts, and literature in Sicily (pp. 297–8). Three years after the publication of this translation, those in Britain who wished to travel to Italy and Sicily could do so once again, as the Napoleonic wars were finally over.

LEGAL THOUGHT ON INTERNATIONAL AGREEMENTS

While Cicero's *Verrines* were on the reading list for travelers to Sicily and gaining increasing scholarly attention, the speeches and Cicero's other extensive writings were also in use to help formulate new approaches to international agreements. A significant contributor to the concept of international law was Hugo Grotius (1583–1645), the great Dutch jurist and humanist.[23] He was a child prodigy who entered the University of Leiden when he was only eleven, published his first book when he was fourteen, and received a doctorate when he was fifteen. He held administrative offices in Rotterdam, but his political associations led to his imprisonment in 1619, from which he was smuggled out in a chest of books and took refuge in Paris. There, he spent the rest of his life as the French King's pensioner, except for brief service as an Ambassador of Sweden on behalf of Queen Christina.

Earlier in Holland, Hugo Grotius was hired by a shipping company to compose a treatise on the legal right to prizes (*De iure praedae*), written circa 1606. A Mennonite member of the company had questioned its ethical and legal right to seize a ship in the Indian Ocean that had belonged to Portugal. Grotius was extraordinarily well read in Hebrew, Greek, and Latin authors and wrote a treatise defending the right to seize the ship, articulating the right of the conqueror to portable goods.

---

[23] W. G. Grewe, *The Epochs of International Law*, trans. M. Byers (Berlin, 2000): 7–12, 191–195. On ancient ideas about international law, see Bederman (2001b).

He published one chapter of the treatise on prizes under the title *Mare liberum* (1609), in which he argued, essentially, for freedom of the seas: Portugal (or any power) did not have the right to bar navigation or trade in the East Indies.[24]

Grotius lived in a turbulent era that included religious controversy, the Thirty Years War, and ongoing Dutch struggles with other powers, as well as the internal dissensions that led to his temporary imprisonment. The issue of booty in warfare and what was customary among warring powers was still emerging from the medieval institution of feuds, so it should not surprise that new thinking was needed about whether taking a ship as booty was proper and justified. (Grotius concludes that it is justified, as is taking in booty on land, based on the precedents he cites of comments made by Cicero, Polybius, Livy, and Tacitus.)

F. Redlich emphasizes that the crucial distinction between a feud and a war is not that one is private and one is public but rather that in feuds, even servants, retainers, subjects, and allies become enemies and lose their legal rights. Maximum damage is inflicted: looting was a weapon of war, and the booty was used for exacting reparations and luring mercenaries; it was even justified by early jurists.[25] By the early eighteenth century, the disadvantages of such widespread looting were recognized, especially for discipline among troops, and the problem of ownership (whether the booty belonged to the individual soldier or to the warring people) became more acute. As we saw in Chapter 1, the Romans gradually developed firm policies on the same issues.[26]

---

[24] H. Bull, "The Importance of Grotius in the Study of International Relations," in H. Bull et al., eds., *Hugo Grotius and International Relations* (Oxford, 1990): 65–93.

[25] F. Redlich, *De praeda militari. Looting and Booty, 1500–1815* (Wiesbaden, 1956): 2–3, 64–65.

[26] P. Contamine, "The Growth of State Control. Practices of War, 1300–1800: Ransom and Booty," in P. Contamine, ed., *War and Competition between States* (Oxford, 2000): 163–193. A related matter is sustaining the army at war: Should they forage and feed off the countryside, thus pillaging the locals, or should food be provided? This issue was pertinent in the Napoleonic wars, especially in the Peninsula, where the French troops were so predatory

Grotius' treatise on ships as prizes, not published separately until 1868 when it was discovered by a book dealer in Amsterdam, was used by Grotius as the centerpiece for his more famous work on international rights on the sea and in time of war (*De iure belli ac pacis* [1625]).[27] Many of Cicero's essays and speeches are quoted in support of Grotius' arguments, including the *Verrines*. In an analysis of the ancient authors used by Grotius for international rights, D. Bederman has counted more than eighty citations from Cicero's writings in the 1625 edition, more than any other single author.[28] As a group, Grotius cites ancient Greek and Roman historians the most, then orators and political commentators (Cicero, Pliny, Quintilian, Seneca), followed by philosophers, especially Aristotle and Plato. Bederman explains that Grotius focused on the practice and customs of ancient states rather than the history of jurisprudence or legal details because he was seeking the principles of "natural justice," which he felt should guide the conduct of states.[29]

The significance of Grotius' contribution was that he thought of international law as having a universal application; in this, he was guided by Cicero's concept of a society of mankind rather than of states (*humane generis societies*).[30] As Bederman points out, in the early seventeenth century, the raw material for views about international

that the local people developed a new style of covert struggle against them (guerilla warfare), and did what they could to assist the British. For British policy, see discussion later in this chapter.

[27] Hugo Grotius, *De iure praedae commentarius* [1604], *Classics of International Law*, J. B. Scott, ed., trans. G. L. Williams (New York, 1964): Scott includes an analysis of the difference between the original *De iure praedae* and its subsequent use in Grotius' widely known treatise (published in his life-time) in the preface to the translation; Bull (1990): 67–71; S. Buckle, *Natural Law and the Theory of Property: Grotius to Hume* (Oxford, 1991).

[28] Bederman (2001): 115.

[29] Bederman (2001): 114–115.

[30] Cicero, *Off.* 1.50–59; 3.21–37; *Fin.* 3.19–22; discussed by Bederman (2001): 116–122, who notes that Grotius was aware of Cicero's debt to Stoic philosophers for this concept. The concept had also emerged in the treatises of Alberco Gentili (1552–1608), an Italian expatriate who lived in England. Gentili too came to similar conclusions, also using ancient authors and

law was derived from ancient authors. Bederman's overall project is a demonstration of the profound significance of classical rhetorical traditions for the development of legal interpretations. The essential concept that can be traced from Cicero to Grotius is the idea of a human community that transcends the state; ultimately, this is derived from philosophy and rhetoric, not specific legal antecedents. Grotius' legal thinking was taken up and expanded by Baron Samuel von Pufendorf (1632–1694), a jurist and philosopher who taught at the University of Heidelberg and in Sweden. He argued that the law of nations (international law) must be based on principles of natural law – that is, not decreed or formulated in courts or legislatures – and he also refined the arguments for interpreting treaties.[31]

Jurists writing on international law and concerned with property rights in time of war had a hope of developing prescriptive agreements in anticipation of a conflict. This had obvious, ongoing practical applications. The theoretical investigations of the seventeenth century were usually inspired by specific events, such as the ship captured in the Indian Ocean that was the original impetus for what became Grotius' important treatise *De iure belli ac pacis* (1625). Part of Grotius' contribution was to define separate categories of property that would be treated in different ways, with different kinds of rights and obligations attached to their possession. In the mid-eighteenth century, the idea of establishing a separate category for art, religious and "cultural" property, with its own conditions of treatment during wartime, emerges in the writings of the Swiss jurist Emmerich de Vattel (1714–1767). His treatise, *Droit des gens, ou principes de la loi naturelle appliqués à la conduit et aux affaires des Nations et des Souverains* of 1758, was to become the essential

---

Cicero as primary sources: P. Haggenmacher, "Grotius and Gentili: A Reassessment of Thomas E. Holland's Inaugural Lecture," in Bull (1990): 133–176.

[31] On the complex development of the concept of "Law of Nations" and the role of Pufendorf, see Grewe (2000): 349–360.

foundation for the concept of cultural property.[32] He uses the term "society of nations" in the treatise, anticipating its use after the First World War.[33] He also uses arguments about what is "humane," such as the following passage:

> ...for whatever cause a country be devastated, these buildings should be spared which are an honour to the human race and which do not add to the strength of the enemy, such as temples, tombs, public buildings and all edifices of remarkable beauty. What is gained by destroying them? It is the act of a declared enemy of the human race thus wantonly to deprive men of these monuments of art and models of architecture....[34]

Vattel took the ideas about "natural law" formulated earlier by Grotius and Pufendorf (and his teacher Christian von Wolff) and carried them further, set on a firmer basis with more specific ways to make international agreements binding. According to Bederman, Vattel's interpretations of treaty law do not overtly rely heavily on classical authorities, but are built implicitly on Grotius.[35] Rather than seeking authority in the distant past, Vattel's focus was on current arguments, yet the ancient ideas still provided the logical underpinning of the arguments.

De Vattel contributed (among several concepts) a new recognition of cultural property as something separate from land, ships, bullion, commodities, arms, or other portable possessions. The concept of cultural property itself is inherently nationalistic, especially as it is used today, and its development depended in part on the emergence of a strong sense

---

[32] [Emmerich de] Vattel, *The Law of Nations*, trans. J. Chitty (Philadelphia, 1852); F. S. Ruddy, *International Law in the Enlightenment. The Background of Emmerich de Vattel's Le Droit des Gens* (Dobbs Ferry, NY, 1975); Grewe (2000): 287–289, passim.

[33] Grewe (2000): 288.

[34] E. de Vattel, *The Law of Nations, or Principles of Natural Law as Applied to the conduct and Affairs of States and Sovereignties* III. Trans. Charles G. Fenwick (Washington, DC, 1916): ch. 9, 293.

[35] Bederman (2001): 138–141.

of cultural patrimony that is contained in the sense of nationhood.[36] While these new ideas still remained in the arena of discussion, however, and had an intellectual impact that may have contributed to social opinions, the new ideas about cultural property as a separate category of possession did not have any force of law.

ADMINISTRATORS ABROAD: THE VERRINE MODEL

Against the international background of the Enlightenment and the views promulgated by Emmerich de Vattel, however, Cicero's ideal portrait of the humane general Scipio Aemilianus, who repatriated Sicilian statuary, took on added contemporary relevance in new political circumstances. In the 1780s, Verres and the *Verrines* would be used extensively by Edmund Burke in his prosecution of Warren Hastings on charges of extortion in India. This political use of Cicero was not new. Even earlier in England, private persons concerned with issues of plundering or extortion also had recourse to ancient sources and Cicero in particular to justify their views. Two pamphlets preserved in the British Library illustrate what must have been an ongoing concern and the familiar recourse to the Classics for authoritative support.

In 1703, a certain Thomas Heskith published *ΛΑΦΥΡΟΛΟΓΙΑ: or, a Discourse concerning Plunder: wherein the Legality of the same is proved by several Presidents* [sic] *and Arguments, brought from the Laws of God, of Nature and Nations ... with some brief Reflections on St. Mary's and Vigo,* in which he seeks to validate the rights of officers and soldiers to the spoils of a public enemy, and their right to keep the spoils themselves. He begins with etymology, then moves on to a discussion of Cicero's *Verrines*, biblical examples of plunder, Xenophon on the Persian King

---

[36] This fundamental point is discussed by J. H. Merryman, *Thinking about the Elgin Marbles. Critical Essays on Cultural Property, Art and Law* (The Hague and London, 2000): 66–91. For a convenient collection of essays on the development of views and legislation about cultural property, see J. H. Merryman and A. E. Elsen, *Law, Ethics, and the Visual Arts*[3] (London and Boston, 1998).

Cyrus (the same passage discussed in Chapter 1), and many other ancient examples of plundering. Heskith then writes at length on the actions in Spain of the Duke of Ormond, and the legalities of a military intervention that had just occurred. The tract seems sincerely written and shows considerable erudition, but the arguments in favor of plundering are not persuasive. The author seeks to justify the old "to the victor go the spoils" argument, supported by his impressive classical learning.

A second, anonymous pamphlet published in 1732, entitled *Verres and his Scribblers: A Satire in Three Cantos*, uses the *Verrines* extensively and more cleverly than Heskith. It was written as a satire in verse on a current political situation. The complaint is about what was perceived as the heavy-handed monetary policies of Sir Robert Walpole (1676–1745), who was then serving as First Lord of the Treasury (in that office 1721–1742). The preface to *Verres and his Scribblers* is humorously defensive and self-exculpatory and claims that the following verses are directed against a "country attorney," who is defined further with the anagram "Lawlope."[37] The author was probably right to apologize for the verses really are doggerel, but are of interest here nevertheless as an example of how the story of Verres was used as political commentary. Here is an extract on Verres/Walpole:

> To every Sense of Worth and Virtue lost,
> The Vultur ravag'd on the Publick Cost;
> Tax'd every Man's and swell'd his own Estate
> Bought Mannors, Pictures, Palaces and Plate,
> By selling, quartring, palming, private jobbing,
> Reversions, Places, Pensions, publick robbing.
> Th'unsated Thief shone with inglorious Fame,
> His Wealth and Honours point out his Shame.[38]

[37] Anonymous, *Verres and His Scribblers; a Satire in Three Cantos. To Which Is Added an Examen of the Piece, and a Key to the Characters and Obscure Passages* (London, 1732): preface, 66–69.
[38] Anonymous, *Verres and His Scribblers* (1732): 8–9.

The verses continue on a great length in a similar style of excoriation. The anonymous author must have read the *Verrines* and, ignited by fresh indignation, felt inspired to create this commentary on his own circumstances.

Verres was brought up as a negative exemplar once again in British public discourse later in the eighteenth century, when administrators in India were considered culpable for greed, corruption, and misadministration in Bengal. A bad precedent had already been set in India by Robert Clive back in 1757, when he intervened in a dynastic competition, fought an unnecessary and lopsided battle at Plassey, and accepted a huge payoff. Bengal, the most wealthy, strong, and fruitful province of the Mughal empire, became a province of the East India Company, "an empire within an empire." Further episodes during the next decades of excessive profits, akin to plundering, triggered investigations by Parliament in the affairs of the Company (founded in 1600). The British public did not like the impugning of their national character, and the social concern was expressed in a series of satires and plays, pamphlets and other forms of public complaint.[39] Returning nabobs were so wealthy they could buy seats in Parliament, as did Clive. There was also the increasingly uneasy and unbalanced relationship between the East India Company and the British government. In 1773, the British government established a new judicial and administrative structure that clarified its rights to govern in India, under a Governor-General.

The new Governor-General, Warren Hastings (1732–1818, served 1773–1784), was sent out to Calcutta. He was an old India hand and had risen through the ranks of the Company. In his new position, he was supposed to collect taxes, keep order, and administer justice, and he did reform the judicial system and make orderly arrangements in his

---

[39] For the events, J. Keay, *India, A History* (New York, 2000): 381–393; for public reaction in England, L. James, *Raj. The Making and Unmaking of British India* (New York, 1997): 42–52. On these events and the view of the west in India, see the excellent discussion of M. Jasanoff, *Edge of Empire. Lives, Culture, and Conquest in the East 1750 – 1850* (New York, 2005).

administration. He was constricted by hostile members on a four-man
council that had some input into decisions; also there was a fair amount
of inertia, since the old ways of laissez-faire administering had been
highly profitable to members of the Company. But by 1782, the House
of Commons demanded his dismissal and impeachment. In addition to
the customary charges of excessive profit, it was alleged that he hanged
people he did not like, he extorted money from the Rajah of Benares
and from a rich widow (the Begum of Oudh), and used British troops
as mercenaries, hiring them out for defensive duties.

Edmund Burke (1729–1797) was his chief prosecutor in a trial that
lasted eight years but finally ended with Hastings' acquittal. Already
widely published, the founder of a periodical, and a member of Dr.
Samuel Johnson's circle of friends, Burke had been a Member of Parliament since 1765, where he was a staunch advocate for better treatment
of the American colonies. He was well regarded for his oratory and,
in preparation for this trial, he read Cicero's *Verrines*, which were his
model.[40] The parallels between the charges are remarkably similar (no
doubt deliberately so, in their formulation). Burke emphasizes what
he perceives as the Verrine character of Hastings at several points in
his speeches. He also assumes a general familiarity with the *Verrines*,
saying, "We have all in our early education read the Verronean [sic] orations . . . " (see epigraph at the beginning of this chapter), and remarks
that in Cicero's "orations you see almost every instance of rapacity and
peculation which we charge upon Mr. Hastings."[41]

---

[40] M. L. Clarke comments that he must have read them in Latin and on his own initiative
because they were not on the curriculum of Trinity College Dublin when he was a student,
and there was not yet an English translation available (Clarke, 1965: 101); however, he may
well have read them as a schoolboy as the passage quoted in this chapter below suggests.
They are still widely used as a school text. For the trial, see P. J. Marshall, *The Impeachment
of Warren Hastings* (Oxford, 1965); on Hastings' life and the trial, J. Bernstein, *Dawning of
the Raj. The Life and Trials of Warren Hastings* (Chicago, 2000); on Burke's use of Cicero, P.
Ayres, *Classical Culture and the Idea of Rome* (Cambridge, 1997): 42–47.

[41] Marshall (2000): 662–663.

It may be argued that for this tactic to be effective, the audience already must have had familiarity with the story of Verres. In fact, the *Verrines* were once again widely read in England as models of rhetoric, just as the speeches of Burke himself would be read by coming generations, whether their interest was in law, oratory, or India. Furthermore, the case against Verres is discussed (briefly) in Plutarch's *Life of Cicero*, very popular then and available in translation, and Plutarch was among the most widely read of ancient authors in this period. The deliberate use of Cicero by Burke is one reflection of the high esteem in which Cicero was held in eighteenth-century England: he expected his parallels and Ciceronian oratory to persuade and prevail in Parliament.[42]

For the uninitiated, the London newspaper *Public Advertiser* carried a series of articles dissecting Cicero's case against Verres.[43] According to the preface to the series, the comparison between Verres and Hastings came originally from the "whisperings" of his accusers' friends, and:

> *From conversation this comparison has travelled to the public papers,*
> *and from the papers to the print-shops, where, under the character of the*
> *Roman Orator, the person and manner of Mr. Burke are too faithfully*
> *delineated to escape the observation of those who have ever once seen*
> *this very distinguished character. To those conversant in the Roman*
> *History, and with the affairs of India (particularly the government of*

---

[42] On the reputation of Cicero in Burke's life-time, see G. Carnall, "Burke as Modern Cicero," in G. Carnall and C. Nicholson, eds., *The Impeachment of Warren Hastings. Papers from a Bicentenary Commemoration* (Edinburgh, 1989): 78–80. On Burke's use of Ciceronian views in other writings, especially *Reflections on the Revolution in France*, see J. Zetzel, "Plato with Pillows: Cicero on the Uses of Greek Culture," in D. Braund and C. Gill, eds., *Myth, History and Culture in Republican Rome* (Exeter, 2003): 135–137.

[43] *Public Advertiser*, 5, 6, 7, 11, 13, 15 February 1788, a six-part series entitled "View of the Character and Conduct of C. Verres, Praetor of Sicily, and Warren Hastings Esq., late Governor General of Bengal, with a parallel between M. Tullius Cicero and the Right Hon. Edmund Burke," signed *Amicus Curiae*. The existence of the series is noted in Marshall (2000): 29.

Bengal for these last twenty years past, or to those who have carefully read over the charges exhibited against Mr. Hastings, with his answers), the glaring injustice of this comparison must evidently appear, but as this knowledge, cannot be possessed by many, I propose, in the course of a few letters, through the channel of your paper, first to state the character and conduct of Verres and Mr. Hastings, for facts; Next to draw a parallel between Marcus Tullius Cicero, the accuser of Verres, and The Right Hon. Edmund Burke, the accuser of Warren Hastings, Esq.; And lastly, to suggest such reasons drawn from the general conduct of Mr. Hastings as, in my opinion, should operate in favour of that Gentleman's exculpation. (signed Amicus Curiae, *Feb. 5, 1788)*

In the series, published throughout the month of February, the *Amicus Curiae* gives an extended and witty comparison between the two pairs of men (Cicero and Burke, Verres and Hastings), with subtle barbs directed against Mr. Burke. The *Amicus Curiae* certainly read the *Verrines* closely and knew Cicero well, for the comparisons are both apt and accurate in detail. The series ends with lengthy exhortations to the Court about proper government abroad, the difficulties of administration, and the significance of the responsibilities and representation of the British government. This series in a London newspaper gives insight into the deep level of public interest in this scandal, at least at the beginning of the trial. By 1795, no doubt the public felt somewhat weary of hearing about it. Most significant, however, is the sophisticated use of the *Verrines* both by Burke (who suggests Hastings had a small sphinx, putting him briefly into the role of Hortensius) and by journalists for a public ready to hear about it.

The other eighteenth-century British official who caused a great public stir and was accused of being a Verres was Thomas Bruce, seventh Earl of Elgin. Once he was appointed in late 1798 as British Ambassador Extraordinary and Minister Plenipotentiary to the Sublime Porte of

Selim III, Sultan of Turkey, Lord Elgin anticipated a trip to Athens, then part of the Ottoman Empire, en route to Constantinople. He already had in mind a serious undertaking concerning antiquities in Athens, for which he hoped to get public funds, but when he was refused, he decided to use his own money. He had not yet seen Athens but wanted to make casts of antiquities to use as models for the architectural decoration of his seat, Broomhall. On the way to Constantinople, the Elgins stopped at Palermo, where they visited Sir William Hamilton (envoy to the Bourbon court in Naples, now evacuated to its second seat in Palermo because of the French seizure of Italy). Sir William suggested that Lord Elgin hire the Italian artist and architect Giovanni Battista Lusieri. Lord Elgin had also hired William R. Hamilton (then twenty-two, no relation to Sir William) as his private secretary and attaché, and W. R. Hamilton helped gather up suitable equipment and assistants for Lusieri. While the main party headed east, Lusieri and his assistants waited in Sicily for passage, passing time by making drawings of some of the temples, including the Temple of Concord at Agrigento and buildings in Syracuse.

In Constantinople, after several persistent requests, Lord Elgin eventually obtained a *firman* (permit) to, among other actions, "contemplate ... measure and draw, take mouldings ... dig in rubbish for inscriptions ... and [take away pieces of old stone with inscriptions] or [figures], without interference" on the Akropolis of Athens.[44] Far from merely making casts or drawings, Lord Elgin's men removed cornice blocks from the Parthenon that were still *in situ* (after some 2,250 years) and forcibly extracted sculpted metopes from the exterior and blocks

---

[44] For the full text of the extant firman, see W. St. Clair, *Lord Elgin & the Marbles*³ (Oxford, 1998): appendix 1, 337–341. For a close commentary on the firman, events in Athens, eyewitnesses, and Elgin's motives, see D. Williams, "'Of publick utility and publick property?': Lord Elgin and the Parthenon Sculptures," in A. Tsingarida, ed., with D. Kurtz, *Appropriating Antiquity, Saisir l'Antique* (Brussels, 2002): 103–164, including contemporary sketches and watercolors of the removal in progress.

of the frieze from the interior wall; in addition, they levied out much of the remaining pedimental sculpture. Some of the sculpture and several cornice blocks were dropped and smashed in the process. A few years later, one whole shipload was sunk on its way to England but then retrieved by sponge divers, thanks to the energy and supervision of W. R. Hamilton.[45]

In the meantime, the pillaging and destruction caused distress and lamentation in Athens. The story of Lord Elgin's spoliation of the Parthenon has been told often, recently, and well, but usually from a perspective outside of Greece, looking at Greece and the Parthenon as the victims. E. Yalouri's book on the Akropolis examines the history of the Greek response to the despoliation and the important role of the Akropolis in the formation of Greek national identity.[46]

Of particular interest for public reaction in England to the event is the role played by the poet and philhellene, George Gordon (1788–1824), Lord Byron. His campaign against Lord Elgin's despoiling of the Parthenon became very well known because he wove it into his poetry, with prose commentary, that was becoming extremely popular. At a time when travel to the Continent was dangerous and limited because of the Napoleonic wars, Byron decided to head farther east to the "Levant," which included Greece and Turkey, accompanied by his friend John Cam Hobhouse. On their way to Malta for the eastward voyage in the early summer of 1809, Byron and Hobhouse first visited Lisbon and explored parts of Portugal, where the British would celebrate Sir

---

[45] St. Clair (1998); general accounts in T. Vrettos, *The Elgin Affair* (New York, 1997); C. Hitchens, *The Elgin Marbles. Should They Be Returned to Greece?* (New York, 1997). For the legal aspect and claims of restitution, see Merryman (2000): 24–65.

[46] E. Yalouri, *The Acropolis. Global Fame, Local Claim* (New York, 2001); see also D. Philippides, "The Parthenon as Appreciated by Greek Society," in P. Tournikiotis, ed., *The Parthenon and Its Impact in Modern Times* (Athens, 1994): 278–309; for Athens and the Parthenon after independence, E. Bastéa, *The Creation of Modern Athens. Planning the Myth* (Cambridge, 2000).

Arthur Wellesley's (the future Duke of Wellington's) important victory at Talavera, won just weeks later in July. After further travels and adventures in Albania, they arrived in Athens on Christmas Day, 1809, and stayed there for about ten weeks.

Byron spent his mornings writing and visiting the sites on horseback in the afternoons. He and Hobhouse became friends with Lusieri, who did not hide the very apparent destruction caused by the removal of sculpture from the Parthenon and architectural pieces such as a caryatid from the Erechtheum on the Akropolis. Byron saw all this with growing anger. When Byron returned to England via Malta, he traveled on the same British ship that took some of the marbles away from Greece. But after his return, he warned Lord Elgin that he planned to publish complaints (the men apparently never met).[47]

In a satire, *English Bards and Scotch Reviewers* (1809), written before he went to Greece, Lord Byron mocks Lord Elgin and also Lord Aberdeen as foolish collectors of broken stones. The trip to Athens changed his view: he now understood the larger significance of "broken stones." After he saw the damage, he became far more pointed and vehement in his criticism. *The Curse of Minerva* was written in Athens in 1811 and depicts Minerva with a broken lance, the gorgoneion missing from her aegis, her eyes filled with tears at the terrible violation of her temple. Her temple had escaped the depredations of Alaric the Goth (said to have respected the temple), only to fall victim to a cold-hearted Scot.

---

[47] L. A. Marchand, *Byron. A Portrait* (Chicago, 1979): 282–283, and 317 for his reaction to an invitation to join the "Athenian Club," in which he states a wish to "immolate Ld. Elgin to Minerva & Nemesis." In a letter written July 31, 1811, to Hobhouse, Byron says, "Lord Elgin has been teazing to see me these last four days. I wrote to him, at his own request, all I knew about his robberies, and at last have written to say that as it is my intention to publish (in Childe Harold) on that topic, I thought proper, since he insisted on seeing me, to give him notice that he might not have an opportunity of accusing me of double dealing afterwards. So you see how matters stand. I believe we differ on Lord E[lgin]'s subject, or else he will be prettily trimmed among us, i.e. Dr. [E. D.] Clarke, you, and my self, prose and verse all rising in revenge of Minerva." Letter published in John Murray, ed., *Lord Byron's Correspondence* II (London, 1922): 43.

Byron's attack on Lord Elgin did not go without answer: W. R. Hamilton, formerly Elgin's attaché, was appointed an undersecretary of state for Foreign Affairs in October 1809, an office he served until 1822 when he was promoted to ambassador to Naples – the same post held by his more famous predecessor with the same name. After Byron's publication of *The Curse of Minerva* caused a stir in London, Hamilton responded with a published *Memorandum on the Subject of the Earl of Elgin's Pursuits in Greece* (1811). In this pamphlet, he outlines the history of Lord Elgin's project (referring to his own role in the third person), giving a detailed account of its background and progress, with appendices containing supporting letters and scholarly notes. He says Mr. [Thomas] Harrison, architect, talked with Elgin about the need for young architects to see casts of antiquities, which would be better than the drawings of J. Stuart and N. Revett as models; he notes that Elgin's group in Athens "witnessed daily destruction of sculpture and architecture by Turks and travellers" and says that statues from the Parthenon were ground for mortar or broken up while looking for treasure. The French had already smashed one metope and taken other objects to France. "The Ilyssus [sic] Temple, intact in Stuart's day [1750s], has disappeared and even its foundations cannot be discerned."[48] Elgin bought fragments of the Nike temple that had been embedded upside down in the wall of a gunpowder magazine. Hamilton tells the story of hiring sponge divers from Syme and Kalymnos to retrieve the sunken cargo of statuary. He refers to Canova's declining the invitation to "complete" the statuary, and how the sculpture made Mrs. Siddons [the most famous actress of the day] cry.[49]

[48] The Ilissos temple was a small marble Ionic temple of ca. 430 BCE similar to the Temple of Athena Nike on the Akropolis; it was thoroughly documented by Stuart and Revett, but by 1768 was dismembered and sold for its marble to be reused as building material for a church. For details of its history, see M. M. Miles, "The Date of the Temple on the Ilissos River," *Hesperia* 49 (1980): 309–325. Some of its sculptured frieze still remains. Illustrations in J. Stuart and N. Revett, *Antiquities of Athens* I (London, 1762): chapter 2.

[49] *Memorandum on the Subject of the Earl of Elgin's Pursuits in Greece* (London, 1811): 1–45.

This defense contains many of the elements that would be repeated over the years, especially in the debates surrounding the purchase of the Parthenon marbles five years later in 1816: the collecting activity is framed in opposition to the French presence in Athens and the ongoing destruction by locals, especially the Turks, with specific horrifying examples of what had been already lost and the generally sad state of the antiquities in Athens.

Fierce competition between western Europeans for possession of new "discoveries" in Greece was also an issue in the acquisition of the pedimental sculpture from the Temple of Aphaia on the island Aegina, near Athens. An international party of young architects led by C. R. Cockerell dug 3 feet down in front of the remains of the temple and found the well-preserved pedimental sculpture, on both front and back sides, in 1811. Cockerell wanted it to go to the British Museum and tried to arrange for its purchase. Preserved correspondence shows that W. R. Hamilton had tried to assist Cockerell in the negotiations; a strong feeling of patriotism, that these finds should be in Britain, runs throughout the letters between him and Cockerell and Cockerell to his parents.[50]

On September 2, 1811, a ship was ordered sent by Lord Wellesley (Richard, Sir Arthur Wellesley's eldest brother), writing from 10 Downing Street as Foreign Secretary, thus offering formal governmental support for the acquisition. Despite this effort, the British representative went to Malta (where the sculptures had been shipped) rather than to Zakynthos, where the auction was being held. In the absence of a British bidder, Ludwig I of Bavaria purchased the Aegina sculptures and today they are part of the collection of the Munich Glyptothek. Cockerell later succeeded in getting another of his discoveries, the entire inner

---

[50] Correspondence preserved among the Cockerell Family Papers in the Royal Institute of British Architects, London. For Cockerell at Aegina, see D. Watkin, *The Life and Work of C. R. Cockerell* (London, 1974): 8–12. Cockerell dedicated his book on Aegina and Bassai to the memory of W. R. Hamilton.

frieze from the Temple of Apollo at Bassai, to the British Museum (in October 1815).

The ongoing Napoleonic war had a far-flung effect, influencing attitudes about these acquisitions, which were viewed as significant discoveries to be rescued from ignorant locals and as a potential benefit for (British, French, or German) artists and architects. After Napoleon Bonaparte's stripping of art from Italy and Egypt in the late 1790s (discussed later in this chapter) and Lord Elgin's precedent of 1801, the scope of what was taken from ancient sites now included whole assemblages, not merely individual pieces. The intensified nationalist spirit transcended the idea of simply augmenting private collections for private houses, since the intended destination shifted to national museums, and the triumphalism implicit in the acquisition was now national, not individual.

By 1812, Lord Byron had completed his next volume of poetry that contained more commentary on Lord Elgin's activities in Greece. *Childe Harold* was the vehicle for his most severe denunciations; I give here two excerpts from Canto II:

> *XI.*
> *But who, of all the plunderers of yon Fane*
> *On high – where Pallas lingered, loth to flee*
> *The latest relic of her ancient reign –*
> *The last, the worst, dull spoiler, who was he?*
> *Blush, Caledonia! Such thy son could be!*
> *England! I joy no child he was of thine:*
> *Thy free-born men should spare what once was free;*
> *Yet they culd violate each saddening shrine,*
> *And bear these altars o'er the long-reluctant brine.*
> *XV.*
> *Cold is the heart, fair Greece! that looks on Thee,*
> *Nor feels as Lovers o'er the dust they loved;*

Dull is the eye that will not weep to see
Thy walls defaced, thy mouldering shrines removed
By British hands, which it had best behoved
To guard those relics ne'er to be restored: –
Curst be the hour when from their isle they roved,
And once again thy hapless bosom gored,
And snatched thy shrinking Gods to Northern climes abhorred!

Aside from references to Lord Elgin's Scottish ancestry (Caledonia), the cold, hard climate that fostered a cold heart, and so forth, the more interesting denunciations involve Lord Byron's use of the *Verrines*. In commentary and notes to his poetry (which went through multiple editions), he refers to Lusieri, Lord Elgin's architect and agent, as his "Finder," an allusion to the "hunting dogs" hired by Verres, the Cibyratans Tlepolemus and Hieron. Again and again, through multiple editions of his poetry and commentary, Byron slams Elgin for raping Athens of the Parthenon sculpture, while pointing to his official role as ambassador to Constantinople as a mark of shameful British maladministration.

The parallel with Verres was telling, and Byron succeeded well in stirring public opinion, using his enormous popularity to good effect. This may have influenced the very close decision made by Parliament and the British Museum in 1816, as they very nearly refused to buy the sculptures from Lord Elgin. There were other reasons for hesitation, detailed at length by W. St. Clair, but public opinion surely played a role as well.[51] For both of these episodes – the trial of Hastings and the pillaging and damage done to the Parthenon – there was strong

[51] St. Clair (1998): 180–200, 245–260; I. Jenkins, *Archaeologists & Aesthetes* (London, 1992): 13–40; D. M. Wilson, *The British Museum. A History* (London, 2002): 71–75. Lord Byron's opposition to Elgin is discussed by Hitchens (1997): 45–48. On Lord Byron in Greece, see E. Kefallineou, *Byron and the Antiquities of the Acropolis of Athens* (Athens, 1999), with texts of all relevant poetry.

public reaction, and in the rhetoric of the time, Verres provided the best parallel for condemnation.

Byron was not himself an antiquarian or particularly interested in the physical recovery of the past. Like others of his time, he left his name as carved graffiti in several spots in Greece, visible still today, such as on a front anta of the Temple of Poseidon at Sounion. Like others, he brought back "souvenirs," but his booty consisted of four skulls, living tortoises, and Greek servants, and no classical works of art. Yet, both Byron and Hobhouse admired Professor E. D. Clarke of Cambridge University, who, while deploring Lord Elgin's actions on the Akropolis, himself took away a caryatid from Appius Claudius Pulcher's propylon at Eleusis still revered by the current residents, despite their protests.[52] While views about antiquities and actual behavior could be inconsistent, still there was strong, widespread disapproval of Lord Elgin's actions because of their large scope and the destruction that resulted to standing temples of special historical importance, well known from literary sources. Byron's contribution was his ability to see through the current circumstances in Greece to a better, independent future and to recognize and publicize the ethical wrong and historical violation perpetrated by Lord Elgin.

Byron's *Childe Harold* combines fiction, autobiographical elements, commentary on current politics and detailed travelogue for an immediate audience kept at home by war and avid for the exotic atmosphere of the Levant. The adulatory reception given to Byron and his poetry was impelled in part by the long history of the Grand Tour, now interrupted, and an ongoing cultural acclamation of the classical past as exemplary

[52] The statue is now in the Fitzwilliam Museum, Cambridge; L. Budde and R. Nichols, *Catalogue of the Greek and Roman Sculpture in the Fitzwilliam Museum* (Cambridge, 1964): 46–49, no. 81; for the reaction of the local people to the removal, E. D. Clarke, *Travels in Various Countries: Greece, Egypt and the Holy Land* VI (London, 1818): 600–602, 615–623; on Clarke, see also Williams (2002): 130.

that was just starting to shift focus from Italy to Greece. (In Britain, the shift in the early nineteenth century was in part a reaction to the French appropriation of Rome as a model and the influence of Winckelmann's views on the superiority of Greek culture.[53]) Rather than simply describing Greece along with classical references, long the custom for travel accounts in Italy and Sicily, Byron introduced a dashing hero (modeled on himself) onto a poetic landscape that was simultaneously classical and contemporary. In his poetry, ancient Greece still lived but was also potentially a modern country that needed to be "freed" from outside rule. His campaign against Lord Elgin as a Verres was only one aspect of his respect for contemporary Greece: he evidently recognized that Greeks themselves would eventually reclaim their antiquities and their history.[54] His philhellenic enthusiasm and inspiration contributed to growing support for the Greek cause, even though official British policy was initially allied with Ottoman rule, especially in the aftermath of the French invasion of Egypt. In 1824, Byron died of fever in Mesolonghi while supporting the war effort for Greek independence, heroically rallying besieged defenders of the town.[55]

ON VANDALISM

Another fierce critic of Lord Elgin's actions in Greece was Edward Dodwell (1776/7–1832), artist and author of several books on travels in Greece and Italy. He devotes many pages to the episode of the

[53] For other factors, see F. Turner, "Why the Greeks and Not the Romans in Victorian Britain?" in G. W. Clarke, ed., *Rediscovering Hellenism. The Hellenic Inheritance and the English Imagination* (Cambridge, 1989): 61–81.

[54] For an overview of Byron's political views, see N. Leask, "Byron and the Eastern Mediterranean: *Childe Harold* II and the 'Polemic of Ottoman Greece,'" in D. Bone, ed., *The Cambridge Companion to Byron* (Cambridge, 2004): 99–117.

[55] For a recent discussion of Byron's role in Greek independence, F. MacCarthy, *Byron, Life and Legend* (London, 2002): 487–522; succinct account of the impact of Byron in Greece, L. Trayianmoudi, "A 'Very Life in … Despair in the Land of Honourable Death': Byron and Greece," in R. A. Cardwell, ed., *The Reception of Byron in Europe, II: Northern, Central and Eastern Europe* (London, 2004): 419–438.

despoliation of the Parthenon (his "inexpressible mortification" is frequently quoted in recent discussions) and also gives valuable information about the conditions of many other ancient monuments in Greece and commentary on how Turks, local Greeks, and foreign visitors were treating them while he was there or in the recent past. He enumerates various kinds of destruction, damage, and neglect, and compares it to the ongoing "Vandalic profanation" of monuments in Italy, especially Rome. In the course of his comments on the damage to the Parthenon, he remarks, "The Athenian temples will thus probably be destroyed for the sake of their ornaments; which, instead of remaining in their original places, as the property of all nations, will be appropriated by the strongest" (full statement in Appendix, no. 9).[56] Here is an early articulation of the view that such monuments should be "the property of all nations" or the cultural heritage of everyone, an argument that is still used today.

The original Vandals migrated out of Germany at the end of 406 and successively entered into Gaul, Spain, and north Africa, where under Gaiseric they established a kingdom centered in Carthage. In 455, they sacked Rome, causing legendary devastation. Eventually, they were defeated by Belisarius, Justinian's general (who was awarded an exceptional, old-style Triumph in 535), and thereafter they were less significant in the Mediterranean. Today, the word "vandalism" has become so worn that we tend to think of broken windows and graffiti as examples. But when the word was first used by the Abbé Henri Grégoire in the 1790s, it served to make a powerful and evocative political statement because the perpetrators of damage and destruction of French

---

[56] E. Dodwell, *A Classical and Topographical Tour through Greece; during the Years 1801, 1805, and 1806* (London, 1819) I: 322; "Vandalic profanation," on p. 327. The context of the quotation on "property of all nations" is given in the Appendix, no. 9. For his biography, see *ODNB* 16: 442–444 [Y. Foote]. Dodwell recommends the use of casts of antiquities for instructive purposes, thus rendering the pillage of originals unnecessary.

monuments were themselves French.[57] The Abbé Grégoire censured
the deliberate and terrible destruction wrought in France of churches
and monasteries, their windows and contents, royal tombs and monuments, and some private property, all committed in the course of the
revolutionary upheavals. He was asked to respond to a proposal to elim-
inate all inscriptions in Latin and wrote a series of reports and essays
in which he articulates why the care and preservation of antiquities,
books, monuments, paintings, and buildings should be a proper concern
and responsibility of the state. In them, he argues against the continuing destruction of cultural property within France and regards all such
damage as (barbaric) vandalism that deprives all of France of her history.

As J. Sax has pointed out in his legal study of Grégoire's publications,
this was the initial articulation of the principle of separating the political, ideological, or religious agenda of the patron (in this case, royals and
the church) from the creation of the artist or architect. Grégoire argues
against wanton destruction even of artistic property closely associated
with the *ancien régime*, saying, "Certainly the temples of the Druids
at Montmorillon, and that of Diana at Nimes, were not built by the
hand of reason; and nevertheless is there any true friend of the arts
who would not want them to be preserved in their entirety[?]. Because
the pyramids of Egypt had been built by tyranny and for tyranny,
ought these monuments of antiquity to be demolished ... [?]."[58] As Sax
notes, the separation of art (as a product) from the motives of the patron
was a thoroughly modern idea, and although Grégoire's ideas about
conservation were not immediately put into place – not until 1830,

[57] The *OED* gives Henri Grégoire, Bishop of Blois, credit for the coining of the word, although it may have been in the air and used by other authors as well (*OED*[2] [1989]19: 425).
[58] J. Sax, "Heritage Preservation as a Public Duty: The Abbé Grégoire and the Origins of
an Idea," *Michigan Law Review* 88, 5 (1990): 1142–1169; see also J. Sax's larger study of the
whole issue, *Playing Darts of with a Rembrandt* (Ann Arbor, 1999). The cited passage (in Sax,
1990: 1155) is from H. Grégoire, *Troisième rapport sur le vandalisme, séance du 24 Frimaire, l'an
III.* For studies of vandalism during the revolution, see the essays in S. Bernard-Griffiths,
et al., eds., *Révolution française et "vandalisme révolutionnaire"* (Paris, 1992).

under a royal regime – nonetheless, his ideas about national patrimony were widely circulated and admired.[59] This separation potentially shifts the responsibility for the maintenance and protection of monuments to the state, and hence it presupposes a nationalistic outlook on such cultural "heritage" that would be under state stewardship. In this view, all of French history is part of French national patrimony and therefore should be preserved and protected. His inclusion of the pyramids of Egypt, like Dodwell's comments on Athenian temples as the property of all nations, edges closer to the idea of international concern with world-wide heritage, and hence international responsibility for its protection. As of 1794, however, the Abbé was involved in assessing and selecting for the new Revolutionary Louvre Museum paintings plundered from Belgium, and he looked forward to the French conquest of Italy and the ancient art that he expected to be taken as booty, including the Apollo Belvedere from the Vatican.[60]

NAPOLEON IN ITALY

This story, like that of the Parthenon Marbles, is a familiar one but so pivotal for the development of ideas about cultural property that I give a brief account here. The courageous individuals who bravely spoke out against Napoleon's actions relied in part on Cicero's *Verrines* for their argumentation, and they deserve to be heard again. On May 18, 1796, Napoleon announced a treaty with the Duke of Parma that included stipulations that twenty paintings should be handed over. This was the

[59] For the impact of Grégoire's writings, see Sax (1990); A. Vidler, "The Paradoxes of Vandalism: Henri Grégoire and the Thermidorian Discourse on Historical Monuments," in J. Popkin and R. Popkin, eds., *The Abbé Grégoire and His World* (Dordrecht, Boston, and London, 2000): 129–156; A. Sepinwall, *The Abbé Grégoire and the French Revolution* (Berkeley, Los Angeles, and London, 2005), esp. 137–139. The Abbé is also known for other innovative ideas on many subjects ranging from abolishing slavery and the treatment of Jews to education and the purity of language.

[60] The Abbé's role is discussed in C. Gould, *Trophy of Conquest, The Musée Napoléon and the Creation of the Louvre* (London, 1965): 31, 41, 49.

start of the extensive, systematic looting of the Italian peninsula, under a thin guise of a series of unequal treaties, including the infamous Treaty of Tolentino with the Papal States (1797).[61] The idea was not totally new; such seizures had occurred a few years earlier, under revolutionary fervor. The French revolutionaries viewed themselves as the political heirs of Rome, and just as the ancient Romans had appropriated Greek art, so too, they thought, should they appropriate art that only they would truly appreciate (e.g., Flemish art from Antwerp): thus they justified their seizures by claiming both status as the true heirs to Rome and superior artistic sensibility.[62] But the scale of plundering of art by Napoleon (to be placed by the victors in the Musée Napoléon) was unprecedented in early modern history: one would have to go back to L. Mummius at Corinth, or perhaps Marcellus at Syracuse – parallels that surely would have pleased Napoleon.

The Louvre Museum had opened in Paris in 1793 and the royal collections had been made available to the public. Napoleon seized on the plans already partially in place for filling it with the "best" art of Europe, and he expected that would make Paris the center of art production. It was now to be called the Musée Napoléon. The aim was an encyclopedic presentation of art history but at the same time a gathering of what were deemed "masterpieces" that would also serve as exemplars for aspiring artists.[63] (In this, he anticipated Hitler's and Stalin's similar plans for museums in Austria and Russia.) Under the

---

[61] The classic account is that of Gould (1965); see also A. McClellan, *Inventing the Louvre* (Cambridge, 1994): 91–123. For recent discussions of the Treaty of Tolentino and its repercussions: *Ideologie e patrimonio storico-culturale nell'età rivoluzionaria e napoleonica: a proposito del Trattato di Tolentino. Atti del convegno Tolentino 18–21 Sept., 1997, Pubblicazioni degli archivi di Stato,* 55 (Rome, 2000). For the earlier history of the idea of using plundered art under the Revolution, see E. Pommier, *L'Art de la liberté. Doctrines et débats de la révolution française* (Paris, 1991): 397–466; D. Poulot, *Musée, nation, patrimonie, 1789–1815* (Paris, 1997): 11–36, 195–277.

[62] Pommier (1991): 93–166; McClellan (1994): 91–108. Napoleon's policy discussed in S. Englund, *Napoleon, A Political Life* (New York, 2004): 114; on French use of Roman imagery, see R. Chevallier, ed., *La Révolution française et l'antiquité* (Tours, 1991).

[63] For the implications of these ideas for art history, the history of museums, and the fate of the concept of "masterpiece," see H. Belting, *The Invisible Masterpiece* (Chicago, 2001):

thinnest veneer of the unequal treaties (what Grotius would have called an "odious promise" of dubious validity because of the conditions under which they were made), Napoleon's soldiers cut paintings out of their frames in churches, emptied private collections, and sent what they did not destroy in a series of convoys pulled by water buffalo and oxen. The crates were then shipped to Marseilles.

They sent off to Paris the Bronze Horses of San Marco in Venice, themselves trophies from Constantinople. Napoleon wanted to take Trajan's Column from Rome, but his engineers advised him that it could not be moved without destroying it. The papal collection was the next target. The Laocoön, discovered in a hole by a farmer in Rome in 1506, was crated up. It was the most famous and at that time the most admired sculpture from antiquity (see Fig. 18). The sculptural group also might have had a particular resonance for the French because Laocoön was the Trojan priest who warned the Trojans not to accept the Wooden Horse left behind by the Greeks as a supposed offering to Athena. He was then killed, together with his sons, when a god hostile to Troy sent serpents that emerged from the sea, a harbinger of the fall of Troy (which in turn led to the eventual foundation of Rome – and France was supposed to be the new Rome). Along with Laocoön and his sons, the Belvedere Apollo from the Vatican and the Dying Gaul from the Musei Capitolini joined the Aphrodite from the Uffizi in Florence (the Medici Venus) in the trip to Paris, along with dozens of other ancient statues from Italian collections. When those items arrived in France in 1798, it was decided that they should be carried into Paris in a triumphal procession, closely modeled on those described by Roman authors. They were featured along with the Venetian Bronze Horses and are represented in a drawing of the procession, which shows them uncrated (see Fig. 19).

27–49. These ideas were not generated by Napoleon but by earlier revolutionaries, and then they were taken up and expanded by Napoleon. For discussion of the ideology and its antecedents in the immediately pre-revolutionary period, see McClellan (1994).

FIGURE 18. Laocoön group, by Hagesandros, Athanodoros, and Polydoros of Rhodes, ca. 40–20 BCE. Museo Pio Clementino, Vatican. Photo credit: Archive Timothy McCarthy / Art Resource, NY.

FIGURE 19. Pierre-Gabriel Berthault, *Entrée triomphale des monuments des sciences et arts en France; Fête a ce sujet; les 9 et 10 thermidor an 6.me de la Republique* (Triumphal entry of monuments of science and art into France), Paris [1802]. Collection Hennin, Bibliothèque Nationale de France. Photo credit: Bibliothèque Nationale de France, département de la reproduction.

Paris was now to be the new Rome, where cultural and political authority would join again. There were triumphal chariots and banners around the crates that read: "Greece relinquished them, Rome lost them, their fate has changed twice, it will never change again."[64] Besides ancient sculpture and a whole range of Italian painting, the papal archive was taken, including papal working files, manuscripts,

[64] On the calculated emulation of antiquity, see H. T. Parker, *The Cult of Antiquity and the French Revolutionaries, A Study in the Development of the Revolutionary Spirit* (1937; repr. New York, 1965); Pommier (1991): 331–396. For the triumphal procession, P. Mainardi, "Assuring the Empire of the Future: The 1798 'Fête de la Liberté'," *ArtJ* 48 (1989): 155–163; D. M. Quynn, "The Art Confiscations of the Napoleonic Wars," *AHR* 50 (1945): 437–460.

and historical documents such as the transcripts of the trial of Giordano Bruno of Nola, the philosopher and metaphysician who was burned at the stake in 1600 for heresy. The triumphal procession also had camels, lions and exotic plants, reminiscent of Pompey's Triumph of 61 BCE and the Flavian Triumph of 71.

The procession was recalled and commemorated by an elaborate vessel, modeled after "Etruscan" (actually Greek) vases, made by the Sèvres porcelain factory fifteen years later in 1813, perhaps for the Louvre or for one of the imperial residences[65] (Fig. 20). A polychrome painting around its middle represents *L'Entrée à Paris des oeuvres destinées au musée Napoléon* (*Entry into Paris of Works Destined for the Napoleonic Museum*). An idealized version of the procession, with the sculpture not in crates and pulled by citizens and soldiers, the painting shows the Laocoön, Apollo Belvedere, Medici Venus and other sculpture, and also piles of books and scrolls of papers, pulled through a triumphal arch labeled *MUSÉE* (Fig. 21). The medallions in relief on the scrolled handles represent Augustus, Napoleon, Pericles, and Lorenzo de' Medici. It is plain that at the time the captured art was regarded first and foremost as military booty on a Roman model, which is one reason why after the defeat of the French, the decision was made to repatriate as much of it as possible.

After Waterloo, Pope Pius VII sent to Paris the artist Antonio Canova as his emissary to ask for the return of his sculpture, and the archives, and not least his working papers. Much had been lost in transit, however, including the records of Bruno's trial. Canova's esteem as an artist and his diplomatic skill contributed to the eventual (even if partial) success of his mission.[66]

---

[65] Details in M.-N. Pinot de Villechenon, *Sèvres. Porcelain from the Sèvres Museum, 1740 to the Present Day* (London, 1997): 54–57.

[66] C. M. S. Johns, *Antonio Canova and the Politics of Patronage in Revolutionary and Napoleonic Europe* (Berkeley, 1998): 171–194; F. Zuccoli, "Le ripercussioni del trattato di Tolentino sull'attività diplomatica di Antonio Canova nel 1815 per il recupero delle opere d'arte," *Ideologie e patrimonio storico-culturale* (2000): 611–632.

FIGURE 20. Antoine Béranger, *The entrance into Paris of the works destined for the Musée Napoléon*, "Etruscan-style" [actually Greek] volute krater, 1813. Porcelain. Musée Nationale de Ceramique, Sèvres. Photo credit: Réunion des Musées Nationaux / Art Resource, NY.

Napoleon's systematic despoliation of Italy was severely criticized by the French artist and architectural theorist Antoine-Chrysostôme Quatremère de Quincy (1755–1849), who branded Napoleon as a Verres in numerous essays published in France. In his open letters (published in 1796), addressed to General Miranda, a revolutionary leader from South America, Quatremère emphasizes the contrast between Napoleon's actions with those of Scipio Aemilianus, who repatriated statuary, using Ciceronian rhetoric as well as several quotations from the *Verrines*.[67] Once again, the sufferings of the Sicilian Greeks under Verres were recalled for a contemporary parallel!

Quatremère believed that the best art had a universal quality and therefore could not be possessed but ought to be held in the original context in which it was nurtured.[68] In his Fourth Letter to Miranda, he credits this idea to Cicero (in fact, it was Polybius', amplified by Cicero). The idea that art (at least the "best" art) does have a context and a setting necessary for its full understanding and appreciation was an older aesthetic issue in France that was discussed in the debates surrounding the opening of the Louvre in 1793.[69] The significance of context is still crucial to ongoing discussions about cultural property, although insistence on context no longer depends on the perceived quality of the item. Now the emphasis is on history and the historical value of artifacts, which can only be known within a particular, archaeological context.

After the *Letters* to Miranda were published, Quatremère's discussion of ethics did stir some public opinion against Napoleon's actions. A

[67] Quatremère de Quincy, *Lettres à Miranda sur le Déplacement des Monuments de l'Art del'Italie* (1796; E. Pommier, ed., Paris 1989): quotes the *Verrines* or mentions Verres at 99, 116, 123, 132 (citing *Verr.* 2.4.73–74), in addition to general rhetorical echoes. This edition also includes the petition against plundering of art, August 16, 1796, with fifty signatories (pp. 141–142).

[68] On Quatremère and his views, see A. Potts, "Political Attitudes and the Rise of Historicism in Art Theory," *ArtHist* 1 (1978): 191–213; Pommier's preface to his edition of Quatremère's letters, Pommier (1989): 7–67; Pommier (1991): 414–432; S. Lavin, *Quatremère de Quincy and the Invention of a Modern Language of Architecture* (Cambridge, MA, 1992): 150–157.

[69] McClellan (1994); Belting (2001): 27–35.

FIGURE 21. Antoine Béranger, *The entrance into Paris of the works destined for the Musée Napoléon* (Detail: the Laocoön), "Etruscan-style" [actually Greek] volute krater, 1813. Porcelain. Musée Nationale de Ceramique, Sèvres. Photo credit: Réunion des Musées Nationaux / Art Resource, NY.

petition was circulated and garnered fifty signatories, including sculptors, painters, architects, and other artists, and even Vivant Denon, the future Director of the Musée Napoleon (Louvre), who was later instrumental in Napoleon's removal of antiquities from Egypt. They called for the looting to stop, and their petition was published. Nonetheless, Napoleon's plundering in Europe continued and then expanded into Egypt.

NAPOLEON IN EGYPT

In his invasion of Egypt in 1798, just two years after invading Italy, Napoleon was again following an idea that had been in the air earlier in revolutionary circles. It was thought that a blow could be made against

British interests in India, via Egypt.[70] At the same time, the campaign was fitted into revolutionary rhetoric with the suggestion that the Egyptians could be "freed" from the tyranny of the Ottoman Empire. The campaign was a military disaster, and Napoleon abandoned his army in Egypt to return to France after defeat by the British. Yet he must be credited with initiating a new European scholarly interest in Egypt and the founding of Egyptology.

The invasion itself was crude and brutal, wasteful and futile as a military campaign. It led to a huge influx of foreign troops into Egypt (French, British, and Ottoman Turkish) within the following five years. The exploratory side of the campaign was far more successful, however, and had far-reaching consequences. Probably at the suggestion of Vivant Denon, Napoleon brought with him 167 scientists and specialists, equipped with the latest tools for surveying, drawing, and recording, and the invaders documented and published a wealth of knowledge about Egypt, ancient and modern. Despite military defeat, their scholarly efforts were soon published in handsome volumes (*Description de l'Égypte*) that provided valuable documentary evidence for both ancient and modern Egypt.[71]

The sculpture and other artifacts gathered together by the French team became spoils of war twice because after the British land army defeated the French in Egypt in 1801, the British claimed the collection

---

[70] This threat was taken very seriously by the British, even after Bonaparte left Egypt; Arthur Wellesley, the future Duke of Wellington, was then in India and in 1801 was supposed to take part in a strike through the Red Sea, but he came down with a tropical ailment that prevented him from sailing. The ship he should have been on sank, and all hands were lost.

[71] For an overview with extensive bibliography, D. Dykstra, "The French Occupation of Egypt, 1798–1801," in M. W. Daly, ed., *The Cambridge History of Egypt*, 2 (Cambridge, 1998): 113–138; on the motivations and politics of the campaign, Y. Laissus, *L'Égypte, une aventure savante, avec Bonaparte, Kléber, Menou 1798–1801* ([Paris], 1998); A. Schom, *Napoleon Bonaparte* (New York, 1997): 71–188; Jasanoff (2005); also still useful is J. C. Herold, *Bonaparte in Egypt* (New York, 1962); J. Benoist-Méchin, *Bonaparte en Égypte, ou le rêve inassouvi (1797–1801)* (Paris, 1978); H. Laurens, et al., *L'Expédition d'Égypte* (Paris, 1989).

in the Treaty of Alexandria, and the pieces are now in the British Museum. The Rosetta Stone was almost smuggled away by the French. W. R. Hamilton, then serving as Lord Elgin's attaché, was present in Alexandria on a diplomatic mission, and when he heard a rumor of this, he found some marines to accompany him and rowed out to the French ship to demand its return, as stipulated in the treaty.[72] They handed it over. At some point someone painted on the side of the Rosetta Stone, "Captured in Egypt by the British Army in 1801."[73] In contrast with the outpouring of negative reaction to the plundering of Italian art, the Egyptian plunder was met with great excitement and interest throughout Europe, and the plunder and the campaign inspired a new round of "Egyptomania."

RESTITUTION OF PLUNDER AND POPULAR REACTIONS

For the first time in early modern history and the first time since Scipio Aemilianus, after Waterloo, the Duke of Wellington made the decision that the art plundered by Napoleon in Italy ought to be returned to its previous owners. This overturned ancient precedents (to the victors go the spoils) enacted by most Romans and moved the issue of the fate of art in war beyond even Ciceronian idealism. Rather than packing off the Laocoön, Apollo Belvedere, Medici Venus, and the Dying Gaul to Windsor Castle, along with other sculpture and hundreds of much-esteemed Italian paintings, the victors decided to repatriate them. Furthermore, France and the Louvre were not plundered of their own artistic possessions, even though previously in the course of more than

---

[72] For W. R. Hamilton's role, *ODNB* 24: 933–934; firsthand account: W. R. Hamilton, *Aegyptica or Some Account of the Antient and Modern State of Egypt, as Obtained in the Years 1801* (London, 1809): 402–403.

[73] Wilson (2002): 63–64; the letters are still visible on the side of the stone. On the other side was painted, "Presented by King George III" [to the British Museum], also still visible. For an argument for the restitution of the Rosetta Stone, see D. N. Osman, "Occupiers' Title to Cultural Property: Nineteenth-Century Removal of Egyptian Artifacts," *Col JTransnatlLaw* 37 (1999): 969–1002.

two decades the French had plundered art in all the countries they had occupied, most notably the Netherlands, Italy, Prussia, and Spain.

After a very long and bitter war, this was a remarkable outcome. In just the battle of Waterloo alone, some forty-seven thousand men on all sides suffered casualities and approximately twenty thousand horses were killed. The cost to all parties in lives and resources of the long struggle against Napoleon was enormous. Moreover, England, allies in Europe, and Russia had already forced Napoleon to abdicate the previous year, after his defeat at Leipzig and the arduous but triumphant campaigns in the Peninsula made his fate clear. The scale of the British generosity, based on principle, to Italy was unprecedented, but the restraint from plundering the French was extraordinary; true, financial reparations were demanded, but artistic treasures are beyond price and their ownership a focal point for national pride.

After Napoleon was defeated in 1814 and sent to Elba, no official provision for the repatriation of Napoleon's European plunder was made in the Treaty of Paris, although a limited number of paintings were returned to Prussia by decree of Louis XVIII.[74] Apparently, the French did try to have past actions validated on the basis of the (unequal, infamous) Treaty of Tolentino, but ratification was refused, even when they tried to offer an exception for all the paintings taken from Prussia (for the details, see the Duke of Wellington's letter in Appendix, no. 11). The Duke of Wellington thought of himself as representing all of the nations of Europe, he says, and felt that what might be done to return art to Prussia should be done for all. A written policy on museums was not set immediately because it was thought best to await the decisions of the various monarchs involved. A short time later, after Napoleon's escape from Elba and after Waterloo, however, the situation seemed quite different. The forbearance that the Allies had shown in 1814,

---

[74] Gould (1965): 116–119.

leaving these matters still possibly subject to negotiation, was no longer felt. The Duke makes this clear in his famous letter, quoted below.

After Waterloo (June 18, 1815), there was a general rush east toward Paris and some pursuit of French troops. Napoleon briefly eluded capture but eventually surrendered in Rochefort to the warship HMS *Bellerophon* (Captain Maitland, RN), which would take him to Plymouth before his final voyage to St. Helena. Of the Allies, the Prussians got to Paris first, and, once they were established, they simply took back their plundered art by force. The French populace seems to have opposed removals from the Louvre in sufficiently great numbers that the Belgians, wishing to reclaim what Napoleon had taken from them, felt obliged to ask the Duke of Wellington for support.

Correspondence among the Duke of Wellington, Lord Castlereagh (then Foreign Secretary), and Lord Liverpool shows that they were considering a range of options over several weeks in the late summer and early autumn of 1815. They were nudged along by Tallyrand, who was very concerned about the return of paintings to the King of the Netherlands. W. R. Hamilton, now Lord Castlereagh's undersecretary, was involved in the negotiations: he urged repatriation of everything, including the Pope's collection. Their correspondence reveals that they considered purchases (everyone definitely *wanted* the art: there was no lack of interest in possessing it) but were concerned about managing public opinion and refuting French charges of hypocrisy. The Duke and Lord Castlereagh resisted hints from the Prince Regent that the Laocoön would make a fine addition to the British royal collections, and instead they persuaded him that the higher course would be to pay for the restitution of the papal collection to Rome, since the Pope could not afford the shipping himself. The Prince Regent generously sent funds, and today the exchange of compliments on the occasion is commemorated by a portrait of Pius VII, painted by Sir Thomas Lawrence, placed among the luminaries of Waterloo in the Waterloo

Chamber in Windsor Castle: a more fitting ornament than ancient art as *spolia*. The same artist painted for the Waterloo Chamber what would become the most repeated representation of the Duke of Wellington (Fig. 22).

The Duke took the view that the looted art might serve as a focal point for French military spirit yet again and, in any case, it was obvious to all that art belonged in its proper context. That had been Quatremère's primary argument (and Polybius' long before him). He also comments on the silence of the Treaty of Paris of May 1814 and notes the various reasons why silence does not mean acquiescence. The Duke wrote a decisive letter on this topic to Lord Castlereagh, from which I quote these paragraphs (full text in Appendix, no. 11):

> The Allies then, having the contents of the museum justly in their power, could not do otherwise than restore them to the countries from which, contrary to the practice of civilized warfare, they had been torn during the disastrous period of the French revolution and the tyranny of Buonaparte.
>
> The conduct of the Allies regarding the museum, at the period of the Treaty of Paris [1814], might be fairly attributed to their desire to conciliate the French army, and to consolidate the reconciliation with Europe, which the army at that period manifested a disposition to effect. But the circumstances are now entirely different. The army disappointed the reasonable expectation of the world, and seized the earliest opportunity of rebelling against their Sovereign, and of giving their services to the common enemy of mankind, with a view to the revival of the disastrous period which had passed, and of the scenes of plunder which the world had made such gigantic efforts to get rid of.
>
> This army having been defeated by the armies of Europe, they have been disbanded by the United Counsel of the Sovereigns, and no reason can exist why the powers of Europe should do injustice to their own subjects with a view to conciliate them again. Neither has it ever appeared to me

FIGURE 22. Sir Thomas Lawrence (1769–1830), The Duke of Wellington, c. 1815. Oil on canvas. Apsley House (Wellington Museum), London. Photo credit: Victoria & Albert Museum, London / Art Resource, NY.

to be necessary that the Allied Sovereigns should omit this opportunity to do justice and to gratify their own subjects in order to gratify the people of France.

The feeling of the people of France upon this subject must be one of national vanity only. It must be a desire to retain these specimens of the arts, not because Paris is the fittest depository for them, as, upon that subject, artists, connoisseurs, and all who have written upon it, agree that the whole ought to be removed to their ancient seat, but because they were obtained by military concessions, of which they are the trophies.

The same feelings which induce the people of France to wish to retain the pictures and statues of other nations would naturally induce other nations to wish, now that success is on their side, that the property

should be returned to their rightful owners, and the Allied Sovereigns
must feel a desire to gratify them.

It is, besides, on many accounts, desirable, as well for their own
happiness as for that of the world, that the people of France, if they do
not already feel that Europe is too strong for them, should be made
sensible of it; and that, whatever may be the extent, at any time, of their
momentary and partial success against any one, or any number of
individual powers in Europe, the day of retribution must come.

Not only, then, would it, in my opinion, be unjust in the Sovereigns to
gratify the people of France on this subject, at the expense of their own
people, but the sacrifice they would make would be impolitic, as it would
deprive them of the opportunity of giving the people of France a great
moral lesson.

(Excerpt from letter of Duke of Wellington to Viscount Castlereagh,
K. G., Paris, September 23, 1815).[75]

The Duke's letter to Lord Castlereagh was published in the London *Times* of October 14, 1815. In Paris, after the letter was made public and the troops began removing and packing items from the Louvre, there was a great public outcry. Ladies were said to have wept over the loss of the Apollo; crowds nearly prevented the removal of the Venetian Bronze Horses. From the French viewpoint, the art was "theirs," won in war. They seemed to think that the most recent part of the war that culminated in the terrible battle at Waterloo was actually against Napoleon personally, not France, so that they should keep their "spoils" from the previous war (even though they had been defeated then, too; that is, they evidently did not fully concede defeat either in 1814 or 1815). They supported their view with the idea that the Louvre should

---

[75] Lieut. Colonel Gurwood, *The Dispatches of Field Marshall the Duke of Wellington*, 12 (London, 1838): 645–646. The original draft of this letter, now in the Wellington Archives at Southampton University, was written by the Duke partly in pencil, partly overwritten in ink, with additions in the Duke's hand, and a secretary's hand; there are few changes.

be encyclopedic in scope and that visitors could see the art better in Paris than in Italy or elsewhere, especially better than foggy England. Their anger was focused specifically on the Duke, who was even booed at the opera.[76] This emotional reaction is captured in an anonymous drawing showing a weeping French artist, with the Laocoön and the Apollo Belvedere being taken away from the museum in the background. His palette is cast forlornly in front of him (see Fig. 23).

This French view is illustrated specifically by a pamphlet published by a M. Hippolyte.[77] The author admits he will not consider whether the war was just but takes up the issue of the "rights" of war; he writes not out of national pride or personally against His Excellency the Duke. He says that throughout the ages and in almost all wars, there has been payment in gold, silver, jewels, precious furniture, statues, and pictures. He argues that the Museum of Paris was the fruit of victory, of legitimate exchange, conceded by treaty and capitulation. Now the Museum offers only debris and ruin, the long galleries denuded and despoiled, smoking from the blow that deprived France of her most precious monuments. What a loss for the arts! All had been brought together in the most magnificent palace of the universe. He cites numerous historical parallels of art as plunder (the actions of Cyrus, Aemilius Paullus, Pompey, Lucullus, and Vespasian) as a justification for stripping Italy and Austria, the Netherlands, and Prussia of art. He notes that the British took Tipu Sahib (Rajah of Mysore)'s crown, throne, diamond bird, rubies, emeralds, and other treasures,[78] and that they have the sacred carriage

---

[76] For the French view, Johns (1998): 183–194; E. Pommier, "Réflexions sur le problème des restitutions d'oeuvres d'art en 1814–1815," in *Dominique-Vivant Denon, L'oeil de Napoleon* (Paris, 1999): 354–357; atmosphere in Paris, P. Mansel, *Paris between Empires. Monarchy and Revolution 1814–1852* (New York, 2001): 93–97.

[77] M. Hippolyte, *Observations d'un Français, sur l'enlevement des chefs-d'oeuvre du Muséum de Pris, en réponse a la lettre du Duc de Wellington au Lord Castelreagh, sous la date du 23 septembre 1815, et publieée, le 18 octobre, dans le Journal des Débats [5th oct. 1815]* (Paris, 1815): 1–39 (British Library). The summary that follows is from this pamphlet.

[78] This is a reference to the battle of Srirangapatam (1799), where the British won a victory with Colonel Wellesley's (the future Duke of Wellington) participation.

of Bonaparte, the precious objects, and immense sums found in his baggage.[79] He concludes by asserting that the French, by creating the Museum, cultivated the arts and performed a greater service than that philosophical nation [Britain] which last year burned the arsenal of New York and the library of the United States. Hence, the argument of this author has at its heart a belief that the encyclopedic museum in Paris is so important it should not have been disturbed and a refusal to concede defeat (because if we follow his logic that the "fruits of victory" should go to the victor, then they should go now to the British and their allies, who won, not to the French, who lost).

The London *Courier, Times,* and *Globe* provided readers with a running account of this issue and details of French opinion that the editors then castigated. In the style of our own contemporary journalism, the newspapers take the story and work many angles, day after day, week after week. For example, the *Courier* takes up the story on July 15, 1815, with breathless speculation over whether Prince Blücher really will blow up the Jena bridge in Paris (because of the offending name) and an account of the pictures and statues in the Louvre. Two days later, the newspaper published a highly detailed descriptive list of plunder taken from Italy in 1797, including ancient sculpture, paintings listed by artist, manuscripts (e.g., Petrarch's copy of Virgil, with annotations in his handwriting, and Galileo's manuscripts) and geological collections, and they note that there is still to be added property from Dusseldorf, Dresden, Berlin, Madrid, the Hague, Antwerp, Florence, and Moscow. On July 24, the editors are concerned more with speculation about

---

[79] Napoleon's carriage was captured at Waterloo: a highly detailed description of it and all its contents and furnishings was published in the London *Courier*, November 30, 1815. His elaborate court sword, evidently intended to be worn in an anticipated victory procession in Brussels, was found in the carriage and today is on display in Apsley House Wellington Museum alongside the Duke's field sword, used at Waterloo, both made by the goldsmith Martin Biennais; with them is Tipu Sahib's sword and dagger.

FIGURE 23. *L'Artiste français pleurant les chances de la guerre* (French artist mourns the fate of war), c. 1815. Collection Hennin, Bibliothèque Nationale de France, Paris. Photo credit: Bibliothèque Nationale de France, département de la reproduction.

Napoleon's behavior on board the *Bellerophon* and about the terms of
the upcoming settlement: Marcellus at Syracuse is invoked, Cicero and
Sallust are quoted on the need for magnanimity to the defeated. A
newspaper from Flanders is quoted, describing Prince Blücher in the
Louvre, with catalogue in hand, reading aloud, "From the Dresden
Gallery! O yes – I recollect it – take it down." In July 29th's paper, the
editors report French laments about the dismembering of the Museum
and retort that the arts made as much progress when the fine collection
was distributed among its lawful owners. These stories are reported
alongside reviews of statistics and facts, including lists of deaths and
injuries from Waterloo and speculations about Napoleon's brothers.

The issue grew more heated in August. On August 21, the editors
comment, "the French say they [pictures and statues] are their's [sic],
not by robbery but by right of conquest. Be it so – By the same right
of conquest then they are ours! What can be clearer than this? And
though we do not mean to say that we should keep them from those
from whom they were taken, yet those Powers might be willing to give
up to us a part of what belongs to them for a valuable consideration ... "
with suggestions for a National Gallery in London. On September 29,
the paper reports news from the Hamburgh [sic] *Mail*, in which plans
for an exhibition of the returned works of art are discussed, with the
proceeds to go to wounded soldiers. Already in Potsdam there are statues
that have been to Paris and back. On October 3, as items are removed
from the Louvre, the paper comments on blank marks on the walls
that contrast with the splendid decorated ceilings, and on the next day
reports that the Austrians are taking down the Bronze Horses; there
is also discussion of the Duke of Wellington's letter. In October 12th's
paper, the petition written nineteen years earlier by Quatremère de
Quincy about Napoleon's plundering of Italy is printed in English
translation, complete with the names of the signatories. Several letters
written by the Italian artist Antonio Canova to a British friend are
featured on October 16, from which I give this extract:

*... What gratitude ought we not to feel towards the magnanimous
British nation! Fully does she deserve that the Arts, in return for this
generous act, should join hand in hand to raise a perpetual monument to
her name; but the best and the more lasting monument will be engraved
in the heart of every Italian, who on beholding the sacred objects torn
from their country, again restored to her, will recollect the nation that
stood forth as their advocate for this restitution, and will call down
upon her the blessing of Providence.*

And a subsequent letter begins with the memorable declaration: "We
are now beginning to drag forth from this great cavern of stolen goods
the precious objects of Art taken from Rome."[80]

The Bronze Horses (see Fig. 17) are given space to speak in the first
person in an article entitled "Adieu of the Bronze Horses to the
Parisians," stated to be "from a French paper" (more typically the name
of the paper is given, so this claim is surely part of the conceit) published in the *Courier* on October 18: "We should not have acted in a
manner becoming the place of our origin, which was one of the cities
of Greece most renown for its politeness, had not our residence among
you taught us to regard it as a duty, not to leave you without returning thanks for the kind reception you have given us. . . . It was always
with reluctance that we were transferred from Corinth to Rome, from
Rome to Byzantium, from Byzantium to Venice, and from Venice to
Paris," they begin. This rather arch piece contains much fulmination
against Napoleon (e.g., "A single man among you reminded us at once
of the baseness of Augustus, the cruelty of Nero, and the dissimulation
of Domitian . . . ") and a warning not to wish to see them again there at
such a price, the blood of two million Frenchmen.

On October 31, the *Courier* reports that the Quatremère de Quincy's
Letters to Miranda were just reprinted in Rome and provides a summary

---

[80] For discussion of Canova's important role in the restitution of art to Italy, see Johns (1998):
171–194.

of their contents, including discussion of Polybius' views, Scipio Aemilianus' repatriation of sculpture taken by the Carthaginians to towns in Sicily, and Quatremère's comparison of "the conduct of those who wished to despoil Italy, to the brutal rapacity of the infamous Verres" and again notes his signed petition to which the "Verreses of the Directory did not deign to give an answer." In November, the paper gave extracts from a travel narrative by a Miss Williams, who describes the reputedly histrionic reaction of the French at the removal of the art from the Louvre. After this account, interest in the story that had lasted five months seems to diminish.

The London *Times* and *Globe* also followed this story closely, with similar stories. The *Times* reprinted on October 13 Quatremère's petition, and on the next day, the Duke's letter of September 23. In the *Times* of October 26, the newspaper printed a translation of an article from the German paper *Rhenish Mercury* on the granite pillars taken from Aachen, tracing their long history back to Charlemagne and beyond to Helena, mother of Constantine.[81] The occasion was the ongoing furor over repatriation that was of equally intense interest in Prussia, where repatriation was keenly supported. Clearly, the public in London must have been quite absorbed by this part of the aftermath of Waterloo. For this public, the views articulated by Polybius and Cicero and taken up by Quatremère unmistakably had considerable relevance and helped to support general opinion.

In a description of his stay in Paris during the autumn after Waterloo, the journalist John Scott reports that he was able to go up on the Arc de Triomph while the Bronze Horses were still there, slipping by the guards because he was British. He gives an eyewitness account to the accumulated artistic plunder (and provides a detailed list of the

---

[81] Napoleon had removed thirty-eight columns from Charlemagne's royal church at Aachen; some were returned at this time, but eight still remain in the Louvre. See D. P. S. Peacock, "Charlemagne's Black Stones: The Re-use of Roman Columns in Early Medieval Europe," *Antiquity* 71 (273): 709–717 and Kinney (2001): 146–147.

sculpture, paintings, and manuscripts taken), and of the public tumult surrounding the repatriation. Without a doubt, this event had great emotional resonance.[82] Subsequent travel accounts "in classical lands" also mention the French plunder and its repatriation – the topic lived on for several decades at least, and British travelers could be quite acidic on the subject.[83] It should be noted, however, that according to recent tallies, only about 55 percent of what was taken was actually returned. V. Denon, the director of the Louvre, had managed to send out to other French towns many of the significant paintings, where they remained.[84] In Venice, the Bronze Horses were received with great jubilation, and a special ceremony with a salute of twenty-one canon was staged for their reinstallation on the Basilica of San Marco, painted by Vincenzo Chilone[85] (see Fig. 24).

The avid interest in the issue of repatriation also helped fuel the foundation and expansion of public museums, in England and continental Europe, a movement that had already begun in the eighteenth century when royal collections began to be opened to the public.[86] The

[82] John Scott, *Paris Revisited in 1815, by way of Brussels; including a Walk over the Field of Battle at Waterloo* (London, 1816): list of plundered items, pp. 362–368.

[83] E.g., the Rev. John Eustace, in *A Classical Tour through Italy in the Year 1802* (London, 1815) II, says, "the French, who in every instance, have been the scourge of Italy, and have rivalled, or rather surpassed the rapacity of the Goths and Vandals, laid their sacrilegious hands on the unparalleled collection of the Vatican, tore its masterpieces from their pedestals, and dragging them from their temples of marble, transported them to Paris and consigned them to the dull sullen halls, or rather stables of the Louvre," p. 59. The account by Joseph Forsyth (*Remarks on Antiquities, Arts, and Letters during an Excursion in Italy in the years 1802 and 1803* [London, 1813]) has similar remarks on the plundering of the French and the suffering of the inhabitants from war, and comments on the burnt shells of their houses on p. 132.

[84] D. Tamblé, "Il ritorno dei beni culturali dalla Francia nello Stato pontificio e l'inizio della politica culturale della Restaurazione nei documenti camerali dell'Archivio di Stato di Roma," *Ideologie e patrimonio storico-culturale* (2000): 457–514; and Pommier (1999).

[85] For details of their return to Venice, see A. Toniato, "The Horses of San Marco Form the Fall of the Republic to the Present Day," in *Horses of San Marco, Venice* (London, 1979): 117–123.

[86] Useful overview in C. Duncan and A. Wallach, "The Universal Survey Museum," *ArtHist* 3 (1980): 448–469; for the Louvre, McClellan (1994); for museums in Germany,

public attention in the autumn of 1815 to the sculpture and paintings that had served as "spoils of war" intensified the appeal of museums and accelerated the nationalistic competition for acquisition. In England, the sculptured frieze from the Temple of Apollo at Bassai found by C. R. Cockerell was purchased for the British Museum in 1814 and arrived in the autumn of 1815, just as the discussion of repatriation of the art in Paris was under way. The Parthenon Marbles taken by Lord Elgin were purchased after extensive debate that began in 1816, and they were exhibited to the public about fifteen months after the repatriation to Italy of what had been regarded as the acme of ancient art (e.g., the Laocoön, Apollo Belvedere, Medici Venus). One consequence of the debate was that new scholarly opinions began to form about the superiority of original Greek art over Roman versions. These views would dominate future studies well into the twentieth century. The Louvre was pleased to acquire the Venus de Milo in 1820, fresh from the island of Melos, but removed with some opposition from the local people. The acquisitions stirred avid public interest in ancient art in both England and France, but the public denunciations that faced Lord Elgin were not brought up in the case of the Venus in Paris or the frieze of the Temple of Apollo in London. In Germany, some museums used casts for exhibits in an effort to fulfill their expected didactic role.

Further into the nineteenth century, the idea of "collecting" antiquities on behalf of a public museum became one of the motivating factors in archaeological explorations and excavations. Even as archaeology was developing as a rigorous discipline and was conducted for the sake of knowledge, not for artistic treasures, the need for financial support of expeditions and excavations abroad meant that the likely acquisition of archaeological finds could be cited to potential backers as a persuasive

see S. Marchand, "The Quarrel of the Ancients and Moderns in the German Museums," in S. A. Crane, ed., *Museums and Memory* (Stanford, 2000): 179–199.

FIGURE 24. Vincenzo Chilone (1758–1839), *Ceremony of the reinstallation of the Bronze Horses on the façade of the Basilica of San Marco, Venice*. Coll. Treves Bonfili, Venice. Photo credit: Cameraphoto Arte, Venice / Art Resource, NY.

reason to support fieldwork. Deals were (usually) worked out with the host country to purchase or divide the finds.

THE DUKE OF WELLINGTON'S VIEWS

The Duke was heard to say in later life that it was impossible to prevent looting when a besieged city was being captured. But on military campaigns, the Duke had always put into place strong policies against casual pilfering by his troops. He was opposed to this for the basic reason that it led to lack of discipline, but he disapproved of it more generally, and in letters we find him complaining about infractions. Beginning with his time in India, he regarded as a part of his own responsibility the planning for the provisioning of his men, and meticulously ordered huge quantities of bullock carts, rice, and other provisions for the campaigns that required them: that careful planning became one of the hallmarks of his success. In the Peninsula, too, considerable effort was made to provide troops with what they needed. For this, the army was dependent on support from the navy, and that cooperation was key to the success of the strategy against Napoleon's generals in Spain. The provisions were not always sufficient or of high quality, but a strong effort was made to keep them moving forward to the front lines, even as the army maneuvered farther inland into Spain.

The strategy of winning support from local inhabitants made it crucial not to offend them with pilfering and to capitalize on the different treatment they would receive from the British, compared to the French, who committed so many atrocities that they drove the Spanish populace into closer alliance with the British. Wellington had standing orders that listed specific punishments for stealing eggs, chickens, wine and other commodities, in a table of offenses, some of which were punishable by hanging. That such punishments were actually carried out is well known from the many published memoirs of the Peninsular campaigns.[87]

The punishments were supposed to set an example, but that was not always sufficient. Weeks after the battle of Vitoria, the Duke received a polite letter of complaint from the Spanish mayor, Josef Garret, listing the many evidently serious abuses committed in the town by the garrisoned English troops and appealing to Wellington to enforce his orders. The Duke enclosed the letter in his own published, much-quoted letter to Lord Bathurst of July 2, 1813, in which he denounces the troops as the "scum of the earth." The reason for the Duke's anger on this

---

[87] The punishments are given in detail in Lt. Col. John Gurwood, ed., *The General Orders of the Field Marshall Duke of Wellington in the Campaigns of 1809 to 1815* (London, 1832). For actual examples of British pilfering of food and livestock, see E. Hathaway, ed., *A Dorset Soldier. The Autobibography of Sergeant William Lawrence, 1790–1869* (Staplehurst, 1993): 58–60, *passim*. The letters of F. S. Larpent, who served as Judge Advocate General for the British army in the Peninsula, illustrate how pilfering and its punishment were a frequent concern for him (*The Private Journal of F. S. Larpent* [London, 1853], 3 vol.).

occasion is usually not included in modern discussions that focus on the Duke's attitude toward his troops and quote that particular phrase as a general denunciation. The British had just won a great victory, but it was not final in part because plunder distracted the troops from proper pursuit of the French. To compound that failure, now there was desertion and a general lack of discipline because of ongoing looting and harassing of locals. The Duke's disparaging view was specific to this occasion.[88]

In the Duke's view, high standards also applied to his officers and himself. When Napoleon's brother, titled King Joseph of Spain, abandoned his carriage and fled on horseback from the battlefield of Vitoria on June 13, 1813, he left behind nearly everything: 151 cannon; massive amounts of ammunition, baggage, and food; many women (courtesans), their children, pet monkeys, and parrots; and nearly a hundred carriages. There were so many chests of bullion and treasure, soon spilled out onto the ground, that the British army was diverted as they stopped to pick it up and allowed most of the French to escape, missing Joseph by about five minutes. Joseph's papers, love letters, a silver chamberpot, and diplomatic pouches were there, and more than two hundred rolled-up canvases that later proved to be the Spanish Royal collection of paintings.[89] Wellington sent the paintings to England, where his brother, Lord Maryborough, had the Keeper of Royal Pictures look at

[88] Letter from Spanish mayor Josef Garret: Wellington Papers 1/373, University of Southampton. Letter to Lord Bathurst: Gurwood (1838) 10: 495–496 (the Duke's letter notes the enclosure of the letter from Vitoria). I thank C. M. Woolgar for bringing the unpublished Spanish letter to my attention.

[89] The plunder is described in numerous eyewitness accounts of the battle and its aftermath: e.g., Larpent (1853): I, 246–248; A. Schaumann, *On the Road with Wellington, The Diary of a War Commissary* (repr. London, 1999): 378–381 (in which the food and wine left by the French were especially appreciated); B. H. Liddell Hart, ed., *The Letters of Private Wheeler, 1809–1829* (Gloucestershire, 1951): 116–120 (soldiers try on French clothing and hold auctions of plunder); J. Weller, *Wellington in the Peninsula* (1962, repr. London, 1992): 263–264, quoting an unnamed officer's account reported by C. W. C. Oman. On the battle, W. E. P. Napier, *History of the War in the Peninsula* (London, 1840 [1993]): 548–581; D. Gates, *The Spanish Ulcer* (Cambridge, MA, 1986): 386–390.

them. Their value and significance was then realized, as among them were works by Correggio, Velasquez, Titian, and Van Dyck. Apparently, Joseph Bonaparte had gathered up the Spanish Royal collection to take to France (and did escape with about twelve paintings including five by Raphael, a Titian, and a Guido Reni). When Wellington learned this, he insisted that the paintings be returned. While still on campaign in southern France, and just before the final confrontation with Soult at Toulouse, Wellington took the time to write about repatriating them. He wrote from Aire, on March 16, 1814, to his brother Sir Henry Wellesley:

> *My dear Henry,*
>
> *The baggage of King Joseph, after the battle of Vitoria, fell into my hands, after having been plundered by the soldiers; and I found among it an imperial [a type of luggage designed for a coach] containing prints, drawings and pictures.*
>
> *From the cursory view which I took of them, the latter did not appear to me to be anything remarkable. There are certainly not among them any of the fine pictures which I saw in Madrid, by Raphael and others; and I thought more of the prints and drawings, all of the Italian school, which induced me to believe that the whole collection was robbed in Italy rather than in Spain. I sent them to England, and, having desired that they should be put to rights, and those cleaned which required it, I have found that there are among them much finer pictures than I conceived there were; and as, if the King's palaces have been robbed of pictures, it is not improbable that some of his may be among them, and I am desirous of restoring them to His Majesty, I shall be much obliged to you if you will mention the subject to Don J. Luyando, and tell him that I request that a person may be fixed upon to go to London to see them and to fix upon those belonging to His Majesty.*
>
> *This may be done either now or hereafter when I shall return to England, as may be most expedient.*

In the meantime the best of them are in the hands of persons who are
putting them to rights, which is an expense necessary for their
preservation, whether they belong to His Majesty or not.

Ever your most affectionately,
WELLINGTON

I will get the catalogue of the pictures which I have got copied, and
will send it to you. It will probably enable the Spanish Government to
form an opinion, without inspection, which of the pictures belong to the
King.[90]

After repeated attempts at communication on this topic, in 1816, the
Duke received a letter from the Spanish King, Ferdinand VII, who
was adamant that he keep the paintings. They are in Apsley House
today, the Duke's London home, now a national museum. Among them,
Correggio's *The Agony in the Garden* was the Duke's favorite.

Was the Duke actually influenced by Cicero's *Verrines*? It seems
unlikely that in Paris in the autumn of 1815 he could have had time for
much reflection. Presumably, he knew the story, at the least from Hastings' trial and Byron's poetry, the public reaction to Napoleon's plunder,
and discussions in newspapers. Paris that autumn was a glittering social
scene at night, after administrative work could be set aside. He might
have heard about these issues further in the salons, where women,
including Claire de Duras and Mme. de Staël (by correspondence that
autumn), would not hesitate to share their opinions on the topic.[91]

The Duke was thought to be an indifferent student of Latin (compared to his oldest brother Richard, at least), but he did know Latin well

---

[90] Letter as published in Gurwood, *Dispatches* 11 (1838), 586–587. For this history and the
correspondence, see C. M. Kauffmann, *Catalogue of Paintings in the Wellington Museum*
(London, 1982): 5–7. On the aftermath of the battle of Vitoria, E. Longford, *Wellington, The
Years of the Sword* (New York: 1969): 314–318.

[91] Correspondence and comments on art cited by P. Delaforce, *Wellington the Beau* (Gloucestershire, 1990): 73. On womens' roles and the tradition of the salons, D. Goodman, *The
Republic of Letters. A Cultural History of the French Enlightenment* (Ithaca, 1994).

enough to read Julius Caesar's *Gallic Wars* because in later life he spoke several times about how valuable it had been to him in the Peninsula, not only for tactics but also for crossing rivers and building bridges in Portugal. For his other reading, some insight to an earlier stage in his life is provided by a bill of purchase for the library that he took with him on the long voyage to India in the late 1790s. Besides many volumes on military history and tactics, he bought numerous books on India, the history of India, and the recent trial of Warren Hastings. Among ancient authors, he had Caesar's commentaries and twelve volumes of Plutarch's *Lives*, which include the lives of Marcellus and Cicero, in which the case of Verres is described briefly.[92]

By now, however, the Duke had his own experiences to draw upon. It seems to me that he dealt with the issue of repatriation as a well-read eighteenth-century gentleman and as a humane general, like Scipio Aemilianus. Today, just inside the front door of Apsley House, we can see his taste: a marble portrait of Cicero that the Duke purchased in 1816 at an art auction in Paris (see Fig. 8).

---

[92] Arthur Wellesley's library for his voyage to India is discussed by P. Guedalla, *The Duke* (1931; repr. Hertfordshire, 1997): 54–65; a list he made later in life of suggested books for his son is discussed by E. Longford, "The Duke of Wellington's Books," *History Today* 17 (1967): 1–28. For the Duke's reflections on his military experience, see P. H. (Earl) Stanhope, *Notes of Conversations with the Duke of Wellington 1831–1851* (London, 1888, repr. 1998).

EPILOGUE: THE CONTINUING PLUNDER OF ART

◉▣◉

Plunder in Time of War

Among the survivors of the battle of Waterloo was a brilliant, idealistic young Prussian, Francis Lieber (1797–1872), who eventually immigrated to the United States. After earning several higher degrees in Classics, he went to Greece, hoping to help in the Greek War of Independence. After spending some time there, mostly in frustration, he arrived penniless in Rome. He was assisted by the distinguished historian, Barthold G. Niebuhr, who was serving as the Prussian ambassador. Lieber tutored Niebuhr's son, and he himself studied Roman history with Niebuhr.[1]

In the United States, Lieber first supported himself by organizing translations of a German encyclopedia and commissioning new articles for an American version, *The Encyclopaedia Americana* (13 vols., 1829–1833). This was a successful project because Lieber asked prominent people to contribute to it, among them, Joseph Bonaparte, Napoleon's brother and the temporary king of Spain who had fled the battlefield of Vitoria (he supplied the entries on his family). Lieber became a professor of history and wrote books on political and legal philosophy while teaching at South Carolina College (now the University of South Carolina), and moved eventually to Columbia College (now Columbia University). He was asked by President Lincoln to write a legal code for use by Union soldiers in 1863, as part of an advisory committee that included four generals, led by General Henry Wager Halleck.[2]

---

[1] Biographical details in F. Freidel, *Francis Lieber, Nineteenth-Century Liberal* (Glouster, MA, 1947 [1968]).

[2] For the historical background to this decision and analysis of the earlier views of Halleck and Leiber, see J. T. Johnson, *Just War Tradition and the Restraint of War* (Princeton, 1981):

General Orders No. 100 contained the first legal recognition of cultural property as a special protected category in war.[3] Its overall purpose, however, was to regulate the behavior of soldiers toward the enemy, an increasing problem because of guerilla-style confrontations that created ambiguities over treatment of prisoners, noncombatants, spies, and property, and it also addressed internal discipline within the army. *General Orders No. 100* has had a very long afterlife within the United States, and many of its provisions, with slight modifications, are still in effect, under different titles.[4] Here, I note the impact of just one set of its provisions, concerning the treatment of cultural property in time of war. For *General Orders No. 100*, or the Lieber Code, as it is often called after its principal author, Lieber and Halleck were drawing on a long tradition and theoretical discussion reaching from Cicero to Emmerich de Vattel, but they were responsible for the first statement that had actual legal force.[5]

The Lieber Code was admired by European legal scholars and became the basis for subsequent international agreements on the issue of cultural property, including the Hague Conventions of 1907 and 1954. Here are excerpts from the Lieber Code:

Article 34

As a general rule, the property belonging to churches, to hospitals, or other establishments of an exclusively charitable character, to

284–306. On the idea of military codes and ethical guidelines, see also N. Fotion and G. Elfstrom, *Military Ethics. Guidelines for Peace and War* (Boston, 1986): 66–79.

[3] *Instructions for the Government of Armies of the United States in the Field*, prepared by Francis Lieber, promulgated as *General Order No. 100* by President Lincoln, April 24, 1863. The relevant sections of the text are printed in E. Simpson, ed., *The Spoils of War. World War II and Its Aftermath: The Loss, Reappearance, and Recovery of Cultural Property* (New York, 1997): 272–273, from L. Friedman, ed., *The Law of War. A Documentary History*, 1 (New York, 1972): 158.

[4] The provisions of *General Orders No. 100* and its descendants in the United States are discussed with commentary in D. A. Wells, *The Laws of Land Warfare. A Guide to the U.S. Army Manuals* (Westport, CT, 1992).

[5] The correspondence and earlier publications of Halleck and Lieber are discussed by Johnson (1981: 306–326), with extensive quotations from archival material in the Huntington Library.

establishments of education, or foundations for the promotion of
knowledge, whether public schools, universities, academies of learning or
observatories, museums of the fine arts, or of a scientific character – such
property is not to be considered public property in the sense of paragraph
31; but it may be taxed or used when the public service may require it.
Article 35
Classical works of art, libraries, scientific collections, or precious
instruments, such as astronomical telescopes, as well as hospitals, must
be secured against all avoidable injury, even when they are contained in
fortified places whilst besieged or bombarded.
Article 36
If such works of art, libraries, collections, or instruments belonging to a
hostile nation or government can be removed without injury, the ruler of
the conquering state or nation may order them to be seized and removed
for the benefit of the said nation. The ultimate ownership is to be settled
by the ensuing treaty of peace.
In no case shall they be sold or given away, if captured by the armies of
the United States, nor shall they ever be privately appropriated, or
wantonly destroyed or injured.

The Hague Convention of 1954, more than one hundred years after the Lieber Code, moved the legal issues forward with more detail and refinement, but the basic issues are the same.[6] Both treat cultural property as exceptional from other kinds of property, to be dealt with in a particular way in time of war. The Hague Convention of 1954 was in part a reiteration and response that was much needed after the atrocities of World War II.

For the U.S. armed forces today, one far-reaching result of Lieber and Halleck's *General Orders No. 100* is that now each U.S. soldier in

---

[6] For the Hague Convention of 1954, see K. Chamberlain, *War and Cultural Heritage. An Analysis of the 1954 Convention for the Protection of Cultural Property in the Event of Armed Conflict and Its Two Protocols* (Leicester, 2004).

combat is issued a two-sided card with the *Standing Rules of Engagement* (ROE). Two of the clauses read:

- Do not attack medical or religious personnel.
- Do not attack schools, museums, national monuments, and any other historical or cultural sites unless they are being used for a military purpose and pose a threat.

The second clause reiterates the familiar exception for the military use of cultural sites that goes back in historical writing at least as far as Josephus Flavius' account of the siege of the Temple of Jerusalem by Titus (Chapter 4), but wholly modern in the clause is the stated consideration to be given to schools, museums, national monuments, and historical and cultural sites.

As is well known, the rapacity of the Nazis in the seizing of art far surpassed what was perpetrated by Napoleon on Europe and Egypt. Adolf Hitler planned an encyclopedic museum in Linz that was supposed to hold all the best art of the world. For this, and for the private collections of his associates such as Hermann Goering, private and public holdings throughout continental Europe and Russia were plundered. This was not just a matter of art as "spoils of war," however. Looting and deliberate destruction of art began well before the war with illegal seizures from Jewish owners that were part of the Nazi religious persecutions, and this extensive art theft was considered a crime at the Nuremberg trials. The calculated, programmatic seizures of art have been thoroughly discussed by Lynn H. Nicholas in *The Rape of Europa*, and in a vast bibliography, with supporting Web sites and registries of lost and stolen art. The legal repercussions, with claims for restitution, are ongoing.[7] Some of the art and artifacts from Nazi holdings and previous

---

[7] L. H. Nicholas, *The Rape of Europa. The Fate of Europe's Treasures in the Third Reich and the Second World War* (New York, 1994); H. Feliciano, *The Lost Museum. The Nazi Conspiracy to Steal the World's Greatest Works of Art* (New York, 1997); legal views in Merryman and Elsen (1998) and P. Gerstenblith, *Art, Cultural Heritage, and the Law. Cases and Materials*

legal German possession have reappeared in Russia, taken there from Berlin after the war, and constitute another focal point for dispute, the subject of an international conference at Bard College in 1995.[8]

Both the British and American armies had "monuments units" during World War II that sought to restrain and direct Allied attacks away from important historical sites, and today the U.S. armed forces receive advice from archaeologists about the location and significance of antiquities in the Middle East in the current conflicts. Having a specific group of military men dedicated to avoiding targets that were of historical and cultural significance was new in warfare.

Deliberate plundering of art in wartime has not ended, but at least there is in place international agreement that seeks to restrain it. Art and architecture, broadly defined to include also archaeological sites, are still vulnerable to plunder, aerial bombing, ground explosives and destructive occupations, and ideological attacks.

Plundering of Archaeological Sites

The new scholarly disciplines of the eighteenth and nineteenth centuries of art history and archaeology had stressed the significance of preserving the context for art. This was a concern not only for scholars who wanted to understand better the historical significance of art (as Quatremère de Quincy argued), but it also was an issue with growing political implications because of the strong ideas about cultural "patrimony" that were tied to concepts of nationhood (as observed by the Abbé Grégoire). Today, nearly two hundred years after the battle

---

(Durham, NC, 2004): 479–534; on restitution of art looted in World War II, see the essays in M.-A. Renold and P. Gabus, eds., *Claims for the Restitution of Looted Art. Studies in Art Law* 15 (Geneva, 2004); an example of a published registry: S. Lillie, *Was einmal war: Handbuch der enteigneten Kunstsammlungen Wiens* (Vienna, 2003), 1,439 pp.

[8] See the essays and papers in Simpson (1997), and comments on the Bard symposium by K. Meyer, "Who Owns the Spoils of War?" in K. D. Vitelli, ed., *Archaeological Ethics* (Walnut Creek, 1996): 137–150. The second edition of 2006, edited by K. D. Vitelli and C. Colwell-Chanthaphonh, present another series of (mostly) different, updated essays.

of Waterloo, these concerns have extended to archaeological sites and artifacts – and not just "art" or "masterpieces" – because we recognize now that when sites are robbed of artifacts, what is lost is not only "patrimony" or "cultural heritage" for a specific country or culture but also history itself, for all of humankind. This is evident, for example, in the looting of the Baghdad Museum. Not only Iraqis but all of us have lost by that looting and damage. [9]

Even in what we like to think of as "peacetime," archaeological sites are exposed to destruction, daily, around the globe. As of this writing, the FBI estimates that the criminal enterprise in stolen art causes losses of at least $6 billion annually.[10] Archaeological remains are exploited and destroyed for commercial interest: locals and criminals illegally hunt them out and dig them up in order to sell them to collectors (individuals and museums) who want the finds as art, or to keep as investments, or to display as decorations. Not only are the artifacts lost to the world if they are in private hands but, more important, the historical context of the objects also is destroyed, even if the illicitly obtained object is purchased and displayed in a museum.

Several studies of Greek pottery, for example, have revealed statistical evidence for a greatly escalated trade in illicit antiquities and a burgeoning market for them among both private collectors and museums. In one of them, R. Elia has shown that 88.4 percent of decorated pottery from Apulia in southern Italy has no provenience.[11] This finding about

---

[9] M. Bogdanos, "The Casualties of War: The Truth about the Iraq Museum," *AJA* 109 (2005): 477–526, and M. Bogdanos with W. Patrick, *Thieves of Baghdad* (New York, 2005). For discussion of competing claims in concepts of heritage, collectors, and efforts to retrieve objects in an archaeological context, see the essays in E. Barkan and R. Bush, eds., *Claiming the Stones, Naming the Bones. Cultural Property and the Negotiation of National and Ethnic Identity* (Los Angeles, 2002); of particular relevance is the lucid analysis of C. Lyons, "Objects and Identities: Claiming and Reclaiming the Past," 116–137.

[10] http://www.fbi.gov/hq/cid/arttheft/arttheft.htm, accessed 6/5/06.

[11] R. Elia, "Analysis of the Looting, Selling, and Collecting of Apulian Red-Figure Vases: A Quantitative Approach," in N. Brodie, et al., eds., *Trade in Illicit Antiquities: The Destruction*

one particular class of objects from one region in Italy is corroborated in a much larger, global study of the whole history of the collecting of Greek vases by V. Nørskov, who discusses the changing focus and interests of collectors of pottery over the centuries.[12] These and other studies clearly show that purchases at auction by collectors and museums (paying increasingly higher prices) have given impetus for yet more clandestine digging. In the nineteenth and earlier twentieth centuries, some objects that were sold from source countries were likely chance finds by farmers, but that is no longer how most objects come on the market: rather, they are deliberately sought and robbed from the ground.

The international agreements that were developed for the protection of cultural property in wartime now are the model for international protective agreements for peacetime as well, such as Convention on the Means of Prohibiting and Preventing the Illicit Import, Export and Transfer of Ownership of Cultural Property adopted by UNESCO in 1970. Hence, 1970 is widely regarded as the basic international "cutoff" date for the movement across borders of antiquities without an earlier history of ownership. Several countries set even earlier dates prohibiting the export of antiquities outside their borders without permission, such as Italy, whose law on exports of antiquities was passed in 1939. Other key international agreements are the UNIDROIT Convention on the International Return of Stolen or Illegally Exported Cultural Objects (1995) and the Convention on the Protection of Underwater Cultural Heritage (2001).[13]

of the World's Archaeological Heritage (Cambridge, 2001): 145–154. For a study of the lack of find-spots of items in museum collections, see C. Chippindale and D. W. J. Gill, "Material Consequences of Contemporary Classical Collecting," *AJA* 104 (2000): 463–511.

[12] V. Nørskov, *Greek Vases in New Contexts. The Collecting and Trading of Greek Vases – An Aspect of the Modern Reception of Antiquity* (Aarhus, 2002).

[13] Their history and intentions are discussed by B. T. Hoffman, "Exploring and Establishing Links for a Balance Art and Cultural Heritage Policy," in B. T. Hoffman, ed., *Art and Cultural Heritage. Law, Policy, and Practice* (Cambridge, 2006): 1–18.

One way to address the problem of looting and destruction of archaeological sites is to find alternative means of making the artifacts "profitable" for local economies. Even if archaeological sites are regarded as a potential resource for commercial exploitation in the more benign form of tourism, for example, still it must be acknowledged that the material remains of the past are a finite, limited resource, never to be renewed or duplicated, and the need for protection is urgent.[14] Despite the UNESCO Convention, the number and extent of robberies of sites have greatly escalated around the world, and they become ever more destructive with more sophisticated tools of intrusion and easier access to formerly remote areas. S. R. M. Mackenzie provides the most thorough and fresh examination of this problem, with suggestions for amelioration and perspectives and interpretive analysis rooted in the field of criminology.[15] Above all, most needed is greater protection of archaeological sites and greater vigilance of authorities in the countries that are the sources of the antiquities.

The primary professional body in the United States for archaeologists specializing in the Classical past of the Mediterranean area is the Archaeological Institute of America, founded in 1879. It has long endorsed the UNESCO Convention that protects cultural property, and its journal, *The American Journal of Archaeology*, has in place an editorial policy that prohibits initial publication of "any object in a private or public collection acquired after December 30, 1973, unless its existence is documented before that date, or it was legally exported from the country of origin." That policy was recently reiterated strongly by

---

[14] This is discussed usefully in N. Brodie and K. W. Tubb, eds., *Illicit Antiquities. The Theft of Culture and the Extinction of Archaeology* (London, 2002); for the view of heritage as a factor to economists, with an emphasis on Sicily, see I. Rizzo and R. Towse, eds., *The Economics of Heritage. A Study in the Political Economy of Culture in Sicily* (Cheltenham, UK, and Northhampton, MA, 2002).

[15] S. R. M. Mackenzie, *Going, Going, Gone: Regulating the Market in Illicit Antiquities* (Leicester, 2005).

the current Editor-in-Chief, Naomi J. Norman.[16] Archaeologists hope that by bringing the destruction of the past and the loss of human history to wide attention, and by taking a firm stand within our own organization, further legal steps will be taken to stop the looting of sites.

Athena's Olive Tree: Repatriation of Art and Artifacts

Considerable attention in the press has been given to a court case in Italy (1995) in which an art dealer, Giacomo Medici, was convicted on various charges of illegal trafficking in antiquities. The case has drawn notice for the relationships between this criminal dealer and the J. Paul Getty Museum in Los Angeles and Malibu and the Metropolitan Museum in New York. The journalists, Peter Watson and Cecilia Todeschini, have reported the extensive evidence found by Italian carabinieri in raids on the Geneva warehouses of Medici and other dealers.[17] Because of the dealers' meticulous records, including Polaroid photographs of antiquities freshly out of the ground (and photographs of the same objects in museums), it has been possible for the governments of Italy and Greece to make successful claims for restitution from the Metropolitan Museum in New York, the Getty Museum, and the Boston Museum of Fine Arts. The ancient objects (statuary, small bronzes, decorated pottery, and wall paintings) were clearly stolen by organized criminals digging and extracting them illegally. In one instance illustrated by Watson and Todeschini, wall paintings from a first-century house in the area of Naples were cut off the wall and cut into several

---

[16] N. J. Norman, "Editorial Policy on the Publication of Recently Acquired Antiquities," *AJA* 109 (2005): 135–136.

[17] P. Watson and C. Todeschini, *The Medici Conspiracy. The Illicit Journey of Looted Antiquities, From Italy's Tomb Raiders to the World's Greatest Museums* (New York, 2006). G. Medici is free on appeal, as of this writing; other trials are underway of other individuals connected to the case and to the evidence found in Geneva.

pieces so as to make them easier to sell. There is no ambiguity in these instances because of the wealth of documentation.

Before the Italian legal case against G. Medici, the Getty Museum had already voluntarily repatriated items that clearly were taken from archaeological sites in Italy, such as a fifth century BCE lead tablet inscribed with legal provisions for religious ritual (*lex sacra*) from the Sanctuary of Demeter Malophoros in Selinous, Sicily; it is now in the Archaeological Museum of Palermo. Such issues are resolved on a case-by-case basis and continue to generate new lawsuits. Some major museums in the United States continue to purchase antiquities of uncertain provenance, with no policy of acquisition in place with a cutoff date, after which no undocumented piece would be acquired. A few, such as the University of Pennsylvania Museum, have a clear policy of not acquiring pieces of uncertain origin: the Penn Museum put its policy into place in 1970. The Getty Museum has recently adopted an acquisition policy that respects the 1970 UNESCO agreement.[18]

The issue of repatriation of art or archaeological artifacts acquired by museums long ago and under very different circumstances, such as the Parthenon Marbles, also has been much discussed in recent publications.[19] Museums have offered defenses of their holdings and point to their important role in educating the public, as in the statement made by the director of the British Museum, Neil MacGregor. Moreover, arguments have been advanced for redefinitions of "cultural heritage" on

---

[18] "The J. Paul Getty Museum Policy for Acquisition – Approved by the Board of Trustees on October 23, 2006," *IJCP* 13 (4) 2006: 423–425.

[19] A number of perspectives are given in, e.g.: R. Atwood, *Stealing History. Tomb Raiders, Smugglers, and the Looting of the Ancient World* (New York, 2004); H. and A. Borowitz, *Pawnshop and Palaces. The Fall and Rise of the Campana Art Museum* (Washington and London, 1991); J. Greenfield, *The Return of Cultural Treasures* (Cambridge, 1995, second edition); D. Lowenthal, *The Heritage Crusade and the Spoils of History* (Cambridge, 1998); S. M. Pearce, *On Collecting. An Investigation into Collecting in the European Tradition* (London and New York, 1995); Colin Renfrew, *Loot, Legitimacy and Ownership. The Ethical Crisis in Archaeology* (London, 2000); Sax (1999); J. H. Merryman, ed., *Imperialism, Art, and Restitution* (Cambridge, 2006). For specifically archaeological issues, see, e.g., the essays in Vitelli (1996, 2006); Brodie and Tubb (2002); Gerstenblith (2004).

the grounds that the nationalism implicit in the concept is too limiting for the conditions of contemporary culture.[20]

As for the best known of all cases of requested repatriation, the Parthenon Marbles, the British have clear legal grounds for possessing them, as John Henry Merryman has argued persuasively.[21] Among the sculpture from the Parthenon now in the British Museum are fragments that represent the Olive Tree given by Athena to the Athenians. The tree was once in the center of the west pediment, the side of the Parthenon first seen by people entering the Acropolis. The goddess gave the tree (and the cultivation of the olive) to the ancient Athenians as a special gift in a contest with Poseidon to determine who would be the patron deity, and she won; an actual tree believed to be descended from the original grew in antiquity outside the Temple of Athena Polias. For Athenians, the tree was symbolic of Athena's protection: the living version by the temple was burned by Xerxes in the sack of Athens of 479 BCE, but put out a long green shoot from the charred stump on the very next day (Herodotus, 8.55); it has been replanted in the modern era. My own view is that the marble fragment of the Olive Tree now in London, and all the other sculpture from the Parthenon, really belong in Athens, reunited with the rest of the sculpture from the temple and exhibited near the temple itself. Some will argue that this is exceptionalism: yes, the Parthenon is exceptional, not least for the history it has acquired in the last two hundred years. The British have

---

[20] N. MacGregor, "The Whole World in Our Hands," cited as appendix 2 in G. Lewis, "The 'Universal Museum': A Case of Special Pleading?" in B. Hoffman (2006): 382–384, originally published in the *Guardian*, Saturday 24 July, 2004. A public debate on repatriation of art from museums was held on March 6, 2006, at the New School in New York and reported in the *New York Times*. For the arguments to reconsider "cultural heritage," see K. Appiah, *Cosmopolitanism. Ethics in a World of Strangers* (New York, 2006): 115–135, an essay originally printed in *The New York Review of Books* (53, 2, February 9, 2006), entitled *Whose Culture Is It?* Appiah makes the good point that new national museums should exhibit examples of art from around the world, not only what is local or indigenous. Ongoing commentary on these issues may be found in *The International Journal of Cultural Property* (see in particular the issues published in 2005, 2006).

[21] Merryman (2000): 24–63.

legal title (and possession) of the sculpture, but I expect that eventually they will return the Parthenon Marbles to Greece. Historically, the British have often been at the forefront in resolving ethical issues.

Nonetheless, the issue is complex and difficult. It should be admitted by all concerned that the British Museum has been a very good steward of the Parthenon Marbles (apart from an episode of overly zealous cleaning of the sculpture during the 1930s). The museum is open seven days a week to the public, free of charge; it takes its didactic role seriously and plays it superbly by mounting a wide range of interesting and engaging exhibits on art of many periods, and it shows self-reflection with frequent, excellent exhibits on the history of the museum and the genesis of modern collecting. It allows scholars ready and full access to its holdings. More than any other museum in the world, the British Museum fulfills the ideals of the "universal museum" that formed part of the Enlightenment in the mid-eighteenth century. While it is no longer possible (or even necessarily desirable) to found or fill a *new* "universal museum," we should cherish and appreciate the few we have.

The deeply important educational role of museums everywhere could be enhanced by more frequent programs of loans of material for exhibition. Newer national museums should not only exhibit the art of their own countries but also find ways to make accessible to their citizens examples from the whole world's artistic heritage. More important than the current geographical location of art already in museums, however, is that all art needs greater protection, both the art in glass cases (still vulnerable, as we saw in Baghdad) and whatever may still lie undiscovered in an archaeological context. Whether in war or by force of commerce, art must no longer be taken as plunder.

APPENDIX: ON ART AS PLUNDER

◎▣◎

1. POLYBIUS ON THE SPOILS OF SYRACUSE

Polybius 9.10: translated by W. R. Paton (Polybius, *The Histories* [Cambridge, MA, and London: Harvard University Press (Loeb)]: IV, 24–29).

A city is not adorned by external splendors, but by the virtue of its inhabitants. . . . [text lost]

The Romans, then, decided for this reason to transfer all these objects to their own city and leave nothing behind. As to whether in doing so they acted correctly and in their own interest or the reverse, there is much to be said on both sides, but the more weighty arguments are in favor of their conduct having been wrong then and still being wrong. For if they had originally relied on such things for the advancement of their country, they would evidently have been right in bringing to their home the kind of things which had contributed to their aggrandizement. But if, on the contrary, while leading the simplest of lives, very far removed from all such superfluous magnificence, they were constantly victorious over those who possessed the greatest number and finest examples of such works, must we not consider that they committed a mistake? To abandon the habits of the victors and to imitate those of the conquered, not only appropriating the objects, but at the same time attracting that envy which is inseparable from their possession, which is the one thing most to be dreaded by superiors in power, is surely an incontestable error. For in no case is one who contemplates such works of art moved so much by admiration of the good fortune of those who have possessed themselves of the property of others, as by pity as well as envy for the original owners. And when opportunities

361

become ever more frequent, and the victor collects around him all the treasures of other peoples, and these treasures may be almost said to invite those who were robbed of them to come and inspect them, things are twice as bad. For now spectators no longer pity their neighbors, but themselves, as they recall to mind their own calamities. And hence not only envy, but a sort of passionate hatred for the favorites of fortune flares up, for the memories awakened of their own disaster move them to abhor the authors of it. There were indeed perhaps good reasons for appropriating all the gold and silver: for it was impossible for them to aim at a world empire without weakening the resources of other peoples and strengthening their own. But it was possible for them to leave everything which did not contribute to such strength, together with the envy attached to its possession, in its original place, and to add to the glory of the native city by adorning it not with paintings and reliefs but with dignity and magnanimity. At any rate these remarks will serve to teach all those who succeed to empire, that they should not strip cities under the idea that the misfortunes of another are an ornament to their own country. The Romans on the present occasion, after transferring all these objects to Rome, used such as came from private houses to embellish their own homes, and those that were state property for their public buildings.

2. LIVY: CATO COMMENTS ON THE BAD EFFECTS OF SPOILS IN ROME

Livy, 34.4. Dramatic date is 195 BCE (Cato complains about the repeal of a sumptuary law, the *lex Oppia*); translated by J. C. Yardley (Livy. *The Dawn of Empire, Books 31–40* [Oxford: Oxford University Press, 2000]: 144).

You have often heard my complaints about the lavish spending of women, and of men as well, and not just private citizens but magistrates, too. You have heard me complain that our state is plagued with two antithetical vices, greed and extravagance, afflictions that have been the downfall of all great empires. The fortunes of our republic are improving and advancing on a daily basis, and our empire is expanding – now we are crossing into Greece and Asia, which are replete with all manner of seductive pleasures, and we are even handling the treasures of kings. The more this happens, the more I shudder at the possibility that these things may have captured us rather than we them. Those statues from Syracuse were enemy standards brought against the city, believe me. Already I hear too many people praising and admiring the artifacts of Corinth and Athens, and ridiculing the earthenware antefixes of the Roman gods. But I prefer to have these gods smiling on us, and I hope they will, if we allow them to remain in their abodes.

3. CICERO COMMENTS ON THE IMPACT ON FOREIGN ENVOYS TO ROME OF VERRES' PLUNDERED ART FROM ASIA MINOR

Cicero, *Verr.* 2.1.58–59, translated by L. H. G. Greenwood (Cicero. *The Verrine Orations* [Cambridge, MA, and London: Harvard University Press (Loeb edition), 1959]: I, 181–183).

You will plead that your statues and pictures, like his [Publius Servilius], have adorned the city and forum of the people of Rome. Paintings have also adorned the city and Forum of the Roman people. Yes: I remember standing among the people of Rome, and looking at the decorated Forum and Comitium; a decoration splendid to the eye, but painful and melancholy to the heart and mind: I looked at the brilliant show that was made by your thefts, by the robbing of our provinces, by the spoliation of our friends and allies. Note that it was then, gentlemen, that Verres received his chief encouragement to continue his misdeeds: he saw that the men who aimed at being called the masters of the courts were the servants of desire for such things as these. And it was then, on the other hand, and only then, that the allied and foreign peoples abandoned their last hope of prosperity and happiness; for a large number of persons from Asia and Achaia, who happened at the time to be in Rome serving on deputations, beheld in our Forum the revered images of their gods that had been carried away from their own sanctuaries, and recognizing as well the other statues and works of art, some here and some there, would stand gazing at them with weeping eyes. What we then heard these people saying was always this, that the ruin of our allies and friends was certain beyond all question; for there in the Forum of Rome, in the place where once those who had wronged our allies used to be prosecuted and found guilty, now stood, openly exposed to view, the objects reft from those allies by criminals and robbers.

4. LIVY COMMENTS ON THE ART TAKEN BY MARCELLUS FROM SYRACUSE

Livy, 25.40.1–3, translated by A. de Sélincourt (Livy. *The War with Hannibal, Books XXI–XXX of the History of Rome from Its Foundation* [Harmondsworth: Penguin Books, 1965]: 350–351).

Meanwhile, after the capture of Syracuse, Marcellus had made a general settlement of affairs in Sicily, and that, too, with such honourable integrity as could not but enhance the dignity of the Roman people as much as it added to his own reputation. This is undeniable: but at the same time he removed to Rome the beautiful statues and paintings which Syracuse possessed in such abundance. These were, one must admit, legitimate spoils, acquired by right of war [*hostium quidem illa spolia et parta belli iure*]; nonetheless their removal to Rome was the origin of our admiration of Greek art and started the universal and reckless spoliation of all buildings sacred and profane which prevails today, and which ultimately turned against our own Roman gods, beginning with the very temple which Marcellus so splendidly adorned. For time was when foreigners used to visit the temples dedicated by Marcellus at the Porta Capena, drawn thither by the magnificent examples of Greek art which they contained; but hardly any of them are to be seen today.

5. Plutarch Comments on the Effects in Rome of Marcellus' Spoils from Syracuse

Plutarch, *Marc.* 21, translated by Ian Scott-Kilvert (Plutarch. *Makers of Rome. Nine Lives by Plutarch* [Harmondsworth: Penguin Books, 1965]: 106–107).

When the Romans recalled Marcellus to carry on the war against Hannibal in Italy, he took back with him most of the statues and other offerings which the Syracusans had dedicated to the gods, including their finest works of art; for he intended that these should not only decorate his Triumph but also adorn the capital. Before this date Rome neither possessed nor indeed was even aware of such elegant and exquisite creations, nor was there any taste for a graceful and delicate art of this kind. Instead, the city was filled with the bloodstained arms and spoils of barbarian tribes, and crowned with the monuments and trophies of victorious campaigns, so that to the unwarlike visitor or the aesthete she offered almost nothing to gladden or reassure the eye . . . At any rate Marcellus greatly pleased the common people, because he adorned the capital with works of art which possessed the Hellenic grace and charm and truth to nature. On the other hand, it was Fabius Maximus who earned the approval of the older generation, because after he had captured Tarentum he neither disturbed nor removed a single monument of this kind. He carried off all the money and valuables which had belonged to the city, but allowed all the statues to remain in their places, and on this occasion made the remark which has since become famous: "Let us leave the Tarentines these angry gods of theirs!' Such people blamed Marcellus in the first place for bringing discredit upon the name of Rome, because he paraded not only men but gods like captives in his triumphal procession; and secondly because hitherto the people had been accustomed to spend their time either in fighting or in agriculture and had never tasted luxury or leisure. . . . Now, on the contrary, he was teaching them to become lazy and glib connoisseurs of art and artists, so that they idled away the greater part of the day in clever and trivial chatter about aesthetics. In spite of such criticisms, Marcellus spoke with pride of what he had done and he liked to claim even to Greeks that he had taught the ignorant Romans to admire and honor the glories of Greek art.

6. Cicero Comments on Scipio Aemilianus' Repatriation of Art Booty from Carthage to Sicilian Cities

Cicero, *Verr.* 2.4.73, translated by L. H. G. Greenwood (Cicero. *The Verrine Orations* [Cambridge, MA, and London: Harvard University Press (Loeb edition), 1959]: II, 371–373).

In the third Punic War, some centuries later, Publius Scipio captured Carthage. In the hour of victory – I would have you observe his scrupulous uprightness, that you may rejoice in the noble patterns of upright conduct that our countrymen afford to us, and may hold Verres' incredible lack of scruple the more detestable on that account – knowing that Sicily had repeatedly and for long periods been ravaged by the Carthaginians, he called all the Sicilians together, and ordered a general search to be made, promising to do his utmost for the restoration to the several communities of all that was once theirs. Then it was that the treasures formerly removed from Himera were, as I have already related, given back to the people of Thermae; others to Gela; others to Agrigentum, including the famous bull said to have belonged to Phalaris, the most cruel of all tyrants, in which he tortured men by thrusting them into it alive and lighting a fire underneath it. When restoring this bull to the people of Agrigentum, Scipio is said to have recommended them to ask themselves whether it were better to be the slaves of their own countrymen or the subjects of Rome, now that they possessed this memorial both of their countrymen's cruelty and of Roman kindness.

7. PAUSANIAS COMMENTS ON AUGUSTUS' THEFTS FROM THE TEMPLE OF ATHENA ALEA AT TEGEA

Pausanias, 8.46, translated by J. G. Frazer (*Pausanias's Description of Greece* [London: Macmillan and Co., Ltd., 1913]: I, 432–433.

The ancient image of Athena Alea, and with the tusks of Calydonian boar, were carried off by the Roman emperor Augustus, after he had defeated Antony and his allies, among whom were all the Arcadians except the Mantineans. It is known that Augustus was not the first to carry off votive offerings and images of the gods from his vanquished foes, but that he only followed a long-established precedent. For when Ilium was taken and the Greeks were dividing up the spoils, the wooden image of Zeus of the Courtyard was given to Sthenelus, the son of Capaneus. And many years afterwards, when Dorians were migrating into Sicily, Antiphemus, the founder of Gela, sacked Omphace, a town of the Sicanians, and carried off to Gela an image made by Daedalus. And we know that Xerxes, the son of Darius, king of Persia, besides what he carried off from the city of Athens, took from Brauron an image of Brauronian Artemis; and moreover, accusing the Milesians of willfully playing the coward in the sea-fights with the Athenians in Greek waters, he took the bronze Apollo of Branchidae. The latter image was afterwards restored to the Ephesians by Seleucus. But down to my time the Argives still preserve the images they took from Tiryns: one of them, a wooden image, stands beside the image of Hera, the other is preserved in the sanctuary of Elean Apollo. When the people of Cyzicus compelled the people of Proconnesus by force of arms to settle in Cyzicus, they took from Proconnesus an image of Mother Dindymene: the image is of gold, and its face is of the teeth of hippopotamuses instead of ivory. Thus the Emperor Augustus merely practiced an ancient custom, which is observed by Greeks and barbarians alike. The image of Athena Alea at Rome is as you go to the Forum of Augustus. There it stands, an image made wholly of ivory, the work of Endoeus. As to the boar's tusks, the keepers of the curiosities say that one of them is broken; but the remaining one is preserved in the imperial gardens, in a sanctuary of Dionysus, and is just half a fathom long.

8. Ammianus Marcellinus Comments on how Constantius was Urged to Move an Obelisk from Egypt to Rome

Ammianus Marcellinus, 17.4.12–13, translated by Walter Hamilton (Ammianus Marcellinus. *The Later Roman Empire (A.D. 354–378)* [London: Penguin Books, 1986]: 122–123).

The flatterers whose habit it was to inflate the pride of Constantius kept dinning into his ears that the emperor Octavian [Augustus], who brought two Egyptian obelisks from Heliopolis and set up one in the Circus Maximus and the other in the Campus Martius, did not dare to disturb or move the one which was brought to Rome in our day because he was daunted by the difficulties presented by its size. But let me tell those who do not know that the reason why that early emperor left this obelisk untouched when he moved some others was that it was dedicated as a special offering to the sun God and placed in the sacred precinct of a magnificent temple, to which access was forbidden. There it towered over the whole structure. Constantine, however, made small account of this and rightly supposed that he would be committing no sacrilege if he removed this wonderful object from one temple and dedicated it at Rome, which may be called the temple of the whole world. So he tore it from its foundations, but then let it lie for a long period on the ground while the necessary preparations were being made for its transport. . . . [and then moved it to Alexandria; after Constantine's death, it lay in Alexandria for a many decades, until Constantius II sent it to Rome, 358 CE].

9. Edward Dodwell Comments on the Damage done to the Parthenon by Lord Elgin's Agents

Edward Dodwell, *A Classical and Topographical Tour through Greece; during the Years 1801, 1805 and 1806* (London, 1819): I, 322–323.

It is painful to reflect that these trophies of human genius, which had resisted the silent decay of time, during a period of more than twenty-two centuries, which had escaped the destructive fury of the Ikonoklasts, the inconsiderate rapacity of the Venetians, and the barbarous violence of the Mohamedans, should at last have been doomed to experience the devastating outrage which will never cease to be deplored. Independent of the moral blame which must necessarily attach to such an act, the authority of the example may henceforth be pleaded as a precedent, and employed as an apology for similar depredations. The Athenian temples will thus probably be destroyed for the sake of their ornaments; which, instead of remaining in their original places, as the property of all nations, will be appropriated by the strongest. When we come to trace the causes which led to this scene of havoc and destruction, the greater share of the odium will naturally, and not unjustly, be referred to those who first exhibited the example of such unhallowed violations of all that the feeling of genuine taste respects and consecrates.

10. QUATREMÈRE DE QUINCY COMMENTS ON THE UNIVERSALITY OF ARTS AND SCIENCES

Excerpt, *Letters to General Miranda*, Quatremère de Quincy, first published 1796 (translated and quoted in S. Lavin, *Quatremère de Quincy and the Invention of a Modern Language of Architecture* [Cambridge, MA: Harvard University Press, 1992]: 154).

In effect, as you know, the arts and sciences in Europe have long since formed a republic. Its members, tied together by the social pact, tend much less to isolate themselves in their respective homelands than they tend to bring their interests together from the very precious point of view of a universal fraternity. This felicitous sentiment, as you also know, cannot be stifled even by the bloody dissensions that push nations to tear each other to pieces. Woe to the senseless and cruel man who would wish to extinguish the spark of the sacred fire of humanity and of philanthropy that the culture of the arts and sciences still keeps alive in the hearts of some. . . . By a happy revolution, the arts and sciences belong to all of Europe and are no longer the exclusive property of any one nation.

11. THE DUKE OF WELLINGTON EXPLAINS WHY THE ART PLUNDERED FROM EUROPEAN COUNTRIES BY NAPOLEON AND THE FRENCH ARMY SHOULD BE REPATRIATED

Letter from the Duke of Wellington to Lord Castlereagh: Paris, September 23, 1815 (Gurwood, Lt.Col. [John]. *The Dispatches of Field Marshal The Duke of Wellington, during his various campaigns, 1799 to 1815.* Vol. 12 [London: John Murray, 1838]: 641–646).

My Dear Lord,

There has been a good deal of discussion here lately respecting the measures which I have been under the necessity of adopting in order to get for the King of the Netherlands his pictures, &c., from the museums; and, lest these reports should reach the Prince Regent, I wish to trouble you, for His Royal Highness's information, with the following statement of what has passed.

Shortly after the arrival of the Sovereigns at Paris, the Minister of the King of the Netherlands claimed the pictures, &c., belonging to his Sovereign equally with those of other powers; and, as far as I could learn, never could get any satisfactory reply from the French Government. After several conversations with me, he addressed your Lordship in an official note, which was laid before the Ministers of the Allied Sovereigns assembled in Conference; and the subject was taken into consideration repeatedly, with a view to discover a mode of doing justice to the claimants of the specimens of the arts in the museums, without hurting the feelings of the King of France. In the mean time the Prussians had obtained from His Majesty not only all the really Prussian pictures, but those belonging to the Prussian territories on the left of the Rhine, and the pictures, &c., belonging to all the allies of His Prussian Majesty; and the subject pressed for an early decision; and your Lordship wrote your note of the 11th instant, in which it was fully discussed.

The Minister of the King of Netherlands, still having no satisfactory answer from the French Government, appealed to me, as the Commander in Chief of the army of the King of Netherlands, to know whether I had any objection to employ His Majesty's troops to obtain possession of what was his undoubted property. I referred this application again to the Ministers of the Allied Courts, and, no objection having been stated, I considered it my duty to take the necessary measures to obtain what was his right.

I accordingly spoke to the Prince de Talleyrand upon the subject, explained to him what had passed in Conference, and the grounds I had for thinking that the King of the Netherlands had a right to the pictures; and begged him to state the case to the King, and to ask His

Majesty to do me the favor to point out the mode of effecting the object of the King of the Netherlands which should be least offensive to His Majesty.

The Prince de Talleyrand promised me an answer on the following evening; which not having received, I called upon him at night, and had another discussion with him upon the subject, in which he informed me that the King could give no orders upon it; that I might act as I thought proper; and that I might communicate with M. Denon.

I sent my aide de camp, Lieut. Colonel Fremantle, to M. Denon in the morning, who informed him that he had no orders to give any pictures out of the gallery, and that he could give none without the use of force.

I then sent Colonel Fremantle to the Prince de Talleyrand to inform him of this answer, and to acquaint him that the troops would go the next morning at twelve o'clock to take possession of the King of the Netherlands' pictures; and to point out that, if any disturbance resulted from this measure, the King's Ministers, and not I, were responsible. Colonel Fremantle likewise informed M. Denon that the same measure would be adopted.

It was not necessary, however, to send the troops, as a Prussia guard had always remained in possession of the gallery, and the pictures were taken without the necessity of calling for those of the army under my command, excepting as a working party to assist in taking them down and packing them.

It has been stated that, in being the instrument of removing the pictures belonging to the King of the Netherlands from the Gallery of the Tuileries, I had been guilty of a breach of a treaty which I had myself made; and, as there is no mention of the museums in the treaty of the 25th of March, and it now appears that the treaty meant is the military Convention of Paris, it is necessary to show how that Convention affects the museum.

It is not now necessary to discuss the question whether the Allies were or not at war with France. There is no doubt whatever that their armies entered Paris under a military convention concluded with an officer of the Government, the Prefect of the Department of the Seine, and an officer of the army being a representative of each of the authorities existing at Paris at the moment, and authorized by those authorities to treat and conclude for them.

The article of the Convention which it is supposed has been broken is the eleventh, which relates to public property. I positively deny that this article referred at all to the museums or galleries of pictures.

The French commissioners in the original project proposed an article to provide for the security of this description of property. Prince Blücher would not consent to it, as he said there were pictures in the gallery which had been taken from Prussia, which His Majesty Louis XVIII had promised to restore, but which had never been restored. I stated this circumstance to the French commissioners, and they then offered to adopt the article with an exception of the Prussian pictures. To this offer I answered that I stood there as the ally of all the nations in Europe, and anything that was granted to Prussia I must claim for other nations. I added that I had no instructions regarding the museum, nor any grounds on which to form a judgment how the Sovereigns would act; that they certainly would insist upon the King's performing his engagements, and that I recommended that the article should be omitted altogether, and that the question should be reserved for the decision of the Sovereigns when they should arrive.

Thus the questions regarding the museum stands under the treaties. The Convention of Paris is silent upon it, and there was a communication upon the subject which reserved the decision for the Sovereigns.

Supposing the silence of the Treaty of Paris of May, 1814, regarding the museum, gave the French Government an undisputed claim to its contents upon all future occasions, it will not be denied that this claim was shaken by this transaction.

Those who acted for the French Government at the time considered that the successful army had a right to, and would, touch the contents of the museum, and they made an attempt to save them by an article in the military Convention. This article was rejected, and the claim of the Allies to their pictures was broadly advanced by the negociators on their part; and this was stated as the ground for rejecting the article. Not only then the military Convention did not in itself guarantee the possession, but the transaction above recited tended to weaken the claim to the possession by the French Government, which is founded upon the silence of the Treaty of Paris of May, 1814.

The Allies then, having the contents of the museum justly in their power, could not do otherwise than restore them to the countries from which, contrary to the practice of civilized warfare, they had been torn during the disastrous period of the French revolution and the tyranny of Buonaparte.

The conduct of the Allies regarding the museum, at the period of the Treaty of Paris [1814], might be fairly attributed to their desire to conciliate the French army, and to consolidate the reconciliation with Europe, which the army at that period manifested a disposition to effect.

But the circumstances are now entirely different. The army disappointed the reasonable expectation of the world, and seized the earliest opportunity of rebelling against their Sovereign, and of giving their services to the common enemy of mankind, with a view to the revival of the disastrous period which had passed, and of the scenes of plunder which the world had made such gigantic efforts to get rid of.

This army having been defeated by the armies of Europe, they have been disbanded by the United Counsel of the Sovereigns, and no reason can exist why the powers of Europe should do injustice to their own subjects with a view to conciliate them again. Neither has it ever appeared to me to be necessary that the Allied Sovereigns should omit this opportunity to do justice and to gratify their own subjects in order to gratify the people of France.

The feeling of the people of France upon this subject must be one of national vanity only. It must be a desire to retain these specimens of the arts, not because Paris is the fittest depository for them, as, upon that subject, artists, connoisseurs, and all who have written upon it, agree that the whole ought to be removed to their ancient seat, but because they were obtained by military concessions, of which they are the trophies.

The same feelings which induce the people of France to wish to retain the pictures and statues of other nations would naturally induce other nations to wish, now that success is on their side, that the property should be returned to their rightful owners, and the Allied Sovereigns must feel a desire to gratify them.

It is, besides, on many accounts, desirable, as well for their own happiness as for that of the world, that the people of France, if they do not already feel that Europe is too strong for them, should be made sensible of it; and that, whatever may be the extent, at any time, of their momentary and partial success against any one, or any number of individual powers in Europe, the day of retribution must come.

Not only, then, would it, in my opinion, be unjust in the Sovereigns to gratify the people of France on this subject, at the expense of their own people, but the sacrifice they would make would be impolitic, as it would deprive them of the opportunity of giving the people of France a great moral lesson.

Believe me, &c.,
WELLINGTON
Viscount Castlereagh, K. G.

BIBLIOGRAPHY

Correspondence in Archives

Cockerell Family Papers, in the Royal Institute of British Architects, London
Wellington Papers, in the Wellington Archives, University of Southampton

Pamphlets in the British Library

Anonymous. 1732. *Verres and his Scribblers; a Satire in Three Cantos. To which is added an Examen of the Piece, and a Key to the Characters and obscure Passages.* London.

Fraguier, Abbé. 1740. *Three Dissertations; one on the character of Augustus, Horace and Agrippa . . . Another on the Gallery of Verres by the Abbé Fraguier, in which many excellent Pieces of ancient Statuary, Sculpture and Painting are described. . . .* Trans. George Turnbull. London.

Hamilton, William R. 1811. *Memorandum on the Subject of the Earl of Elgin's Pursuits in Greece.* London.

Heskith, Thomas. 1703. *ΛΑΦΥΡΟΛΟΓΙΑ: or, a Discourse concerning Plunder: wherein the Legality of the same is proved by several Presidents [sic] and Arguments, brought form the Laws of God, of Nature and Nations . . . with some brief Reflections on St. Mary's and Vigo.* London.

Hippolyte, M. 1815. *Observations d'un Français, sur l'enlevement des chefs-d'oeuvre du Muséum de Paris, en response a la letter du Duc de Wellington au Lord Castlereagh, sous la date du 23 septembre 1815, et publiée, le 18 octobre, dans le Journal des Débats [5th oct. 1815].* Paris: 1–39.

Books and Articles

Aberson, Michel. 1994. *Temples votifs et butin de guerre dans la Rome républicaine.* Biblioteca helvetica Romana, 26. Rome.

Adams, J. N. 2003. *Bilingualism and the Latin Language.* Cambridge: Cambridge University Press.

Agora 3 = Wycherley, R. E. 1957. *The Athenian Agora, III. Literary and Epigraphical Testimonia.* Princeton: American School of Classical Studies.

Agora 31 = Miles, Margaret M. 1998. *The Athenian Agora, XXXI. The City Eleusinion.* Princeton: American School of Classical Studies.

Alcock, Susan E. 2002. *Archaeologies of the Greek Past. Landscape, Monuments, and Memories.* Cambridge: Cambridge University Press.

Alcock, Susan E., John F. Cherry, and Jas. Elsner, eds. 2001. *Pausanias. Travel and Memory in Roman Greece.* Oxford: Oxford University Press.

Alexander, Michael C. 1976. "Hortensius' Speech in Defense of Verres," *Phoenix* 30: 46–53.

Alexander, Michael C. 1990. *Trials in the Late Roman Republic, 149 B.C. to 50 B.C. Phoenix* Supp. 26. Toronto: Toronto University Press.

Alexander, Michael C. 2002. *The Case for the Prosecution in the Ciceronian Era.* Ann Arbor: University of Michigan Press.

Alföldi, G. 1995. "Eine Bauinschrift aus dem Colosseum." *ZPE* 109: 195–226.

Ambler, W. 2001. *Xenophon. The Education of Cyrus.* Ithaca and London: Cornell University Press.

Anderson, M. J. 1997. *The Fall of Troy in Early Greek Poetry and Art.* Oxford: Clarendon Press.

Antonetti, C. 1990. *Les Étoliens. Image et religion. Centre de recherches d'histoire ancienne, 92. Annales Littéraires de l'Université de Besançon, 405.* Paris: Les Belles Lettres.

Appiah, Kwame Anthony. 2006. *Cosmopolitanism. Ethics in a World of Strangers.* New York: Norton.

Arafat, K. 1996. *Pausanias' Greece. Ancient Artists and Roman Rulers.* Cambridge: Cambridge University Press.

Astin, A. E. 1967. *Scipio Aemilianus.* Oxford: Clarendon Press.

Atwood, R. 2004. *Stealing History. Tomb Raiders, Smugglers, and the Looting of the Ancient World.* New York: St. Martin's Press.

Austin, M. M. 1986. "Hellenistic Kings, War, and the Economy." *CQ* 36: 465.

Ayres, Philip. 1997. *Classical Culture and the Idea of Rome.* Cambridge: Cambridge University Press.

Badian, Ernst. 1958. *Foreign Clientelae* (264–70 B.C.). Oxford: Clarendon Press.

Badian, Ernst. 1983. *Publicans and Sinners.* Ithaca and London: Cornell University Press.

Baldassarri, P. 1998. *Sebastoi Soteri: Ediliza Monumentale ad Atene durante il Saeculum Augustum.* Rome.

Baldo, Gianluigi. 2004. *M. Tulli Ciceronis.* In *C. Verrem actionis secundae. Liber Quartus (De Signis).* Florence.

Bardill, J. 1997. "The Palace of Lausus and Nearby Monuments in Constantinople: A Topographical Study." *AJA* 101: 67–95.

Barkan, Elazar and Ronald Bush, eds. 2002. *Claiming the Stones, Naming the Bones. Cultural Property and the Negotiation of National and Ethnic Identity.* Los Angeles: Getty Research Institute.

Barkan, Leonard. 1999. *Unearthing the Past. Archaeology and Aesthetics in the Making of Renaissance Culture.* New Haven: Yale University Press.

Barnes, J. 1997. "Roman Aristotle," in J. Barnes and M. Griffin, eds., *Philosophia Togata II. Plato and Aristotle at Rome.* Oxford: Clarendon Press: 1–21.

Barnes, T. D. 2005. "The Sack of the Temple in Josephus and Tacitus," in Edmonson et al. (2005): 129–144.

Barr-Sharrar, Beryl. 1998. "Some Observations Concerning Late Hellenistic Bronze Production on Delos," in Olga Palagia and William Coulson, eds., *Regional Schools in Hellenistic Sculpture. Oxbow Monograph 90*. Oxford: Oxbow Books: 185–198.

Bartman, Elizabeth. 1986. "Lysippos' Huge God in Small Shape," *Bulletin of the Cleveland Museum of Art* 73: 298–311.

Bartman, Elizabeth. 1991. "Sculptural Collecting and Display in the Private Realm," in Gazda (1991): 71–88.

Bartman, Elizabeth. 1992. *Ancient Sculptural Copies in Miniature*. Leiden: Brill.

Bassett, Sarah. 2004. *The Urban Image of Late Antique Constantinople*. Cambridge: Cambridge University Press.

Bastéa, E. 2000. *The Creation of Modern Athens. Planning the Myth*. Cambridge: Cambridge University Press.

Beagon, Mary. 1992. *Roman Nature: The Thought of Pliny the Elder*. Oxford: Oxford University Press.

Beard, Mary, et al. 1991. *Literacy in the Roman World. JRA* Supp. 3. Ann Arbor.

Beard, Mary. 2003a. "The Triumph of Flavius Josephus," in Boyle and Dominik (2003): 543–558.

Beard, Mary. 2003b. "The Triumph of the Absurd: Roman Street Theatre," in C. Edwards and G. Woolf, eds., *Rome the Cosmopolis*. Cambridge: Cambridge University Press: 21–43.

Beard, Mary. 2004. "Writing Ritual: The Triumph of Ovid," in A. Barchiesi, J. Rüpke, and S. Stephens, eds., *Rituals in Ink*. Stuttgart: Franz Steiner: 115–126.

Becatti, G. 1956. "Letture Pliniane: Le opere d'arte nei monumenta Asini Pollionis e negli Horti Serviliani," in *Studi in Onore di Calderini e Paribeni*, 3 (Milan 1956): 199–210.

Bederman, David J. 2001a. *Classical Canons. Rhetoric, Classicism and Treaty Interpretation*. Aldershot: Ashgate.

Bederman, David J. 2001b. *International Law in Antiquity*. Cambridge: Cambridge University Press.

Belting, Hans. 1994. *Likeness and Presence*. Chicago and London: University of Chicago Press.

Belting, Hans. 2001. *The Invisible Masterpiece*. Chicago: University of Chicago Press.

Benoist-Méchin, J. 1978. *Bonaparte en Égypte, ou le rêve inassouvi (1797–1801)*. [Paris]: Perrin.

Bergmann, Bettina. 1991. "Painted Perspectives of a Villa Visit: Landscape and Status and Metaphor," in Gazda (1991): 49–70.

Bergmann, Bettina and Christine Kondoleon, eds. 1999. *The Art of Ancient Spectacle. Studies in the History of Art, 56*. New Haven and London: Yale University Press.

Bernard-Griffiths, Simone, Marie-Claude Chemin, and Jean Ehrard, eds. 1992. *Révolution française et "vandalisme révolutionnaire."* Paris: Universitas.

Bernstein, Jeremy. 2000. *Dawning of the Raj. The Life and Trials of Warren Hastings.* Chicago: Ivan R. Dee.

Berve, H. 1956. *Koenig Hieron II.* Munich: Bayerisch Akademie der Wissenschaften.

Berve, H. 1967. *Die Tyrannis bei den Griechen.* Munich: C. H. Beck.

Bethemont, J. and J. Pelletier. 1983. *Italy. A Geographical Introduction.* London and New York: Longman.

Bivonia, Livia. 1994. *Iscrizioni latine lapidarie del Museo Civico di Termini Imerese. Kokalos,* Supp. 9. Rome.

Black, Jeremy. 1992. *The British Abroad. The Grand Tour in the Eighteenth Century.* New York: St. Martin's Press.

Bloomer, W. M. 1992. *Valerius Maximus & the Rhetoric of the New Nobility.* Chapel Hill and London: University of North Carolina Press.

Boardman, J. and C. E. Vafopoulou-Richardson. 1986. "Diomedes I," in *LIMC* 3: 396–409.

Bodel, John. 1997. "Monumental Villas and Villa Monuments," *JRA* 10: 5–35.

Bogdanos, Matthew. 2005. "The Casualties of War: The Truth about the Iraq Museum," *AJA* 109 (2005): 477–526.

Bogdanos, Matthew, with W. Patrick. 2005. *Thieves of Baghdad.* New York: Bloomsbury.

Borowitz, H. and A. 1991. *Pawnshop and Palaces. The Fall and Rise of the Campana Art Museum.* Washington and London: Smithsonian Institution Press.

Bosman, Lex. 2004. *The Power of Tradition. Spolia in the Architecture of St. Peter's in the Vatican.* Hilversum: Uitgeverij Verloren.

Bosworth, B. 1999. "Augustus, the Res Gestae and Hellenistic Theories of Apotheosis." *JRS* 89: 1–18.

Bounia, A. 2004. *The Nature of Classical Collecting. Collectors and Collections, 100 BCE–100 CE.* Aldershot: Ashgate.

Bowman, A. K. and G. Woolf, eds. 1994. *Literacy and Power in the Ancient World.* Cambridge: Cambridge University Press.

Boyle, A. J. 2003. "Introduction: Reading Flavian Rome," in Boyle and Dominik (2003): 60–67.

Boyle, A. J. and W. J. Dominik, eds. 2003. *Flavian Rome. Culture, Image, Text.* Leiden: Brill.

Bradley, Keith R. 1989. *Slavery and Rebellion in the Roman World, 140 B.C.–70 B.C.* Bloomington and Indianapolis: Indiana University Press.

Bradley, Keith R. 1994. *Slavery and Society at Rome.* Cambridge: Cambridge University Press.

Brauer, G. C., Jr. 1986a. *Taras. Its History and Coinage.* New Rochelle, NY: Caratzas.

Braund, S. H. 1989. *Beyond Anger: A Study of Juvenal's Third Book of Satires.* Cambridge: Cambridge University Press.

Bremmer, J. N. and N. M. Horsfall. 1987. *Roman Myth and Mythography. BICS* Supp. 52. London.

Brenk, Beat. 1987. "Spolia from Constantine to Charlemagne: Aesthetics versus Ideology." *DOP* 41: 103–109.

Brennan, *Praetors* = Brennan (2000).

Brennan, T. Corey. 1996. "Triumphus in Monte Albano," in Robert Wallace and Edward M. Harris, eds. *Transitions to Empire. Essays in Greco-Roman History, 360–146 B.C., in honor of E. Badian.* Norman and London: University of Oklahoma Press: 315–337.

Brennan, T. Corey. 2000. *The Praetorship in the Roman Republic.* Oxford: Oxford University Press.

Brodie, Neil and Kathryn W. Tubb, eds. 2002. *Illicit Antiquities. The Theft of Culture and the Extinction of Archaeology.* London and New York: Routledge.

Broughton, *MRR* = Broughton, T. Robert S. 1968. *The Magistrates of the Roman Republic*, I. 509 B.C.–100 B.C. *APA Monograph*, 15. Cleveland, OH: Press of Case Western Reserve University.

Brunt, P. A. 1980. "Patronage and Politics in the 'Verrines'." *Chiron* 10: 273–289.

Brunt, P. A. 1988. "Clientela," in *The Fall of the Roman Republic and Related Essays.* Oxford: Clarendon Press.

Brunt, P. A. 1988. *The Fall of the Roman Republic.* Oxford: Clarendon Press.

Brunt, P. A. and J. M. Moore. 1967. *Res Gestae Divi Augusti.* Oxford: Oxford University Press.

Brydone, Patrick. 1798. *A Tour through Sicily and Malta, in a Series of Letters to William Beckford, esq. of Sommerly in Suffolk.* Greenfield, MA.

Bryson, Norman. 1984. *Tradition and Desire. From David to Delacroix.* Cambridge: Cambridge University Press.

Buchner, E. 1982. *Die Sonnenuhr des Augustus.* Mainz.

Büchner, K. 1984a. *De re publica, Kommentar.* Heidelberg: Winter.

Büchner, K. 1984b. *M. Tullius Cicero. De Re Publica. Kommentar.* Heidelberg: Carl Winter.

Buckle, S. 1991. *Natural Law and the Theory of Property: Grotius to Hume.* Oxford: Oxford University Press.

Buckler, J. 1989. *Philip II and the Sacred War. Mnemosyne* Supp. 109. Leiden: Brill.

Budde, L. and Richard Nichols. 1964. *Catalogue of the Greek and Roman Sculpture in the Fitzwilliam Museum.* Cambridge: Cambridge University Press.

Bull, Hedley. 1990. "The Importance of Grotius in the Study of International Relations," in Hedley Bull, Bendict Kingsbury, and Adam Roberts, eds., *Hugo Grotius and International Relations*. Oxford: Oxford University Press.

Bussmann, Klaus and Heinz Schilling, eds. 1998. *1648. War and Peace in Europe II* [Münster: Westfälisches Landesmuseum].

Butler, Shane. 2002. *The Hand of Cicero*. London and New York: Routledge.

CAH 7.2 = Walbank, F. W., et al., eds. 1989. *The Cambridge Ancient History. 2. The Rise of Rome to 220 B.C.* Cambridge: Cambridge University Press.

CAH 8 = Astin, A. E., et al., eds. 1989. *The Cambridge Ancient History. 8. Rome and the Mediterranean to 133 B.C.* Cambridge: Cambridge University Press.

CAH 9 = Crook, J. A., Andrew Lintott, and Elizabeth Rawson, eds. 1994. *The Cambridge Ancient History. 9. The Last Age of the Roman Republic, 146–43 B.C.* Cambridge: Cambridge University Press.

CAH 13 = Cameron, Averil and Peter Garnsey, eds. 1998. *The Cambridge Ancient History. 13. The Late Empire, A.D. 337–425.* Cambridge: Cambridge University Press.

Cahill, Nicholas. 2002. *Household and City Organization at Olynthus*. New Haven and London: Yale University Press.

Calciati, Romolo. 1983, 1986, 1987. *Corpus Nummorum Siculorum*. I–III. Novara. I (1983), II (1986), III (1987).

Cambiano, G. 2006. "Cicerone in Inghilterra nella prima metà del Settecento," in Narducci (2006).

Carey, Sorcha. 2003. *Pliny's Catalogue of Culture. Art and Empire in the Natural History*. Oxford: Oxford University Press.

Carnall, Geoffrey. 1989. "Burke as Modern Cicero," in Geoffrey Carnall and Colin Nicholson, eds. *The Impeachment of Warren Hastings. Papers from a Bicentenary Commemoration*. Edinburgh: Edinburgh University Press: 76–90.

Casson, Lionel. 1974. *Travel in the Ancient World*. Baltimore and London: The Johns Hopkins University Press [repr. 1994].

Cavallo, G. and P. Fedeli in G. Cavallo, et al., eds. 1989. *Lo spazio letterario de Roma antica, II, La Circolazione del testo*. Rome.

Caven, Brian. 1990. *Dionysius I. War-Lord of Sicily*. New Haven and London: Yale University Press.

Cavenaile, Robert. 1958. *Corpus Papyrorum Latinarum*. Wiesbaden: Otto Harrassowitz.

Ceserani, Giovanna. 2000. "The Charm of the Siren: The Place of Classical Sicily in Historiography," in Smith and Serrati (2000): 174–193.

Chamberlain, K. 2004. *War and Cultural Heritage. An Analysis of the 1954 Convention for the Protection of Cultural Property in the Event of Armed Conflict and Its Two Protocols*. Leicester: The Institute of Art and Law.

Champlin, Edward. 2003. *Nero*. Cambridge, MA: Harvard University Press.

Chaney, Edward. 1998. *The Evolution of the Grand Tour*. London: Frank Cass.

Chaplin, Jane D. 2000. *Livy's Exemplary History*. Oxford: Oxford University Press.

Chastel, André. 1983. *The Sack of Rome, 1527*. Trans. Beth Archer. *Bollingen*, 26. Princeton: Princeton University Press.

Chevallier, Raymond, ed. 1984. *Présence de Cicéron. Actes du Colloque des 25, 26 septembre 1982. Homage au R. P. M. Testard*. Paris

Chevallier, Raymond. 1991. *L'Artiste, le collectionneur & le faussaire. Pour une sociologie de l'art romain*. Paris: Armand Colin.

Chevallier, Raymond, ed. 1991. *La Révolution française et l'antiquité. Collection Caesarodunum*. Vol. XXVbis. Tours: Centre de recherces A. Piganiol.

Chippendale, C. and D. W. J. Gill. 2000. "Material Consequences of Contemporary Classical Collecting." *AJA* 104: 463–511.

Churchill, J. B. 1999. "*Ex qua quod vellent facerent*: Roman Magistrates' Authority over *Praeda* and *Manubiae*." *TAPA* 129: 85–116.

CIL = *Corpus Inscripitonum Latinarum*. (1863–)

Clarke, E. D. 1818. *Travels in Various Countries: Greece, Egypt and the Holy Land*. London.

Clarke, John. 1991. *The Houses of Roman Italy 100 B.C.–A.D. 250: Ritual, Space and Decoration*. Berkeley and Oxford: University of California Press.

Clarke, M. L. 1965. "'*Non hominis nomen, sed eloquentiae*,'" in T. A. Dorey, ed. *Cicero*. London: Routledge & Kegan Paul.

Classen, C. J. 1985. *Recht – Rhetorik – Politik*. Darmstad.

Cline, Eric. 2004. *Jerusalem Besieged*. Ann Arbor: The University of Michigan Press.

Coarelli, Filippo. 1983. *Il foro romano, I: Periodo arcaico*. Rome.

Coarelli, Filippo. 1988. *Il foro Boario*. Rome: Edizioni Quasar.

Coarelli, Filippo. 1990. "Cultura artistica e società," in A. Schiavone, ed. *Storia di Roma, 2.1: La repubblica imperiale*. Rome: G. Einaudi: 159–185, 633–670.

Coarelli, Filippo. 1993. *Dintorni de Roma*. Rome: Laterza.

Coarelli, Filippo. 1996 [1982]. "La *Pugna Equestris* di Agatocle nell'Athenaion di Siracusa," in *Revixit Ars. Arte e ideologia a Roma. Dai modelli ellenistici alla tradizione repubblicana*. Rome: 85–101. (Reprinted from L. Beschi, ed., *Aparchai. Nuove ricerche e studi sulla Magna Grecia e la Sicilia antica in onore de Paolo Enrico Arias*. Pisa, 1982: 547–557.)

Coleman, K. M. *Statius. Silvae IV*. Oxford: Clarendon Press.

Constantine, D. 1984. *Early Greek Travellers and the Hellenic Ideal*. Cambridge and New York: Cambridge University Press.

Contamine, Philippe. 2000. "The Growth of State Control. Practices of War, 1300–1800: Ransom and Booty," in Philippe Contamine, ed. *War and Competition between States*. Oxford: Clarendon Press: 163–193.

Conte, G. B. 1994a. *Genres and Readers: Lucretius, Love Elegy, Pliny's Encyclopedia.* Baltimore: The Johns Hopkins University Press.

Conte, G. B. 1994b. *Latin Literature, A History.* Baltimore and London: The Johns Hopkins University Press.

Cooper, J. S. 1983. *The Curse of Agade.* Baltimore and London: The Johns Hopkins University Press.

Cornell, T. J. 1986. "The Value of the Literary Tradition Concerning Archaic Rome," in Raaflaub (1986): 52–76.

Cornell, T. J. 1995. *The Beginnings of Rome. Italy and Rome from the Bronze Age to the Punic Wars (c. 1000–264 BC).* London and New York: Routledge.

Cowles, Frank H. 1917. *Gaius Verres: An Historical Study.* Cornell Studies in Classical Philology, 20. Ithaca, NY.

Crawford, Jane W. 1984. *M. Tullius Cicero: The Lost and Unpublished Orations. Hypomnemata*, 80. Göttingen.

Crawford, Jane W. 1994. *M. Tullius Cicero. The Fragmentary Speeches. An Edition with Commentary.* Atlanta: Scholars Press.

Crawford, Jane W. 2002. "The Lost and Fragmentary Orations," in May (2002): 305–330.

Crawford, M. H. 1985. *Coinage and Money under the Roman Republic.* Berkeley: University of California Press.

Crawford, M. H. 1989. "Aut sacrom aut poublicom," in P. Birks, ed. *New Perspectives in the Roman Law of Property. Essays for Barry Nicholas.* Oxford: Clarendon Press: 93–98.

Crawford, M. H., ed. 1996. *Roman Statutes. BICS* Supp. 64. London.

Curran, John R. 1994. "Moving statues in late antique Rome: Problems of perspective," *ArtHist* 17: 46–58.

Curran, John R. 2000. *Pagan City and Christian Capital. Rome in the Fourth Century.* Oxford: Clarendon Press.

D'Alton, Martina. 1993. *The New York Obelisk, or How Cleopatra's Needle Came to New York and What Happened When It Got Here.* New York: Metropolitan Museum.

D'Arms, John H. 1970. *Romans on the Bay of Naples.* Cambridge, MA: Harvard University Press.

D'Arms, John H. 1981. *Commerce and Social Standing in Ancient Rome.* Cambridge, MA: Harvard University Press.

D'Onofrio, C. 1965. *Gli obelischi di Roma.* Rome: Bulzoni.

Dagron, Gilbert. 1974. *Naissance d'une capitale. Constantinople et ses institutions de 330 à 451.* Paris: Presses Universitaires de France.

Dalby, Andrew. 1996. *Siren Feasts. A History of Food and Gastronomy in Greece.* London and New York: Routledge.

Dalby, Andrew. 2000. *Empire of Pleasures. Luxury and Indulgence in the Roman World*. London and New York: Routledge.

Davies, Jason P. 2004. *Rome's Religious History: Livy, Tacitus and Ammianus on Their Gods*. Cambridge: Cambridge University Press.

Delaforce, P. 1990. *Wellington the Beau*. Gloucestershire.

Demouliez, A. 1976. *Cicèron et son goût: Essai sur une definition d'une aesthetique romaine à la fin de la République*. Collection Latomus, 150. Bruxelles: Latomus.

de Souza, Philip. 1999. *Piracy in the Greco-Roman World*. Cambridge: Cambridge University Press.

Dillon, Sheila and Katherine E. Welch, eds. 2006. *Representations of War in Ancient Rome*. Cambridge: Cambridge University Press.

Dix, T. Keith. 2000. "The Library of Lucullus," *Athenaeum* 88: 441–464.

Dodwell, Edward. 1819. *A Classical and Topographical Tour through Greece; during the Years 1801, 1805 and 1806*. 2 vols. London: Rodwell and Martin.

Dolan, Brian. 2001. *Ladies of the Grand Tour*. New York: HarperCollins.

Donohue, A. A. 1995. "Winckelmann's History of Art and Polyclitus," in W. G. Moon, ed., *Polykleitos, the Doryphoros, and Tradition*. Madison: University of Wisconsin Press: 327–353.

Donohue, A. and M. Fullerton, eds. 2003. *Ancient Art and Its Historiography*. Cambridge: Cambridge University Press.

Donahue, J. F. 2004. *The Roman Community at Table, during the Principate*. Ann Arbor: University of Michigan Press.

Dubois, Laurent. 2004. *Avengers of the New World. The Story of the Haitian Revolution*. Cambridge, MA: Harvard University Press.

Ducrey, P. 1968. *Le traitement des prisonniers de guerre dans la Grèce antique*. Paris: Boccard.

Ducrey, P. 1986. *Warfare in Ancient Greece*. Trans. J. Lloyd. New York: Schocken Books.

Dugan, J. 2005. *Making a New Man. Ciceronian Self-fashioning in the Rhetorical Works*. Oxford: Oxford University Press.

Dunbabin, Katherine M. D. 2003. *The Roman Banquet. Images of Conviviality*. Cambridge: Cambridge University Press.

Duncan, Carol and Alan Wallach, 1980. "The Universal Survey Museum," *ArtHist* 3: 448–469.

Dyck, Andrew. 1996. *A Commentary on Cicero, De Officiis*. Ann Arbor: University of Michigan Press.

Dykstra, D. 1998. "The French occupation of Egypt, 1798–1801," in M. W. Daly, ed. *The Cambridge History of Egypt*, 2. Cambridge: Cambridge University Press.

Dyson, Stephen. 1985. *The Creation of the Roman Frontier*. Princeton: Princeton University Press.

Edmonson, Jonathan C. 1999. "The Cultural Politics of Public Spectacle in Rome and the Greek East, 167–166 BCE," in Bergmann and Kondoleon (1999): 77–95.

Edmonson, Jonathan, Steve Mason, and James Rives, eds. 2005. *Flavius Josephus and Flavian Rome*. Oxford: Oxford University Press.

Edwards, Catherine. 1993. *The Politics of Immorality in Ancient Rome*. Cambridge: Cambridge University Press.

Edwards, C. and G. Woolf, eds. 2003. *Rome the Cosmopolis*. Cambridge: Cambridge University Press.

Ehlers, W. 1939. "Triumphus." *RE* VIIIA, col. 493–511.

Eigler, Ulrich. 2003. "Aemilius Paullus: ein Feldherr auf Bildungsreise?" in Eigler (2003): 250–267.

Eigler, Ulrich, Ulrich Gotter, Nino Luraghi, and Uwe Walter, eds. 2003. *Formen römische Geschichtsschreibung von den anfängen bis Livius. Gattungen – Autoren – Kontexte*. Darmstadt: Wissenschaftliche Buchgesellschaft.

Eilers, Claude. 2002. *Roman Patrons of Greek Cities*. Oxford: Oxford University Press.

Elia, Ricardo J. 2001. "Analysis of the Looting, Selling and Collecting of Apulian Red-Figure Vases: A Quantitative Approach," in Neil Brodie, Jennifer Doole, and Colin Renfrew, eds., *Trade in Illicit Antiquities: The Destruction of the World's Archaeological Heritage*. Cambridge: McDonald Institute Monographs: 145–154.

Elsner, Jas. 1994. "Constructing Decadence: The Representation of Nero as Imperial Builder," in Jas Elsner and Jamie Masters, eds., *Reflections of Nero, Culture, History & Representation*. Chapel Hill and London: University of North Carolina Press: 112–127.

Elsner, Jas. 1995. *Art and the Roman Viewer: The Transformation of Art from the Pagan World to Christianity*. Cambridge: Cambridge University Press.

Elsner, Jas. 1996. "Image and Ritual: Reflection on the Religious Appreciation of Classical art," *CQ* 46: 515–531.

Elsner, Jas. 2000. "From the Culture of *spolia* to the Cult of Relics: The Arch of Constantine and the Genesis of Late Antique Forms," *PBSR* 68: 149–184.

Elsner, Jas. and R. Cardinal, eds. 1994. *The Cultures of Collecting*. Cambridge, MA: Harvard University Press.

Englund, Steven. 2004. *Napoleon, A Political Life*. New York: Scribner.

Enos, Richard L. 1988. *The Literate Mode of Cicero's Legal Rhetoric*. Carbondale and Edwardsville: Southern Illinois University Press.

Eustace, Rev. John. 1813. *A Classical Tour through Italy in the Year 1802*. London.

Fant, J. Clayton. 1993. "A Distribution Model for the Roman Imperial Marbles," in Harris (1993): 146–147.

Faraone, Christopher A. 1992. *Talismans and Trojan Horses. Guardian Statues in Ancient Greek Myth and Ritual*. Oxford: Oxford University Press.

Favro, Diane. 1996. *The Urban Image of Augustan Rome*. Cambridge: Cambridge University Press.

Feldherr, Andrew. 1998. *Spectacle and Society in Livy's History*. Berkeley and London: University of California Press.

Feliciano, Hector. 1997. *The Lost Museum. The Nazi Conspiracy to Steal the World's Greatest Works of Art*. New York: Basic Books.

Ferchiou, N. 1994. "Recherches sur les éléments architecturaux," in Hellenkemper Salies (1994) 1: 195–207.

Ferrary, J.-L. 1988. *Philhellénisme et Impérialisme. Aspects idéologiques de la conquête romaine du mond hellénistique. BEFAR*, 271. Rome: Bretschneider.

Finley, M. I. 1968. *A History of Sicily. Vol. I. Ancient Sicily to the Arab Conquest*. New York: The Viking Press.

Flower, Harriet I. 1996. *Ancestor Masks and Aristocratic Power in Roman Culture*. Oxford: Clarendon Press.

Flower, Harriet I. 2000. "The Tradition of the Spolia Opima: M. Claudius Marcellus and Augustus," *ClAnt* 19: 34–64.

Flower, Harriet I. 2003. "'Memories' of Marcellus. History and Memory in Roman Republican Culture," in Eigler (2003): 39–52.

Flower, Harriet I., ed. 2004. *The Cambridge Companion to the Roman Republic*. Cambridge: Cambridge University Press.

Forsyth, Joseph. 1813. *Remarks on Antiquities, Arts, and Letters during an Excursion in Italy in the years 1802 and 1803*. London.

Fothergill, Brian. 1969. *Sir William Hamilton, Envoy Extraordinary*. New York: Harcourt, Brace & World.

Fotion, N. and G. Elfstrom. 1986. *Military Ethics. Guidelines for Peace and War*. Boston: Routledge & Kegan Paul.

Frank, Tenney, ed. 1933. *Economic Survey of Ancient Rome, I*. Baltimore: The Johns Hopkins University Press.

Frazel, T. D. 2004. "The Composition and Circulation of Cicero's *In Verrem*," *CQ* 54: 128–142.

Frazer, J. G. 1898. *Pausanias's Description of Greece*. 6 vols. New York: Biblo and Tannen [repr. 1968].

Freidel, Frank B. 1947. *Francis Lieber, Nineteenth-Century Liberal*. Glouster, MA: P. Smith [repr. 1968].

Friedman, Leon. 1972. *The Law of War. A Documentary History*. 2 vols. New York: Random House.

Fuciková, Eliska. 2001. "The Collection of Rudolf II at Prague: Cabinet of Curiosities or Scientific Museum?" in Impey and MacGregor (2001): 63–70.

Fuhrmann, M. 1992. *Cicero and the Roman Republic*. Trans. W. E. Yuill. Oxford and Cambridge: Blackwell.

Galinski, K. 1996. *Augustan Culture*. Princeton: Princeton University Press.

Galsterer, H. 1994. "Kunstraub und Kunsthandel im republikanischen Rom," in Hellenkemper Salies (1994) 2: 857–866.

Gantz, Timothy. 1993. *Early Greek Myths. A Guide to Literary and Artistic Sources*. Baltimore and London: The Johns Hopkins University Press.

Garlan, Yvon. 1975. *War in the Ancient World. A Social History*. London: Chatto & Windus.

Gasparri, C. and A. Veneri. 1986. "Dionysos/Bacchus," *LIMC* 3: 414–420, 496–514, 541–558.

Gates, David. 1986. *The Spanish Ulcer*. Cambridge, MA: Da Capo Press.

Gauer, W. 1968. *Weihgeschenke aus den Perserkriegen. AM Beiheft 2*.

Gavrilov, A. K. 1997. "Techniques of Reading in Classical Antiquity," *CQ* 47: 56–76.

Gazda, Elaine K., ed. 1991. *Roman Art in the Private Sphere. New Perspectives on the Architecture and Decor of the Domus, Villa and Insula*. Ann Arbor: University of Michigan Press.

Gazda, Elaine K., ed. 2002. *The Ancient Art of Emulation*. Ann Arbor: University of Michigan Press.

Geiger, Joseph. 1985. *Cornelius Nepos and Ancient Political Biography. Historia Einzelschr*, 47. Stuttgart.

Gelzer, M. 1969. *Cicero, ein biographischer Versuch*. Wiesbaden: Franz Steiner Verlag.

Gera, D. L. 1993. *Xenophon's Cyropaedia. Style, Genre, and Literary Technique*. Oxford: Clarendon Press.

Gerstenblith, Patty. 2004. *Art, Cultural Heritage, and the Law. Cases and Materials*. Durham, NC: Carolina Academic Press.

Gibbon, Edward. 1776. *The History of the Decline and Fall of the Roman Empire*. London.

Giuliano, A. 2001. "Signum Cereris," in *Scritte Minori. Xenia Antiqua*, 9: 203–214 (= *Atti della Accademia nazionale dei Lincei. Rendiconti*. Serie IX, iv, 1993; 50–65).

Goethe, J. W. von. 1989. *Italian Journey, Goethe's Collected Works*, 6. Trans. R. R. Heitner. New York: Suhrkamp.

Goldsworthy, A. K. 1996. *The Roman Army at War. 100 BC–AD 200*. Oxford: Clarendon Press.

Goodman, Dena. 1994. *The Republic of Letters. A Cultural History of the French Enlightenment*. Ithaca and London: Cornell University Press.

Goodman, M. D. and A. J. Holladay. 1986. "Religious Scruples in Ancient Warfare," *CQ* 36: 151–171.

Gordon, R. 1979. "The Real and the Imaginary: Production and Religion in the Graeco-Roman World," *Art History* 2: 5–34.

Gould, C. 1965. *Trophy of Conquest, The Musée Napoléon and the Creation of the Louvre*. London: Faber and Faber.

Graindor, Paul. 1931. *Athènes de Tibère a Trajan. Recueil de travaux*, 8. Cairo.

Graverini, L. 2001. "L. Mummio Acaico." *Maecenas* 1: 105–148.

Green, Peter. 1978. "Caesar and Alexander, Aemulatio, Imitatio, Comparatio." *AJAH* [1978]: 1–26, repr. in *Classical Bearings* [Berkeley and London, 1989]: 193–209.

Green, Peter. 2006. *Diodorus Siculus, Books 11–12.37.1. Greek History, 480–431 BC. The Alternative Version*. Austin: University of Texas Press.

Greene, M. T. 1992. *Natural Knowledge in Preclassical Antiquity*. Baltimore and London: The Johns Hopkins University Press.

Greenfield, Jeanne. 1995. *The Return of Cultural Treasures*. 2. Cambridge: Cambridge University Press.

Greenidge, A. H. J. 1901. *The Legal Procedure of Cicero's Time*. Oxford: Clarendon Press [repr. 1999, Union, NJ: Lawbook Exchange, Ltd.].

Grendler, P. F. 1989. *Schooling in Renaissance Italy. Literacy and Learning, 1300–1600*. Baltimore: The Johns Hopkins Press.

Grewe, Wilhelm G. 2000. *The Epochs of International Law*. Trans. M. Byers. Berlin: Walter de Gruyter.

Griffin, Miriam and Jonathan Barnes, eds. 1989. *Philosophia Togata. Essays on Philosophy and Roman Society*. Oxford: Clarendon Press.

Gros, Pierre. 1976. *Aurea Templa: Recherches sur l'architecture religieuse de Rome à l'époque d'Auguste. BEFAR* 231. Rome.

Gros, Pierre. 1979. "Les Statues de Syracuse et les "dieux" de Tarente," *REL* 57: 85–114.

Grotius, Hugo. 1604. *De iure praedae commentarius [1604]. Classics of International Law*. J. B. Scott, ed. Trans. G. L. Williams. New York: Oceana.

Gruen, Erich S. 1968. *Roman Politics and the Criminal Courts, 149–78 B.C.* Cambridge, MA: Harvard University Press.

Gruen, Erich S. 1984. *The Hellenistic World and the Coming of Rome*. Berkeley and London: University of California Press.

Gruen, Erich S. 1990. *Studies in Greek Culture and Roman Policy*. Berkeley and London: University of California Press.

Gruen, Erich S. 1992. *Culture and National Identity in Republican Rome*. Ithaca, NY: Cornell University Press.

Guberti Bassett, Sarah. 2000. "'Excellent Offerings': The Lausos Collection in Constantinople." *ArtB* 82: 6–25.

Guedalla, Philip. 1931 [1997]. *The Duke*. Hertfordshire: Wordsworth.

Gunderson, E. 2003. "The Flavian Amphitheatre: All the World as Stage," in Boyle and Dominik (2003): 637–658.

Gurwood, Lt. Col. [John]. 1838. *The Dispatches of Field Marshall the Duke of Wellington*, 12. London: John Murray.

Gutzwiller, Katherine. 2004. "Gender and Inscribed Epigram: Herennia Procula and the Thespian Eros," *TAPA* 134: 383–418.

Habermehl, H. 1958. "C. Verres." *RE* VIII A/2, col. 1561–1633.

Habicht, Christian. 1984. "Pausanias and the Evidence of Inscriptions," *ClAnt* 3: 40–56.

Habicht, Christian. 1990. *Cicero the Politician*. Baltimore and London: The Johns Hopkins University Press.

Habicht, Christian. 1985. *Pausanias' Guide to Ancient Greece*. Berkeley and London: University of California Press.

Habinek, Thomas N. 1998. *The Politics of Latin Literature. Writing, Identity, and Empire in Ancient Rome*. Princeton: Princeton University Press.

Haggenmacher, P. 1990. "Grotius and Gentili: A Reassessment of Thomas E. Holland's Inaugural Lecture," in Bull (1990): 133–176.

Hales, Shelley. 2000. "At Home with Cicero," *G & R* 47: 44–55.

Hales, Shelley. 2003. *The Roman House and Social Identity*. Cambridge: Cambridge University Press.

Hallett, Christopher H. 2005. "Emulation versus Replication: Redefining Roman Copying," *JRA* 18: 419–435.

Hamilton, William R. 1809. *Aegyptica or Some Account of the Ancient and Modern State of Egypt, as obtained in the years 1801*. London.

Hannestad, Niels. 1994. *Tradition in Late Antique Sculpture. Conservation – Modernization – Production. Acta Jutlandica* 69: 2. Aarhus: Aarhus University Press.

Harris, Diane. 1995. *The Treasures of the Parthenon and Erechtheion*. Oxford: Clarendon Press.

Harris, William V. 1979. *War and Imperialism in Republican Rome*. Oxford: Clarendon Press.

Harris, William V. 1989. *Ancient Literacy*. Cambridge, MA, and London: Harvard University Press.

Harris, William V. 1993. "Between Archaic and Modern: Problems in Roman Economic History," in W. V. Harris, ed., *The Inscribed Economy. JRA* Supp. 6. Ann Arbor: 11–30.

Hartswick, Kim J. 2004. *The Gardens of Sallust*. Austin: University of Texas Press.

Haselberger, *MAR* = Haselberger, Lothar, et al. 2002. *Mapping Augustan Rome. JRA* Supp. 50. Portsmouth, RI.

Haskell, F. and N. Penny. 1981. *Taste and the Antique. The Lure of Classical Sculpture, 1500–1900*. New Haven: Yale University Press.

Hathaway, Eileen, ed. 1993. *A Dorset Soldier. The Autobibography of Sergeant William Lawrence, 1790–1869*. Staplehurst: Spellmount.

Hatzfeld, J. 1912. "Les italiens résident à Délos." *BCH* 36: 1–218.

Havelock, C. 1995. *The Aphrodite of Knidos and Her Successors: A Historical Review of the Female Nude in Greek Art*. Ann Arbor: University of Michigan Press.

Head, Barclay V. 1911. *Historia Numorum. A Manual of Greek Numismatics*. Chicago: Argonaut, Inc. [repr. 1967].

Heibges, U. 1968. "Religion and Rhetoric in Cicero's Speeches," *Latomus* 28: 833–849.

Heinrich, H. 1994. "Die Chimärenkapitelle," in Hellenkemper Salies (1994) 1: 209–237.

Hellenkemper Salies, Gisela, et al., eds. 1994. *Das Wrack. Der antike Schiffsfund von Mahdia*, 2 vols. Köln: Rheinland Verlag.

Herold, J. C. 1962. *Bonaparte in Egypt*. New York.

Higbie, Carolyn. 2003. *The Lindian Chronicle and the Greek Creation of Their Past*. Oxford: Oxford University Press.

Higginbotham, James. 1997. *Piscinae. Artificial Fishponds in Roman Italy*. Chapel Hill and London: University of North Carolina Press.

Hinz, Valentina. 1998. *Der Kult von Demeter und Kore auf Sizilien und in der Magna Graecia. Palilia* 4. Wiesbaden.

Hitchens, Christopher. 1997. *The Elgin Marbles. Should They be Returned to Greece?* New York: Verso.

Hodkinson, S. 2000. *Property and Wealth in Classical Sparta*. London: Duckworth and The Classical Press of Wales.

Hoff, Michael C. 1994. "The So-called Agoranomion and the Imperial Cult in Julio-Claudian Athens," *AA* 93: 93–117.

Hoff, Michael C. 1997. "*Laceratae Athenae*: Sulla's Siege of Athens in 87/6 B.C. and its Aftermath," in Hoff and Rotroff (1997): 33–51.

Hoff, Michael C. and Susan I. Rotroff, eds. 1997. *The Romanization of Athens. Oxbow Monograph* 94. Oxford: Oxbow Press.

Hoffman, Barbara T. 2006. *Art and Cultural Heritage. Law, Policy, and Practice*. Cambridge: Cambridge University Press.

Holliday, Peter J. 2002. *The Origins of Roman Historical Commemoration in the Visual Arts*. Cambridge: Cambridge University Press.

Hölscher, Tonio. 2004. *The Language of Images in Roman Art*. [Trans. from original German ed., 1987.] Cambridge: Cambridge University Press.

Hölscher, Tonio. 2006. "The Transformation of Victory into Power: From Event to Structure," in Dillon and Welch (2006): 27–48.

Horden, P. and N. Purcell. 2000. *The Corrupting Sea. A Study of Mediterranean History.* London: Blackwell.

Horsfall, Nicholas. 1989. *Cornelius Nepos. A Selection, including the Lives of Cato and Atticus.* Oxford: Clarendon Press.

Horsfall, Nicholas. 1995. "Rome without Spectacles." *G&R* 42: 49–56.

Horsfall, Nicholas. 2003. *The Culture of the Roman Plebs.* London: Duckworth.

Howgego, C. 1992. "The Supply and Use of Money in the Roman World." *JRS* 82: 1–31.

HWCR = Gruen (1984).

ID = *Inscriptions de Délos.* Paris: H. Champion. (1926–).

Ideologie e patrimonio storico-culturale nell'età rivoluzionaria e napoleonica: a proposito del Trattato di Tolentino. 2000. *Atti del convengo Tolentino 18–21 Sept., 1997, Pubblicazioni degli archivi di Stato,* 55. Rome.

IG = *Inscriptiones Graecae.* (1873–)

ILLRP = Degrassi, A., ed. 1963, 1965. *Inscriptiones Latinae Liberae Rei Publicae.* Berlin: De Gruyter.

ILS = Dessau, H. 1962. *Inscriptiones Latinae Selectae.* Berlin: Weidmann.

Imber, M. 2001. "Practised Speech: Oral and Written Conventions in Roman Declamation," in J. Watson, ed. *Speaking Volumes. Orality and Literacy in the Greek and Roman World.* Leiden: Brill: 201–212.

Impey, Oliver and Arthur MacGregor, eds. 2001. *The Origins of Museums. The Cabinet of Curiosities in Sixteenth- and Seventeenth-Century Europe.* London: House of Stratus.

Ingamell, John. 1997. *A Dictionary of British and Irish Travellers in Italy, 1701–1800. Compiled from the Brinsley Ford Archive.* New Haven and London: Yale University Press.

Isager, Jacob. 1991. *Pliny on Art and Society. The Elder Pliny's Chapters on the History of Art.* London and New York: Routledge.

Isager, Jacob, ed. 2001. *Foundation and Destruction: Nikopolis and Northwestern Greece.* Aarhus.

Iversen, Eric. 1968. *Obelisks in Exile, I.* Copenhagen: G. E. C. Gad.

Jacobson, D. M. and M. P. Weitzman. 1992. "What Was Corinthian Bronze?" *AJA* 96: 237–247.

Jaeger, Mary. 1997. *Livy's Written Rome.* Ann Arbor: University of Michigan Press.

Jaeger, Mary. 2002. "Cicero and Archimedes' Tomb." *JRS* 92: 49–61.

Jaeger, Mary. 2003. "Livy and the Fall of Syracuse," in Eigler (2003): 213–234.

Jaeger, Mary. 2006. "Livy, Hannibal's Monument, and the Temple of Juno at Croton." *TAPA* 136: 389–414.

James, Lawrence. 1997. *Raj. The Making and Unmaking of British India.* New York: St. Martin's Griffin.

Jameson, Michael. 1990. "Private Space and the Greek City," in O. Murray and S. Price, eds. *The Greek City from Homer to Alexander*. Oxford: 171–195.

Jasanoff, Maya. 2005. *Edge of Empire. Lives, Culture, and Conquest in the East, 1750–1850*. New York: Alfred A. Knopf.

Jenkins, Ian and Kim Sloan. 1996. *Vases and Volcanoes. Sir William Hamilton and his Collection*. London: British Museum.

Jenkins, Ian. 1992. *Archaeologists & Aesthetes in the Sculpture Galleries of the British Museum 1800–1939*. London: British Museum.

Johns, Christopher M. S. 1998. *Antonio Canova and the Politics of Patronage in Revolutionary and Napoleonic Europe*. Berkeley: University of California Press.

Johnson, James Turner. 1981. *Just War Tradition and the Restraint of War*. Princeton: Princeton University Press.

Jolivet, V. 1987. "*Xerxes togatus*: Lucullus en Campanie," *MEFRA* 99: 823–846.

Jones, C. P. 2003. "Editing and understanding Pausanias," *JRA* 16: 673–676.

Jucker, Hans. 1950. *Vom Verhältnis der Römer zur bildensen Kunst der Griechen*. Frankfurt: V. Klostermann.

Kauffmann, C. M. 1982. *Catalogue of Paintings in the Wellington Museum*. London: Her Majesty's Stationery Office.

Keaveney, A. 1992. *Lucullus. A Life*. London and New York: Routledge.

Keay, John. 2000. *India, A History*. New York: Grove Press.

Kefallineou, Eugenia. 1999. *Byron and the Antiquities of the Acropolis of Athens. The Archaeological Society at Athens Library, 192*. Athens.

Kellum, Barbara. "The City Adorned: Programmatic Display at the *Aedes Concordiae Augustae*," in Raaflaub and Toher (1990): 276–307.

Kelsall, Charles, trans. 1812. *The Two Last Pleadings of Marcus Tullius Cicero against Caius Verres; Translated and Illustrated with Notes*. London.

Kennedy, G. A. 2002. "Cicero's Oratorical and Rhetorical Legacy" in May (2002): 481–501.

Kenney, E. J. and W. V. Clausen. 1982. *Cambridge History of Classical Literature, II. Latin Literature*. Cambridge: Cambridge University Press.

Kinney, Dale. 1995. "Rape or Restitution of the Past? Interpreting *Spolia*," in Susan C. Scott, ed. *The Art of Interpreting. Papers in Art History from The Pennsylvania State University*, 9: 52–67.

Kinney, Dale. 1997. "Spolia. Damnatio and renovatio memoriae," *MAAR* 42: 117–148.

Kinney, Dale. 2001. "Roman Architectural Spolia," *ProcAPS* 145 (2001): 138–150.

Kleiner, Diana. 1992. *Roman Sculpture*. New Haven and London: Yale University Press.

Kleiner, F. S. 1989. "The Study of Roman Triumphal and Honorary Arches 50 years after Kähler" (review article), *JRA* 2: 196–206.

Kleiner, F. S. 2001. "Who Really Built the Arch of Constantine?" (review article), *JRA* 14: 661–663.

Kolbert, Elizabeth. 2005. "Annals of Science. The Climate of Man, II," *The New Yorker*. May 2: 64–73.

Kolbert, Elizabeth. 2006. *Field Notes from a Catastrophe: Man, Nature and Climate Change*. New York: Bloomsbury.

Kondoleon, Christine. 1991. "Signs of Privilege and Pleasure: Roman Domestic Mosaics," in Gazda (1991): 105–115.

Kraus, C. S. and A. J. Woodman. *Latin Historians. Greece & Rome*, Survey 27. Oxford: Oxford University Press.

Krautheimer, Richard. 1980, 2000. *Rome, Profile of a City, 312–1308*. Princeton: Princeton University Press.

Krautheimer, Richard. 1983. *Three Christian Capitals*. Berkeley: University of California Press.

Künzl, Ernst. 1988. *Der römische Triumph. Siegesfeiern im antiken Rom*. Munich: Beck.

Kuttner, Ann. 1995. "Republican Rome Looks at Pergamon," *HSCP* 97: 157–178.

Kuttner, Ann. 1999. "Culture and History at Pompey's Museum," *TAPA* 129: 343–373.

Lafon, X. 2001. *Villa Maritima. Recherches sur les villas littorales de l'Italie romaine (IIIe siècle av. J.-C./IIIᵉ siècle ap. J.-C.). BEFAR* 307. Rome.

Laissus, Yves. 1998. *L'Égypte, une aventure savânte avec Bonaparte, Kléber, Menou 1798–1801*. Paris: Fayard.

Lancel, S. 1998. *Hannibal*. Trans. A. Nevill. Oxford: Blackwell.

Lapatin, Kenneth D. S. 2001. *Chryselephantine Statuary in the Ancient Mediterranean World*. Oxford: Oxford University Press.

La Rocca, Eugenio. 1985. *Amazzonomachia: Le sculture frontonali del tempio di Apollo Sosiano*. Rome.

La Rocca, Eugenio. 1996. "Le tegole del tempio de Hera Lacinia ed it tempio della Fortuna Equestre: tra spoliazioni e restauri in età tardo-repubblicana," in R. Spada, ed. *Il tesoro di Hera. Scoperte ne santuario di Hera Lacinia a Capo Colonna di Crotone*. Milan: 89–98.

La Rocca, Eugenio. 1998. "Artisti rodii negli *horti* romani," in M. Cima and E. La Rocca, eds., *Horti romani: atti del convegno internazionale*, Roma, 4–6 maggio 1995 [1998]: 203–274.

Laroche, Didier. 1989. "Nouvelles observations sur l'offrande de Platées," *BCH* 113: 183–198.

Larpent, F. S. 1853. *The Private Journal of F. S. Larpent, Esq. Judge Advocate General of the British Forces in the Peninsula, attached to the Head-quarters of*

Lord Wellington during the Peninsular War, from 1812 to its Close. London: Richard Bentley.

Larsen, J. A. O. 1968. *Greek Federal States. Their Institutions and History.* Oxford: Clarendon Press.

Laurens, Henry, Charles C. Gillispie, Jean-Claude Golvin, Claude Traunecker. 1989. *L'Expédition d'Égypte.* Paris: Armand Colin.

Lavagnini, Bruno. 1985. "Sulle orme dell'epigrafista Georg Walther," *RömMittHist* 27: 339–355.

Lavin, Sylvia. 1992. *Quatremère de Quincy and the Invention of a Modern Language of Architecture.* Cambridge, MA: Harvard University Press.

Leask, Nigel. 2004. "Byron and the Eastern Mediterranean: *Childe Harold* II and the 'Polemic of Ottoman Greece'," in Drummond Bone, ed. *The Cambridge Companion to Byron.* Cambridge: Cambridge University Press: 99–117.

Leeman, A. D. 1986. Orationis Ratio. *The Stylistic Theories and Practice of the Roman Orators Historians and Philosophers.* Amsterdam: Adolf M. Hakkert.

Leen, Anne. 1991. "Cicero and the Rhetoric of Art." *AJP* 112: 229–245.

Lemosse, M. 1972. "Les éléments techniques de l'ancien triomphe romain et le problème de son origine." *ANRW* 1.2. Berlin and New York.

Levene, D. S. 1993. *Religion in Livy.* Mnemosyne, Supp. 127. Leiden: Brill.

Levens, R. C. G. 1946. *Cicero, Verrine V.* Bristol: Bristol Classical Press [repr. 1980].

Levick, Barbara. 1999. *Vespasian.* London and New York: Routledge.

Liddell Hart, B. H., ed. 1951. *The Letters of Private Wheeler 1809–1828.* Gloucestershire: Windrush Press.

Lillie, Sophie. 2003. *Was einmal war: Handbuch der enteigneten Kunstsammlungen Wiens.* Vienna: Czernin Verlag.

LIMC = *Lexicon Iconographicum Mythologiae Classicae.* 1981–1999. Zurich and Stuttgart: Artemis Verlag.

Lindsay, H. 1998. "The Biography of Atticus: Cornelius Nepos on the Philosophical and Ethical Background of Pomponius Atticus," *Latomus* 57.2: 324–336.

Linfert, A. 1994. "Boethoi," in Hellenkemper Salies (1994) 2: 831–848.

Ling, Roger. 1991. *Roman Painting.* Cambridge: Cambridge University Press.

Lintott, Andrew W. 1992. *Judicial Reform and Land Reform in the Roman Republic.* Cambridge: Cambridge University Press.

Lintott, Andrew W. 1993. *Imperium Romanum. Politics and Administration.* London and New York: Routledge.

Lintott, Andrew W. 1999. *The Constitution of the Roman Republic.* Oxford: Clarendon Press.

Lomas, Kathryn. 2004. "Hellenism, Romanization and Cultural Identity in Massalia," in Kathryn Lomas, ed., *Greek Identity in the Western*

Mediterranean. Papers in honour of Brian Shefton. Mnemosyne Supp. 246. Leiden: Brill: 475–498.

Longford, Elizabeth. 1967. "The Duke of Wellington's Books," *History Today* 17: 1–28.

Longford, Elizabeth. 1969. *Wellington, The Years of the Sword.* New York: Harper & Row.

Lowenthal, David. 1998. *The Heritage Crusade and the Spoils of History.* Cambridge: Cambridge University Press.

LTUR = Steinby, E. M., ed. 1993–2000. *Lexicon Topographicum Urbis Romae.* Rome: Edizioni Quasar.

Luce, T. James. 1977. *Livy. The Composition of His History.* Princeton: Princeton University Press.

Luce, T. James. 1990. "Livy, Augustus, and the Forum Augustum," in Raaflaub and Toher (1990): 123–138.

Lyons, Claire. 2002. "Objects and Identities: Claiming and Reclaiming the Past," in Barkan and Rush (2002): 116–137.

MacCarthy, Fiona. 2002. *Byron, Life and Legend.* London: John Murray.

Mackenzie, Simon R. M. 2005. *Going, Going, Gone: Regulating the Market in Illicit Antiquities.* Leicester: Institute of Art and Law.

Mainardi, Patricia. 1989. "Assuring the Empire of the Future: The 1798 'Fête de la Liberté'," *ArtJ* 48(1989): 155–163.

Malcovati, H. 1976. *Oratorum Romanorum* Fragmenta.[4] Turin: Paravia.

Malkin, I. 1991. "What Is an Aphidruma?" *ClAnt* 10: 77–96.

Mango, Cyril. 1963. "Antique Statuary and the Byzantine Beholder," *DOP* 17: 53–75.

Mango, Cyril. 1990. *Le développement urbain de Constantinople (IVe–VIIe siècles).* Paris: De Boccard.

Mango, Cyril, Michael Vickers and E. D. Francis. 1992. "The Palace of Lausos at Constantinople and Its Collection of Ancient Statues," *JournHistColl* 4: 89–98.

Manni, E. 1981. *Geografia fisica e politica della Sicilia antica.* Rome.

Mansel, Philip. 2001. *Paris Between Empires. Monarchy and Revolution 1814–1852.* New York: St. Martin's Press.

Marchand, L. A. 1979. *Byron. A Portrait.* Chicago: University of Chicago Press.

Marchand, Suzanne L. 1996. *Down from Olympus. Archaeology and Philhellenism in Germany, 1750–1970.* Princeton: Princeton University Press.

Marchand, Suzanne L. 2000. "The Quarrel of the Ancients and Moderns in the German Museums." In Susan A. Crane, ed., *Museums and Memory.* Stanford: Stanford University Press: 179–199.

Marchetti, S. 1991. *Plinio il Vecchio e la tradizione del moralismo Romano.* Pisa.

Marinatos, Nanno and Robin Hägg, eds. 1993. *Greek Sanctuaries. New approaches.* London and New York: Routledge.

Marinone, N. 1950. *Quaestines Verrinae.* Torino: Università di Torino.

Marshall, B. A. 1985. *A Historical Commentary on Asconius.* Columbia, MS.

Marshall, P. J. 1965. *The Impeachment of Warren Hastings.* Oxford: Oxford University Press.

Marshall, P. J. ed., 2000. *The Writings and Speeches of Edmund Burke, Vol. 7: India: The Hastings Trial 1789–1794.* Oxford: Oxford University Press.

Marvin, Miranda. 1989. "Copying in Roman Sculpture: The Replica Series," in *Retaining the Original. Multiple Originals, Copies, and Reproductions,* Vol. 20, *Studies in the History of Art.* Washington, DC: 29–25 [repr. in E. D'Ambra, ed. *Roman Art in Context.* Englewood Cliffs, NJ, 1993: 161–188].

Marvin, Miranda. 1997. "Roman Sculptural Reproductions or Polykleitos: The Sequel," in A. Hughes and E. Ranfft, eds. *Sculpture and Its Reproductions.* London: Reaktion Books.

Mattusch, Carol C. 1988. *Greek Bronze Statuary, From the Beginnings through the Fifth Century B.C.* Ithaca and London: Cornell University Press.

Mattusch, Carol C. 1994. "Bronze Herm of Dionysos," in Hellenkemper Salies (1994) I: 431–450.

Mattusch, Carol C. 1996. *Classical Bronzes. The Art and Craft of Greek and Roman Statuary.* Ithaca and London: Cornell University Press.

May, James M. 1988. *Trials of Character. The Eloquence of Ciceronian Ethos.* Chapel Hill and London: University of North Carolina Press.

May, James M., ed. 2002. *Brill's Companion to Cicero. Oratory and Rhetoric.* Leiden: Brill.

Mayor, Adrienne. 2000. *The First Fossil Hunters. Paleontology in Greek and Roman Times.* Princeton: Princeton University Press.

McClellan, Andrew. 1994. *Inventing the Louvre. Art, Politics, and the Origins of the Modern Museum in Eighteenth-Century Paris.* Cambridge: Cambridge University Press.

McDermott, W. C. 1977. "The Verrine Jury," *RhM* 120: 64–75.

McDonnell, Myles. 2006. "Roman Aesthetics and the Spoils of Syracuse," in Dillon and Welch (2006): 68–90.

Meier, C. 1982. *Caesar, A Biography.* New York: Basic Books. (Trans. D. McLintock.) Meiggs, Russell. 1980. "Sea-borne Timber Supplies to Rome," in J. H. D'Arms and E. C. Kopff, eds. *The Seaborne Commerce of Ancient Rome: Studies in Archaeology and History. MAAR* 36, 185–196.

Merryman, John H. 2000. *Thinking about the Elgin Marbles. Critical Essays on Cultural Property, Art and Law.* The Hague and London: Kluwer Law International.

Merryman, John H., ed. 2006. *Imperialism, Art and Restitution.* Cambridge: Cambridge University Press.

Merryman, John H. and A. E. Elsen. 1998. *Law, Ethics, and the Visual Arts.*³ London and Boston: Kluwer Law International.

Mertens, Dieter. 1984. "Aspetti dell'architettura crotoniate," in *Crotone, Atti del XXIII Convegno di Studi sulla Magna Grecia.* Taranto, 1983 [1984]: 189–230.

Meyer, Karl E. 1996. "Who Owns the Spoils of War?" in Vitelli (1996): 137–150.

Michelini, Chiara. 2000. "Il patrimonio artistico de alcune *poleis* siceliote nel *de Signis* ciceroniano," in *Terze gionate internazionali di studi sull'area elima (Gibellina-Erice-Contessa Entellina, 23–26 ottobre 1997). Atti.* II. Pisa: 777–808.

Miles, Gary B. 1995. *Livy. Reconstructing Early Rome.* Ithaca and London: Cornell University Press.

Miles, Margaret M. 1980. "The Date of the Temple on the Ilissos River," *Hesperia* 49 (1980): 309–325.

Miles, Margaret M. 1989. "A Reconstruction of the Temple of Nemesis at Rhamnous," *Hesperia* 58: 133–249.

Miles, Margaret M. 1998. *The Athenian Agora,* XXXI. *The City Eleusinion.* Princeton: American School of Classical Studies.

Miles, Margaret M. 2002. "Cicero's Prosecution of Gaius Verres: A Roman View of the Ethics of Acquisition of Art," *IJCP* 11: 28–49.

Miles, Margaret M. 2005. "Kunstraub – von Odysseus bis Saddam Hussein." *Schweitzer Monatsheft. Zeitschrift für Politik Wirtschaft Kultur.* March/April: 16–20. (Trans. R. Fischer.)

Millar, Fergus. 1986. "Politics, Persuasion and the People before the Social War (150–90 BC)," *JRS* 76 (1986): 1–11; repr. in Millar (2002).

Millar, Fergus. 1998. *The Crowd in Rome in the Late Republic. Jerome Lectures,* 22. Ann Arbor: University of Michigan Press.

Millar, Fergus. 2002. "Cornelius Nepos, "Atticus," and the Roman Revolution," in Millar (2002): 183–199 [repr. from *G & R* 35(1988): 40–55].

Millar, Fergus. 2002a. *The Roman Republic and the Augustan Revolution, I. Rome, The Greek World, and the East.* H. M. Cotton and G. M. Rogers, eds. Chapel Hill and London: University of North Carolina Press.

Millar, Fergus. 2002b. "Popular Politics at Rome in the Late Republic," in Millar (2002): 169–170.

Millar, Fergus. 2005. "Last Year in Jerusalem: Monuments of the Jewish War in Rome," in Edmonson et al. (2005): 101–128.

Miller, Margaret C. 1997. *Athens and Persia in the Fifth Century BC. A Study in Cultural Receptivity.* Cambridge: Cambridge University Press.

Mitchell, Thomas N. 1979. *Cicero, The Ascending Years.* New Haven and London: Yale University Press.

Mitchell, Thomas N. 1986. *Cicero: Verrines II.1.* Warminster: Aris & Phillips.

Mitchell, Thomas N. 1991. *Cicero, The Senior Statesman*. New Haven and London: Yale University Press.

ML = Meiggs, R. and D. Lewis, eds. 1969, 1988. *A Selection of Greek Historical Inscriptions to the End of the Fifth Century B.C.* Oxford: Clarendon.

Moles, J. L. 1988. *Plutarch. The Life of Cicero*. Warminster: Aris & Phillips.

Momigliano, Arnaldo. 1980. "La riscoperta della Sicilia antica da T. Fazello a P. Orsi," in E. Gabba and G. Vallet, eds. *La Sicilia Antica* 1.3. Naples: 767–780.

Momigliano, Arnaldo. 1984. "The Theological Efforts of the Roman Upper Classes in the First Century BC," in C. Ando, ed. *Roman Religion*. Edinburgh, 2003 [repr. *CPh* 79 (1984): 19–211].

Momigliano, Arnaldo. 1990. *The Classical Foundations of Modern Historiography*. Berkeley: University of California Press.

Morgan, L. 2000. "The Autopsy of C. Asinius Pollio," *JHS* 90: 51–69.

Morstein Kallet-Marx, Robert. 1995. *Hegemony to Empire. The Development of the Roman Imperium in the East from 148 to 62 B.C.* Berkeley and Oxford: University of California Press.

Morstein-Marx, Robert. 2004. *Mass Oratory and Political Power in the Late Roman Republic*. Cambridge: Cambridge University Press.

Mouritsen, H. 2001. *Plebs and Politics in the Late Roman Republic*. Cambridge: Cambridge University Press.

Muensterberger, W. 1994. *Collecting, An Unruly Passion. Psychological Perspectives*. Princeton: Princeton University Press.

Murphy, Trevor. 1998. "Cicero's First Readers: Epistolary Evidence for the Dissemination of His Works," *CQ* 48: 492–505.

Murphy, Trevor. 2004. *Pliny the Elder's* Natural History. *The Empire in the Encyclopedia*. Oxford: Oxford University Press.

Murray, O., ed. 1990. *Sympotica. A Symposium on the Symposium*. Oxford: Clarendon Press.

Murray, William M. 2003. "Foundation and destruction: Nikopolis and northwestern Greece" (review article), *JRA* 16: 475–478.

Myrone, M. and L. Peltz. 1999. Producing the Past. Aspects of Antiquarian Culture and Practice, 1700–1850. Aldershot: Ashgate.

Naas, V. 2002. *Le projet encyclopédique de Pline l'Ancien. Collection de l'Ecole français de Rome*, 303. Paris: Ecole français de Rome.

Napier, W. E. P. 1840. *History of the War in the Peninsula*. London: Constable [repr. 1993].

Narducci, E. 1997. *Cicerone e l'eloquenza romana: Retorica e progetto culturale*. Rome and Bari: Laterza.

Narducci, E. 2003. "La memoria dell grecità nell'immaginario delle ville ciceroniane," in M. Citroni, ed. *Memoria e identità. La cultura romana costuisce la sua immagine. Studi e testi*, 21. Firenze: G. Pasquali: 119–148.

Narducci, E. 2006. *Cicerone nella tradizione europea: dalla tarda antichità al Settecento. Atti del VI Symposium Ciceronianum Arpinas.* Firenze: Felice le Monnier.

Nevett, Lisa. 2002. "Continuity and Change in Greek Households under Roman Rule: The Role of Women in the Domestic Context," in Erik Nis Ostenfeld, ed. *Greek Romans and Roman Greeks.* Aarhus: Aarhus University Press.

Newlands, Carole E. 2002. *Statius'Silvae and the Poetics of Empire.* Cambridge: Cambridge University Press.

Nicholas, Lynn H. 1994. *The Rape of Europa. The Fate of Europe's Treasures in the Third Reich and the Second World War.* New York: Vintage Books.

Norman, Naomi J. 2005. "Editorial Policy on the Publication of Recently Acquired Antiquities," *AJA* 109: 135–136.

Nørskov, Vinnie. 2003. *Greek Vases in New Contexts. The Collecting and Trading of Greek Vases – An Aspect of the Modern Reception of Antiquity.* Aarhus: Aarhus University Press.

ODNB = Matthew, H. C. G. and B. Harrison, eds. 2004. *Oxford Dictionary of National Biography.* Oxford: Oxford University Press.

Ogilvie, R. M. 1965. *A Commentary on Livy, Books 1–5.* Oxford: Clarendon Press.

Orlin, Eric. 1997. *Temples, Religion and Politics in the Roman Republic.* Mnemosyne, Supp. 164. Leiden: Brill.

Osman, D. N. 1999. "Occupiers' Title to Cultural Property: Nineteenth-Century Removal of Egyptian Artifacts." *ColJTransnatlLaw* 37 (1999): 969–1002.

Overbeck, J. 1868. *Die antiken Schriftquellen zur Geschichte de bildenden Künste bei den Griechen.* Leipzig: Hildesheim [repr. 1959].

Packer, James. 2003. "*Plurima et amplissima opera*: Parsing Flavian Rome," in Boyle and Dominik (2003): 167–198.

Pape, M. 1975. *Griechische Kunstwerke aus Kriegebeute und ihre öffentliche Aufstellung in Rom.* Hamburg: Diss. Universität Hamburg.

Parke, H. W. and D. E. W. Wormell. 1956. *The Delphic Oracle.* Oxford: Basil Blackwell.

Parker, A. J. 1992. *Ancient Shipwrecks of the Mediterranean & the Roman Provinces. BAR,* 580. Oxford: Tempus Reparatum.

Parker, H. T. 1937 [1965]. *The Cult of Antiquity and the French Revolutionaries, A Study in the Development of the Revolutionary Spirit.* New York: Octagon Books.

Parker, Robert. 1983. *Miasma. Pollution and Purification in Early Greek Religion.* Oxford: Clarendon Press.

Paterson, Jeremy. 1998. "Trade and Traders in the Roman World: Scale, Structure, and Organisation," in H. Parkins and C. Smith, eds., *Trade, Traders and the Ancient City.* London and New York: Routledge, 149–167.

Peacock, D. P. S. 1997. "Charlemagne's Black Stones: The Re-use of Roman Columns in Early Medieval Europe," *Antiquity* 71 (273): 709–717.

Pearce, Susan M. 1995. *On Collecting. An Investigation into Collecting in the European Tradition.* London and New York: Routledge.

Pelling, Christopher. 1989. "Plutarch: Roman Heroes and Greek Culture," in Griffin and Barnes (1989): 199–208.

Pelling, Christopher. 2002. *Plutarch and History. Eighteen Studies.* London: Duckworth.

Perlwitz, Olaf. 1992. *Titus Pomponius Atticus. Untersuchungen zur Person eines einglussreichen Ritters in der ausgehenden römischen Republik. Hermes Einzelschr.* 58. Stuttgart: Franz Steiner.

Perry, Ellen. 2005. *The Aesthetics of Emulation in the Visual Arts of Ancient Rome.* Cambridge: Cambridge University Press.

Philipp, H. and W. Koenigs. 1979. "Zu den basen des L. Mummius in Olympia," *AM* 94: 193–216.

Philippides, Dimitris. 1994. "The Parthenon as Appreciated by Greek Society," in P. Tournikiotis, ed. *The Parthenon and its Impact in Modern Times.* Athens: Melissa, 278–309.

Phillips, Jonathan. 2004. *The Fourth Crusade and the Sack of Constantinople.* New York: Viking.

Phillipson, Coleman. 1911. *The International Law and Custom of Ancient Greece and Rome.* 2 vols. London: Macmillan and Co., Ltd.

Pietilä-Castrén, Leena. 1987. Magnificentia publica: *The Victory Monuments of the Roman Generals in the Era of the Punic Wars. Commentationes Humanarum Litterarum,* 84. Helsinki: Societas Scientiarum Fennica.

Pinot de Villechenon, Marie-Noëlle. 1997. *Sèvres. Porcelain from the Sèvres Museum, 1740 to the Present Day.* Trans. John Gilbert [French ed. 1993]. London: Lund Humphries.

Pollitt, J. J. 1974. *The Ancient View of Greek Art: Criticism, History and Terminology.* New Haven and London: Yale University Press.

Pollitt, J. J. 1978. "The Impact of Greek Art on Rome," *TAPA* 108: 155–174.

Pollitt, J. J. 1983. *The Art of Rome c. 753 B.C.–A.D. 337. Sources and Documents.* Cambridge: Cambridge University Press.

Pollitt, J. J. 1986. *Art in the Hellenistic Age.* Cambridge: Cambridge University Press.

Pollitt, J. J. 1990. *The Art of Ancient Greece. Sources and Documents.* Cambridge: Cambridge University Press.

Pommier, Édouard. 1989. *Lettres à Miranda sur le Déplacement des Monument de l'Art de l'Italie. Introduction et notes.* Paris: Macula.

Pommier, Édouard. 1991. *L'Art de la liberté. Doctrines et débats de la révolution française.* Paris: Gallimard.

Pommier, Édouard. 1999. "Réflexions sur le problème des restitutions d'oeuvres d'art en 1814–1815," in *Dominique-Vivant Denon, L'oeil de Napoléon*. Paris: 254–257.

Potter, David. 2004. "The Roman Army and Navy," in Flower (2004): 66–88.

Potts, Alex. 1978. "Political Attitudes and the Rise of Historicism in Art Theory," *ArtHist* 1: 191–213.

Potts, Alex. 1994. *Flesh and the Ideal: Winckelmann and the Origins of Art History*. New Haven: Yale University Press.

Poulot, Dominique. 1997. *Musée, nation, patrimonie, 1789–1815*. Paris: Gallimard.

Powell, J. and J. Paterson, eds. 2004. *Cicero the Advocate*. Oxford: Oxford University Press.

Pritchard, R. T. 1970. "Cicero and the *Lex Hieronica*," *Historia* 19: 352–368.

Pritchard, R. T. 1971. "Gaius Verres and the Sicilian Farmers," *Historia* 20: 229–238.

Pritchard, R. T. 1972. "Some Aspects of First-Century Sicilian Agriculture," *Historia* 21: 646–660.

Pritchett, W. K. 1971. *The Greek State at War*, 1. Berkeley and London: University of California Press.

Pritchett, W. K. 1979. *The Greek State at War*, 3. Berkeley and London: University of California Press.

Pritchett, W. K. 1991. *The Greek State at War*, 5. Berkeley and Oxford: University of California Press.

Quincy, Quatremère de. 1796 [1989]. *Lettres à Miranda sur le Déplacement des Monuments de l'Art del'Italie*. E. Pommier, ed., Paris: Éditions Macula.

Quynn, D. M. 1945. "The Art Confiscations of the Napoleonic Wars," *AHR* 50 (1945): 437–460.

Raaflaub, Kurt A., ed. 1986. *Social Struggles in Archaic Rome. New Perspectives on the Conflict of the Orders*. Berkeley and London: University of California Press.

Raaflaub, Kurt A. 1996. "Born to Be Wolves? Origins of Roman Imperialism," in Wallace and Harris (1996): 273–314.

Raaflaub, Kurt A. and M. Toher, eds. 1990. *Between Republic and Empire*. Berkeley: University of California Press.

Rambaud, M. 1953. *Cicéron et l'histoire romaine*. Paris: Les Belles Lettres.

Rasmussen, S. W. 2003. *Public Portents in Republican Rome. Analecta Roman Instituti Danici*. Suppl. 34. Rome: Bretschneider.

Rauh, N. 1993. *The Sacred Bonds of Commerce*. Amsterdam: J. C. Gieben.

Rawson, Elizabeth. 1975. *Cicero, A Portrait*. London: Allen Lane.

Rawson, Elizabeth. 1985. *Intellectual Life in the Late Roman Republic*. London: Duckworth.

Rawson, Elizabeth. 1990. "The Antiquarian Tradition: Spoils and Representations of Foreign Armor," in *Roman Culture and Society. Collected Papers*. Oxford, 1991: 582–598 [repr. from *Staat und Staatlichkeit in der frühen römischen Republik*. Stuttgart, 1990: 157–173].

Rawson, Elizabeth. 1991. *Roman Culture and Society: Collected Papers*. Oxford: Clarendon Press.

RE = A. Pauly and G. Wissova. *Realencyclopädie der classischen Altertumswissenschaft. 1893–1980*.

Redlich, Fritz. 1956. *De praeda militari. Looting and Booty 1500–1815*. Wiesbaden: Franz Steiner.

Reiter, W. 1988. *Aemilius Paullus. Conqueror of Greece*. London, New York, and Syndey: Croom Helm.

Renfrew, C. 2000. *Loot, Legitimacy and Ownership. The Ethical Crisis in Archaeology*, London: Duckworth.

Renold, Marc-André and Pierre Gabus, eds. 2004. *Claims for the Restitution of Looted Art. Studies in Art Law 15*. Geneva: Schulthess.

Reynolds, L. D., ed. 1983. *Texts and Transmissions, A Survey of the Latin Classics*. Oxford: Clarendon Press.

Reynolds, L. D. and N. G. Wilson. 1991. *Scribes and Scholars. A Guide to the Transmission of Greek and Latin Literature.*³ Oxford: Clarendon Press.

Rich, John. 1993. "Fear, Greed and Glory: The Causes of Roman War-Making in the Middle Republic," in Rich and Shipley (1993): 38–68.

Rich, John and Graham Shipley, eds. 1993. *War and Society in the Roman World*. London and New York: Routledge.

Richardson, Lawrence. 1992. *A New Topographical Dictionary of Ancient Rome*. Baltimore and London: The John Hopkins University Press.

Ridgway, Brunilde Sismondo. 1997. *Fourth-Century Styles in Greek Sculpture*. Madison: University of Wisconsin Press.

Ridgway, Brunilde Sismondo. 1984. *Roman Copies of Greek Sculpture: The Problem of the Originals*. Ann Arbor: University of Michigan Press.

Ridgway, Brunilde Sismondo. 2002. *Hellenistic Sculpture III. The Styles of ca. 100–31 B.C.* Madison: University of Wisconsin Press.

Riggsby, Andrew M. 1997. "'Public' and 'Private' in Roman Culture: The Case of the Cubiculum," *JRA* 10: 36–56.

Riggsby, Andrew M. 1999. *Crime and Community in Ciceronian Rome*. Austin: University of Texas Press.

Rigsby, K. J. 1996. *Asylia. Territorial Inviolability in the Hellenistic World*. Berkeley and London: University of California Press.

Rives, James. 1993. "Marcellus and the Syracusans," *CPh* 88: 32–35.

Rives, James. 2005. "Flavian Religious Policy and the Destruction of the Jerusalem Temples," in Edmonson et al. (2005): 145–166.

Rivet, A. L. F. 1988. *Gallia Narbonesis. Southern France in Roman Times.* London: B. T. Batsford, Ltd.

Rizzo, Idle and Ruth Towse, eds. 2002. *The Economics of Heritage. A Study in the Political Economy of Culture in Sicily.* Cheltenham, UK, Northampton, MA, USA: Edward Elgar.

Robert, L. 1965. Hellenica. *Recueil d'épigraphie de numismatique et d'antiquités greques, 13, d'Aphrodisias à la Lycaonie.* Paris.

Robinson, O. F. 1995. *The Criminal Law of Ancient Rome.* London: Duckworth.

Rohrbacher, D. 2002. *The Historians of Late Antiquity.* London and New York: Routledge.

RoR = Beard, Mary, John North and Simon Price. 1998. *Religions of Rome.* Cambridge: Cambridge University Press.

Rossi, A. 2000. "The Tears of Marcellus. History of a Literary Motif in Livy," *G&R* 47: 56–66.

Rotroff, Susan I. 1994. "The Pottery," in Hellenkemper Salies (1994): 133–152.

Roullet, A. 1972. *The Egyptian and Egyptianizing Monuments of Imperial Rome.* Leiden: Brill.

Rouse, W. H. D. 1902 [1975]. *Greek Votive Offerings.* New York: Arno Press.

Roussel, D. 1970. *Les Siciliens entre les Romains et les Carthaginois a l'epoque de la premiere guerre punique.* Centre de recherches d'histoire ancienne, 3. Paris.

Rudd, Niall and William Barr. 1991. *Juvenal. The Satires.* Trans. N. Rudd; introduction and notes by W. Barr. Oxford: Clarendon Press.

Ruddy, F. S. 1975. *International Law in the Enlightenment. The Background of Emmerich de Vattel's Le Droit des Gens.* Dobbs Ferry, NY: Oceana.

Ruga, A. 1996. "La copertura dell'edificio A," in Spada (1996): 99–105.

Sacks, K. 1990. *Diodorus Siculus and the First Century.* Princeton: Princeton University Press.

Salzman, Michele. 1999. "The Christianization of Sacred Time and Sacred Space," in W. V. Harris, ed. *The Transformations of Urbs Roma in Late Antiquity. JRA* Supp. 33. Portsmouth, RI: 123–134.

Sanders, L. J. 1987. *Dionysios I of Syracuse and Greek Tyranny.* London, New York, Sydney: Croom Helm.

Sanders, L. J. 1991. "Dionysius I of Syracuse and the Origins of the Ruler Cult in the Greek World," *Historia,* 40: 275–287.

Saradi-Mendelovici, H. 1990. "Christian Attitudes toward Pagan Monuments in Late Antiquity and Their Legacy in Later Byzantine Centuries," *DOP* 44: 47–60.

Sax, Joseph L. 1990. "Heritage Preservation as a Public Duty: The Abbé Grégoire and the Origins of an Idea," *Michigan Law Review* 88, 5: 1142–1169.

Sax, Joseph L. 1999. *Playing Darts with a Rembrandt. Public and Private Rights in Cultural Treasures.* Ann Arbor: University of Michigan Press.

Scardigli, Barbara, ed. 1995. *Essays on Plutarch's Lives.* Oxford: Clarendon Press.

Schaps, D. M. 2004. *The Invention of Coinage and the Monetization of Ancient Greece.* Ann Arbor: University of Michigan Press.

Schaumann, August L. F. 1999. *On the Road with Wellington. The Diary of a War Commissary.* London and Philadelphia: Greenhill Books, Stackpole Books. (Trans. from German ed., 1924.)

Scheer, Tanja S. 2000. *Die Gottheit und ihr Bild. Untersuchungen zur Funktion griechischer Kultbilder in Religion und Politik* (*Zetemata*, 105). Munich: C. H. Beck.

Schilling, Robert. 1992. "Cicero as Theologian," in Y. Bonnefoy, et al., eds. *Roman and European Mythologies.* Chicago: University of Chicago Press: 123–125.

Schnapp, Alain. 1996. *The Discovery of the Past.* London: British Museum.

Schneider, W. J. 2001. "Phidiae Putavi Martial und der Hercules Epitrapezios des Novius Vindex." *Mnemosyne* 54.6: 697–720.

Scholten, Joseph B. 2000. *The Politics of Plunder. Aitolians and Their Koinon in the Early Hellenistic Era, 279–217 B.C.* Berkeley and London: University of California Press.

Schom, Alan. 1997. *Napoleon Bonaparte.* New York: HarperCollins.

Scott, Jonathan. 2003. *The Pleasures of Antiquity. British Collectors of Greece and Rome.* New Haven: Yale University Press.

Scott, John. 1816. *Paris Revisited in 1815, by way of Brussels; including a walk over the field of battle at Waterloo.* London: Longman, Hurst, Rees, Orme, and Brown.

Sehlmeyer, Markus. 1999. *Stadtrömische Ehrenstatuen der republikanischen Zeit. Historia*, Einzelsch. 130. Stuttgart.

Sepinwall, Alyssa Goldstein. 2005. *The Abbé Grégoire and the French Revolution.* Berkeley, Los Angeles, and London: University of California Press.

Serrati, John. 2000. "Garrisons and Grain: Sicily between the Punic Wars," in Smith and Serrati (2000): 115–133.

Sérullaz, Maurice. 1963. *Les peintures murales de Delacroix.* Paris: Les Éditions du Temps.

Settle, J. S. 1962. *The Publication of Cicero's Orations.* Diss. University of North Carolina, Chapel Hill.

Shackleton Bailey, D. R. 1965. *Cicero's Letters to Atticus I.* Cambridge: Cambridge University Press.

Shackleton Bailey, D. R. 1971. *Cicero*. London: Duckworth.

Shackleton Bailey, D. S. 1977. *Cicero: Epistulae ad familiares*. 2 vols. Cambridge: Cambridge University Press.

Shatzman, Israël. 1972. "The Roman General's Authority over Booty," *Historia* 21: 177–205.

Shatzman, Israël. 1975. *Senatorial Wealth and Roman Politics. Collection Latomus*, 142. Brussels.

Shaw, B. D. 2001. *Spartacus and the Slave Wars. A Brief History with Documents*. Boston, New York: Bedford/St. Martin's.

Shear, T. Leslie, Jr. 1993. "The Persian Destruction of Athens: Evidence from Agora Deposits," *Hesperia* 62: 383–482.

Sherk, Robert K. 1984. *Rome and the Greek East to the death of Augustus*. Cambridge: Cambridge University Press.

Simpson, Elizabeth, ed. 1997. *The Spoils of War. World War II and Its Aftermath: The Loss, Reappearance, and Recovery of Cultural Property*. New York: Harry N. Abrams, Inc.

Sinn, Ulrich. 1993. "Greek Sanctuaries as Places of Refuge," in Marinatos and Hägg (1993): 88–109.

Skidmore, C. 1996. *Practical Ethics for Roman Gentlemen. The Work of Valerius Maximus*. Exeter: University of Exeter Press.

Slater, W. J., ed., 1991. *Dining in a Classical Context*. Ann Arbor: University of Michigan Press.

Small, Jocelyn P. 1997. *Wax Tablets of the Mind. Cognitive Studies of Memory and Literacy in Classical Antiquity*. London and New York: Routledge.

Smith, Christopher and John Serrati, eds. 2000. *Sicily from Aeneas to Augustus*. Edinburgh: Edinburgh University Press.

Solin, H., O. Salomies, and U.-M. Liertz, eds. 1995. *Acta colloquii epigraphici Latini, Helsingiae, 3.-6. Sept. 1991 habiti*. Helsinki.

Spada, R., ed. 1996. *Il tesoro di Hera. Scoperte ne santuario di Hera Lacinia a Capo Colonna di Crotone*. Milan.

Spaeth, Barbette S. 1996. *The Roman Goddess Ceres*. Austin: University of Texas Press.

Speck, Paul. 1995. "*Urbs quam Deo donavimus*. Konstantins des Grossen Konzept für Konstantinopel." *Boreas* 18 (1995): 143–173.

Stangl, T. 1909. *Ciceronis orationum scholiastae, II*. Paterborn: F. Schoningh.

Stanhope, Philip Henry, Earl. 1998. *Notes of Conversations with the Duke of Wellington 1831–1851*. With a new Introduction by Elizabeth Longford. London: Prion. (First public edition, 1888.)

Starr, Raymond J. 1987. "The Circulation of Literary Texts in the Roman World," *CQ* 37: 213–223.

St. Clair, William. 1998. *Lord Elgin & the Marbles.*³ Oxford: Oxford University Press.

Steel, C. E. W. 2001. *Cicero, Rhetoric, and Empire.* Oxford: Oxford University Press.

Steel, C. E. W. 2004. "Being Economical with the Truth: What Really Happened at Lampsacus?" in J. Powell and J. Paterson, eds. *Cicero the Advocate.* Oxford: Oxford University Press: 233–251.

Steinhart, Matthias. 1997. "Bemerkungen zu Rekonstruktion, Ikonographie und Inschrift des plataïschen Weihgeschenkes," *BCH* 121: 33–69.

Stenhouse, William. 2000. "Classical Inscriptions and Antiquarian Scholarship in Italy, 1600–1650," in Alison E. Cooley, ed. *The Afterlife of Inscriptions. Reusing, Rediscovering, Reinventing & Revitalizing Ancient Inscriptions. BICS,* Supp. 75. London: 77–89.

Stewart, Andrew. 1990. *Greek Sculpture, An Exploration.* New Haven and London: Yale University Press.

Stewart, Peter. 2003. *Statues in Roman Society. Representation and Response.* Oxford: Oxford University Press.

Stockton, D. 1971. *Cicero, A Political Biography.* Oxford: Oxford University Press.

Stroh, Wilfried. 1975. *Taxis und Taktik: die advokatische Dispositionskunst in Ciceros Gerichtsreden.* Stuttgart: B. G. Teubner.

Stroh, Wilfried. 2004. "De Domo Sua: *Legal Problem and Structure,*" in Jonathan Powell and Jeremy Paterson, eds. *Cicero the Advocate.* Oxford: Oxford University Press: 313–370.

Strong, D. E. 1966. *Greek and Roman Gold and Silver Plate.* London: Methuen.

Stuart, James and Nicholas Revett. 1762. *The Antiquities of Athens, as measured and delineated by James Stuart and Nicholas Revett.* London: J. Haberkorn.

Stumpf, Claudia. 1787. *Richard Payne Knight. Expedition into Sicily.* London: British Museum.

Swain, S. C. R. 1995. "Hellenic Culture and the Roman Heroes of Plutarch," in Scardigli (1995): 229–264.

Swain, Simon. 1996. *Hellenism and Empire. Language, Classicism, and Power in the Greek World AD 50–250.* Oxford: Clarendon Press.

Swain, Simon. 1997. "Biography and Biographic in the Literature of the Roman Empire," in M. J. Edwards and S. Swain, eds., *Portraits. Biographical Representation in the Greek and Latin Literature of the Roman Empire.* Oxford: Oxford University Press, 1–38.

*Syll.*³ = W. Dittenberger, ed. (1915–1924). *Sylloge Inscriptionum Graecarum.* Leipzig: S. Hirzel.

Syme, Ronald. 1961. "Who Was Vedius Pollio?" *JRS* 51: 24–30.

Tamblé, D. 2000. "Il ritorno dei beni culturali dalla Francia nello Stato pontificio e l'inizio della politica culturale della Restaurazione nei documenti camerali dell'Archivio di Stato di Roma," in *Ideologie e patrimonio storico-culturale* (2000): 457–514.

Tanner, J. 2000. "Portraits, Power and Patronage in the Late Roman Republic," *JRS* 90: 18–50.

Tanner, J. 2006. *The Invention of Art History in Ancient Greece. Religion, Society and Artistic Rationalism.* Cambridge: Cambridge University Press.

Taylor, L. R. 1966. *Party Politics in the Age of Caesar.* Berkeley and Los Angeles: University of California Press.

Teyssier, M.-L. 1984. "Cicéron et les arts plastiques, peinture et sculpture," in R. Chevallier, ed., *Présence de Cicéron. Actes du Colloque des 25, 26 septembre 1982. Homage au R. P. M. Testard.* Paris: 67–76.

Titchener, F. 2003. "Cornelius Nepos and the Biographical Tradition," *G & R* 50: 85–99.

Toniato, Anna Guidi. 1979. "The Horses of San Marco from the Fall of the Republic to the Present Day," in *Horses of San Marco, Venice.* Trans. John Wilton-Ely [Italian ed. 1977]. London: 117–123.

Toynbee, Arnold J. 1965. *Hannibal's Legacy. The Hannibalic War's Effects on Roman Life.* 2 vols. London: Oxford University Press.

Trayianmoudi, Litsa. 2004. "A 'Very Life in . . . Despair in the Land of Honourable Death': Byron and Greece," in R. A. Cardwell, ed. *The Reception of Byron in Europe, II: Northern, Central and Eastern Europe. The Athlone Critical Traditions Series: The Reception of British Authors in Europe.* London: Thoemmes Continuum: 419–438.

Treggiari, Susan. 1969. *Roman Freedmen during the Late Republic.* Oxford: Clarendon Press.

Treggiari, Susan. 1998. "Home and Forum: Cicero between 'Public' and 'Private'," *TAPA* 128: 1–23.

Trevor Hodge, A. 1998. *Ancient Greek France.* London: Duckworth.

Trevor-Roper, Hugh. 1970. *The Plunder of the Arts in the Seventeenth Century.* London: Thames and Hudson.

Trombley, Frank R. 1993. *Hellenic Religion and Christianization, c. 370–529.* Leiden: Brill.

Trompf, G. W. 2000. *Early Christian Historiography. Narratives of Retributive Justice.* London and New York: Continuum.

Trouard, M. A. 1942. *Cicero's Attitude towards the Greeks.* Chicago: Diss. University of Chicago.

Tsingardia, Athena, ed., with Donna Kurtz. 2002. *Appropriating Antiquity, Saisir l'Antique. Collections et collectionneurs d'antiques en Belgique et en*

Grande-Bretagne au XIXe siècle. Lucernae Novantiquae, 2. Bruxelles: Le Livre Timperman.

Turner, Frank M. 1989. "Why the Greeks and Not the Romans in Victorian Britain?" in G. W. Clarke, ed. *Rediscovering Hellenism. The Hellenic Inheritance and the English Imagination.* Cambridge: Cambridge University Press: 61–81.

Tuzet, H. 1955. *La Sicile au XVIIIe siècle vue par les voyageurs étrangers.* Strasbourg: P. H. Heitz.

Vai, G. B. and I. P. Martini, eds. 2001. *Anatomy of an Orogen: The Apennines and Adjacent Mediterranean Basins.* Dordrecht, Boston, and London: Kluwer.

Van De Mieroop, M. 2005. *King Hammurabi. A Biography.* Malden, MA: Blackwell.

Vasaly, Ann. 1993. *Representations. Images of the World in Ciceronian Oratory.* Berkeley and London: University of California Press.

Vasaly, Ann. 2002. "Cicero's Early Speeches," in May (2002): 71–111.

Vattel, Emmerich de. 1758. *The Law of Nations.* Trans. J. Chitty. Philadelphia: T. and J. W. Johnson.

Versnel, H. S. 1970. *Triumphus. An Inquiry into the Origin, Development and Meaning of the Roman Triumph.* Leiden: E. J. Brill.

Vickers, Michael. 2001. "Greek and Roman Antiquities in the Seventeenth Century," in Impey and MacGregor (2001): 309–318.

Vickers, Michael and David Gill. 1994. *Artful Crafts, Ancient Greek Silverware and Pottery.* Oxford: Clarendon Press.

Vidler, A. 2000. "The Paradoxes of Vandalism: Henri Grégoire and the Thermidorian Discourse on Historical Monuments," in J. Popkin and R. Popkin, eds. *The Abbé Grégoire and His World.* Dordrecht, Boston, and London: Kluwer, 129–156.

Villehardouin, Geoffroy de. 1963 [written c.1207, first published 1585]. "The Conquest of Constantinople," *Chronicles of the Crusades*, trans. Margaret R. B. Shaw. London: Penguin Classics.

Vitelli, Karen D., ed. 1996. *Archaeological Ethics.* Walnut Creek, CA: Altamira Press.

Vitelli, Karen D. and Chip Colwell-Chanthaphonh, eds. 2006. *Archaeological Ethics.*² Lanham, MD: Altamira Press.

Vitruvius. 1999. *Ten Books on Architecture.* Trans. I. D. Rowland, with commentary by T. N. Howe. Cambridge: Cambridge University Press.

Vogt, J. 1975. *Ancient Slavery and the Ideal of Man.* Trans. R. Wiedemann. Cambridge, MA: Harvard University Press.

von Albrecht, M. 2003. *Cicero's Style. A Synopsis.* Leiden and Boston: Brill.

von der Mühll, F. *RE* VIII, 2, s.v. *Hortensius* (13), col. 2470–2481 [1913].

von Hesberg, H. 1994. "Die Architekturteile," in Hellenkemper Salies (1994)1: 175–194.

Vrettos, Theodore. 1997. *The Elgin Affair*. New York: Arcade.

Walbank, F. W. 1940. *Philip V of Macedon*. Cambridge: Cambridge University Press.

Walbank, F. W. 1957, 1967, 1979. *A Historical Commentary on Polybius*, I, II, III. Oxford: Clarendon Press.

Walker, H. J. 2004. *Valerius Maximus. Memorable Deeds and Sayings. One Thousand Tales from Ancient Rome*. Indianapolis and Cambridge: Hackett.

Wallace-Hadrill, Andrew. 1989. "Patronage in Roman Society: From Republic to Empire," in A. Wallace-Hadrill, ed. *Patronage in Ancient Society*. London and New York: Routledge: 63–87.

Wallace-Hadrill, Andrew. 1990. "Pliny the Elder and Man's Unnatural History," *G & R* 37: 80–96.

Wallace-Hadrill, Andrew. 1994. *Houses and Society in Pompeii and Herculaneum*. Princeton: Princeton University Press.

Walsh, P. G. 1961. *Livy. His Historical Aims and Methods*. Cambridge: Cambridge University Press.

Wardle, D. 1998. *Valerius Maximus. Memorable Deeds and Sayings*, Book I. Oxford: Clarendon Press.

Watkin, David. 1874. *The Life and Work of C. R. Cockerell*. London.

Watson, Alan. 1968. *The Law of Property in the Later Roman Republic*. Oxford: Clarendon Press.

Watson, Alan. 1992. *The State, Law and Religion. Pagan Rome*. Athens, GA, and London: University of Georgia Press.

Watson, Peter and Cecilia Todeschini. 2006. *The Medici Conspiracy. The Illicit Journey of Looted Antiquities from Italy's Tomb Raiders to the World's Greatest Museums*. New York: Public Affairs.

Waurick, G. 1975. "Kunstraub der Römer: Untersuchungen zu seinen anfängen anhand der Inschriften." *JRGZ* 22: 1–46.

Weigel, D. 1998. "Roman Generals and the Vowing of Temples, 500–100 B.C.," *C&M* 49: 119–142.

Weinstock, Stefan. 1971. *Divus Julius*. Oxford: Clarendon Press.

Weis, Anne. 2003. "Gaius Verres and the Roman Art Market: Consumption and connoisseurship in Verrine II.4," in A. Haltenhoff et al., eds. *O tempora, o mores! Römische Werte und römische Literatur in den letzten Jahrzehnten der Republik*. Saur: 359–365.

Weiss, H. 1997. "Late Third Millennium Abrupt Climate Change and Social Collapse in West Asia and Egypt," in H. N. Dalfes, G. Kukla, and H. Weiss, eds. *Third Millennium BC Climate Change and Old World Collapse*. Berlin: Springer: 711–723.

Weiss, Peter. 2003. "The Vision of Constantine," *JRA* 16: 237–259.

Weitzman, S. 2005. *Surviving Sacrilege. Cultural Persistence in Jewish Antiquity.* Cambridge, MA: Harvard University Press.

Welch, Katherine. 2003. "A New View of the Origins of the Basilica: The Atrium Regium, Graecostasis, and Roman Diplomacy," *JRA* 16: 5–34.

Welch, Katherine E. 2006. "*Domi Militiaeque*: Roman Domestic Aesthetics and War Booty in the Republic," in Dillon and Welch (2006): 91–161.

Weller, Jac. 1962. *Wellington in the Peninsula.* London: Greenhill [repr. 1992].

Wells, Donald A. 1992. *The Laws of Land Warfare. A Guide to the U.S. Army Manuals. Contributions in Military Studies, 132.* Westport, CT: Greenwood Press.

Williams, Dyfri. 2002. "'Of publick utility and publick property?': Lord Elgin and the Parthenon Sculptures," in Tsingarida and Kurtz (2002): 103–164.

Williams, Stephen and Gerard Friell. 1994. *Theodosius, The Empire at Bay.* New Haven and London: Yale University Press.

Wilson, David M. 2002. *The British Museum. A History.* London: British Museum.

Wilson, R. J. A. 1990. *Sicily under the Roman Empire.* Warminster: Aris and Philips.

Wilson, R. J. A. 2000. "Ciceronian Sicily: An archaeological Perspective," in Smith and Serrati (2000): 134–160.

Wilton-Ely, J. and V., trans. *The Horses of San Marco.* London: Thames and Hudson.

Winterbottom, M. 1982. "Cicero and the Silver Age," in W. Ludwig, ed., *Éloquence et rhétorique chez Cicéron (Entretiens sur l'Antiquité classique, 28).* Geneva: 237–266.

Wiseman, T. P. 1971. *New Men in the Roman Senate, 139B.C.–A.D. 14.* Oxford: Oxford University Press.

Woolgar, C. M. 1984. *A Summary Catalogue of the Wellington Papers. Occasional Paper, 8.* University of Southampton.

Wörner, E. s.v. "Palladion" Roscher III.1 (1897–1909): 1301–1309.

Yalouri, Eleana. 2001. *The Acropolis. Global Fame, Local Claim.* New York: Berg.

Young, Gary K. 2001. *Rome's Eastern Trade. International Commerce and Imperial Policy, 31 BC–AD 305.* London and New York: Routledge.

Zanker, Paul. 1978. "Zur Funktion und Bedeutung griechischer Skulptur in der Römerzeit," in *Le classicisme à Rome aux I^{ers} siécles avant et après J. C. Entretiens Hardt* 25: 283–306.

Zanker, Paul. 1990. *The Power of Images in the Age of Augustus.* Ann Arbor: University of Michigan Press.

Zeiner, Noelle K. 2005. *Nothing Ordinary Here. Statius as Creator of Distinction in the Silvae.* New York and London: Routledge.

Zetzel, James E. G. 1973. "Emendari ad Tironem: Some Notes on Scholarship in the Second Century AD," *HSCP* 77: 225–243.

Zetzel, James E. G. 2003. "Plato with Pillows: Cicero on the Uses of Greek Culture," in D. Braund and C. Gill, eds. *Myth, History and Culture in Republican Rome. Studies in honour of T. P. Wiseman.* Exeter: University of Exeter Press: 119–138.

Zielinski, T. 1912. *Cicero im Wandel der Jahrhunderte⁵* Darmstadt: Wissenschaftliche Buchgesellschaft [repr. 1967].

Zimmer, G. 1989. "Das Sacrarium des C. Heius. Kunstraub und Kunstgeschmack in der späten Republik," *Gymnasium* 96: 493–531.

Zimmer, G. 1994. "Republikanisches kunstverständnis: Cicero gegen Verres," in Hellenkemper Salies (1994) 2: 867–874.

Ziolkowski, Adam. 1992. *The Temples of Mid-Republican Rome and Their Historical and Topographical Context.* Rome: Bretschneider.

Ziolkowski, Adam. 1993. "*Urbs direpta*, or how the Romans sacked cities," in Rich and Shipley (1993): 69–91.

Zuccoli, F. 2000. "Le ripercussioni del trattato di Tolentino sull'attività diplomatica di Antonio Canova nel 1815 per il recupero delle opere d'arte," in *Ideologie e patrimonio storico-culturale* (2000): 611–632.

Zulueta, Francis de. 1946. *The Institutes of Gaius.* 2 vols. Oxford: Clarendon Press [repr. 1953–58].

INDEX

Page numbers in italics refer to illustrations.